Agricultural Production Economics

Agricultural Production Economics

David L. Debertin
University of Kentucky

Macmillan Publishing Company
New York

Collier Macmillan Publishers
London

Cultivation north of Berthold, North Dakota (Photo Courtesy Richard H. Debertin)

Copyright © 1986, Macmillan Publishing Company, a division of Macmillan, Inc.

Printed in the United States of America

All rights reserved. No part of this book may be reproduced or transmitted in any form or by any means, electronic or mechanical, including photocopying, recording, or any information storage and retrieval system, without permission in writing from the publisher.

Macmillan Publishing Company
866 Third Avenue, New York, New York 10022

Collier Macmillan Canada, Inc.

Library of Congress Cataloging in Publication Data

Debertin, David L.
   Agricultural production economics.

   Bibliography: p.
   Includes index.
   1. Agricultural productivity—Econometric models.
2. Agriculture—Economic aspects—Econometric models.
I. Title.
HD1433.D43   1986   338.1'0724   85-13918
ISBN 0-02-328060-3

Printing: 1 2 3 4 5 6 7 8   Year: 6 7 8 9 0 1 2 3 4 5

ISBN 0-02-328060-3

Preface

This book was designed to fill a gap in currently available textbooks in production economics with applications to agriculture. Undergraduates in agricultural economics departments at most universities spend a great deal of time in introductory courses learning production economics using graphical and tabular presentations. At the same time, undergraduates in most departments are required to take one or more courses in introductory calculus and other mathematics. Too frequently, however, mathematics in undergraduate programs becomes only a requirement that must be fulfilled by the student, rather than a tool that can increase understanding of production theory and its application to agriculture in upper-division courses.

This book provides the student with a detailed presentation of production theory, with emphasis on the linkages between the graphical and the mathematical approaches of presentation. Applications to agriculture are stressed throughout. In the past, instructors of undergraduate courses in agricultural production economics have sometimes been hesitant to use mathematical tools for fear of going over the heads of the students. The undergraduate wonders why the department required the calculus and other mathematics. If the undergraduate enters graduate school, he or she discovers that most production theory makes heavy use of mathematics as a vehicle for model presentation and analysis. The graduate student frequently wonders if there is any linkage between what was learned using a graphical and tabular approach in the undergraduate program and what is being taught at the graduate level.

The student for which this text is designed is one who was required to take a course or two in introductory calculus, and one or two courses in microeconomics that relied primarily on a graphical and tabular presentation, perhaps a number of semesters before taking a course dealing with agricultural production economics. The student might either be an upper-division undergraduate or a first-year graduate student.

Any good textbook should provide threads that link the familiar to the unfamiliar. Some upper-division undergraduates, and most graduate students will find the tabular and graphical presentations contained in the book to be review material. However, since the book stresses the linkages between the tabular, graphical, and mathematical approaches to production theory, many students will find the parallel presentations an effective learning aid. A thorough understanding of production theory can be achieved only if one understands tabular, graphical, and mathematical presentations.

This book is designed primarily as a textbook for a course in agricultural production economics within agricultural economics, rather than as a general production economics textbook. Applications to agriculture are used as illustrations for many of the theoretical concepts that are developed. Policy implications relative to agriculture are stressed throughout. Production theory is better understood if its applications to real-world problems and policies within agriculture are stressed.

Most students will want to take at least one course in introductory microeconomics and one course in differential calculus before taking a course that uses this book. It was not possible to incorporate an entire course on differential calculus, but many basic mathematical concepts are briefly reviewed as their application to agricultural production economics is made apparent. More emphasis is placed on reviewing those mathematical concepts used in production theory that have not received much emphasis in introductory calculus courses, such as topics in constrained optimization and maximization in the several-variable case.

The linkages between production economics and the assumptions of the model of pure competition are stressed in Chapter 1. Chapter 2 to 18 present an in-depth treatment of production theory related to the traditional factor-product, factor-factor, and product-product models. Throughout these chapters, illustrations and applications from agriculture are used, and the relationship between theory taught at the introductory level and the advanced material is stressed. Each model is approached on a very simple, basic level, and, in addition, many advanced topics are treated in detail.

A course relying primarily on a tabular and graphical approach could be taught from the book by concentrating on certain chapters or chapter sections and omitting others. The graphical treatment is complete and detailed. For example, Chapters 7 and 8 deal with very similar economic concepts. Chapter 7 consists of a presentation using primarily detailed graphics. Chapter 8 presents many of the same concepts with the aid of basic calculus. Certain chapters, such as 10 and 11, will be of primary interest to graduate students.

Chapter 19 is devoted to the linkages between marginal analysis and enterprise budgeting. Chapters 20 and 21 provide an introduction to risk and uncertainty and to agricultural production over time. Chapter 22 provides a basic presentation of linear programming and its relationship to the models developed in Chapters 2 to 18. The treatment of the material in Chapters 20 to 22 is of necessity less thorough than the treatment of marginal analysis in Chapters 2 to 18, for a separate textbook could easily be written on each chapter topic. These chapters should be sufficient to provide an introduction to each topic area as a basis for further study. The reading list provides a number of references for a more advanced treatment of these topics. Chapter 23 provides

Preface

an introduction to some unresolved research issues in agricultural production economics.

The author is heavily indebted to his reviewers, Loren Tauer of Cornell, DeLane Welsch of Minnesota, and James Cornelius of Oregon State. James Cornelius deserves special recognition for his enthusiasm and willingness to devote an extra measure of effort in making the book better. E. C. Pasour, Jr. (North Carolina State University), Melvin D. Skold (Colorado State University), Stephen Hatchett (North Carolina State University), and William C. Nelson (North Dakota State University) provided valuable final reviews of the manuscript. Any errors and omissions are the fault of the author, not those of the excellent reviewers.

The author thanks his colleagues Angelos Pagoulatos for many of the ideas which became chapters and for his able assistance in checking mathematical derivations throughout the text; Garnett Bradford, who rendered particular assistance with respect to ideas contained in Chapters 19 and 21; and Larry Jones, for stimulating ideas related to the linkages between firm-level production and the macro economy. Mary Webster performed a valuable service in preparing the various drafts of the text. Finally, the author thanks his parents, Harold and Margaret Debertin, for their continued support.

D.L.D.

Dedication

To Tanya, Kyle, and Tamara

Contents

1. An Introduction   1

1.1	Economics Defined	1
1.2	The Logic of Economic Theory	2
1.3	Economic Theory as Abstraction	3
1.4	Economic Theory Versus Economic Model	3
1.5	Representing Economic Relationships	4
1.6	Consumption Versus Production Economics	4
1.7	Microeconomics Versus Macroeconomics	5
1.8	Statics Versus Dynamics	6
1.9	Economics Versus Agricultural Economics	7
1.10	Agricultural Production Economics	7
1.11	The Assumptions of Pure Competition	9
1.12	Why Retain the Purely Competitive Model?	11
1.13	Concluding Comments	11

2. Production with One Variable Input   14

2.1	What Is a Production Function?	14
2.2	Fixed Versus Variable Inputs and the Length of Run	18
2.3	The Law of Diminishing Returns	20
2.4	Marginal and Average Physical Product	22
2.5	*MPP* and the Marginal Product Function	24
2.6	The Neoclassical Production Function	28
2.7	*MPP* and *APP* for the Neoclassical Function	29
2.8	Sign, Slope, and Curvature	31
2.9	A Single-Input Production Elasticity	34
2.10	Elasticities of Production for the Neoclassical Production Function	36
2.11	Further Topics on the Elasticity of Production	37
2.12	Concluding Comments	38

3. Profit Maximization with One Input and One Output 40

3.1	Total Physical Product Versus Total Value of the Product	40
3.2	Total Factor or Resource Cost	41
3.3	Maximizing the Difference Between Returns and Costs	41
3.4	Value of the Marginal Product and Marginal Factor Cost	44
3.5	Equating *VMP* and *MFC*	44
3.6	Calculating the Exact Level of Input Use to Maximize Output or Profits	46
3.7	General Conditions for Profit Maximization	51
3.8	Necessary and Sufficient Conditions	52
3.9	The Three Stages of the Neoclassical Production Function	53
3.10	Further Topics on Stages of Production	57
3.11	The Imputed Value of an Additional Unit of an Input	58
3.12	Concluding Comments	60

4. Costs, Returns, and Profits on the Output Side 62

4.1	Some Basic Definitions	62
4.2	Simple Profit Maximization from the Output Side	69
4.3	The Duality of Cost and Production	72
4.4	The Inverse of a Production Function	73
4.5	Some Further Illustrations of the Linkages Between Cost and Production Functions	76
4.6	The Supply Function for the Firm	77
4.7	Concluding Comments	79

5. Production with Two Inputs 81

5.1	Introduction	81
5.2	An Isoquant and the Marginal Rate of Substitution	85
5.3	Isoquants and Ridge Lines	89
5.4	*MRS* and Marginal Product	91
5.5	Partial and Total Derivatives and the Marginal Rate of Substitution	93
5.6	Concluding Comments	96

6. Maximization in the Two Input Case 99

6.1	An Introduction to Maximization	99
6.2	The Maximum of a Function	101
6.3	Some Illustrative Examples	102

6.4	Some Matrix Algebra Principles	107
6.5	A Further Illustration	108
6.6	Maximizing a Profit Function with Two Inputs	109
6.7	A Comparison with Output- or Yield-Maximization Criteria	111
6.8	Concluding Comments	112

7. Maximization Subject to Budget Constraints 114

7.1	Introduction	114
7.2	The Budget Constraint	115
7.3	The Budget Constraint and the Isoquant Map	117
7.4	Isoclines and the Expansion Path	119
7.5	General Expansion Path Conditions	120
7.6	The Production Function for the Bundle	122
7.7	Pseudo Scale Lines	124
7.8	Summary of Marginal Conditions and Concluding Comments	127

8. Further Topics in Constrained Maximization and Minimization 130

8.1	Simple Mathematics of Global Profit Maximization	130
8.2	Constrained Revenue Maximization	132
8.3	Second-Order Conditions	136
8.4	Interpretation of the Lagrangian Multiplier	137
8.5	Constrained Output Maximization	138
8.6	Cost-Minimization Subject to a Revenue Constraint	140
8.7	An Application in the Design of a Lease	142
	8.7.1 Cash Rent	142
	8.7.2 Shared Rental Arrangements	142
8.8	An Application to an Acreage Allotment Problem	145
8.9	Concluding Comments	148

9. Returns to Scale, Homogeneous Production Functions, and Euler's Theorem 151

9.1	Economies and Diseconomies of Size	151
9.2	Economies and Diseconomies of Scale	153
9.3	Homogeneous Production Functions	155
9.4	Returns to Scale and Individual Production Elasticities	157
9.5	Duality of Production and Cost for the Input Bundle	158
9.6	Euler's Theorem	162
9.7	Concluding Comments	163

10. The Cobb–Douglas Production Function 166

10.1	Introduction	166
10.2	The Original Cobb–Douglas Function	167
10.3	Early Generalizations	169
10.4	Some Characteristics of the Cobb–Douglas Type of Function	170
10.5	Isoquants for the Cobb–Douglas Type of Function	171
10.6	The Production Surface of the Cobb–Douglas Production Function	173
10.7	Profit Maximization with the Cobb–Douglas Function	175
10.8	Duality and the Cobb–Douglas Function	176
10.9	Constrained Output or Revenue Maximization	179
10.10	Concluding Comments	180

11. Other Agricultural Production Functions 183

11.1	Introduction	183
11.2	The Spillman Production Function	184
11.3	The Transcendental Production Function	185
11.4	The Two-Input Transcendental	187
11.5	Illustrations and Applications of the Transcendental	190
11.6	Cobb–Douglas with Variable Input Elasticities	191
11.7	de Janvry Modifications	191
11.8	Polynomial Forms	192
11.9	Concluding Comments	193

12. The Elasticity of Substitution 195

12.1	An Introduction to the Concept	195
12.2	Elasticities of Substitution and the Cobb–Douglas Function	200
12.3	Policy Applications of the Elasticity of Substitution	201
12.4	The CES Production Function	202
12.5	Elasticities of Substitution and the Translog Production Function	206
12.6	Concluding Comments	209

13. The Demand for Inputs to the Production Process 212

13.1	Introduction	212
13.2	A Single-Input Setting	213
13.3	The Elasticity of Input Demand	215

Contents

13.4	Technical Complements, Competitiveness, and Independence	218
13.5	Input Demand Functions in a Two-Input Setting	219
13.6	Input Demand Functions Under Constrained Maximization	223
13.7	Concluding Comments	224

14. Variable Product and Input Prices   226

14.1	Relaxing the Assumptions of Pure Competition	226
14.2	Variation in Output Prices from the Output Side	227
14.3	Variation in Output Prices from the Input Side	230
14.4	Variable Input Prices	233
14.5	A General Profit-Maximization Statement	234
14.6	Concluding Comments	236

15. Production of More Than One Product   238

15.1	Production Possibilities for a Society	238
15.2	Production Possibilities at the Farm Level	240
15.3	General Relationships	242
15.4	Competitive, Supplementary, Complementary, and Joint Products	244
15.5	Product Transformations from Single-Input Production Functions	246
15.6	Product Transformation and the Output Elasticity of Substitution	249
15.7	Concluding Comments	250

16. Maximization in a Two-Output Setting   252

16.1	The Family of Product Transformation Functions	252
16.2	Maximization of Output	253
16.3	The Isorevenue Line	254
16.4	Constrained Revenue Maximization	255
16.5	Simple Mathematics of Constrained Revenue Maximization	258
16.6	Second-Order Conditions	262
16.7	An Additional Example	264
16.8	Minimization of Input Use Subject to a Revenue Constraint	266
16.9	An Output Restriction Application	268
16.10	Concluding Comments	270

17. Two Outputs and Two Inputs 272

17.1	Introduction	272
17.2	Two Inputs and Two Outputs: A Basic Presentation	273
17.3	Some General Principles	274
17.4	The Constrained Maximization Problem	277
17.5	An Intermediate Product Model	278
17.6	Concluding Comments	283

18. General Multiple-Product and Multiple-Input Conditions 284

18.1	Introduction	284
18.2	Multiple Inputs and a Single Product	285
18.3	Many Outputs and a Single Input	288
18.4	Many Inputs and Many Outputs	289
18.5	Concluding Comments	292

19. Enterprise Budgeting and Marginal Analysis 294

19.1	The Development of an Enterprise Budget	294
19.2	The Level of Output to Be Produced	296
19.3	The Variable-Input Levels	298
19.4	The Fixed-Input Allocation	298
19.5	The Economies of Size and Farm Budgets	299
19.6	Price and Output Uncertainty	300
19.7	Concluding Comments	300

20. Decision Making in an Environment of Risk and Uncertainty 302

20.1	Risk and Uncertainty Defined	302
20.2	Farmer Attitudes Toward Risk and Uncertainty	303
20.3	Actions, States of Nature, Probabilities, and Consequences	305
20.4	Risk Preference and Utility	306
20.5	Risk, Uncertainty, and Marginal Analysis	309
20.6	Strategies for Dealing with Risk and Uncertainty	311
	20.6.1 Insure Against Risk	311
	20.6.2 Contracts	312
	20.6.3 Flexible Facilities and Equipment	312
	20.6.4 Diversification	313
	20.6.5 Government Programs	314
20.7	Concluding Comments	315

21. Time and Agricultural Production Processes 316

21.1	Introduction	316
21.2	Alternative Goals of a Farm Manager over Many Seasons	317
	21.2.1 Long-Run Profit Maximization	317
	21.2.2 Accumulation of Wealth	318
	21.2.3 Other Goals	318
21.3	Time as an Input to the Production Process	319
21.4	Time, Inflation, Interest Rates, and Net Worth	321
21.5	Discounting Revenues and Costs	322
	21.5.1 The Present Value of a Dollar	322
	21.5.2 Discounting Revenues with the Present Value Formula	323
	21.5.3 Compounding Revenues and Costs	324
21.6	Polyperiod Production and Marginal Analysis	325
21.7	Concluding Comments	329

22. Linear Programming and Marginal Analysis 330

22.1	Introduction	330
22.2	Classical Optimization and Linear Programming	331
22.3	Assumptions of Linear Programming	332
22.4	Technical Requirements and Fixed-Proportion Production Functions	333
22.5	A Simple Constrained Maximization Problem	334
22.6	Other Approaches for Solving Linear Programming Models	337
22.7	The Simplex Method	338
22.8	Duality	341
22.9	An Application	343
22.10	Concluding Comments	345

23. Frontiers in Agricultural Production Economics Research 347

23.1	Management and Agricultural Production Functions	347
	23.1.1 Alternative Approaches to Management	348
	23.1.2 Management and Profit Maximization	349
23.2	New Technology and the Agricultural Production Function	350
	23.2.1 Some Examples	351
	23.2.2 Time and Technology	352

23.3	Conceptual Issues in Estimating Agricultural Production Functions		354
23.4	Concluding Comments		356

Suggested Readings 357

Index 362

1 Introduction

This chapter introduces some basic concepts fundamental to the study of production economics and provides a brief review of fundamental terms used in economics. These terms are usually presented as part of an introductory economics or agricultural economics course, and provide a starting point for the further study of agricultural production economics. The fundamental assumptions of the purely competitive model and the relationship of these assumptions to agricultural production economics are outlined.

Key Terms and Definitions:

Economics
Wants
Resources
Theory
Model
Consumption Economics
Production Economics
Utility

Profit
Microeconomics
Macroeconomics
Statics
Dynamics
Agricultural Economics
Pure Competition

1.1 Economics Defined

Economics is defined as the study of how limited resources can best be used to fulfill unlimited human wants. Whereas the wants or desires of human beings are unlimited, the means or resources available for meeting these wants or desires are not unlimited. Economics thus deals with making the best use of available resources to fulfill these unlimited wants.

An entire society, an entire country, or for that matter, the world, faces constraints and limitations in the availability of resources. When the word *re-*

source is used, people usually think of basic natural resources, such as oil and gas, and iron ore. However, the term has a much broader economic meaning, and economists include not only basic natural resources, but a broad array of other items that would not occur to those who have not studied economics.

An important resource is the amount of labor that is available within a society. The money that is invested in industrial plants used to produce items consumers want is another basic resource within a society. A resource can be defined still more broadly. Human beings vary in their skill at doing jobs. A society consisting primarily of highly educated and well-trained individuals will be a much more productive society than one in which most people have few skills. Thus the education and skills of jobholders within an economy must be viewed as a limiting resource.

Students may attend college because they hope to obtain skills that will allow them to earn higher incomes. They view the lack of a college degree to be a constraint or limitation on their ability to earn income. Underlying this is the basic driving force of unlimited human wants. Because human wants and desires are unlimited, whereas the resources useful in fulfilling these wants are limited, the basic problem that must be faced, both by individuals and by societies, is how best to go about utilizing scarce resources to fulfill these unlimited wants.

1.2 The Logic of Economic Theory

Economists and others have made numerous attempts to define the word *theory*. A definition widely accepted by economists is that a theory is a representation of a set of relationships. Economic theory can represent either the set of relationships governing the behavior of individual producers and consumers, or the set of relationships governing the overall economy of the society or nation.

However, some scientists, including economists, also use the term *theory* as a synonym for a hypothesis, a proposition about how something operates. Some theories may be based on little if any observation. An example is a theory of how the universe was formed. Theories in physics often precede actual observation. Physicists have highly developed theories about how electrons, protons, and neutrons in atoms behave, despite the lack of actual observation. Although theories may be used as a basis for explaining phenomena in the real world, they need not be based on actual observation.

An *economic theory* can be defined as a representation of a set of relationships that govern human behavior within some portion of an economy. An economic theory can also be defined as a hypothesis or set of hypotheses about how a particular aspect of an economy operates. These hypotheses might be tested by observing if they are consistent with the observed behavior within the economy. Theory as such is not tested; rather, what is tested is the applicability of a theory for explaining the behavior of a particular individual or group of individuals. The conclusion by a social scientist that a theory does not adequately explain the behavior of a particular group of people does not render the theory invalid. The same theory might be quite applicable to other people under a slightly different set of circumstances.

1.3 Economic Theory as Abstraction

The real world is highly complex. Economists spend very little time in the real world, but rather, spend a lot of time attempting to uncover fundamental theories that govern human behavior as it relates to production and consumption. If the real world is highly complex, so is the economy of any industrialized society, or for that matter, the economy of nearly any society or nation. There is so much complexity that it is often difficult to see clearly the fundamental relationships.

In an effort to see more clearly the relationships that are important, economists abstract from reality in developing theories. They leave out relationships identified as unimportant to the problem, in an effort to focus more closely on the relationships which they feel are important. Economic theory often becomes a simplification of reality that may seem unrealistic or even silly to someone with no training in economics.

Moreover, economists appear to argue continually. To a person without a background in economics, economists never seem to agree on anything. The development of an economic theory as a formal set of relationships governing some aspect of an economy will invariably involve simplification. Some relationships will be included: others will be left out. The relationships included are those that the economist developing the theory felt were important and which represented the key features of the particular economic problem the economist wanted to study.

However, economists can and do engage in heated debate with regard to whether or not a particular theory (one that includes some relationships but omits others) is the correct representation. Debate is a very normal and ordinary part of the behavior of economists and is the driving force that results in a continual improvement in economic theories over time. Without it, economics as a discipline within the social sciences would not progress.

1.4 Economic Theory Versus Economic Model

Economists sometimes use the terms *theory* and *model* interchangeably. A child might think of a model as a miniature or toy version of, say, an automobile or farm tractor. This is not a bad way to think about an economic model. To be realistic, a model must have a degree of detail. The model must contain a representation of the principal parts of the real thing, or it would not be recognizable.

At the same time, the model would not be expected to perform the same functions as the real thing. Just as one would not expect to make a journey in a toy automobile, an economist would not expect to control the workings of the U.S. economy with a model of the economy. However, just as an automobile designer might construct a model of a new automobile before the real thing is built in an effort to obtain a better understanding of how the real thing might look, so might an economist construct a model of the U.S. economy to better understand how a particular government policy, if implemented, might affect individuals and firms within the economy.

Economists use models as a way to measure or simulate the effects of a policy without actually having to implement the policy. The key question is "What would happen if ... ?" The model can be used to answer the question and to assess the impact of numerous alternative policies without actually implementing them. Hence a model can also be thought of as a set of relationships (or theory) that lends itself to answering "what would happen if" types of questions.

1.5 Representing Economic Relationships

Economic theories and models can be represented in a variety of ways. Beginning in the 18th century with Adam Smith's famous work *The Wealth of Nations*, economists have relied heavily on words to express economic relationships. Increasingly, words did not lend themselves very well to answering specific "what if" types of questions. Economists in the late nineteenth and early twentieth centuries relied increasingly on graphical tools as the major means of expressing economic relationships. Graphics could often be used to make complex verbal arguments precise, but graphical tools had disadvantages as well. For example, a graph representing a production function on a farm was limited to no more than two inputs and a single output, since it is not possible to draw in more than three dimensions.

The use of mathematics as the means of describing economic theories and models got an important boost with the publication of Paul Samuelson's *Foundations of Economic Analysis* in 1947. Since that time, mathematics has become increasingly important as a tool for the development of theory and models. Fuzzy relationships cannot be part of a theory posed in mathematical terms. Moreover, mathematics opened new doors for expressing complicated relationships. On the production side, there were no longer any limits as to the number of inputs that a production function might use or the number of outputs that could be obtained.

Concomitant with increased use of mathematics for describing economic relationships was increased use of statistics for estimating economic relationships from real-world data. An entirely new subdiscipline, econometrics—economic measurement—appeared. The relationships contained within the mathematically based theoretical model could now be measured.

The final event having an impact on economics over the second half of the twentieth century was rapid growth in the use of the computer as a device for estimating or measuring relationships within an economy. Economists now routinely use techniques for estimating models in which the computational requirements would have been considered impossible to achieve only five or ten years ago.

1.6 Consumption Versus Production Economics

Economics involves choices. A person who faces a limited income (and no one does not) must choose to purchase those items that make him or her feel most satisfied, subject to an income limitation or constraint. Choice is the heart of consumption economics. Economists say that a person derives utility from an item from which he or she receives satisfaction. The basic consumer economics problem involves the maximization of utility (satisfaction) subject to the constraint imposed by the availability of income.

This book deals with another set of choices, however, the set of choices faced by the producer of goods and services desired by the consumer. The producer also attempts to maximize utility. To maximize utility, the producer is motivated by a desire to make money, again in order better to fulfill unlimited wants. Although the producer may have other goals, the producer frequently attempts to maximize profit as a means of achieving utility or satisfaction. Profit is the difference between the revenues obtained from what is sold and the costs incurred in producing the goods. However, producers face constraints, too. If producers did not face constraints, the solution to the profit-maximization problem for the producer would be to produce as much as possible of anything that could be sold for more than the cost of production.

Producers may attempt to maximize something other than profit as a means of achieving the greatest utility or satisfaction. Some farmers might indeed have the objective of maximizing profits on their farms given resources such as land, labor, and farm machinery. The underlying motivation for maximizing profits on the farm is that some of these profits will be used as income to purchase goods and services for which the farmer (and his or her family) obtain satisfaction or utility. Such a farmer behaves no differently from any other consumer. Other farmers might attempt to maximize something else, such as the amount of land owned, as a means to achieve satisfaction.

The producer faces an allocation problem analogous to that faced by the consumer. The consumer frequently is interested in allocating income such that utility or satisfaction is maximized. The producer frequently is interested in allocating resources such that profits are maximized. Economics is concerned with the basic choices that must be made to achieve these objectives. Consumption economics deals primarily with the utility-maximization problem, whereas production economics is concerned primarily with the profit-maximization problem. However, profits are used by the owner of the firm to purchase goods and services that provide utility or satisfaction.

1.7 Microeconomics Versus Macroeconomics

Economics can be broadly divided into two categories: microeconomics and macroeconomics. *Microeconomics* is concerned with the behavior of individual decision-making units. The prefix *micro-* is often used in conjunction with things that are small. Microeconomics deals with the behavior of the individual consumer as income is allocated and the individual firm manager (such as a farmer) who attempts to allocate his or her resources consistent with his or her goals.

The prefix *macro-* is often used in conjunction with things that are large. *Macroeconomics* deals with the big picture. For example, a person studying macroeconomics might deal with issues confronting an entire economy. Inflation and unemployment are classical areas of concern for macroeconomists. They are concerned with how producers and consumers interact in total in a society, nation, or for that matter, the world.

6 Introduction

Macroeconomists are also concerned with the role that government policy might play in determining answers to the fundamental questions that must be answered by any society. These questions include: (1) What should be produced? (2) How much should be produced? (3) How should available goods and services be allocated?

Although microeconomics and macroeconomics are often considered to be separate branches of economics, they are really very closely intertwined. The macroeconomy is made up of individual producers and consumers. Moreover, the decisions made by individual producers and consumers are not at all independent of what is happening at the macro level. Tax cuts and tax increases by the federal government influence income available to the individual consumer to spend. Prices received by individual farmers for the commodities they produce are in large measure determined by the aggregate production of all farmers in producing a particular commodity, yet to a great extent affect decisions made by the farmer as an individual firm manager.

This text deals with production economics and the central focus is on the farm firm as an individual decision-making unit. At the same time, the individual farm firm does not operate in a vacuum, but is affected in large measure by what happens in the aggregate. Moreover, decisions made by individual firms such as farms, when taken together, can have a substantial impact in a macroeconomic setting.

1.8 Statics Versus Dynamics

Economics can also be classified as static economics or dynamic economics. *Static economics* can be thought of as one or more still snapshots of events taking place in an economy. *Dynamic economics* can be thought of as a moving picture of the economy. Economists rely heavily on what is sometimes called *comparative statics*.

The economic relationships are often represented by a graph: for example, a graph showing a supply curve and a demand curve. An event or shock affecting demand or supply is assumed to take place. For example, suppose that consumer incomes increase. A second demand curve might be drawn on the same graph to represent what happens as a result. The snapshot comparison of prices and quantities that would prevail under the old and new levels of consumer incomes is referred to as *comparative statics* (Figure 1.1).

With an analysis using comparative statics, no attempt is made to uncover the processes that caused incomes to rise, nor is time important. This is sometimes referred to as a static, timeless environment. It is a useful means of analysis when the focus is on the impact of an economic shock, not the processes by which the shock takes place. Notice also that comparative statics can be used to shed light on either microeconomic or macroeconomic issues.

In contrast with statics, time is the important element of dynamics. Dynamic economics attempts to show the processes by which an individual consumer, firm, or economy moves from one equilibrium to another. Suppose, for example, that the price of a good or commodity decreases. Dynamic economics might attempt to uncover changes in the quantity that would be taken from the market one hour, one day, one week, and one month from the point in time

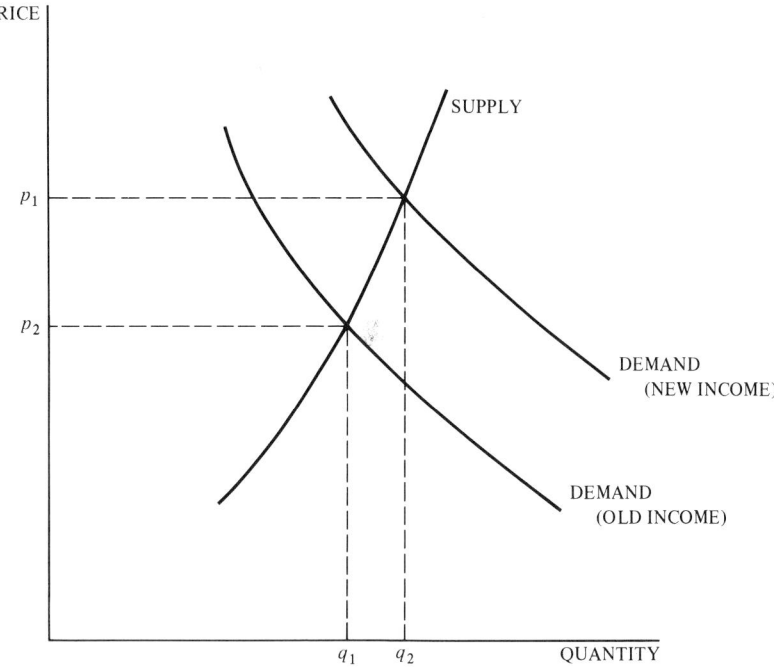

Figure 1.1 Supply and Demand

in which the initial price decrease took place. Another problem in dynamics might be the path of machinery investments made by a farmer over a 20-year period.

1.9 Economics Versus Agricultural Economics

Until now, little has been said about agricultural economics and its relationship to economics. There has been a reason for this. An agricultural economist is, first, an economist, in that an agricultural economist knows economic theory intimately. However, an agricultural economist is also an economist with a specialization in agriculture. The primary interest is in applying economic logic to problems that occur in agriculture. An agricultural economist needs to know economics, but a knowledge of agriculture is also important. If an agricultural economist is to portray relationships accurately using a model of some component of an agricultural sector, the agricultural economist must know these relationships. Otherwise, the salient or important elements of the theory would be missed.

1.10 Agricultural Production Economics

Agricultural production economics is concerned primarily with economic theory as it relates to the producer of agricultural commodities. Some major concerns in agricultural production economics include the following.

Goals and objectives of the farm manager. Agricultural economists often assume that the objective of any farm manager is that of maximizing profits, a measurement of which is the difference between returns from the sale of crops and livestock less the costs of producing these commodities. However, individual farmers have unique goals. One farmer might be more interested in obtaining ownership of the largest farm in the county. Another might have as his or her goal that of owning the best set of farm machinery. Still another might be interested in minimizing his or her debt load.

The goals and objectives of a farm manager are closely intertwined with a person's psychological makeup, and the goals selected by a particular person may have very little to do with profit maximization. Nonetheless, most economic models used for representing the behavior of farm managers assume that the manager is interested in maximizing profits, or at minimum is interested in maximizing revenue subject to constraints imposed by the availability of resources.

Choice of outputs to be produced. A farm manager faces an array of options with regard to what to produce given available land, labor, machinery, and equipment. The manager must not only decide how much of each particular commodity to be produced, but also how available resources are to be allocated among alternative commodities. The farmer might be interested in maximizing profits but may have other goals as well. Often other constraints enter. For example, the government may permit the farmer to grow only a certain number of acres of a particular commodity. The farmer may have a particular knowledge of, or preference for, a certain commodity. The farmland may be better suited for certain types of crops or livestock than for other types.

Allocation of resources among outputs. Once decisions have been made with regard to what commodity or commodities are to be produced, the farmer must decide how his or her available resources are to be allocated among outputs. A simple question to be answered is which field is to be used for the production of each crop, but the questions quickly become far more complex. The amount of farm labor and machinery on each farm is limited. Labor and machinery time must be allocated to each crop and livestock activity, consistent with the farmer's overall objective. The greatest share of this text is devoted to dealing with issues underlying the problems faced by farm managers in the allocation of resources or inputs across alternative outputs or enterprises.

Assumption of risk and uncertainty. Models in production economics frequently assume that the manager knows with certainty the applicable production function (for example, the yield that would result for a crop if a particular amount of fertilizer were applied) and the prices both for inputs to be purchased and outputs to be sold. However, in agriculture, the assumption of knowledge with respect to the production function is almost never met. Weather is, of course, the key variable, but nature presents other challenges. Cattle develop diseases and die, and crops are affected by insects and disease. Most farmers would scoff at economic theory that assumes that a production function is known with certainty.

Although farmers may be fully aware of the prices they must pay for inputs such as fuel, fertilizer, and seed at the time each input is purchased, they are almost never aware at the beginning of the production season of prices that will prevail when outputs are sold. Price uncertainty is a result of the biological lag facing the producer of nearly any agricultural commodity, and production in agriculture takes time.

Economists have often made a simplifying assumption that production takes place instantaneously—that inputs are, upon acquisition, immediately and magically transformed into outputs. The transformation does not instantaneously take place in agricultural production. Production of most crops takes several months. The time may be measured in years from when a calf is conceived to when the fattened steer is placed on the market. Hence farmers must make production decisions with less than perfect knowledge with regard to the price at which the product will sell when it is actually placed on the market.

The competitive economic environment in which the farm firm operates. Economists often cite farming as the closest real-world example of the traditional model of pure competition. But the competitive environment under which a farmer operates depends heavily on the particular commodity being produced.

1.11 The Assumptions of Pure Competition

Economists often use the theory of pure competition as a basic model for explaining the behavior of firms in an industry. At this point, it is useful to review the assumptions of the classical economic model of pure competition and assess the degree to which these assumptions might apply to farming in the United States. The purely competitive model assumes the following:

A large number of buyers and sellers in the industry exist. Few would feel that there are not a large number of sellers in farming. The United States Department of Agriculture (USDA) reported over 2.4 million farms in the United States in 1980, but farm numbers are far fewer for selected agricultural commodities. Only a few farms supply the entire nation's parsley needs, for example.

The assumption of a large number of buyers may be met to a degree at a local livestock auction market or at a central grain exchange in Minneapolis or Chicago, but many agricultural products move in markets in which only a comparatively few buyers exist. The tobacco producer may face only buyers from the three or four major cigarette manufacturers, and prices are determined in an environment that is not very competitive. In the livestock sector, broiler production has been dominated in recent years by only a few major producers. Production of hogs and cattle in the United States is often closer to a purely competitive environment in which a large number of farm firms take prices generated by overall supply and demand for hogs and cattle. However, there are a relatively small number of buyers for hogs and cattle, which again means that the model of pure competition does not strictly apply.

The firm can sell as much as it wants at the going market price, and no single firm is large enough to influence the price for the commodity being produced. For many agricultural commodities, the farmer can sell as much as he or she wants at the market price. Farmers are price takers, not price setters, in the production of commodities such as wheat, corn, beef, and pork. However, for certain commodities, the sparcity of farms means that the producers might exert a degree of control over the price obtained.

The product is homogeneous. The homogeneity assumption implies that the product produced by all firms in the industry is identical. As a result, there is no need for advertising, for there is nothing to distinguish the output of one firm from another. For the most part, this assumption is true in farming. There is little to distinguish one producer's number 2 corn from another's number 2 corn. For a few commodities, there have been some attempts at product differentiation—for example, Sunkist oranges by the growers' cooperative, and branded chicken by the individual broiler producer.

There is free entry and exit, and thus free mobility of resources (inputs or factors of production) exists both in and out of farming. The free-mobility assumption is currently seldom met in agriculture. At one time it may have been possible for a farmer to begin with very little money and a lot of ambition. Nowadays, a normal farm may very well be a business with a million-dollar investment. It is difficult to see how free entry and exit can exist in an industry that may require an individual firm to have a million dollars in startup capital. Inflation over the past decade has drastically increased the startup capital requirements for farming, with resultant impacts on the mobility of resources.

Free mobility of resources in linked to an absence of artificial restraints, such as government involvement. There exist a number of artificial restraints in farming. The federal government has been and continues to be involved in influencing production decisions with respect to nearly every major agricultural commodity and numerous minor commodities as well. Agricultural cooperatives have had a significant impact on production levels for commodities such as milk and oranges.

Grain production in the United States is often heavily influenced by the presence of government programs. The wheat and feed grain programs are major examples. In milk production, the government has largely determined the prices to be received by dairy farmers.

The government is involved not only in major agricultural commodities, but is also heavily involved in the economic environment for many commodities with limited production. For example, the hops producer in Washington state, or the burley tobacco producer in central Kentucky, produces in an environment in which the federal government largely determines both who will produce as well as how much each grower will produce. This is anything but competitive.

All variables of concern to the producer and the consumer are known with certainty. Some economists distinguish between pure competition and perfect competition. These economists argue that *pure competition* can exist even if all variables are not known with certainty to the producer and consumer. However, *perfect competition* will exist only if the producer knows not only the prices for which outputs will be sold, but also the prices for inputs. Moreover, with perfect competition, the consumer has complete knowledge with respect to prices.

Most important, with perfect competition the producer is assumed to have complete knowledge of the production process or function that transforms inputs or resources into outputs or commodities. Nature is assumed not to vary from year to year. Of course, this assumption is violated in agriculture. The vagaries of nature enter into nearly everything a farmer does, and influence not only output levels, but the quantity of inputs used as well.

1.12 Why Retain the Purely Competitive Model?

As has been indicated, the assumptions of the purely competitive model are not very closely met by farming in the United States. The next logical question is: Why retain it? The answer to this question is simple. Despite its weaknesses, the purely competitive model comes closer to representing farming than any other comprehensive model of economic behavior. An individual farm is clearly not a monopoly if a *monopoly* is thought of as being a model in which a single firm is the industry. Nor, for most commodities, do farmers constitute an oligopoly, if an *oligopoly* is defined as a model in which only a few firms exist in a competitive environment where price and output decisions by one firm are strongly affected by the price and output decisions of other firms. Nor does farming usually meet the basic assumption of monopolistic competition, where slight differences in product prices can be maintained over the long term because individual producers are somewhat successful in slightly differentiating their product from products made by a rival firm.

In summary, the purely competitive model has been retained as the basic model for application within agricultural production economics to farming because it comes closer than any of the remaining models of competitive behavior. This does not mean that other models of competitive behavior are unimportant in the remainder of the text. Rather, reliance will be placed on the purely competitive model as the starting point for much of our analysis, with modifications made as needed to meet the particular features of the problem.

1.13 Concluding Comments

The *purely competitive model* provides the basic starting point for much of the remainder of the text. The assumptions of the purely competitive model are fundamental to microeconomic or firm-oriented models of agricultural production processes.

The *factor-product model* is used in instances where one input is varied in the production of a single output. Key features of the factor-product model are outlined in detail in Chapters 2 to 4.

The *factor-factor model* deals with a situation in which two inputs are varied in the production of a single output. The fundamental technical relationships underlying the factor-factor model are presented primarily with graphics in Chapter 5. The mathematics of maximization and minimization are developed in Chapter 6. Chapters 7 and 8 introduce prices and present the complete factor-factor model using the graphical presentation developed in Chapter 5 as well as the mathematics outlined in Chapter 6 as a basis. Linkages between graphical and mathematical presentations are stressed. Chapter 9 provides some extensions of the basic factor-factor model using two inputs and a single output.

Chapter 10 is devoted to the Cobb–Douglas production function, which is perhaps the best known algebraic form used to represent agricultural production processes. Chapter 11 is devoted to some other closely related functional forms which are perhaps more closely linked to traditional production theory and provide better representations of true agricultural production processes, but are more difficult to work with algebraically.

Chapter 12 introduces the concept of the elasticity of substitution between input pairs. The chapter makes use of the constant elasticity of substitution (CES) production function as the means for illustrating this concept.

Chapter 13 shows how the demand functions for inputs or factors of production can be derived from the profit-maximizing conditions for the firm. These input demand functions are derived under varying assumptions with respect to the characteristics of the production function underlying the profit-maximizing conditions.

Chapter 14 relaxes some of the assumptions of the purely competitive model and illustrates how the relaxation of these assumptions can affect profit-maximizing conditions for the firm. Models in which product prices and input prices are allowed to vary are considered.

Chapters 15 and 16 are devoted to the *product-product model,* in which a single input or resource is used to produce two different products. Linkages to the production possibilities curve are outlined. Profit-maximization conditions for the firm are derived.

Chapters 17 and 18 extend the factor-factor and product-product models to situations in which many different inputs are used in order to produce many different outputs. The conditions required to maximize or minimize the manager's objective function subject to limitations in the availability of resources are formally derived using mathematics for many different inputs and outputs in Chapter 18.

Some linkages between marginal analysis and enterprise budgeting are discussed in Chapter 19. Chapters 20 and 21 are devoted to topics that involve dynamic as well as static theory. Chapter 20 presents models that take into account risk and uncertainty. Models in Chapter 21 include time as an explicit element.

Chapter 22 shows how linear programming might be used as a tool for operationalizing concepts related to the factor-factor and product-product models presented in the earlier chapters. Specific applications to agriculture are presented.

Chapter 23 poses some questions and unsolved problems in agricultural production economics which provide the basis for research in agricultural economics. These are used as a vehicle useful as a basis for further study in agricultural production economics.

Questions for Thought and Class Discussion

   1. Discuss the role of microeconomics versus macroeconomics in agricultural economics. Does microeconomics have a greater impact than macroeconomics on the farm manager? Explain.

   2. If pure competition is not an adequate representation of the economic model that underlies farming in the United States, why do the assumptions of pure competition continue to be important to agricultural economists?

   3. Nowadays, is mathematics essential for understanding economic principles?

4. The real world is dynamic. If so, why do agricultural economists continue to rely so heavily on comparative statics?

5. Agricultural economists are frequently accused of spending too little time in the real world. A preoccupation with abstract theoretical issues means that agricultural economists are sometimes unable or unwilling to look at the fundamental issues linked to the production and marketing of agricultural commodities. Do you agree or disagree?

6. To become an agricultural economist, is it more important to know agriculture or to know economic theory?

References

Samuelson, Paul A. *Foundations of Economic Analysis.* New York: Atheneum, 1970 (originally published in 1947).

Smith, Adam, *The Wealth of Nations,* Edwin Cannan ed. New York: The Modern Library, 1937 (originally written in 1776).

U.S. Department of Agriculture, "Economic Indicators of the Farm Sector," *ECIFS-1.* Washington D.C., Aug. 1982.

2 Production with One Variable Input

This chapter introduces the concept of a production function and uses the concept as a basis for the development of the factor-product model. An agricultural production function in presented using graphical and tabular approaches. Algebraic examples of simple production functions with one input and one output are developed. Key features of the neoclassical production function are outlined. The concept of marginal and average physical product is introduced. The use of the first, second, and third derivatives in determining the shape of the underlying total, marginal, and average product is illustrated, and the concept of the elasticity of production is presented.

Key Terms and Definitions:

Production Function
Domain
Range
Continuous Production Function
Discrete Production Function
Fixed Input
Variable Input
Short Run
Long Run
Intermediate Run
Sunk Costs
Law of Diminishing (Marginal) Returns

Total Physical Product (*TPP*)
Marginal Physical Product (*MPP*)
Average Physical Product (*APP*)
$\Delta y/\Delta x$
Sign
Slope
Curvature
First Derivative
Second Derivative
Third Derivative
Elasticity of Production

2.1 What Is a Production Function?

A production function describes the technical relationship that transforms inputs (resources) into outputs (commodities). A mathematician defines a *function* as a rule for assigning to each value in one set of variables (the domain

2.1 What Is a Production Function?

of the function) a single value in another set of variables (the range of the function).

A general way of writing a production function is

$$y = f(x) \tag{2.1}$$

where y is an output and x is an input. All values of x greater than or equal to zero constitute the domain of this function. The range of the function consists of each output level (y) that results from each level of input (x) being used. Equation (2.1) is a very general form for a production function. All that is known about the function $f(x)$ so far is that it meets the mathematician's definition of a function. Given this general form, it is not possible to determine exactly how much output (y) would result from a given level of input (x). The specific form of the function $f(x)$ would be needed, and $f(x)$ could take on many specific forms.

Suppose the simple function

$$y = 2x \tag{2.2}$$

For each value of x, a unique and single value of y is assigned. For example if $x = 2$, then $y = 4$; if $x = 6$, then $y = 12$; and so on. The domain of the function is all possible values for x, and the range is the set of y values corresponding to each x. In equation (2.2), each unit of input (x) produces 2 units of output (y).

Now consider the function

$$y = \sqrt{x} \tag{2.3}$$

It is not possible to take the square root of a negative number and get a real number. Hence the domain (x) and range (y) of equation (2.3) includes only those numbers greater than or equal to zero. Here again the function meets the basic definition that a single value in the range be assigned to each value in the domain of the function. This restriction would be all right for a production function, since it is unlikely that a farmer would ever use a negative quantity of input. It is not clear what a negative quantity of an input might be.

Functions might be expressed in other ways. The following is an example

If $x = 10$, then $y = 25$.
If $x = 20$, then $y = 50$.
If $x = 30$, then $y = 60$.
If $x = 40$, then $y = 65$.
If $x = 50$, then $y = 60$.

Notice again that a single value for y is assigned to each x. Notice also that there are two values for x (30 and 50) that get assigned the same value for y (60). The mathematician's definition of a function allows for this. But one value for y must be assigned to each x. It does not matter if two different x values are assigned the same y value.

Production with One Variable Input

The converse, however, is not true. Suppose that the example were modified only slightly

If $x = 25$, then $y = 10$.
If $x = 50$, then $y = 20$.
If $x = 60$, then $y = 30$.
If $x = 65$, then $y = 40$.
If $x = 60$, then $y = 50$.

This is an example that violates the definition of a function. Notice that for the value $x = 60$, two values of y are assigned, 30 and 50. This cannot be. The definition of a function stated that a single value for y must be assigned to each x. The relationship described here represents what is known as a *correspondence*, but not a function. A correspondence describes the relationship between two variables. All functions are correspondences, but not all correspondences are functions.

Some of these ideas can be applied to hypothetical data describing the production of corn in response to the use of nitrogen fertilizer. Table 2.1 represents the relationship and provides specific values for the general production function $y = f(x)$. For each nitrogen application level, a single yield is defined. The yield level is sometimes referred to as the total physical product (*TPP*) resulting from the nitrogen that is applied.

From Table 2.1, 160 pounds of nitrogen per acre will result in a corn yield or *TPP* of 123 bushels per acre. The concept of a function has a good deal of impact on the basic assumptions underlying the economics of agricultural production.

Another possible problem exists with the interpretation of the data contained in Table 2.1. The exact amount of corn (*TPP*) that will be produced if a farmer decides to apply 120 pounds of nitrogen per acre can be determined from Table 2.1, but what happens if the farmer decides to apply 140 pounds of nitrogen per acre? A yield has not been assigned to this nitrogen application level. A mathematician might say that our production function $y = f(x)$ is discontinuous at any nitrogen application level other than those specifically listed in Table 2.1.

A simple solution might be to interpolate between the known values. If 120 pounds per acre produces 115 bushels of corn, and 160 pounds of nitrogen

Table 2.1 Corn Yield Response to Nitrogen Fertilizer

Quantity of Nitrogen (lb/acre)	Yield (bu/acre)
0	50
40	75
80	105
120	115
160	123
200	128
240	124

2.1 What Is a Production Function?

produces 123 bushels of corn, the yield at 140 pounds might be $(115 + 123)/2$ or 119 bushels per acre. However, incremental increases in nitrogen application do not provide equal incremental increases in corn production throughout the domain of the function. There is no doubt that some nitrogen is available in the soil from decaying organic material and nitrogen applied in previous seasons, and nitrogen need not be applied in order to get back the first 50 bushels of corn.

The first 40 pounds of nitrogen applied produces 25 additional bushels, for a total of 75 bushels; the next 40 pounds produces 30 bushels of corn, for a total of 105 bushels; but the productivity of the remaining 40-pound increments in terms of corn production declines. The next 40 pounds increases yield by only 10 bushels per acre, the 40 pounds after that by only 8 bushels per acre, and the final 40 pounds by only 5 bushels per acre.

Following this rationale, it seems unlikely that 140 pounds of nitrogen would produce a yield of 119 bushels; and a more likely guess might be 120 or 121 bushels. These are only guesses. In reality, no information about the behavior of the function is available at nitrogen application levels other than those listed in Table 2.1. A yield of 160 bushels per acre at a nitrogen application level of 140 pounds per acre could result—or, for that matter, any other yield.

Suppose instead that the relationship between the amount of nitrogen that is applied and corn yield is described as

$$y = 0.75x + 0.0042x^2 - 0.000023x^3 \tag{2.4}$$

where y = corn yield (total physical product) in bushels per acre
x = nitrogen applied in pounds per acre

Equation (2.4) has some advantages over the tabular function presented in Table 2.1. The major advantage is that it is possible to calculate the resultant corn yield at any fertilizer application level. For example, the corn yield when 200 pounds of fertilizer is applied is $0.75(200) + 0.0042(200^2) - 0.000023(200^3)$ = 134 bushels per acre.

Moreover, a function such as this is continuous. There are no nitrogen levels where a corn yield cannot be calculated. The yield at a nitrogen application level of 186.5 pounds per acre can be calculated exactly. Such a function has other advantages, particularly if the additional output resulting from an extra pound of nitrogen is to be calculated. The yields of corn at the nitrogen application rates shown in Table 2.1 can be calculated and are presented in Table 2.2.

The corn yields (*TPP*) generated by the production function in Table 2.2 are not the same as those presented in Table 2.1. There is no reason for both functions to generate the same yields. A continuous function that would generate exactly the same yields as those presented in Table 2.1 would be very complicated algebraically. Economists like to work with continuous functions, rather than discrete production functions from tabular data, in that the yield for any level of input use can be readily obtained without any need for interpolation. However, a tabular presentation would probably make more sense to farmers.

18   Production with One Variable Input

Table 2.2 Corn Yields at Alternative Nitrogen Application Rates for the Production Function y = $0.75x + 0.00042x^2 - 0.000023x^3$

Quantity of Nitrogen, x (lb/acre)	Corn Yield, y or *TPP* (bu/acre)
0	0.0
20	16.496
40	35.248
60	55.152
80	75.104
100	94.000
120	110.736
140	124.208
160	133.312
180	136.944
200	134.000
220	123.376
240	103.968

The yields generated in Table 2.2 also differ from those in Table 2.1 in another important way. Table 2.1 states that if a farmer applied no nitrogen to corn, a yield of 50 bushels per acre is obtained. Of course, nitrogen is absolutely essential for corn to grow. As indicated earlier, the data contained in Table 2.1 assume that there is some residual nitrogen in the soil on which the corn is grown. The nitrogen is in the soil because of decaying organic material and leftover nitrogen from fertilizers applied in years past. As a result, the data in Table 2.1 reveal higher yields at low nitrogen application levels than do the data contained in Table 2.2.

The mathematical function used as the basis for Table 2.2 could be modified to take this residual nitrogen into account by adding a constant such as 50. The remaining coefficients of the function (the 0.75, the 0.0042, and the -0.000023) would also need to be altered as well. Otherwise, the production function would produce a possible but perhaps unrealistic corn yield of $50 + 136.944 = 186.944$ bushels per acre when 180 pounds of fertilizer were applied. For many production processes in agriculture, no input produces no output. Consider the case of the production of beef using feed as an input. No feed would indeed produce no beef. In the case of crop production, some yield will normally result without chemical fertilizers.

A production function thus represents the relationship that exists between inputs and outputs. For each level of input use, the function assigns a unique output level. When a zero level of input is used, output might be zero, or, in some instances, output might be produced without the input.

2.2 Fixed Versus Variable Inputs and the Length of Run

So far, examples have included only one input or factor of production. The general form of the production function was

2.2 Fixed Versus Variable Inputs and the Length of Run

$$y = f(x) \quad (2.5)$$

where y = an output
x = an input

Equation (2.5) is an ultrasimplistic production function for agricultural commodities. Such a function assumes that the production process can be accurately described by a function in which only one input or factor of production is used to produce an output. Few, if any, agricultural commodities are produced in this manner. Most agricultural commodities require several, if not a dozen or more, inputs. As an alternative, suppose a production function where there are several inputs and all but one are assumed to be held fixed at some constant level. The production function would thus become

$$y = f(x_1 | x_2, x_3, x_4, x_5, x_6, x_7) \quad (2.6)$$

For example, y might be the yield of corn in bushels per acre, and x_1 might represent the amount of nitrogen fertilizer applied per acre. Variables $x_2, \ldots, x_7$ might represent each of the other inputs used in the production of corn, such as land, labor, and machinery.

Thus, in this example, the input x_1 is treated as the "variable" input, while the remaining inputs ($x_2, \ldots, x_7$) are assumed to be held constant at some fixed level. The "|" can be read as the word "given." As the use of x_1 is "varied" or increased, units of the variable input x_1 are added to units of the fixed inputs $x_2, \ldots, x_7$.

How can it be determined if an input should be treated as fixed or variable? A *variable input* is often thought of as an input that the farm manager can control or for which he or she can alter the level of use. This implies that the farmer has sufficient time to adjust the amount of input being used. Nitrogen in corn production has often been cited as an example of a variable input, in that the farmer can control the amount to be applied to the field.

A *fixed input* is usually defined as an input which for some reason the farmer has no control over the amount available. The amount of land a farmer has might be treated as a fixed input.

However, these distinctions become muddy and confused. Given sufficient time, a farmer might be able to find additional land to rent or purchase, or the farmer might sell some of the land owned. If the length of time were sufficient to do this, the land input might be treated as a variable input.

The categorization of inputs as either fixed or variable is closely intertwined with the concept of time. Economists sometimes define the *long run* as time of sufficient length such that all inputs to the production function can be treated as variable. The *very short run* can be defined as a period of time so short that none of the inputs are variable. Other lengths of time can also be defined. For example, the *short run* is a period of time long enough such that a few of the inputs can be treated as variable, but most are fixed. The *intermediate run* is long enough so that many, but not all inputs are treated as variable.

These categories again are somewhat arbitrary. If an economist were asked "How long is the short run?", the answer would probably be that the short run is a period of time sufficiently long that some inputs can be treated as variable, but sufficiently short such that some inputs can be treated as fixed. Does this imply a length of time of a day, a week, a month, or a crop production season? The length of time involved could be any of these.

Once fertilizer has been applied, a farmer no longer has control over application levels. The input that was previously classified as variable becomes fixed. Seed before planting is classified as a variable input. Once it is planted in the ground, seed can no longer be treated as a variable input.

Some production economists have argued that inputs should not be arbitrarily categorized as either fixed or variable. These arbitrary categories can be highly misleading. Production economists argue that in the case of crop production, prior to planting, nearly all inputs are variable. Farmers might rent additional land, buy or sell machinery, or adjust acreages of crops. Here is where real decision making can take place. Once planting begins, more and more of the inputs previously treated as variable become fixed. Tractor time and labor for tillage operations cannot be recovered once used. Acreages of crops once planted largely cannot be altered. Insecticides and herbicides are variable inputs before application, but must be treated as fixed or "sunk" once they have been applied. At the start of harvest, the only variable input is the labor, fuel, and repairs to run the harvesting equipment and to move the grain to market.

This view treats the input categories as a continuum rather than as a dichotomy. As inputs are used, costs are treated as sunk. Inputs, once used, can no longer be sold, or used on the farm for a different enterprise, such as another crop.

2.3 The Law of Diminishing Returns

The law of diminishing returns is fundamental to all of production economics. The law is misnamed. It should be called the law of diminishing *marginal* returns, for the law deals with what happens to the incremental or marginal product as units of input or resource are added. The *law of diminishing marginal returns* states that as units of an variable input are added to units of one or more fixed inputs, after a point, each incremental unit of the variable input produces less and less additional output. As units of the variable input are added to units of the fixed inputs, the proportions change between fixed and variable inputs. The law of diminishing returns has sometimes been referred to as the law of variable proportions.

For example, if incremental units of nitrogen fertilizer were applied to corn, after a point, each incremental unit of nitrogen fertilizer would produce less and less additional corn. Were it not for the law of diminishing returns, a single farmer could produce all the corn required in the world, merely by acquiring all of the available nitrogen fertilizer and applying it to his or her farm.

The key word in the law of diminishing returns is *additional*. The law of diminishing returns does not state that as units of a variable input are added, each incremental unit of input produces less output in total. If it did, a pro-

2.3 The Law of Diminishing Returns

duction function would need to have a negative slope in order for the law of diminishing returns to hold. Rather, the law of diminishing returns refers to the rate of change in the slope of the production function. This is sometimes referred to as the *curvature* of the production function.

Figure 2.1 illustrates three production functions. The production function labeled A has no curvature at all. The law of diminishing returns does not hold here. Each incremental unit of input use produces the exact same incremental output, regardless of where one is at on the function. An example of a function such as this is

$$y = 2x \qquad (2.7)$$

Each incremental unit of x produces 2 units of y, regardless of the initial value for x, whether it be 0, 24, 100, or 5000.

A slightly more general form of this function is

$$y = bx \qquad (2.8)$$

where b is some positive number. If b is a positive number, the function is said to exhibit *constant marginal returns* to the variable input x, and the law of diminishing returns does not hold. Each incremental unit of x produces bx units of y.

The production function labeled B represents another kind of relationship. Here each incremental unit of x produces more and more additional y. Hence the law of diminishing returns does not hold here either. Notice that as the use of input x is increased, x becomes more productive, producing more and more additional y. An example of a function that would represent this kind of a relationship is

$$y = x^2 \qquad (2.9)$$

A slightly more general form of the function might be

$$y = ax^b \qquad (2.10)$$

where both a and b are positive numbers, and b is greater than 1. Notice that if $b = 1$, the function is the same as the one depicted in diagram A of Figure 2.1. The value of a must be positive if the input is to produce a positive quantity of output.

The production function labeled C represents the law of diminishing returns throughout its range. Here each incremental unit of x produces less and less additional y. Thus each unit of x becomes less and less productive. At some point, total output may actually start to decline. An example of a function that represents this kind of relationship is

$$y = \sqrt{x} \qquad (2.11)$$

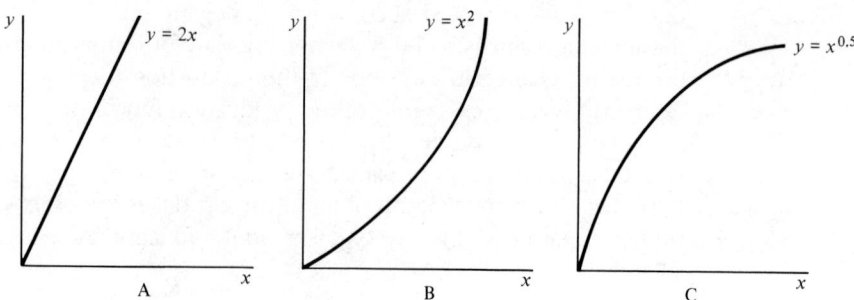

Figure 2.1 Three Production Functions

Another way of writing equation (2.11) is

$$y = x^{0.5} \tag{2.12}$$

Both are exactly the same thing. For this production function, total product (*TPP* or *y*) will never decline.

A slightly more general form of the function is

$$y = ax^b \tag{2.13}$$

where *a* and *b* are positive numbers. However, here *b* must be less than 1 but greater than zero, if diminishing (marginal) returns are to hold. This function will forever increase, but at a decreasing rate.

2.4 Marginal and Average Physical Product

The *marginal physical product (MPP)* refers to the change in output associated with an incremental change in the use of an input. The incremental increase in input use is usually taken to be 1 unit. Thus *MPP* is the change in output associated with a 1-unit increase in the input. The *MPP* of input x_i might be referred to as $MPPx_i$. Notice that *MPP*, representing the incremental change in *TPP*, can be either positive or negative.

Average physical product (APP) is defined as the ratio of output to input. That is, $APP = y/x$. For any level of input use (*x*), *APP* represents the average amount of output per unit of *x* being used.

Suppose that the production function is

$$y = f(x) \tag{2.14}$$

One way of expressing *MPP* is by the expression $\Delta y/\Delta x$, where the Δ denotes change. The expression $\Delta y/\Delta x$ can be read as "the change in *y* (Δy) with respect to a change in *x* (Δx)." For the same function *APP* is expressed either as y/x or as $f(x)/x$.

For the production function

$$y = 2x \tag{2.15}$$

2.4 Marginal and Average Physical Product

MPP is equal to 2. The change in y with respect to a 1-unit change in x is 2 units. That is, each additional or incremental unit of x produces 2 additional or incremental units of y. For each additional unit of x that is used, TPP increases by 2 units. In this example APP equals y/x, or APP equals $2x/x$, or APP equals 2. For this simple production function MPP = APP = 2 for all positive values for x.

For the production function

$$y = bx \qquad (2.16)$$

MPP is equal to the constant coefficient b. The change in y with respect to a change in x is b. Each incremental or additional unit of x produces b incremental or additional units of y. That is, the change in TPP resulting from a 1-unit-change in x is b. Moreover, APP = bx/x. Thus, MPP = APP = b everywhere.

Marginal and average physical products for the tabular data presented in Table 2.1 may be calculated based on the definition that MPP is the change in output (Δy) arising from an incremental change in the use of the input (Δx) and that APP is simply output (y) divided by input (x). These data are presented in Table 2.3. MPP is calculated by first making up a column representing the rate of change in corn yield. This rate of change might be referred to as Δy or perhaps ΔTPP. Then the rate of change in nitrogen use is calculated. This might be referred to as Δx. Since 40-pound units were used in this example, the rate of change in each case for x is 40. The corresponding MPP over the increment is $\Delta y/\Delta x$. MPP might also be thought of as $\Delta TPP/\Delta x$. The corresponding calculations are shown under the column labeled MPP in Table 2.3. For example, if nitrogen use increases from 120 to 160 pounds per acre, or 40 pounds, the corresponding increase in corn yield will be from 123 to 128 bushels per acre, or 5 bushels. The MPP over this range is approximately 5/40 or 0.125.

The MPP's are positioned at the midpoint between each fertilizer increment. The MPP's calculated here are averages that apply only approximately at the midpoints between each increment, that is, at nitrogen application levels of approximately 20, 60, 100, 140, and 180 pounds per acre. Since no information is available with respect to what corn might have yielded at these midpoints, the calculated MPP's are at best approximations that might in certain instances not be very accurate.

Table 2.3 MPP and APP for Corn Yield Response to Nitrogen Fertilizer

Quantity of Nitrogen (lb/acre)	Δx	Yield of Corn (bu/acre)	Δy	MPP	APP
0		50			50/0 = undefined
	40		25	25/40 = 0.625	
40		75			75/40 = 1.875
	40		30	30/40 = 0.75	
80		105			105/80 = 1.313
	40		10	10/40 = 0.25	
120		115			115/120 = 0.958
	40		8	8/40 = 0.20	
160		123			123/160 = 0.769
	40		5	5/40 = 0.125	
200		128			128/200 = 0.640
	40		−4	−4/40 = −0.100	
240		124			124/240 = 0.517

Table 2.3 also includes calculations for average physical product. Average physical product (*APP*) is defined as the ratio of output to input; that is, $APP = y/x$. For any level of input use (x), *APP* represents the average amount of output per unit of x being used. In Table 2.3, *APP* is calculated by dividing corn yield by the amount of nitrogen. These calculations are presented in the column labeled *APP*. The values for *APP* are exact at the specified levels of input use. For example, the exact *APP* when 120 pounds of nitrogen is applied is 115/120 or 0.958.

2.5 *MPP* and the Marginal Product Function

The procedure described in Section 2.5 for calculating *MPP*'s is tedious and time consuming. There exists a quicker and more accurate means for calculating *MPP* and *APP* if the production function is given.

The *MPP* ($\Delta y/\Delta x$) represents the slope or rate of change in the production function. The production function itself is sometimes referred to as total physical product (or *TPP*) function. The *MPP* function refers to the function representing the rate of change in the *TPP* function. If the slope of the *TPP* function were to be graphed, the result would be the *MPP* function, representing the rate of change in the *TPP* or the underlying production function as the use of variable input x is varied.

Given the *TPP* function (or production function), the *MPP* function (or marginal product function) might easily be obtained. Suppose again that the *TPP* or production function is represented by

$$y = 2x \qquad (2.17)$$

Again, the incremental increase in y associated with a 1-unit increase in the use of x is 2 units. Hence $MPP = 2$. Moreover, $\Delta y/\Delta x = 2$. In this case the marginal product function is equal to the constant 2.

For functions that do not have a constant slope, the expression $\Delta y/\Delta x$ can only approximate the slope of the function at a given point (Figure 2.2). The approximation can be very crude and inaccurate if a large value for Δx is chosen for the incremental change in x. This approximation improves as the value for Δx is chosen to be smaller and smaller. If the exact slope or *MPP* of a production function is to be found at a specific point, the magnitude of Δx must become infinitely small. That is, Δx must approach zero.

One way for finding the exact slope of a production function at a particular point is shown in Figure 2.2. Suppose that the exact *MPP* at point *D* is desired. A line is drawn tangent to the production function at *D*, which intersects the vertical axis at point *B*. The exact *MPP* at point *D* is equal to the slope of this line. This slope can be expressed as *BC/OA*. The graphical approach is time consuming, particularly if the *MPP* at several points along the function are to be calculated. A better way might be to find the first derivative of the production function. The *first derivative* of the production function is defined as the limit of the expression $\Delta y/\Delta x$ as Δx approaches zero. As Δx becomes smaller and smaller, $\Delta y/\Delta x$ becomes a better and better approximation of the true slope of the function. The first derivative, *dy/dx*, represents the exact slope of the

2.5 MPP and the Marginal Production Function

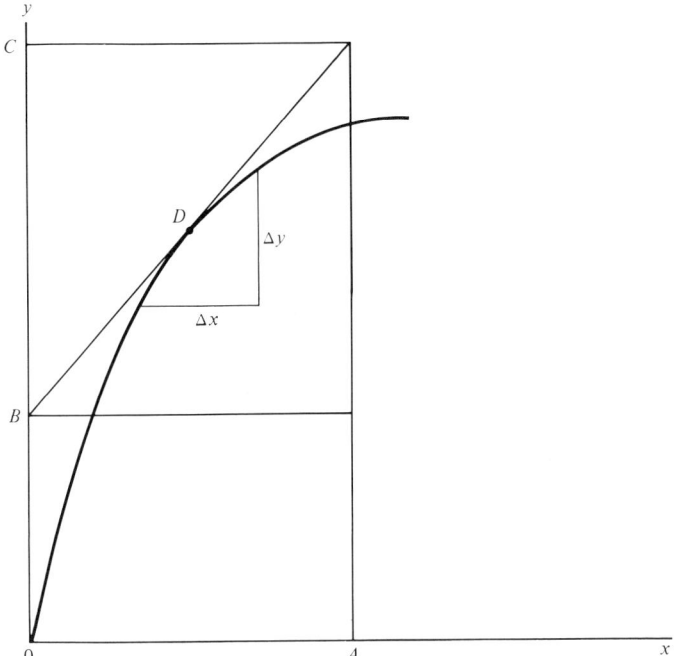

Figure 2.2 Approximate and Exact *MPP*

production function at a particular point. In Figure 2.2, at point D, $dy/dx = BC/OA$.

For the production function

$$y = f(x) \tag{2.18}$$

The first derivative, dy/dx, of equation (2.18) is a function that represents the slope, or rate of change, in the original production function and is sometimes written as

$$dy/dx = f'(x) \text{ or } f_1 \tag{2.19}$$

where $f'(x)$ or f_1 represents the first derivative of, or the rate of change in, the original function. Another way of expressing these relationships is

$$dy/dx = f'(x) = f_1 = dTPP/dx = MPP \tag{2.20}$$

All expressions refer to the rate of change in the original production or *TPP* function.

For the production function

$$y = 2x \tag{2.21}$$

$$dy/dx = dTPP/dx = MPP = 2 \tag{2.22}$$

Throughout the domain of this production function, the rate of change is a constant 2. Each additional unit of x produces 2 additional units of y. The first derivative of this production function [$f'(x)$ or f_1] is 2 for all values of x. Note that in this case dy/dx is exactly the same as $\Delta y/\Delta x$. This is because the slope of the function is a constant 2, not dependent on the value of x.

Suppose the production function

$$y = bx \qquad (2.23)$$

where b is any positive number. Again b is the MPP of x. The derivative of the production function dy/dx is b. Each incremental unit of x will produce b units of y. If x is increased by 1 unit from any initial level, TPP will increase by b units. If b were negative, then TPP would decrease, but this would be a silly production function because positive amounts of x would result in negative amounts of y. It is not entirely clear what a negative bushel of corn would look like. Again, b is constant, and dy/dx will always equal $\Delta y/\Delta x$.

Now suppose that the production function is represented by the equation

$$y = 50 + 5.93x^{0.5} \qquad (2.24)$$

The MPP of x for this function is not the same for every value of x. To calculate the MPP at a particular value for x, not only the derivative of the production function is needed, but also how much x is applied. Two simple rules can be used to find the derivative of any production function similar to the one above.

The first rule states that the derivative of any constant value in a function is 0. In this case, the derivative of 50 is 0. The constant is an intercept term that places the function at $x = 0$ on the y axis at 50. A constant does not affect the slope of the function.

The second rule is that the derivative of any function of the general form

$$y = bx^n \qquad (2.25)$$

can be found by the rule

$$dy/dx = nbx^{n-1} \qquad (2.26)$$

where n and b are any numbers. For example, the derivative of the function $y = x^2$ is $dy/dx = 2x$; the derivative of the function $y = 3x^4$ is $dy/dx = 3 \cdot 4 \cdot x^3$ or $12x^3$. If these functions were production functions, their corresponding derivatives would be the corresponding marginal product functions, representing the slopes or rates of change in the original production functions. The derivative for the production function representing corn yield response to nitrogen fertilizer [equation (2.1)] is $dy/dx = 0 + 0.5 \cdot 5.93 \cdot x^{-0.5}$, or $dy/dx = 2.965x^{-0.5}$.

A number raised to a negative power is 1 over the number raised to the corresponding positive power: for example,

$$x^{-2} = 1/x^2 \qquad (2.27)$$

2.5 MPP and the Marginal Production Function

In this case

$$dy/dx = 2.965/x^{0.5} \tag{2.28}$$

or

$$dy/dx = 2.965/\sqrt{x} \tag{2.29}$$

If the amount of x to be applied is known, the corresponding TPP is $50 + 5.93x^{0.5}$, and the corresponding MPP is $2.965/x^{0.5}$. In this case, MPP is specifically linked to the amount of x that is used, as x appears in the first derivative. If this is the case, dy/dx will provide the exact MPP but will not be the same as the approximation calculated by $\Delta y/\Delta x$.

Table 2.4 presents MPP's calculated by two methods from yield data obtained from this production function [equation (2.24)]. The first method computes the rate of change in the yields for 40-pound fertilizer increments as was done in the earlier example (Table 2.3). The second method inserts values for nitrogen application levels into the MPP function obtained by taking the derivative of the original production function. The values chosen are at the midpoints (20, 60, 100, 140, and 180 pounds of nitrogen per acre).

As is evident from Table 2.4, the results using the two methods are not the same. Method 1 provides the approximate MPP at the midpoint. However, for certain fertilizer application levels (for example, at 20 pounds per acre) the MPP using this first method is very different from the MPP obtained by inserting the actual midpoint value into the MPP function. This is because the production function is curvilinear, and the slope calculated using method 1 is only a crude approximation of the exact slope of the production function over each 40-pound increment of fertilizer use.

The derivative of the function will provide the exact slope of the function at any selected nitrogen application level. Therefore, the calculated MPP values from method 2 are highly accurate for the assumed levels of nitrogen use. Using method 2, the MPP can be calculated at any selected level of fertilizer use (including the application levels of 40, 80, 140, 160, and 200 pounds per acre). Basic differential calculus is a powerful tool in agricultural production economics.

Table 2.4 MPP of Nitrogen in the Production of Corn Under Two Alternative Approaches

Quantity of Nitrogen (lb/acre)	Corn Yield (y or TPP) (bu/acre)	Average MPP, Method 1	Exact MPP, Method 2
0	50		
		0.9375	0.6630 (N = 20 lb/acre)
40	87.5		
		0.3875	0.3827 (N = 60 lb/acre)
80	103.0		
		0.3000	0.2965 (N = 100 lb/acre)
120	115.0		
		0.2500	0.2506 (N = 140 lb/acre)
160	125.0		
		0.2225	0.2212 (N = 180 lb/acre)
200	133.9		

Production with One Variable Input

Table 2.5 Corn Yields, *APP*, and *MPP* for $y = 0.75x + 0.0042x^2 - 0.000023x^3$

x (Nitrogen)	y (Corn) or TPP	APP of x, y/x	MPP of x, dy/dx
0	0	Undefined	0.75
20	16.496	0.8248	0.8904
40	35.248	0.8812	0.9756
60	55.152	0.9192	1.0056
80	75.104	0.9388	0.9804
100	94.000	0.9400	0.9000
120	110.736	0.9228	0.7644
140	124.208	0.8872	0.5736
160	133.312	0.8332	0.3276
180	136.944	0.7608	0.0264
200	134.000	0.6700	−0.3300
220	123.376	0.5608	−0.7416
240	103.968	0.4332	−1.2084

Finally, assume that the production function describing corn yield response to nitrogen fertilizer is the one used as the basis for the data contained in Table 2.5. That function was

$$y = 0.75x + 0.0042x^2 - 0.000023x^3 \tag{2.30}$$

Following the rules for differentiation, the marginal product function corresponding to equation (2.30) is

$$dy/dx = 0.75 + 0.0084x - 0.000069x^2 \tag{2.31}$$

Since *APP* is y/x, the corresponding *APP* function is

$$y/x = (0.75x + 0.0042x^2 - 0.000023x^3)/x$$
$$= 0.75 + 0.0042x - 0.000023x^2 \tag{2.32}$$

Table 2.5 illustrates the exact *APP* and *MPP* values for equation (2.30) obtained by inserting the amount of x (nitrogen) appearing in the first column of the table into the *APP* [equation (2.31)] and *MPP* [equation (2.32)].

2.6 The Neoclassical Production Function

The neoclassical production function has long been popular for describing production relationships in agriculture. Figure 2.3 illustrates the neoclassical production function. As the use of input x_1 increases, the productivity of the input at first also increases. The function turns upward, or increases, at first at an increasing rate. Then a point called the *inflection point* occurs. This is where the function changes from increasing at an increasing rate to increasing at a decreasing rate. Another way of saying this is that the function is convex to the horizontal axis prior to the inflection point, but concave to the horizontal axis after the inflection point. The inflection point marks the end of increasing marginal returns and the start of diminishing marginal returns. Finally, the

2.7 MPP and APP for the Neoclassical Function

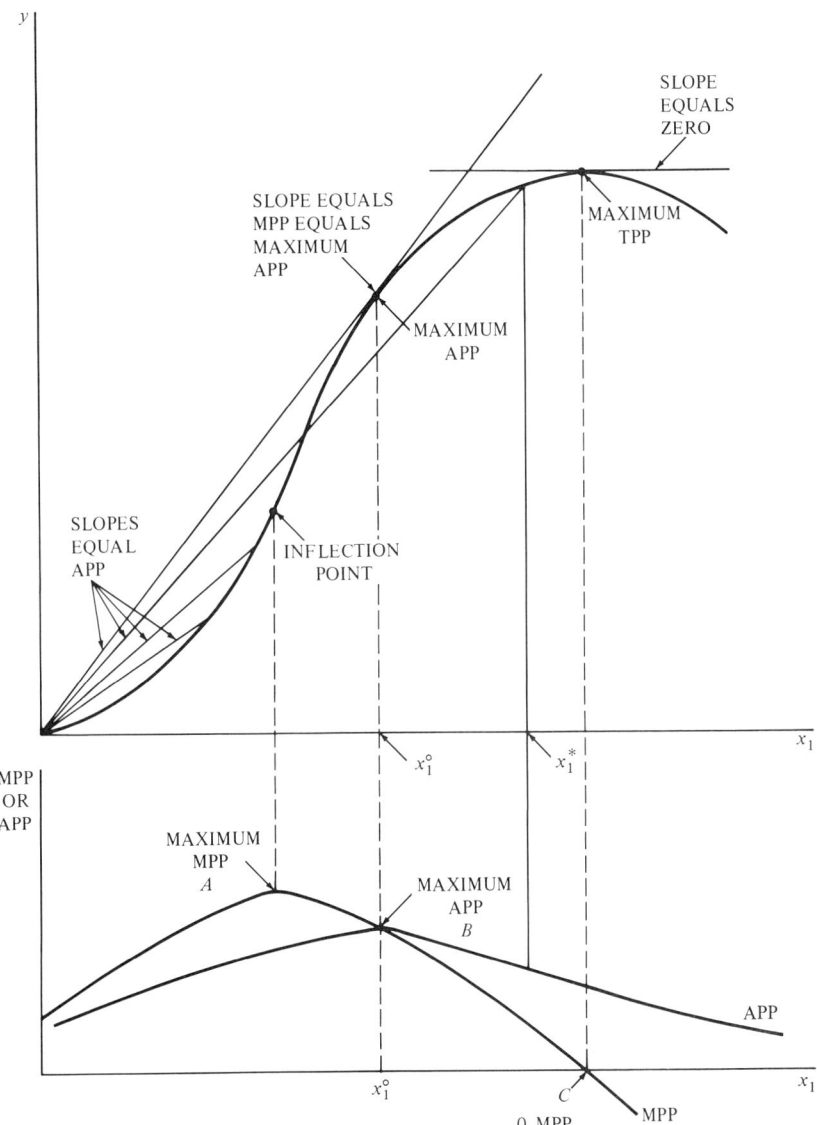

Figure 2.3 Neoclassical Three-Stage Production Function

function reaches a maximum and begins to turn downward. Beyond the maximum, increases in the use of the variable input x_1 result in a decrease in total output (*TPP*). This would occur in an instance where a farmer applied so much fertilizer that it was actually detrimental to crop yields.

2.7 *MPP* and *APP* for the Neoclassical Function

The *MPP* function changes as the use of input x_1 increases. At first, as the productivity of input x_1 increases, so does its marginal product, and the corresponding *MPP* function must be increasing (Figure 2.3). The inflection point marks the maximum marginal product. It is here that the productivity of the incremental unit of the input x_1 is at its greatest. After the inflection point, the marginal product of x_1 declines and the *MPP* function must also be decreasing. The marginal product of x_1 is zero at the point of output maximization, and negative at higher levels. Therefore, the *MPP* function is zero at the point of output maximization, and negative thereafter.

Average physical product (*APP*) also changes as the use of x_1 increases, although *APP* is never negative. As indicated earlier, *APP* is the ratio of output to input, in this case y/x_1 or TPP/x_1. Since this is the case, *APP* for a selected point on the production function can be illustrated by drawing a line (ray) out of the origin of the graph to the selected point. The slope of this line is y/x_1 and corresponds to the values of y and x_1 for the production function. If the point selected on the function is for some value for x_1 called x_1^*, then the *APP* at x_1^* is y/x_1^*.

APP reaches a maximum at a point after the inflection point but before the point in which output is maximized. Figure 2.3 illustrates several lines drawn out of the origin. The line with the greatest slope is tangent to the production function at that point. Therefore, it also represents the slope of the production function at that point. The slope of each line drawn from the origin to a point on the production function represents the *APP* for the function at that point, but only one line is tangent to and thus also represents the slope of the production function at that point. It is here where marginal product must equal average product, *APP* must equal *MPP*, and $y/x = dy/dx$.

Call the point x_1^0 where $y/x = dy/dx$. At any point less than x_1^0, the slope of the production function is greater than the slope of the line drawn from the origin to the point. Hence *APP* must be less than *MPP* prior to x_1^0.

As the use of x_1 increases toward x_1^0, *APP* increases, as does the slope of the line drawn from the origin. After x_1^0, the slope of the production function is less than the slope of the line drawn from the origin to the point. Hence *MPP* must be less than *APP* after x_1^0. As the use of x_1 increases beyond x_1^0, the slope of the line drawn from the origin to the point declines, and *APP* must decline beyond x_1^0. The slope of that line never becomes negative, and *APP* never becomes negative.

However, a line drawn tangent to the production function represents *MPP* and will have a negative slope beyond the point of output maximization. *APP* is always positive, but *MPP* is negative beyond the point of output maximization.

Figure 2.3 also illustrates the relationships that exist between the *APP* and the *MPP* function for the neoclassical production function. The *MPP* function first increases as the use of the input is increased, until the inflection point of the underlying production function is reached (point *A*). Here the *MPP* function reaches its maximum. After this point, *MPP* declines, reaches zero when output is maximum (point *C*), and then turns negative. The *APP* function increases past the inflection point of the underlying production function until it reaches the *MPP* function (point *B*). After point *B*, *APP* declines, but never becomes negative.

The relationships that hold between *APP* and *MPP* can be proven using the composite function rule for differentiation.

Notice that

$$y = (y/x)x \tag{2.33}$$

or $TPP = APP \cdot x$ in the original production or TPP function.

$$dy/dx = y/x + [d(y/x)/dx]x \tag{2.34}$$

or, equivalently, $MPP = APP + $ (slope of APP)x.

If APP is increasing and therefore has a positive slope, MPP must be greater than APP. If APP is decreasing and therefore has a negative slope, MPP must be less than APP. If APP has a zero slope, such as would be the case where it is maximum, MPP and APP must be equal.

2.8 Sign, Slope, and Curvature

By repeatedly differentiating a production function, it is possible to determine accurately the shape of the corresponding MPP function. For the production function

$$y = f(x) \tag{2.35}$$

the first derivative represents the corresponding MPP function:

$$dy/dx = f'(x) = f_1 = MPP \tag{2.36}$$

Insert a value for x into the function $f'(x)$ [equation (2.36)]. If $f'(x)$ (or dy/dx or MPP) is positive, incremental units of input produce additional output. Since MPP is negative after the production function reaches its maximum, a positive sign on $f'(x)$ indicates that the underlying production function has a positive slope and has not yet achieved a maximum. If $f'(x)$ is negative, the production function is downsloping, having already achieved its maximum. The sign on the first derivative of the production function indicates if the slope of the production function is positive or negative and if MPP lies above or below the horizontal axis. If MPP is zero, then $f'(x)$ is also zero, and the production function is likely either constant or at its maximum. Figure 2.4 illustrates seven instances where the first derivative of the TPP function is positive [(a) to (g)] and three instances where the first derivative is negative [(h) to (j)].

The first derivative of the TPP function could also be zero at the point where the TPP function is minimum. The sign on the second derivative of the TPP function is used to determine if the TPP function is at a maximum or a minimum. If the first derivative of the TPP function is zero and the second derivative is negative, the production function is at its maximum. If the first derivative of the TPP function is zero, and the second derivative is positive, the production function is at its minimum point. If both the first and second derivatives are zero, the function is at an inflection point, or changing from convex to the horizontal axis to concave to the horizontal axis. However, all inflection points do not necessarily have first derivatives of zero. Finally, if the first deriv-

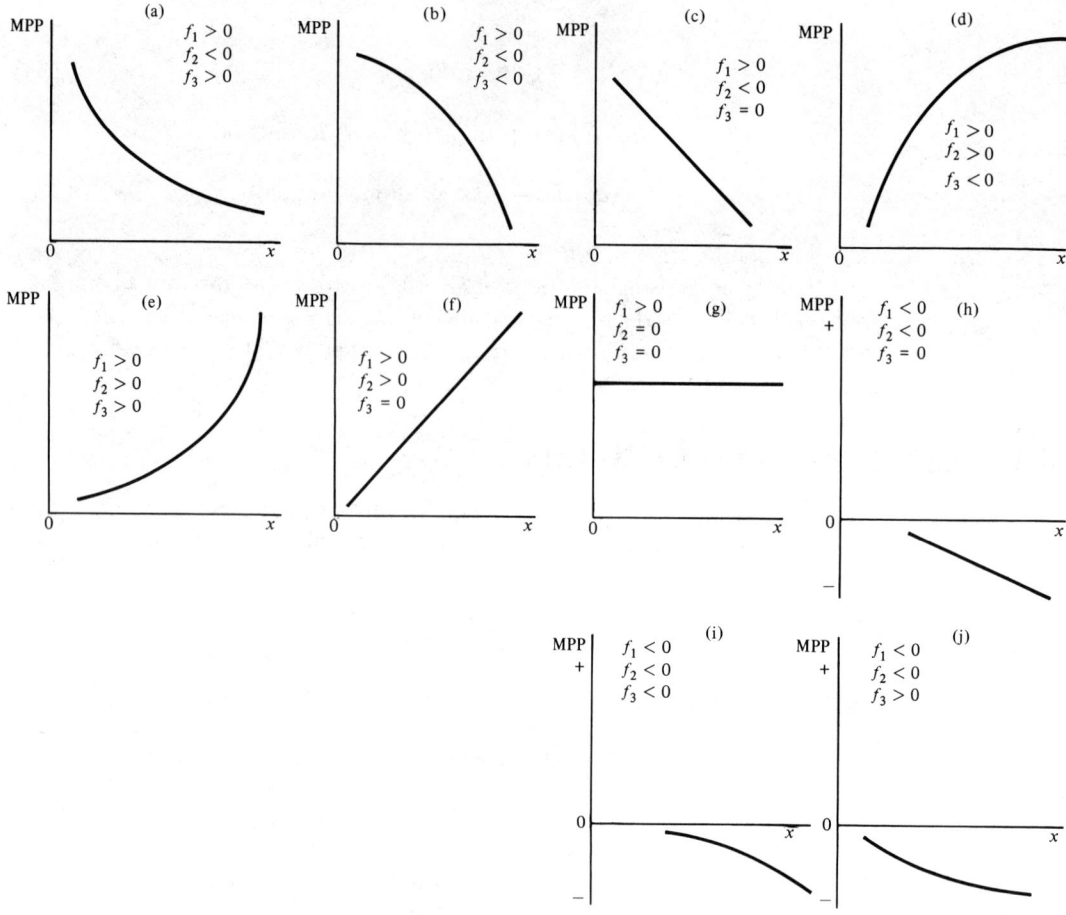

Figure 2.4 Possible *MPP*'s for the Production Function $y = f(x)$; $f_1 = MPP$; $f_2 =$ slope of *MPP*; $f_3 =$ curvature of *MPP*

ative is zero and the second derivative does not exist, the production function is constant.

The second derivative of the production function is the first derivative of the *MPP* function, or slope of the *MPP* function. The second derivative $[d^2y/dx^2$ or $f''(x)$ or $f_2]$ is obtained by again differentiating the production function:

$$d^2y/dx^2 = f''(x) = f_2 = dMPP/dx \qquad (2.37)$$

If equation (2.37) is positive for a particular value of x, *MPP* is increasing at that particular point. A negative sign indicates that *MPP* is decreasing at that particular point. If $f''(x)$ is zero, *MPP* is likely at a maximum at that point. In Figure 2.4, the first derivative of the *MPP* function (second derivative of the *TPP* function is positive in (d), (e), and (f), negative in (a), (b), (c), (h), (i), and (j), and zero in (g).

The second derivative of the *MPP* function represents the curvature of *MPP* and is the third derivative of the original production (or *TPP*) function. It is

2.8 Sign, Slope, and Curvature

obtained by again differentiating the original production function:

$$d^3y/dx^3 = f'''(x) = f_3 = d^2MPP/dx^2 \quad (2.38)$$

The sign on $f'''(x)$ for a particular value of x indicates the rate of change in *MPP* at that particular point. If $f'''(x)$ is positive, *MPP* is increasing at an increasing rate [Figure 2.4(e)] or decreasing at a decreasing rate [(a) or (j)]. A negative sign indicates that *MPP* is increasing at a decreasing rate [(d)], or decreasing at an increasing rate [(b) and (i)]. If $f'''(x)$ is zero, *MPP* has a constant slope with no curvature [(f), (g) and (h)].

A similar approach might be used for *APP*. *APP* equals y/x, and if y and x are positive, *APP* must also be positive. As indicated earlier, the slope of *APP* is

$$d(y/x)/dx = f'(y/x) = dAPP/dx \quad (2.39)$$

For a particular value of x, a positive sign indicates a positive slope and a negative sign a negative slope.

The curvature of *APP* can be represented by

$$d^2(y/x)/dx^2 = f''(y/x) = d^2APP/dx^2 \quad (2.40)$$

For a particular value of x, a positive sign indicates that *APP* is increasing at an increasing rate, or decreasing at a decreasing rate. A negative sign on equation (2.40) indicates that *APP* is increasing at a decreasing rate, or decreasing at an increasing rate. A zero indicates an *APP* of constant slope. The third derivative of *APP* would represent the rate of change in the curvature of *APP*.

Here are some examples of how these rules can be applied to a specific production function representing corn yield response to nitrogen fertilizer. Suppose the production function

$$y = 50 + 5.93x^{0.5} \quad (2.41)$$

where y = corn yield in bushels per acre
x = pounds of nitrogen applied per acre

$$MPP = f'(x) = 2.965\, x^{-0.5} > 0 \quad (2.42)$$

For equation (2.41), *MPP* is always positive for any positive level of input use, as indicated by the sign on equation (2.42). If additional nitrogen is applied, some additional response in terms of increased yield will always result. If x is positive, *MPP* is positive and the production function has not reached a maximum.

$$dMPP/dx = f''(x) = -1.48x^{-1.5} < 0 \quad (2.43)$$

If equation (2.43) is negative, *MPP* slopes downward. Each additional pound of nitrogen that is applied will produce less and less additional corn yield. Thus the law of diminishing (marginal) returns holds for this production function throughout its range.

$$d^2MPP/dx^2 = f'''(x) = 2.22x^{-2.5} > 0 \qquad (2.44)$$

If equation (2.44) holds, the MPP function is decreasing at a decreasing rate, coming closer and closer to the horizontal axis but never reaching or intersecting it. This is not surprising, given that incremental pounds of nitrogen always produce a positive response in terms of additional corn.

$$APP = y/x = 50/x + 5.93x^{0.5}$$
$$= 50x^{-1} + 5.93x^{-0.5} > 0 \qquad (2.45)$$

If x is positive, APP is positive. Corn produced per pound of nitrogen fertilizer is always positive [equation (2.45)].

$$dAPP/dx = d(y/x)/dx = -50x^{-2} - 2.97x^{-1.5} < 0 \qquad (2.46)$$

If x is positive, APP slopes downward. As the use of nitrogen increases, the average product per unit of nitrogen declines [equation (2.46)].

$$d^2APP/dx^2 = d^2(y/x)/dx^2 = 100x^{-3} + 4.45x^{-2.5} > 0 \qquad (2.47)$$

If x is positive, APP is also decreasing at a decreasing rate. As the use of nitrogen increases, the average product per unit of nitrogen decreases but at a decreasing rate [equation (2.47)].

2.9 A Single-Input Production Elasticity

The term *elasticity* is used by economists when discussing relationships between two variables. An elasticity is a number that represents the ratio of two percentages. Any elasticity is a pure number in that it has no units.

The elasticity of production is defined as the percentage change in output divided by the percentage change in input, as the level of input use is changed. Suppose that x' represents some original level of input use that produces y' units of output. The use of x is then increased to some new amount called x'', which in turn produces y'' units of output. The elasticity of production (E_p) is defined by the formula

$$E_p = [(y' - y'')/y]/[(x' - x'')/x] \qquad (2.48)$$

where y', y'', x', and x'' are as defined previously, and x and y represent midvalues between the old and new levels of inputs and outputs. Thus

$$x = (x' + x'')/2$$

and

$$y = (y' + y'')/2 \qquad (2.49)$$

2.9 A Single-Input Production Elasticity

Since the elasticity of production is the ratio of two percentages, it does not depend on the specific units in which the input and output are measured. For example, suppose that y represents corn yield in bushels per acre, and x represents nitrogen in pounds per acre. Then suppose that corn yield is instead measured in terms of liters per hectare, and nitrogen was measured in terms of kilograms per hectare. If the same amount of nitrogen is applied in both instances, the calculated value for the elasticity of production will be the same, regardless of the units in which y and x are measured.

Another way of expressing the elasticity of production is

$$E_p = (\Delta y/y)/(\Delta x/x) \tag{2.50}$$

where $\Delta y = y' - y''$
$\Delta x = x' - x''$

The elasticity of production is one way of measuring how responsive the production function is to changes in the use of the input. A large elasticity (for example, an elasticity of production greater than 1) implies that the output responds strongly to increases in the use of the input. An elasticity of production of between zero and 1 suggests that output will increase as a result of the use of x, but the smaller the elasticity, the less the response in terms of increased output. A negative elasticity of production implies that as the level of input use increases, output will actually decline, not increase.

The elasticity of production can also be defined in terms of the relationship between *MPP* and *APP*. The following relationships hold. First,

$$E_p = (\Delta y/y)/(\Delta x/x) \tag{2.51}$$

Equation (2.51) might also be written as

$$E_p = (\Delta y/\Delta x)(x/y) \tag{2.52}$$

Notice that

$$\Delta y/\Delta x = MPP \tag{2.53}$$

and that

$$x/y = 1/APP \tag{2.54}$$

Thus

$$E_p = MPP/APP \tag{2.55}$$

Notice that a large elasticity of production indicates that *MPP* is very large relative to *APP*. In other words, output occurring from the last incremental unit of fertilizer is very great relative to the average output obtained from all units of fertilizer. If the elasticity of production is very small, output from the last incremental unit of fertilizer is small relative to the average productivity of all units of fertilizer.

2.10 Elasticities of Production for the Neoclassical Production Function

A unique series of elasticities of production exist for the neoclassical production function, as a result of the relationships that exist between *MPP* and *APP*. These are illustrated in Figure 2.5 and can be summarized as follows:

1. The elasticity of production is greater than 1 until the point is reached where $MPP = APP$ (point A).
2. The elasticity of production is greatest when the ratio of *MPP* to *APP* is greatest. For the neoclassical production function, this normally occurs when *MPP* reaches its maximum at the inflection point of the production function (point B).
3. The elasticity of production is less than 1 beyond the point where $MPP = APP$ (point A).
4. The elasticity of production is zero when *MPP* is zero. Note that *APP* must always be positive (point C).
5. The elasticity of production is negative when *MPP* is negative and, of course, output is declining (beyond point C). If the production function is decreasing, *MPP* and the elasticity of production are negative. Again, *APP* must always be positive.

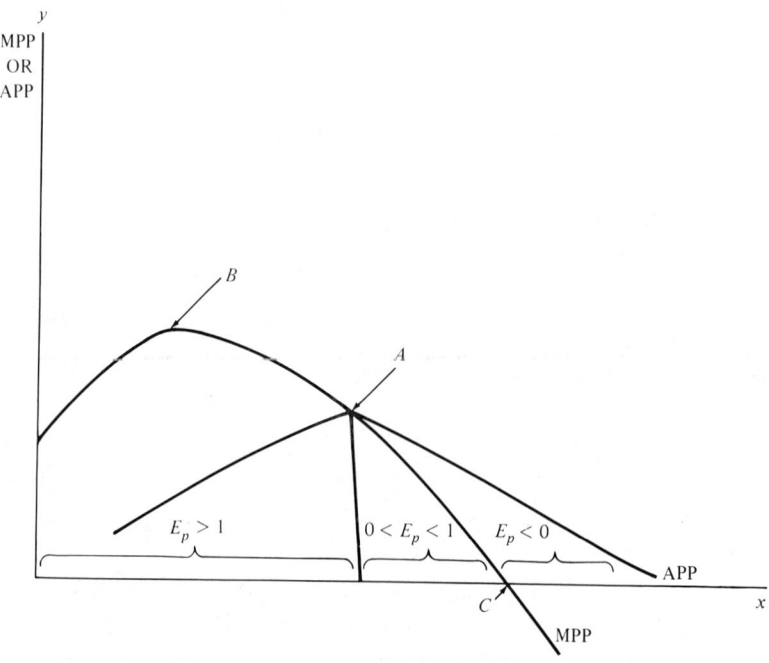

Figure 2.5 *MPP, APP, and the Elasticity of Production*

6. A unique characteristic of the neoclassical production function is that as the level of input use is increased, the relationship between *MPP* and *APP* is continually changing, and therefore the ratio of *MPP* to *APP* must also vary. Since $E_p = MPP/APP$, the elasticity of production too must vary continually as the use of the input increases. This is a characteristic of the neoclassical production function, which in general is not true for some other production functions.

2.11 Further Topics on the Elasticity of Production

The expression $\Delta y/\Delta x$ is only an approximation of the true *MPP* of the production function for a specific amount of the input *x*. The actual *MPP* at a specific point is better represented by inserting the value of *x* into the marginal product function dy/dx.

The elasticity of production for a specific level of *x* might be obtained by determining the value for dy/dx for that level of *x* and then obtaining the elasticity of production from the expression

$$E_p = (dy/dx)y/x \qquad (2.56)$$

Now suppose that instead of the neoclassical production function, a simple linear relationship exists between *y* and *x*. Thus

$$TPP = y = bx \qquad (2.57)$$

where *b* is some positive number. Then $dy/dx = b$, but note also that since $y = bx$, then $y/x = bx/x = b$. Thus *MPP* (dy/dx) = *APP* $(y/x) = b$. Hence, $MPP/APP = b/b = 1$.

The elasticity of production for any such function is 1. This means that a given percentage increase in the use of the input *x* will result in exactly the same percentage increase in the output *y*. Moreover, any production function in which the returns to the variable input are equal to some constant number will have an elasticity of production equal to 1.

Now suppose a slightly different production function

$$y = a\sqrt{x} \qquad (2.58)$$

Another way of writing eqtuation (2.58) is

$$y = ax^{0.5} \qquad (2.59)$$

In this case

$$dy/dx = 0.5\, ax^{-0.5} \qquad (2.60)$$

And

$$y/x = ax^{-0.5} \qquad (2.61)$$

Thus, $(dy/dx)/(y/x) = 0.5$. Hence the elasticity of production is 0.5. This means that for any level of input use MPP will be precisely one half of APP. In general, the elasticity of production will be b for any production function of the form

$$y = ax^b \qquad (2.62)$$

where a and b are any numbers. Notice that

$$dy/dx = bax^{b-1} \qquad (2.63)$$

and that

$$y/x = ax^b/x = ax^b x^{-1} = ax^{b-1} \qquad (2.64)$$

(Another way of writing the expression $1/x$ is x^{-1}. Therefore, $y/x = yx^{-1}$. But $y = ax^b$, and, as a result, $x^b x^{-1} = x^{b-1}$.)

Thus the ratio of MPP to APP—the elasticity of production—for such a function is always equal to the constant b. This is not the same as the relationship that exists between MPP and APP for the neoclassical production function in which the ratio is not constant but continually changing as the use of x increases.

2.12 Concluding Comments

This chapter has outlined in considerable detail the physical or technical relationships underlying the factor-product model. A production function was developed using tabular, graphical, and mathematical tools, with illustrations from agriculture. The law of diminishing marginal returns was introduced. Marginal and average physical product concepts were developed. The rules of calculus for determining if a function is at a maximum or minimum were outlined, using a total physical product and marginal physical product concepts to illustrate the application. Finally, the concept of an elasticity of production was introduced, and the elasticity of production was linked to the marginal and average product functions.

Problems and Exercises

1. Suppose the following production function data. Fill in the blanks.

x (Input)	y (Output)	MPP	APP
0	0		
10	50	___	___
25	75	___	___
40	80	___	___
50	85	___	___

2. For the following production functions, does the law of diminishing returns hold?

a. $y = x^{0.2}$
b. $y = 3x$

2.12 Concluding Comments

    c. $y = x^3$
    d. $y = 6x - 0.10x^2$

3. Find the corresponding *MPP* and *APP* functions for the production functions given in problem 2.

4. Assume a general multiplicative production function of the form

$$y = 2x^b$$

Derive the corresponding *MPP* and *APP* functions, and draw on a sheet of graph paper *TPP*, *APP*, and *MPP* when the value of *b* is

    a. 5
    b. 3
    c. 2
    d. 1.5
    e. 1.0
    f. 0.7
    g. 0.3
    h. 0
    i. -0.5
    j. -1

Be sure to show the sign, slope, and curvature of *MPP* and *APP*. What is the value for the elasticity of production in each case?

Notice that the curves remain at fixed proportion from each other.

5. Graph the production function

$$y = 0.4x + 0.09x^2 - 0.003x^3$$

for values of *x* between 0 and 20. Derive and graph the corresponding *MPP* and *APP*. What is the algebraic expression for the elasticity of production in this case? Is the elasticity of production constant or variable for this function? Explain.

6. Suppose that the coefficients or parameters of a production function of the polynomial form are to be found. The production function is

$$y = ax + bx^2 + cx^3$$

where *y* = corn yield in bushels per acre
        x = nitrogen application in pounds per acre
        a, b and *c* are coefficients or unknown parameters

The production function should produce a corn yield of 150 bushels per acre when 200 pounds of nitrogen is applied to an acre. This should be the maximum corn yield (*MPP* = 0). The maximum *APP* should occur at a nitrogen application rate of 125 pounds per acre. Find the parameters *a, b,* and *c* for a production function meeting these restrictions. *Hint:* First find the equation for *APP* and *MPP* and the equations representing maximum *APP* and zero *MPP*. Then insert the correct nitrogen application levels in the three equations representing *TPP*, maximum *APP*, and zero *MPP*. There are three equations in three unknowns (*a, b,* and *c*). Solve this system for *a, b,* and *c*.

3
Profit Maximization with One Input and One Output

This chapter introduces the fundamental conditions for profit maximization in the single input–single output or factor-product case. The concept of the total value of the product and the value of the marginal product is introduced. The value of the marginal product and the marginal factor cost are equal at the point of profit maximization. Profits are normally maximum when the implicit value of the last dollar spent on an input is one dollar. Stages of production are described, and an explanation of why a farmer would choose to operate in stage II is given.

Key Terms and Definitions

Total Value of the Product (*TVP*)
Profit
Revenue
Cost Function
Value of the Marginal Product (*VMP*)
Total Factor Cost (*TFC*)
Marginal Factor Cost (*MFC*)
Average Value of the Product (*AVP*)
First-Order Condition
Second Order Condition

Necessary Condition
Sufficient Condition
Maximum Profits
Minimum Profits
Stages of Production (I, II, and III)
Rational Stage
Irrational Stage
Implicit Worth
Imputed Value
Shadow Price

3.1 Total Physical Product Versus Total Value of the Product

As indicated in Chapter 2, the output (y) from a production function can be also called total physical product (*TPP*). If a firm such as a farm is operating under the purely competitive conditions, the individual farm firm can sell as

3.3 Maximizing the Difference Between Returns and Costs

little or as much output as desired at the going market price. The market price, p, does not vary. A constant price might be called $p°$. Since

$$TPP = y \tag{3.1}$$

both sides of equation (3.1) can be multiplied by the constant price $p°$. The result is

$$p°TPP = p°y \tag{3.2}$$

The expression $p°y$ is the total revenue obtained from the sale of the output y and is the same as $p°TPP$. The expression $p°TPP$ is sometimes referred to as the *total value of the product* (*TVP*). It is a measure of output (*TPP*) transformed into dollar terms by multiplying by $p°$. For a farmer it represents the revenue obtained from the sale of a single commodity, such as corn or beef cattle. If the output price is constant, the *TVP* function has the same shape as the *TPP* function, and only the units on the vertical axis have changed (Figure 3.1).

3.2 Total Factor or Resource Cost

Suppose that production requires only one input. Suppose also that a farmer can purchase as much of this input as is needed at the going market price v. The purely competitive environment is again assumed to exist. The market price for the input, factor, or resource does not vary with the amount that an individual farmer purchases. Thus the market price might be designated as $v°$. The term $v°x$ can be referred to as *total factor cost* or *total resource cost*. These terms are sometimes abbreviated as *TFC* or *TRC*. Hence

$$TRC = TFC = v°x \tag{3.3}$$

The *TFC* function has a constant slope, in this case equal to $v°$. Another way of looking at $v°$ is that it is the increase in cost associated with the purchase of an additional unit of the input. The increase in cost is equal to the price of the input $v°$

3.3 Maximizing the Difference Between Returns and Costs

A farmer might be interested in maximizing net returns or profit. Profit (Π) is the total value of the product (*TVP*) less the total factor cost (*TFC*). The profit function for the farmer can be written as

$$\Pi = TVP - TFC \tag{3.4}$$

or, equation (3.4) might be written as

$$\Pi = p°y - v°x \tag{3.5}$$

42 Profit Maximization with One Input and One Output

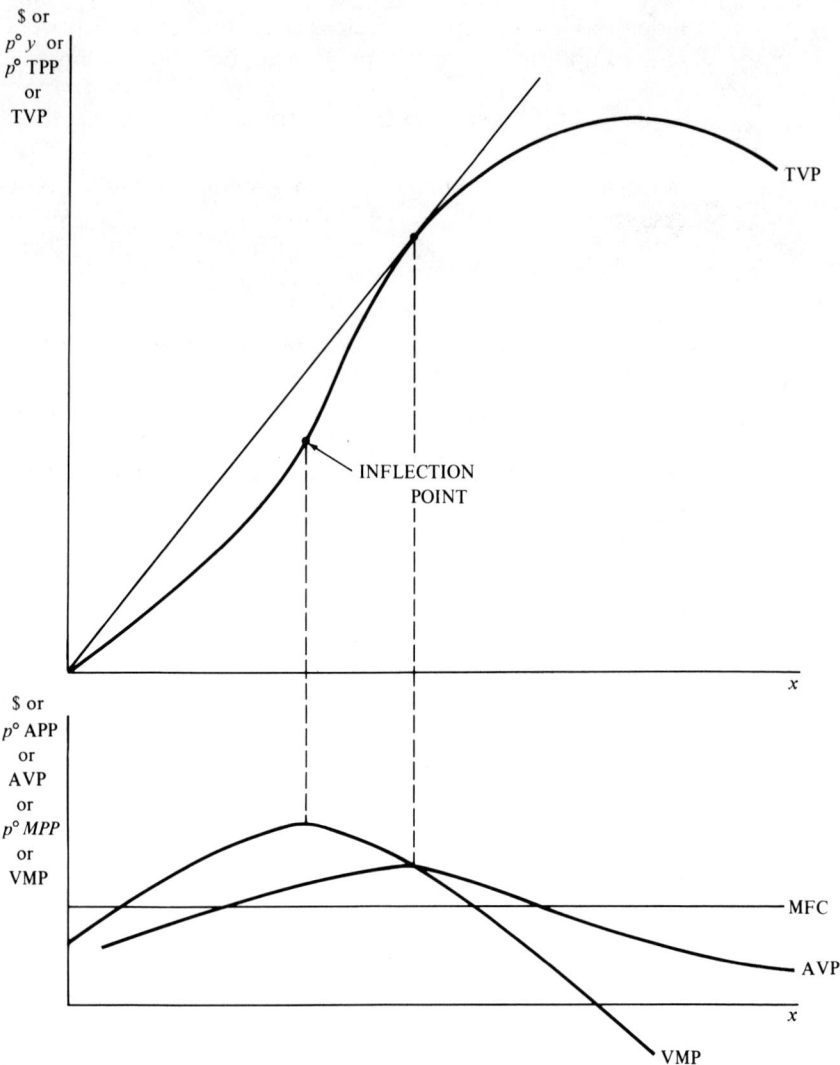

Figure 3.1 *TVP, VMP, AVP,* and *MFC*

Figure 3.2 illustrates the *TVP* function, the *TFC* function, and the profit function, assuming that the underlying production function is of the neoclassical form as described in detail in Chapter 2. The profit function is easily drawn, since it is a graph representing the vertical difference between *TVP* and *TFC*. If *TFC* is greater than *TVP*, profits are negative and the profit function lies below the horizontal axis. These conditions hold at both the very early stages as well as the late stages of input use. Profits are zero when *TVP* = *TFC*. This condition occurs at two points on the graph, where the profit function cuts the horizontal axis. The profit function has a zero slope at two points. Both of these points correspond to points where the slope of the *TVP* curve equals the slope of the *TFC* curve. The first of these points corresponds to a point of profit minimi-

3.3 Maximizing the Difference Between Returns and Costs

zation, and the second is the point of profit maximization, which is the desired level of input use.

These relationships might also be expressed by

$$\Pi = TVP - TFC \tag{3.6}$$

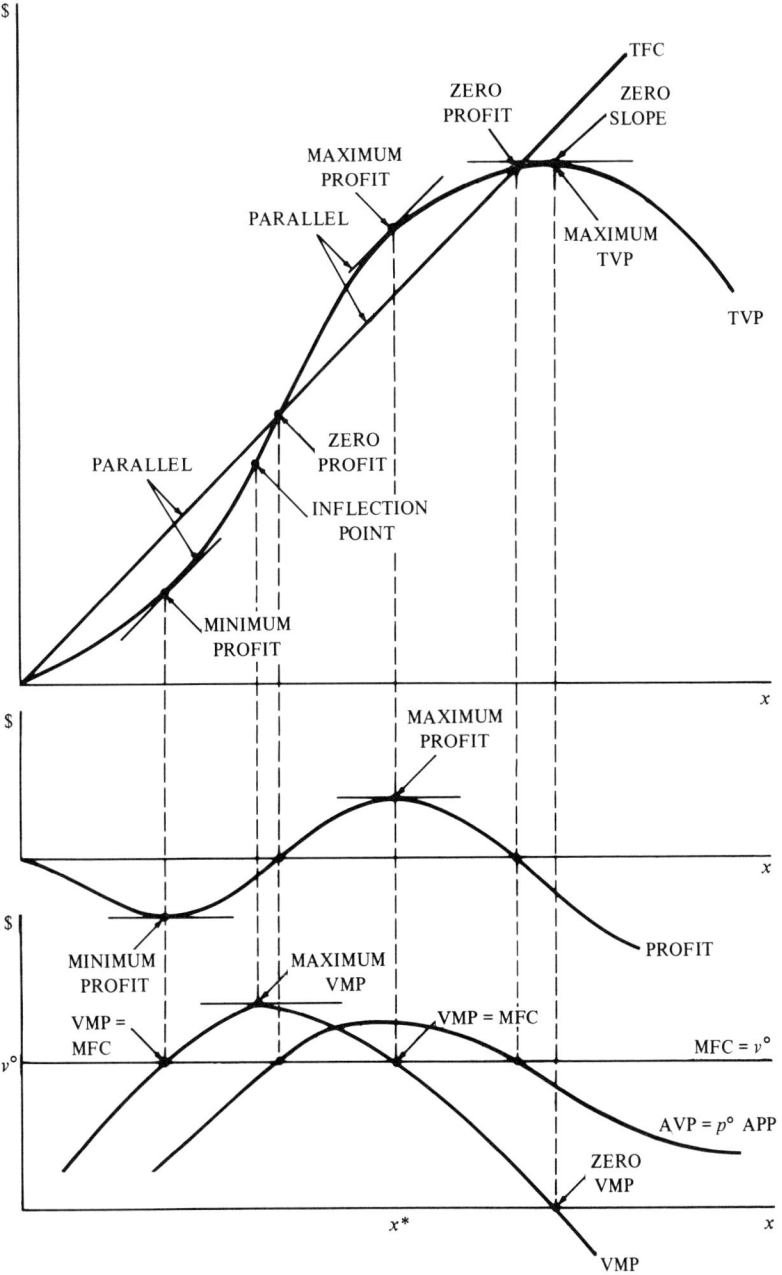

Figure 3.2 *TVP, TFC, VMP, MFC,* and Profit

The slope of the profit function can be expressed (using Δ notation) as $\Delta\Pi/\Delta x$. Hence

$$\Delta\Pi/\Delta x = \Delta TVP/\Delta x - \Delta TFC/\Delta x \tag{3.7}$$

The slope of the function is equal to zero at the point of profit maximization (and at the point of profit minimization—more about this later). Therefore, the slope of the *TVP* function ($\Delta TVP/\Delta x$) must equal the slope of the *TFC* function ($\Delta TFC/\Delta x$) at the point of profit maximization.

3.4 Value of the Marginal Product and Marginal Factor Cost

The value of the marginal product (*VMP*) is defined as the value of the incremental unit of output resulting from an additional unit of x, when y sells for a constant market price $p°$. The *VMP* is another term for the slope of the *TVP* function under a constant product price assumption. In other words, *VMP* is another name for $\Delta TVP/\Delta x$. Since $TVP = p°TPP$, the *VMP* must equal $p° \Delta TPP/\Delta x$. But $\Delta TPP/\Delta x = MPP$. Therefore, *VMP* must be equal to $p°MPP$.

The *marginal factor cost* (*MFC*), sometimes called *marginal resource cost* (*MRC*), is defined as the increase in the cost of inputs associated with the purchase of an additional unit of the input. The *MFC* is another name for the slope of the *TFC* function. Note that if the input price is assumed to be constant at $v°$, then $MFC = v°$.

3.5 Equating *VMP* and *MFC*

The points where the slope of *TVP* equals the slope of *TFC* corresponds either to a point of profit minimization or a point of profit maximization. These points are also defined by

$$p° \, MPP = VMP = MFC = v° \tag{3.8}$$

Figure 3.2 also illustrates these relationships. *MFC*, being equal to a constant $v°$, is a straight line. Notice that *APP* can be multiplied by the price of the product $p°$, and is sometimes referred to as average value of the product (*AVP*). It is equal to $p°$ *APP* or $p°y/x$, or in this case $4.00(APP)$.

There are many ways of rearranging the equation $p° \, MPP = v°$. One possibility is to divide both sides of the equation by the output price $p°$. Then at the point of maximum profit, *MPP* must be equal to $v°/p°$, the factor/product price ratio. Another possibility is to divide both sides of the equation by average physical product (*APP*) or y/x. The profit-maximizing condition would then be given by

$$MPP/APP = (v°x)/(p°y) \tag{3.9}$$

However, *MPP/APP* is the elasticity of production for x. The term $v°x$ represents total factor cost. The term $p°y$ represents total revenue to the farm,

3.5 Equating VMP and MFC

since it is the price of the output times output. At the point of profit maximization, the elasticity of production will be exactly equal to the ratio of total factor cost to total revenue for the farm.

The data contained in Table 2.5 can be used to determine how much nitrogen fertilizer should be applied to the corn. To do this, prices must be assigned both to corn and to the nitrogen fertilizer. Assume that the price of corn is $4.00 per bushel and that nitrogen costs $0.15 per pound. These data are presented in Table 3.1.

Several comments can be made with regard to the data contained in Table 3.1. First, at a nitrogen application level of 180 pounds per acre, the *MPP* of nitrogen is calculated to be 0.0264. The number is very close to zero and suggests that maximum yield is very close to an application rate of 180 pounds per acre. The *MPP* is calculated by first differentiating the *TPP* or production function to find the corresponding *MPP* function:

$$y = 0.75x + 0.0042x^2 - 0.000023x^3 \qquad (3.10)$$

$$dy/dx = 0.75 + 0.0084x - 0.000069x^2 \qquad (3.11)$$

Then the *MPP* at $x = 180$ is

$$MPP = 0.75 + 0.0084(180) - 0.000069(180)^2 = 0.0264$$

However, since at the point where $x = 180$, *MPP* is still positive, the true yield maximum must be at a nitrogen application level of slightly greater than 180 pounds per acre, where $dy/dx = MPP = 0$.

Profits appear to be greatest at a nitrogen application rate of 180 pounds per acre. However, at 180 pounds per acre, the return from the incremental unit of nitrogen (the *VMP* of x) is $0.1056, whereas its cost is $0.15. The results suggest that the last unit of nitrogen that was used returned less than it cost. The profit-maximizing level of nitrogen use must be at slightly less than 180

Table 3.1 Profit Maximization in the Application of Nitrogen to Corn

Quantity of Nitrogen	Corn Yield (bu/acre)	MPP of Nitrogen	$p°$ ($)	VMP ($p° $ MPP)	MFC ($v°$) ($)	Profit ($)
0	0	0.75	4.00	3.0000	0.15	0
20	16.496	0.8904	4.00	3.5616	0.15	62.98
40	35.248	0.9756	4.00	3.9024	0.15	134.99
60	55.152	1.0056	4.00	4.0224	0.15	211.61
80	75.104	0.9804	4.00	3.9216	0.15	288.42
100	94.000	0.9000	4.00	3.6000	0.15	361.00
120	110.736	0.7644	4.00	3.0576	0.15	424.94
140	124.208	0.5736	4.00	2.2944	0.15	475.83
160	133.312	0.3276	4.00	1.3104	0.15	509.25
180	136.944	0.0264	4.00	0.1056	0.15	520.78
200	134.000	-0.3300	4.00	-1.3200	0.15	506.00
220	123.376	-0.7416	4.00	-2.9664	0.15	460.50
240	103.968	-1.2084	4.00	-4.8336	0.15	379.87

pounds per acre. If the input is not free, the profit-maximizing level of input use will always be somewhat less than the level of input use that maximizes the production function. In many instances, however, the difference between the profit-maximizing level of input use and the yield-maximization level of input use may not be very large. In this case the incremental pound of nitrogen must return corn worth only $0.15 in order to cover its cost. If corn sells for $4.00 per bushel, this is but $0.15/$4.00 = 0.0375 bushel of corn from the incremental pound of N.

The difference between the level of nitrogen needed to maximize profits versus the amount needed to maximize output and total revenue does not appear to be very great. If nitrogen were free, there would be no difference at all. As the price of nitrogen increases, the level of nitrogen required to maximize profits is reduced. For example, if nitrogen sold for $1.00 per pound, the last pound of nitrogen applied would need to produce 0.25 bushel of corn at $4.00 per bushel. In general, the distinction between the point representing maximum profit and the point representing maximum revenue becomes more and more important as input prices increase.

If the price of fertilizer is very cheap, the farmer will lose little by fertilizing at a level consistent with maximum yield rather than maximum profit. However, if fertilizer is expensive, the farmer needs to pay close attention to the level of input use that maximizes profits. The same analysis holds true for other inputs used in agricultural production processes for both livestock and crops.

Profits per acre of corn in this example appear to be extraordinarily high, but remember that the production function describing corn yield response to the application of nitrogen assumes that all other inputs are fixed and given. The cost per acre for these inputs could be calculated. Suppose that this turns out to be $450 per acre. This value could be subtracted from each value in the profit column. Conclusions with regard to the profit-maximizing level of nitrogen use would in no way be altered by doing this.

3.6 Calculating the Exact Level of Input Use to Maximize Output or Profits

The exact level of input use required to maximize output (y) or yield can sometimes be calculated. Several examples will be used to illustrate problems in doing this with various production functions. From the earlier discussion it is apparent that if output is to be at its maximum, the *MPP* of the function must be equal to zero. The last unit of input use resulted in no change in the output level and requires that $MPP = dy/dx = 0$ at the point of output maximization.

Suppose the production function

$$y = 2x \tag{3.12}$$

In this case

$$MPP = dy/dx = 2 \text{ and not zero} \tag{3.13}$$

The *MPP* is always 2, and 2 cannot be equal to zero, and the production function

3.6 Calculating Exact Level of Input Use to Maximize Output or Profits

has no maximum. A more general case might be the production function

$$y = bx \tag{3.14}$$

$$MPP = dy/dx = b = 0 \quad ? \tag{3.15}$$

If b were zero, regardless of the amount of x that was produced, no y would result. For any positive value for b, the function has no maximum. Now suppose the production function

$$y = x^{0.5} \tag{3.16}$$

$$MPP = dy/dx = 0.5x^{-0.5} = 0 \quad ? \tag{3.17}$$

The only value for x is 0, for which the MPP would also be equal to 0. Again, this function has no maximum. In general, any function of the form

$$y = ax^b \tag{3.18}$$

where a and b are positive numbers, has no maximum.

Now suppose a production function

$$y = 10 + 8x - 2x^2 \tag{3.19}$$

$$dy/dx = 8 - 4x = 0 \tag{3.20}$$

$$4x = 8 \tag{3.21}$$

$$x = 2 \tag{3.22}$$

Equation (3.19) has a maximum at $x = 2$. In general, a production function of the form

$$y = a + bx + cx^2 \tag{3.23}$$

where $a \geq 0$
$\quad\quad\quad b > 0$
$\quad\quad\quad c < 0$

will have a maximum at some positive level of x.

Finally, the output-maximizing level of input use can be found for the production function used in Chapter 2:

$$y = 0.75x + 0.0042x^2 - 0.000023x^3 \tag{3.24}$$

First, differentiate to find MPP, and then set MPP equal to 0:

$$MPP = dy/dx = 0.75 + 0.0084x - 0.000069x^2 = 0 \tag{3.25}$$

Profit Maximization with One Input and One Output

Now recall from basic algebra that a polynomial of the general form

$$y = ax^2 + bx + c \qquad (3.26)$$

has two solutions for x. These solutions are

$$x = (-b \pm \sqrt{b^2 - 4ac})/2a \qquad (3.27)$$

For this production function [equation (3.24)], $a = -0.000069$, $b = 0.0084$, and $c = 0.75$. One solution generates a negative value for x, which can be ruled out as economically impossible. The second solution is 181.169 units of x, which is the output-maximizing level of nitrogen use (or a slightly greater value than 180, where MPP was 0.0264).

The exact amount of nitrogen required to maximize profits in corn production can be calculated by using a similar approach. A few production functions that do not have an output maximum do have a profit-maximizing solution. First, if profits are maximum or minimum, the slope of the profit function must be equal to zero.

The total value of the product (TVP) is equal to

$$TVP = p°y \qquad (3.28)$$

where $p° = \$4.00$ per bushel
y = yield of corn in bushels per acre

The relationship between corn yield and nitrogen use is again given by the production function written in the general form as

$$y = f(x) \qquad (3.29)$$

where x is the amount of nitrogen fertilizer applied in pounds per acre. Thus

$$TVP = p°f(x) \qquad (3.30)$$

The total factor cost is

$$TFC = v°x \qquad (3.31)$$

where $v° = \$0.15$ per pound of nitrogen. The profit function is

$$\Pi = TVP - TFC \qquad (3.32)$$

or

$$\Pi = (4.00)f(x) - 0.15x \qquad (3.33)$$

To find the maximum or minimum of the profit function, it is necessary to locate the points on the profit function in which the slope is zero. If the

3.6 Calculating Exact Level of Input Use to Maximize Output or Profits

slope of a function is equal to zero, its first derivative must also be equal to zero, because the first derivative of any function is an equation that represents the slope of the function. The first derivative of the profit function can be set equal to zero

$$d\Pi/dx = 4.00(df/dx) - 0.15 = 0 \tag{3.34}$$

or

$$4.00(df/dx) = 0.15 \tag{3.35}$$

The term on the left-hand side of equation (3.35) is $p°MPP$. The price of the product is multiplied times the amount produced by the incremental unit in order to obtain the value of the marginal product (VMP). The term on the right-hand side of the expression is MFC. The conclusion reached here is the same conclusion that was reached from the tabular data. Profits can be maximized at the point where the slope of TVP = the slope of TFC, or $VMP = MRC$.

Several examples are again used to illustrate these ideas for specific production functions. Suppose that $f(x) = bx$, where b is any positive number. Then the production function is

$$y = bx \tag{3.36}$$

and

$$TVP = p°bx \tag{3.37}$$

$$TFC = v°x$$

$$profit = \Pi = TVP - TFC = p°bx - v°x \tag{3.38}$$

If profit is to be maximized, then the slope of the profit function must be equal to zero. That is,

$$d\Pi/dx = p°b - v° = 0 \tag{3.39}$$

or

$$p°b = v° \tag{3.40}$$

but $p°$, $v°$, and b are all constants. The value for $p°b$ either equals $v°$ or it does not equal $v°$. If $p°b$ does not equal $v°$, the profit-maximizing position has not been found. The value for $p°b$ can be looked upon as the return from the incremental unit of x, and of course, $v°$ is the cost or price of x. If $p°b$ is greater than $v°$, profit could be increased by increasing the use of x by ever larger amounts. If $p°b$ is less than $v°$, any incremental increase in the use of x will not cover the incremental cost, and the farmer would be better off to shut down the operation. If $p°b$ equals $v°$, this is true for any level of input use, since VMP

is a constant and not a function of x. VMP is equal to MRC everywhere and the farmer is indifferent as to the level of production.

Now consider a case where the production function is given by

$$y = ax^b \tag{3.41}$$

The corresponding profit function is

$$\text{profit} = \Pi = p°ax^b - v°x$$

The profit-maximizing condition is

$$d\Pi/dx = bp°ax^{b-1} - v° = 0 \tag{3.42}$$

Suppose first that b is greater than 1. Each incremental unit of x produces more and more additional y. Thus MPP is increasing, and as a result, VMP must also be becoming larger and larger. As a result, the more input that is used by the farmer, the greater the incremental return. As a result the farmer will make the most profit by increasing the use of the input without limit.

Now suppose that b is less than 1 but greater than zero. In this case, MPP will decline as the amount of x used is increased. The exact amount of input that will be used to maximize profits can be determined by solving the equation for x:

$$bp°ax^{b-1} = v° \tag{3.43}$$

$$x^{b-1} = v°/(bp°a) \tag{3.44}$$

$$x = [v°/(bp°a)]^{1/(b-1)} \tag{3.45}$$

For example, if $b = 0.5$, then $1/(b - 1) = -2$ and $x = [(0.5p°a)/v°]^2$. If a is positive and b is positive but less than 1, and with constant input and output prices, there will be a finite profit-maximizing level of input use. This is true despite the fact that the underlying production function has no maximum.

Now consider the case for the neoclassical production function used earlier to represent corn yield response to nitrogen as a polynomial [equation (3.10)]. From equation (3.10), it is also possible to determine specifically how much nitrogen would be required to exactly maximize profits.

$$y = 0.75x + 0.0042x^2 - 0.000023x^3 \tag{3.46}$$

$$\text{profit} = \Pi = p°(0.75x + 0.0042x^2 - 0.000023x^3) - v°x \tag{3.47}$$

$$d\Pi/dx = p°(0.75 + 0.0084x - 0.000069x^2) - v° = 0 \tag{3.48}$$

Now suppose that $p° = \$4.00$ and $v° = \$0.15$. The first derivative of the profit equation [equation (3.47)] can be rewritten as

$$4.00(0.75 + 0.0084x - 0.000069x^2) = 0.15$$

or

$$3 + 0.0336x - 0.000276x^2 = 0.15 \quad (3.49)$$

or

$$2.85 + 0.0336x - 0.000276x^2 = 0$$

Using again the formula for finding solutions to polynomials

$$x = [-0.0336 \pm \sqrt{0.0336^2 - 4(-0.000276)(2.85)}]/[2(-0.000276)]$$

$$= 179.322 \text{ pounds of nitrogen per acre to maximize profits.} \quad (3.50)$$

(The only root solution with economic meaning is one that generates a positive value for the input x.)

To ensure that profits are maximized rather than minimized, the second-derivative test, or second-order conditions, are sometimes used. The first derivative of the profit function is again differentiated. In this case

$$d\Pi/dx = 2.85 + 0.0336x - 0.000276x^2 \quad (3.51)$$

$$d^2\Pi/dx^2 = 0.0336 - 0.000552x \quad (3.52)$$

If $x = 179.322$, the value for the second derivative is

$$0.0336 - 0.000552(179.322) = -0.0653857 \quad (3.53)$$

The negative number indicates that profits are at a maximum. A positive number implies a point of profit minimization.

3.7 General Conditions for Profit Maximization

The following are a set of rules for profit maximization. The total value of the product function is given as

$$r = h(x)$$

or

$$r = TVP \quad (3.54)$$

The cost function is given as

$$c = g(x)$$

or

$$c = TFC \quad (3.55)$$

Profits are defined by

$$\Pi = r - c$$

or

$$\Pi = h(x) - g(x)$$

or

$$\Pi = TVP - TFC \qquad (3.56)$$

The first-order conditions for profit maximization require that

$$d\Pi/dx = h'(x) - g'(x) = 0 \qquad (3.57)$$

$$= dr/dx - dc/dx = 0 \qquad (3.58)$$

$$= dTVP/dx - dTFC/dx = 0 \qquad (3.59)$$

$$= VMP - MFC = 0 \qquad (3.60)$$

$$VMP = MFC \qquad (3.61)$$

$$VMP/MFC = 1 \qquad (3.62)$$

The second-derivative test is often used to ensure that profits are maximum, not minimum at this point. The second-derivative test requires that

$$d^2\Pi/dx^2 = h''(x) - g''(x) < 0 \qquad (3.63)$$

$$h''(x) < g''(x) \qquad (3.64)$$

$$d^2TVP/dx^2 < d^2TFC/dx^2 \qquad (3.65)$$

$$dVMP/dx < dMFC/dx \qquad (3.66)$$

The slope of the *VMP* function must be less than the slope of *MFC*. This condition is met if *VMP* slopes downward and *MFC* is constant.

3.8 Necessary and Sufficient Conditions

The terms *necessary* and *sufficient* are used to describe conditions relating to the maximization or minimization of a function. These terms have a very special meaning. The term *necessary* means that the condition must hold for the event to occur. In this case, the slope of the profit function must be equal to zero if the function is to be maximized. In equations (3.57) to (3.66), the condition is the slope of the function, and the event is the maximization of the function.

The necessary condition for the maximization of the function is that the slope be equal to zero. However, if the slope of the profit function is equal to zero, the profit function might also be at a minimum value. A necessary condition does not ensure that the event will occur but only describes a circumstance under which the event could take place. A necessary condition is required for profit maximization, but taken alone, a necessary condition does not ensure that profits will be maximum, only that profits could be maximum.

If the sufficient condition is present, the event will always occur. Thus a sufficient condition for profit maximization means that if the condition holds, profits will always be maximum. The term *sufficient* does not rule out the possibility that there may be other conditions under which the event will take place, but only states that if a particular condition is present, the event will always take place.

The terms *necessary* and *sufficient* are regularly used together. The necessary condition for the maximization of a profit function for corn is that the slope of the function be equal to zero. The necessary and sufficient condition for the maximization of a profit function for corn is that the slope of the function be equal to zero, and that the rate of change in the slope, or the second derivative of the profit function, be negative.

Requirements with respect to signs on first derivatives are sometimes called the first-order conditions, or first-derivative tests for a maximum or minimum. Requirements with respect to signs on second-derivatives are sometimes called the second-order conditions, or second-derivative tests. A necessary condition is sometimes, but not always, the same as a first-derivative test. A second-derivative test is normally only part of the requirements for a sufficient condition.

It is not a sufficient condition for a maximum if only the second derivative is negative. There are many points on the profit function that have negative second derivatives which are neither a minimum nor a maximum. Only when the necessary and sufficient conditions are taken together is a maximum achieved. Finally, necessary and sufficient conditions taken together will ensure that the event will always occur and that no other set of conditions will result in the occurrence of the event.

3.9 The Three Stages of the Neoclassical Production Function

The neoclassical production function described in Chapter 2 can be divided into three stages or regions of production (Figure 3.3). These are designated by Roman numerals I, II, and III. Stages I and III have traditionally been described as irrational stages of production. The terminology suggests that a farm manager would never choose levels of input use within these regions unless the behavior were irrational. Irrational behavior describes a farmer who chooses a goal inconsistent with the maximization of net returns, or profit. Stage II is sometimes called the rational stage, or economic region of production. This terminology suggests that rational farmers who have as their goal profit maximization will be found operating within this region. However, in certain instances, such as when dollars available for the purchase of inputs are limited, a rational farmer may not always operate in stage II of the production function.

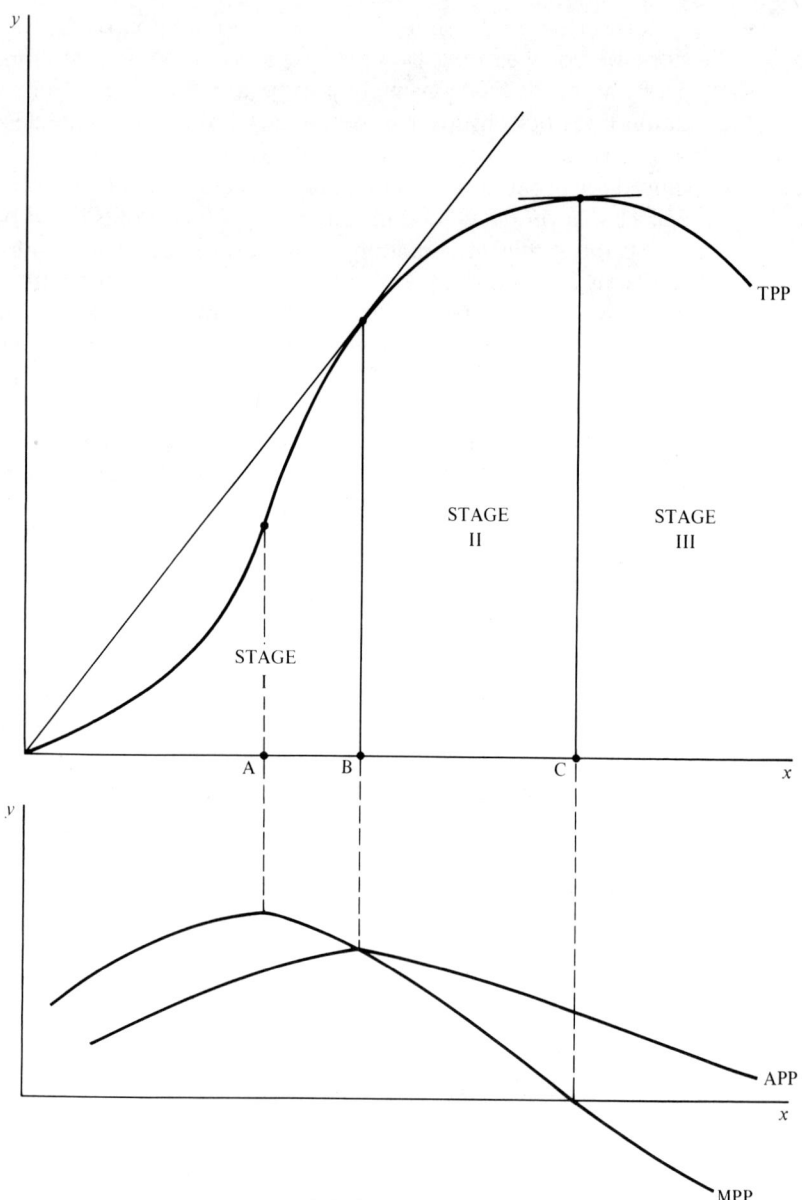

Figure 3.3 Stages of Production for the Neoclassical Production Function

Stage I of the neoclassical production function includes input levels from zero units up to the level of use where *MPP* = *APP*. *Stage II* includes the region from the point where *MPP* = *APP* to the point where the production function reaches its maximum and *MPP* is zero. *Stage III* includes the region where the production function is declining and *MPP* is negative.

The stages of production can also be described in terms of the elasticity of production. For the neoclassical production function, as the level of input use increases, the elasticity of production (E_p) also changes because the elasticity

3.9 The Three Stages of the Neoclassical Production Function

of production is equal to the ratio of *MPP* to *APP*. The value for the elasticity of production identifies the stage of production. If E_p is greater than 1, then *MPP* is greater than *APP* and we are in stage I. Stage I ends and stage II begins at the point where $E_p = 1$ and *MPP* = *APP*. Stage II ends and stage III begins at the point where E_p equals zero and *MPP* is also zero. Stage III exists anywhere that E_p is negative and hence *MPP* is also negative. Notice that the first stage of the neoclassical production function ends and the second stage begins at the point where the marginal product of the incremental or last unit of the input *x* just equals the average product for all units of the input *x*.

It is easy to understand why a rational farmer interested in maximizing profits would never choose to operate in stage III (beyond point C, Figure 3.3). It would never make sense to apply inputs if, on so doing, output was reduced. Even if fertilizer were free, a farmer would never apply fertilizer beyond the point of output maximum.

Output could be increased and costs reduced by reducing the level of input use. The farmer would always make greater net returns by reducing the use of inputs such that he or she were operating instead in stage II.

It is also easy to see why a farmer would not choose to produce in the region where *MPP* is increasing (line *OA*, Figure 3.3) in the first part of stage I, if output prices were constant and sufficient funds were available for the purchase of *x*. In this region, the marginal product of the input is increasing as more and more of the input is used. Diminishing marginal returns have not yet set in, and each additional unit of input used will produce a greater and greater additional net return. The additional return occurs despite the fact that for the first few units, the *MPP* for the incremental unit might still be below the cost of the incremental unit, as represented by the constant *MFC* function.

It is difficult to see why a farmer would not choose to operate in the second part of stage I, where *MPP* is declining but *APP* is increasing (line *AB*, Figure 3.3), if output prices were constant and sufficient funds were available to purchase additional units of *x*. However, using the definition

$$AVP = p°APP = p°y/x. \tag{3.67}$$

the total value of the product (*TVP*) might then be defined as

$$TVP = xAVP = xp°y/x = p°TPP \tag{3.68}$$

Look at Figure 3.4. Pick any level of input use and call that level x^*. Now draw a vertical line from the horizontal axis to the corresponding point on the *AVP* curve. The value of the *AVP* curve at x^* represents the average revenue obtained from the sale of output per unit of *x* used, assuming that the total amount of used was x^*. With constant output prices, *AVP* might be thought of as the average revenue expressed per unit of *x* used. Now draw a horizontal line from the point on the *AVP* curve to the vertical axis. The length of the horizontal line represents the total amount of *x* used, or x^*. A rectangle has now been formed, with the lower sides being the axes of the graph. The area of this rectangle is equal to *TVP* for $x = x^*$. This is because the length of the rectangle is x^* and its height is *AVP*.

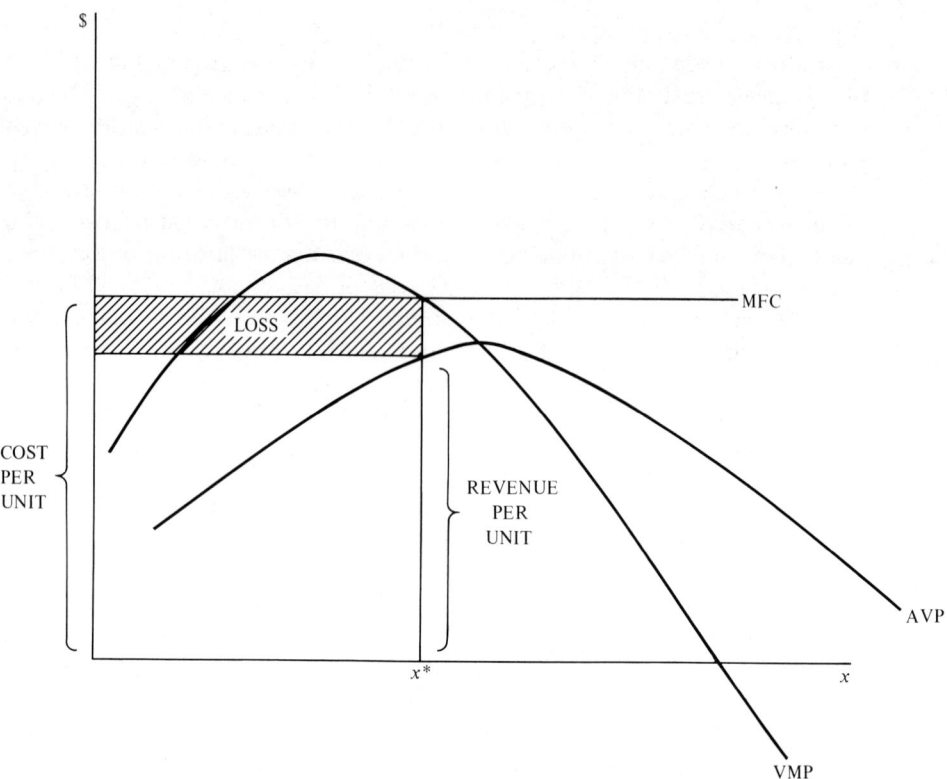

Figure 3.4 If *VMP* Is Greater Than *AVP*, the Farmer Will Not Operate

Now draw a line from x^* to *MFC*. Another rectangle is formed. Input prices are assumed to be constant $v° = MFC$. Since $v°$ is constant, $v°$ is equal to the average cost of a unit of x; or $TFC = v°x$ and $AFC = (v°x)/x = v° = dTFC/dx = MFC$. Then *TFC* at $x = x^*$ is equal to the area contained in the second rectangle.

Profit equals returns less costs.

$$\Pi = TVP - TFC. \tag{3.69}$$

In Figure 3.4, the first rectangle is *TVP* and the second rectangle is *TFC*. Suppose now that the input price is lower than the maximum value for *VMP* but higher than the maximum value for *AVP*. These conditions describe the second part of stage I. The farmer equates *VMP* and *MFC* and finds the resulting profit maximizing level of input use x^*. However, since *AVP* is less than *VMP*, the first rectangle representing *TVP* would necessarily be less than the second rectangle representing *TFC*. This would imply that

$$\Pi = TVP - TFC < 0 \tag{3.70}$$

Moreover, $TVP < TFC$ occurs everywhere in stage *I* of the production function. The farmer would lose money if operation were continued in stage

I. If the price of the input is higher than the maximum *AVP*, there is no way that the incremental unit of input can produce returns sufficient to cover its incremental cost. Under such circumstances a rational solution would be to use 0 units of the input. This situation will be remedied if either of two events occurs: (1) the price of the input declines to a level below the maximum *APP*, or (2) the price of the output increases such that *AVP* rises. New technology might also cause *APP* to increase, and the result would be an increase in *AVP*.

If *MFC* were below *AVP* in stage I, the farmer could always increase profit by increasing the use of the input. However, a farmer might not be able to always get the funds needed for the purchase of the input. In the special case, the farmer could operate in stage *I* if funds for the purchase of input *x* were restricted or limited. In this instance, the profit-maximizing level of input use would occur in stage II. Revenues exceed costs at many points within stage I, and the farmer may be better off to use available revenue for the purchase of *x* and to produce in stage I, even if the profit-maximizing point in stage II cannot be achieved. However, the farmer would never want to operate in stage III of the production function, or, for that matter, to the right of the point in stage II representing the profit-maximizing level of input use, assuming positive input and output prices. The profit-maximizing point is most desired, but other points to the left of the profit-maximizing point may also generate a positive profit for the farmer.

3.10 Further Topics on Stages of Production

One of the reasons for the popularity of the neoclassical production function is that it includes all three stages of production. It is worthwhile to examine some features of other production functions in an effort to determine whether or not the various stages of production are accurately represented. As a starting point, a simple function might be

$$y = bx \qquad (3.71)$$

As indicated earlier, The *MPP*(dy/dx) for this function is b and so the *APP*(y/x) equal to b. The elasticity of production (*MPP/APP*) is b/b, which is 1 everywhere. This implies that this function does not have any identifiable stages. The curious conclusion is that the function is at the dividing point between stages *I* and II throughout its range. No wonder this function has not proven popular with economists. If py [output (y) times its price (p)] were greater than bx [input (x) times its marginal product], profit maximization would entail obtaining as much x as one could possibly obtain, and producing as much y as possible. At some point, input prices would not hold constant, and hence the purely competitive assumptions would break down.

A production function with a constant slope produces *VMP* and *MFC* curves that are both horizontal lines, with *VMP* above *MFC*. For a given level of input use, the area under *VMP* represents returns, and the area under the *MFC* represents costs. The portion of the rectangles that do not overlap represents profits. If py were less than bx, returns would not cover costs and the farm would maximize profits by shutting down and producing no output. If py exactly equaled bx, the farmer would be indifferent toward producing or shutting down, since zero profit would result in either case.

Now consider the case where the production function is

$$y = \sqrt{x} \qquad (3.72)$$

As indicated earlier, the elasticity of production in this case is 0.5 throughout the range of the function, since the ratio MPP/APP is 0.5. This suggests that the farm is in stage II of the production function everywhere. Notice that this stage II is not a simple representation of stage II from the neoclassical production function. The elasticity of production for the neoclassical function decreases from 1 (at the start of stage II) to 0 (at the end of stage II) as the use of the input is increased.

For this production function, the elasticity of production remains constant. For any production function of the form $y = bx^a$, the elasticity of production is equal to the constant a. If a is greater than 1, the production function is in stage I everywhere. If a is less than zero, the function is in stage II everywhere. The function $y = bx$ is a special case of this function with a equal to 1.

3.11 The Imputed Value of an Additional Unit of an Input

For profits to be maximum, a necessary condition is that the slope of the TVP function be equal to the slope of the total factor cost function. This might also be expressed as

$$VMP = MFC = v° \qquad (3.73)$$

$$p°MPP = MFC = v° \qquad (3.74)$$

$$p°dTPP/dx = dTFC/dx \qquad (3.75)$$

or

$$p°dy/dx = v° \qquad (3.76)$$

Equations (3.73) to (3.76) all describe the necessary condition for profit maximization. (The sufficient condition requires that VMP equal MFC and that the VMP curve intersect the MFC curve from above.)

Another way of expressing the relationship $VMP = MFC$ is

$$VMP/MFC = 1 \qquad (3.77)$$

VMP is the return obtained from the incremental unit of x, or the value to the manager of the incremental unit of x. MFC is the cost of the incremental unit of x. The equation $VMP = MFC$ is a decision rule that tells the farmer how much input should be used to maximize profits. This decision rule states that the use of the input should be increased until the point is reached whereby

3.11 The Imputed Value of an Additional Unit of an Input

the last dollar spent on the input returns exactly its incremental cost. This is one of the fundamental marginal rules of economics. Many if not most of the previous incremental dollars spent on the input paid back more than the cost of the input. These units, taken together, generate the profit for the farm (Figure 3.5).

Now suppose that

$$VMP/MFC = 3 \qquad (3.78)$$

Equation (3.78) states that the value of the last dollar spent on the input in terms of its contribution to revenue for the farm is three times its cost. Moreover, the last dollar spent on the input returns $3 to the farm. This number is sometimes referred to as the *imputed value* or *implicit worth* of the incremental dollar spent on the input. Both terms refer to the same concept.

There is no particular reason to believe that the imputed value or implicit worth of the last dollar spent on an input should necessarily be a dollar. The implicit worth of the last dollar spent on an input may be greater than, equal to, or less than a dollar. However, a necessary condition for profit maximization is for VMP to equal MFC. Profit maximization requires that the value of the last dollar spent on the input be a dollar. If profits are maximized, the imputed value of an input will be 1, since its contribution to revenue exactly covers its cost. If the imputed value is 3, as in this instance, profits could be further increased by increasing the use of the input until the imputed value is reduced to 1.

Now suppose that

$$VMP/MFC = 0.5 \qquad (3.79)$$

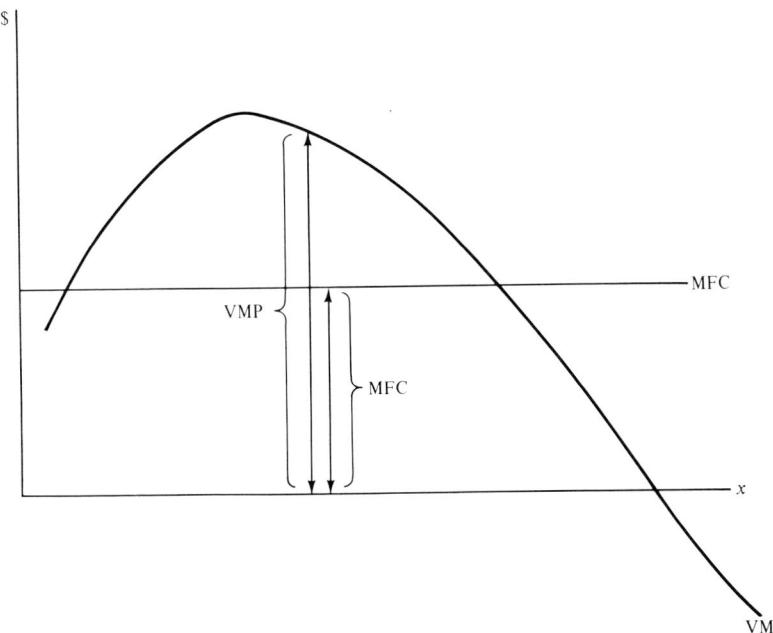

Figure 3.5 Relationship Between *VMP* and *MFC*

Equation (3.79) states that the value of the last dollar spent on the input in terms of its contribution to revenue for the farm is only one-half its cost. This is a point to the right of the profit-maximizing point, although it is still in stage II. Revenue from the sale of the output produced by the last unit of input only covers 50 percent of the cost or price of the input. The last dollar spent returns only 50 cents. The other 50 cents is loss. In this case, profits to the farm could probably be increased by reducing the use of the input. Since the *MPP* of the input usually increases as its use decreases, this has the effect of raising *MPP* and thus increasing *VMP* for the input.

Now suppose that

$$VMP/MFC = 0 \qquad (3.80)$$

Assuming constant positive prices for both the input and output, the only way this could happen is if *MPP* were zero. In this instance, the last dollar contributes nothing to revenue. The only point where this could happen is at the maximum of the production (*TPP* or *TVP*) function, the dividing point between stages II and III.

Finally, suppose that

$$VMP/MFC = -5 \qquad (3.81)$$

Assuming constant positive prices for both the input and the output, the only way this could happen is for *MPP* to be negative. This implies stage III of the production function. In this case, the last dollar spent on the input results in a loss in revenue of $5. This is a point in stage III where the farmer would never produce.

The implicit worth or imputed value of an input or factor of production has also sometimes been called the *shadow price* for the input. It is called a shadow price because it is not the price that the farmer might pay for the input, but rather the value of a dollar spent on the input to the farmer in his or her operation. A farmer might be willing to purchase an input at prices up to but not exceeding the imputed value or shadow price of the input on the farm.

Diagrammatically, the shadow price or imputed value of an input can easily be seen (Figure 3.5). The *VMP* represents the value of the input: the *MFC*, its price or cost per unit. The shadow price is the ratio of value to price. If *MFC* and product prices are constant, the shadow price usually increases until *MPP* reaches its maximum and then decreases. The shadow price is 1 where *MPP* (and *VMP*) intersects *MFC*, and zero where *MPP* intersects the horizontal axis of the graph.

3.12 Concluding Comments

Profit-maximization conditions for the factor-product model have been introduced. Profits are maximum when the necessary and sufficient conditions for a maximum have been met. The necessary conditions for profit maximization require that the profit function have a slope of zero. The necessary condition for profit maximization can be determined by finding the point on the profit function where the first derivative is zero. The sufficient condition, ensuring profit maximization, holds if the first derivative of the profit function is zero and the second derivative of the profit function is negative.

Alternatively, the level of input use that maximizes profits can be found by equating the VMP of the input with the MFC, which in pure competition is the price of the input. The slope of the total value of the product curve will be equal to the slope of the total factor cost curve. The slope of the total value of the product curve is its derivative, which if output prices are constant, is the VMP curve. If the price of x is constant, the slope of the total factor cost curve is the MFC.

Under the assumptions of pure competition, with constant, positive input and output prices, a farmer interested in maximizing profits would never operate in stage III of the production function, where MPP and VMP are declining. A farmer would operate in stage I of the production function only if sufficient funds were not available for the purchase of inputs needed to reach stage II. A farmer would not produce at all if the price of x exceeded the maximum average value of the product.

Problems and Exercises

1. Suppose that the output sells for $5 and the input sells for $4. Fill in the blanks in the following table.

x (Input)	y (Output)	VMP	AVP
0	0		————
10	50	————	————
25	75	————	————
40	80	————	————
50	85	————	————

2. In Problem 1, what appears to be the profit-maximizing level of input use? Verify this by calculating TVP and TFC for each level of input use as shown in the table.

3. Suppose that the production function is given by

$$y = 2x^{0.5}$$

The price of x is $3 and the price of y is $4. Derive the corresponding VMP and AVP functions. What is MFC? Solve for the profit-maximizing level for input use x.

4. When the input price is constant, the slope of the total factor cost function will also be constant. Is this statement true or false? Explain.

5. Whenever the total factor cost function and the total value of the product function are parallel to each other, profits will be maximized. Is this statement true or false? Explain.

6. Suppose that the production function is the one found in Problem 5, Chapter 2. Corn sells for $4.00 per bushel and nitrogen sells for $0.20 per pound. At what nitrogen application rate are profits maximized?

7. Explain the terms *necessary* and *sufficient* in terms of a farmer seeking to maximize profits in the feeding of dairy cattle for milk production.

8. Is the shadow price of a dairy feed ration different from the price the farmer pays per pound of the ration? Explain. Of what importance is a shadow price to a farmer seeking to maximize profits from a dairy herd?

9. Explain the consequences to the farmer if the production function for milk were a linear function of the amount of feed fed to each cow.

4. Costs, Returns, and Profits on the Output Side

In this chapter the concept of a cost function defined in terms of units of output is introduced. Total, variable, and marginal cost curves are illustrated using graphics and derived using mathematics. The necessary conditions for determining the level of output that maximizes profits are derived. The cost functions are shown to be closely linked to the parameters of the underlying production function. The supply function for the firm is derived.

Key Terms and Definitions:

Total Cost (TC)
Total Variable Cost (VC)
Marginal Cost (MC)
Total Fixed Cost (FC)
Average Cost (AVC)
Average Fixed Cost (AFC)
Average Variable Cost (AVC)
Inverse Production Function
Duality of Cost and Production

4.1 Some Basic Definitions

In Chapter 3, a very simple cost equation was defined. This cost equation was

$$TFC = v°x \qquad (4.1)$$

Equation (4.1) states that the total cost for an input or factor of production is the constant price of the input ($v°$) multiplied by the quantity that is used.

However, the costs of production might also be defined not in terms of the use of the input, but in terms of the output. To do this, some basic terms need to be explained.

Variable costs (VC) are the costs of production that vary with the level of output produced by the farmer. For example, in the production of corn, with the time period being a single production season, variable costs might be thought

4.1 Some Basic Definitions

of as the costs associated with the purchase of the variable inputs used to produce the corn. Examples of variable costs include the costs associated with the purchase of inputs such as seed, fertilizer, herbicides, insecticides, and so on. In the case of livestock production within a single production season, a major variable cost item is feed.

Fixed costs (FC) are the costs that must be incurred by the farmer whether or not production takes place. Examples of fixed-cost items include payments for land purchases and depreciation on farm machinery, buildings, and equipment.

The categorization of a cost item as fixed or variable is often not entirely clear. The fertilizer and seed a farmer uses can only be treated as a variable cost item prior to the time in which it is placed in the ground. Once the item has been used, it is sometimes called a sunk, or unrecoverable, cost, in that a farmer cannot decide to sell seed and fertilizer already used and recover the purchase price.

Although depreciation on farm machinery is normally treated as a fixed cost, given sufficient time, the farmer does have the option of selling the machinery so that the depreciation would no longer be incurred. Payments for the purchase of land would not be made if the farmer elected to sell the land. The categorization of farm labor is very difficult. A farm laborer on an annual salary might be treated as a fixed cost which the farmer incurs whether or not production takes place. But if the laborer is laid off, the cost is no longer fixed. Temporary workers hired on an hourly basis might be more easily categorized as a variable cost.

The categorization of a particular input as a fixed cost or variable cost item is thus closely intertwined with the particular period involved. Over very long periods, a farmer is able to buy and sell land, machinery, and other inputs into the production process that would normally be considered fixed. Thus, over very long periods, all costs are normally treated as variable.

Over a very short period of time, perhaps during a few weeks within a single production season, a farmer might not be able to make any adjustment in the amounts of any of the inputs being used. For this length of time, all costs could be treated as fixed. Thus the categorization of each input as a fixed- or variable-cost item cannot be made without explicit reference to the particular period involved. A distinction between fixed and variable costs has thus been made on the basis of the period involved, with the proportion of fixed to variable costs increasing as the length of time is shortened, and declining as the length of time increases.

Some economists define the long run as a period of time of sufficient length such that the size of plant (in the case of farming, the farm) can be altered. Production takes place on a short-run average cost curve ($SRAC$) that is U shaped, with the manager equating marginal revenue (the price of the output in the purely competitive model) with short-run marginal cost ($SRMC$). There exists a series of short run-marginal and average cost curves corresponding to the size of the particular plant (farm). Given sufficient time, the size of the plant can be altered. Farmers can buy and sell land, machinery, and equipment. Long-run average cost ($LRAC$) can be derived by drawing an envelope curve which comes tangent to each short-run average cost curve (Figure 4.1).

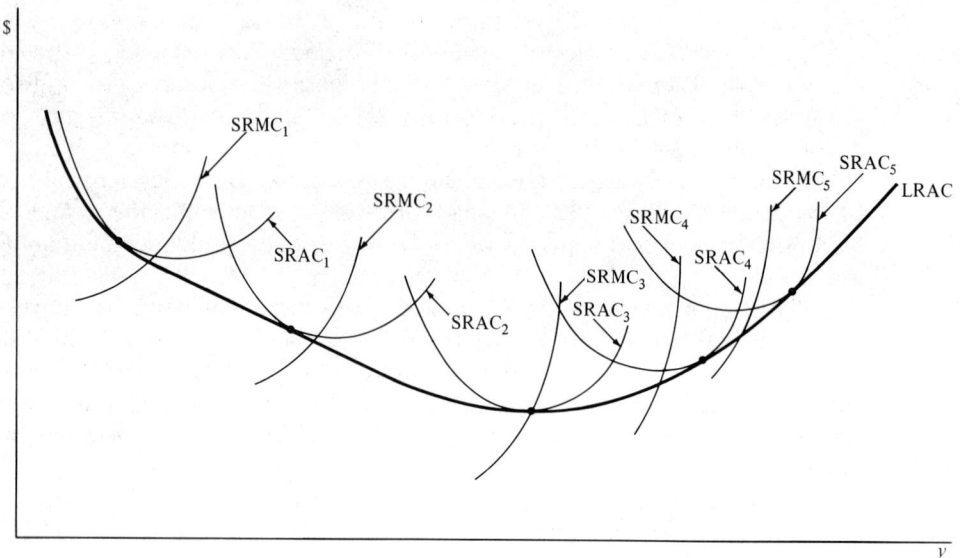

Figure 4.1 Short- and Long-Run Average and Marginal Cost with Envelope Long-Run Average Cost

A classic argument in economics was that between the economist Jacob Viner and his draftsman. Viner insisted that such a long-run average cost curve must necessarily come tangent to the minimum points on each short-run average cost curve. The draftsman argued that this was impossible—that plants operating with less capacity than that represented by the minimum point on the *LRAC* curve must necessarily be tangent to a point on the *LRAC* at higher than minimum *SRAC*. Plants operating at greater than the capacity suggested by the minimum *LRAC* would have a *SRAC* tangent to *LRAC* at a point at greater than minimum *SRAC*. Only for the plant operating with its *SRAC* curve at the point of minimum *LRAC* would the *LRAC* be tangent to the minimum point on the *SRAC*. The draftsman was, of course, correct (Figure 4.1).

In long-run equilibrium, producers discover and select a plant size at the minimum point on *LRAC*. Hence *MR* equals *LRMC* and there is no profit. In the short run, however, *MR* can exceed *MC*. Each producer would equate *MR* to his own *SRMC*. For the producers operating in the short run, this would entail using the plant beyond its point of minimum *SRAC*. No producer would ever be observed operating at the minimum *SRAC* and *LRAC*, save the firms in long-run equilibrium.

Variable costs are normally expressed per unit of output (y) rather than per unit of input (x). This is because there is usually more than one variable cost item involved in the production of agricultural commodities. A general expression for a variable cost function is

$$VC = g(y) \qquad (4.2)$$

Since fixed costs do not vary with output, fixed costs are equal to some constant dollar value k; that is,

$$FC = k \qquad (4.3)$$

4.1 Some Basic Definitions

Total costs (*TC*) are the sum of fixed plus variable costs:

$$TC = VC + FC \tag{4.4}$$

or

$$TC = g(y) + k \tag{4.5}$$

Average variable cost (*AVC*) is the variable cost per unit of output

$$AVC = VC/y = g(y)/y \tag{4.6}$$

Average fixed cost is equal to fixed cost per unit of output:

$$AFC = FC/y = k/y \tag{4.7}$$

The output level y is divided into the constant k, where k represents total fixed costs (*FC*).

There are two ways to obtain average cost (*AC*), sometimes also called average total cost (*ATC*). One way is to divide total cost (*TC*) by output (y):

$$AC = ATC = TC/y \tag{4.8}$$

Another way is to sum average variable cost (*AVC*) and average fixed cost (*AFC*):

$$AC = AVC + AFC \tag{4.9}$$

or

$$TC/y = VC/y + FC/y \tag{4.10}$$

Marginal cost is defined as the change in total cost, or total variable cost, resulting from an incremental change in output.

$$MC = \Delta TC/\Delta y = \Delta VC/\Delta y \tag{4.11}$$

Since the value for fixed costs (*FC*) is a constant k, *MC* will be the same irrespective of whether it is based on total costs or total variable cost.

Marginal cost (*MC*) at a particular point is the slope of the total cost function. Marginal cost can be defined in terms of derivatives. In this instance

$$MC = dTC/dy = dVC/dy \tag{4.12}$$

The marginal cost function is a function representing the slope of the total cost function. For example, a value for *MC* of $5.00 indicates that the last or incremental unit of output cost an additional $5.00 to produce.

Figure 4.2 illustrates the cost functions that have been defined. The illustration of *VC* looks like a production function that has been inverted. Output,

Costs, Returns, and Profits on the Output Side

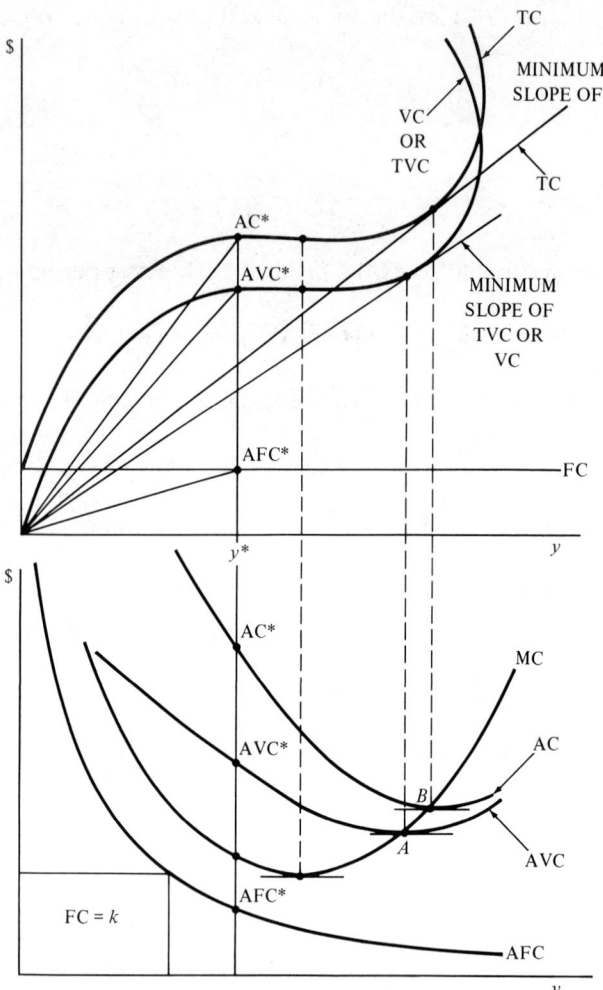

Figure 4.2 Cost Functions on the Output Side

rather than input, is on the horizontal axis. The vertical axis is dollars, not units of input. Moreover, the slope of the *VC* function appears to be exactly the inverse of the slope on a production function. The production function increased initially at an increasing rate until the inflection point was reached, then it increased at a decreasing rate. The cost function first increases at a decreasing rate until the inflection point is reached. Then the cost function increases at an increasing rate.

The cost curves look rather strange when output reaches its technical maximum. Suppose that the maximum yield a farmer can achieve in the production of corn is 140 bushels per acre. Suppose that despite the farmer's best efforts to increase yields further by applying more seed, fertilizer, and pesticides, the additional yield is just not there. The additional seed results in more plants that become overly crowded in the field, and the additional plants become so crowded that yield is reduced. The additional fertilizer starts to do damage to the crop.

4.1 Some Basic Definitions

The additional herbicides kill the corn plants. As more and more variable inputs are used, yield starts to drop off to 130, 120, or even 110 bushels per acre. Costs for the additional variable inputs are incurred even at yield levels that could have been achieved with a much lower level of input use and a corresponding reduction in the cost for seed, fertilizer, and pesticide. The variable-cost function must turn back on itself once the maximum yield is achieved. This is actually stage III of variable cost.

Once variable cost turns back on itself, it is no longer technically a function. This is because for some yield levels, two rather than one value for variable cost is assigned. Thus VC might be thought of in this case as a cost correspondence rather than a cost function.

Fixed cost (FC), being constant, is a horizontal line positioned at the corresponding dollar value on the vertical axis. Total cost (TC) appears nearly the same as variable cost (VC). Total cost has been shifted vertically by the fixed-cost amount. The difference between TC and VC at any point is FC. TC and VC are not parallel to each other, because FC is represented by the vertical distance between TC and VC. At each level of output, however, the slope of TC equals the slope of VC.

Any point on the average cost curves (AC, AVC, and AFC) can be represented by the slope of a line drawn from the origin of the graph to the corresponding point on TC, VC or FC. Suppose that the value for AC, AVC and AFC at some output level called y^* is to be determined. Draw a vertical line from y^* to the corresponding point on TC, VC, and FC. Call these points TC^*, VC^*, and FC^*. Now draw a line from each of these points to the origin of the graph. Three triangles will result. The slope of each of these triangles represents the corresponding AC^*, AVC^*, and AFC^* for the output level y^* (Figure 4.2).

Marginal cost (MC) at any point is represented by the slope of a line drawn tangent to either TC or VC. The minimum slope for both TC and VC occurs at the respective inflection points of TC and VC. The inflection points for both TC and VC correspond to the same level of output. Thus MC is minimum at the inflection point of either the TC or the VC curve, and there is but one MC curve that can be derived from either the TC or the VC curve.

Minimum AVC occurs where a line drawn from the origin comes tangent to VC. Minimum AC occurs where a line drawn from the origin comes tangent to TC. The point of tangency on TC occurs to the right of the point of tangency on VC. Thus the minimum AC will occur to the right of the minimum AVC. Since these lines are tangent to TC and VC, they also represent the slopes of the curves at the two points. Hence they also represent MC at the two points. Therefore, MC must be equal to and cut AVC and AC at each respective minimum (points A and B, Figure 4.2).

The relationship that must exist between AC and MC can be proven:

$$TC = (AC)y \qquad (4.13)$$

$$dTC/dy = AC(1) + y(dAC/dy) \qquad (4.14)$$

$$MC = AC + y(\text{the slope of } AC) \qquad (4.15)$$

If the slope of *AC* is positive, *MC* must be greater than *AC*. If the slope of *AC* is negative, *MC* must be less than *AC*. If the slope of *AC* is zero, *AC* is at its minimum and *MC* must equal *AC*. The reader can verify that the same relationship must hold between *MC* and *AVC*.

AFC is a rectangular hyperbola. Draw a straight line from any point on the *AFC* curve to the corresponding vertical ($) and horizontal ($y$) axis. The area of the enclosed rectangle is equal to *FC*, which is the constant k (Figure 4.2). To the point of maximum output, as y becomes larger and larger, *AFC* comes closer and closer to the horizontal axis but does not reach it. Similarly, as y becomes smaller and smaller, *AFC* becomes larger and larger and gets closer and closer to the vertical axis. Again *AFC* never reaches the vertical axis.

Since *AC* is the sum of *AVC* + *AFC*, and *AFC* becomes smaller and smaller to the point of maximum output, as output increases, *AC* should be drawn closer and closer to *AVC*. The minimum slope of a line drawn from the origin of the graph to the *TC* curve occurs at an output level smaller than the output level associated with the minimum slope of a line drawn from the origin to the *VC* curve. Therefore, minimum *AVC* occurs at an output level smaller than the level at which minimum *AC* occurs.

The behavior of the average cost curves beyond the point of output maximization is somewhat complicated. Beyond the point of output maximization, y is reduced. Since *FC* remains constant, *AFC* returns along the exact same

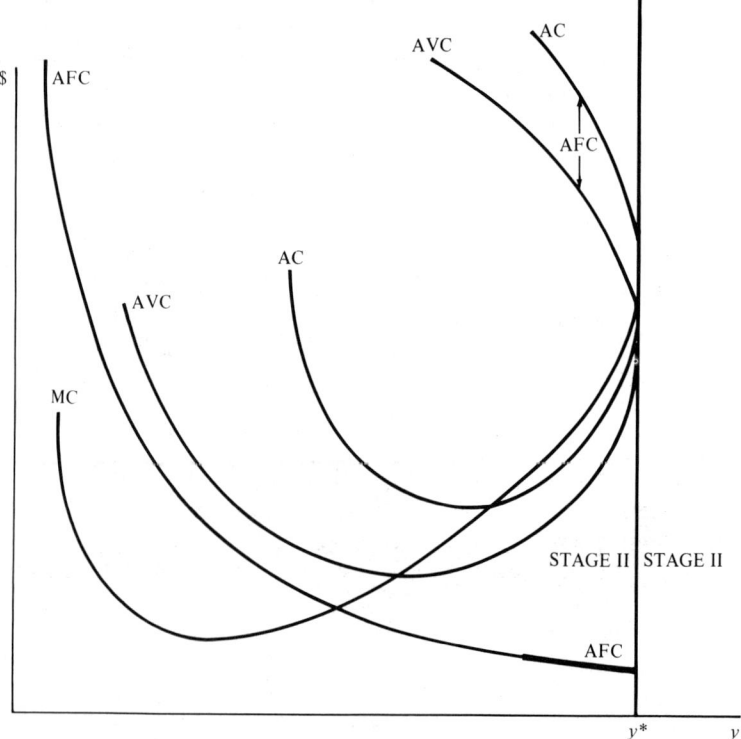

Figure 4.3 Behavior of Cost Curves As Output Approaches a Technical Maximum y^*

curve. *AVC* and *AC* are increasing even as *y* is reduced, when inputs are used beyond the point of output maximization. Moreover, if there are any fixed costs, *AC* must remain above *AVC*. Both *AVC* and *AC* must turn back on themselves to represent the new higher average costs associated with the reduction in output when inputs are used beyond the point of output maximization. If this is to occur, *AC* must cross over *AVC* at the point where output is maximum. At the point of output maximum, both *AC* and *AVC* have a perfectly vertical or infinite slope (Figure 4.3). In stage III, *MC* goes into the negative quadrant when *MPP* is negative.

4.2 Simple Profit Maximization from the Output Side

Perhaps no criterion is more famous in economics than the expression "marginal cost equals marginal revenue." This simple rule is the basic requirement for selecting the level of output that maximizes profit.

If a farmer can sell all the output that he or she produces at the going market price, the resulting total revenue (*TR*) function is a line with a constant positive slope of $p°$:

$$TR = p°y \qquad (4.16)$$

where $p°$ is some constant market price and *y* is the output.

The farmer's profit is equal to total revenue (*TR*) minus total cost (*TC*):

$$\Pi = TR - TC \qquad (4.17)$$

The greatest profit will be achieved when the difference between *TR* and *TC* is greatest (Figure 4.4). Superimpose the *TR* function on the previously defined *TC*. The greatest vertical distance between *TR* and *TC* occurs at points where the slope of *TR* and *TC* are the same. There are two points where this occurs. At the first point, *TC* is above *TR*, so this point represents the minimum profit. The second point represents maximum profit, which is the desired point.

Maximum (or minimum) profit is achieved at the points where the slope of the profit function is equal to zero. Thus

$$\Pi/dy = dTR/dy - dTC/dy = 0 \qquad (4.18)$$

Notice that dTR/dy represents the slope of *TR* and dTC/dy is the slope of *TC*. The slope of *TR* is referred to as marginal revenue (*MR*). The slope of *TC* has already been defined as marginal cost (*MC*). Hence equation (4.18) can be rewritten as

$$MR - MC = 0 \qquad (4.19)$$

or the famous

$$MR = MC \qquad (4.20)$$

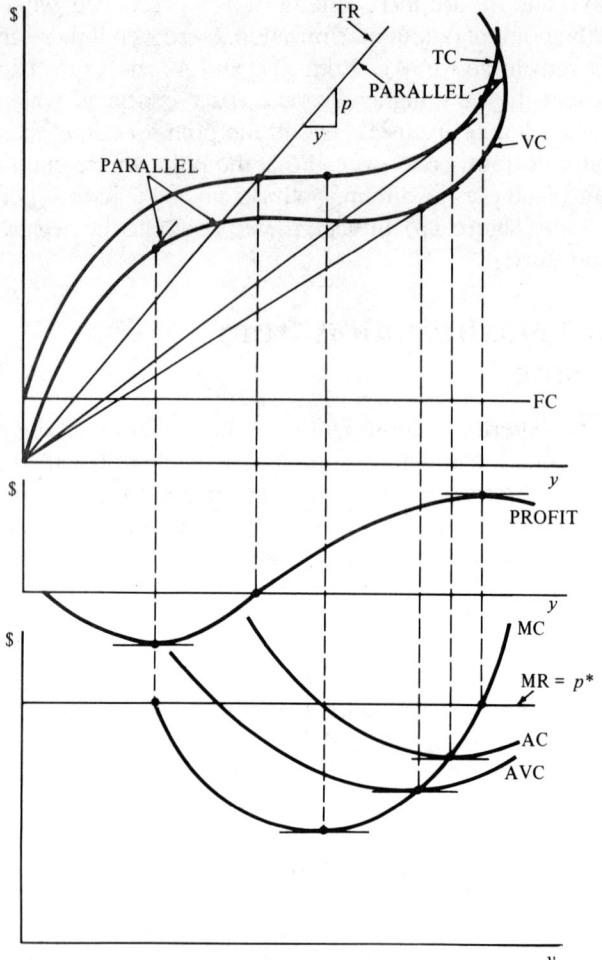

Figure 4.4 Cost Functions and Profit Functions

Under the assumptions of pure competition, the output price is constant. Incremental units of the output can be sold at the going market price $p°$. Hence MR must be $p°$:

$$dTR/dy = p° = MR \tag{4.21}$$

Figure 4.4 illustrates the average and marginal cost curves with marginal revenue included. Marginal cost equals marginal revenue at two points. The first point corresponds to the point of profit minimization, the second to the point of profit maximization. The second derivative test can be used to confirm this.

Differentiate the equation

$$MR - MC = 0 \tag{4.22}$$

which results in

$$dMR/dy - dMC/dy = + \text{ or } - ? \tag{4.23}$$

4.2 Simple Profit Maximization from the Output Side

The sign on equation (4.23) tells if the point is a maximum or a minimum on the profit function. A negative sign indicates a maximum, and a positive sign is a minimum. Another way of looking at equation (4.23) is that the slope of MC must be greater than the slope of MR for profits to be maximized.

The term dMR/dy represents the slope of the the marginal revenue curve. In this case, marginal revenue is a constant with a zero slope. The sign on equation (4.23) is thus determined by the slope of MC, which is dMC/dy. If the slope of MC is negative, equation (4.23) will be positive. This condition corresponds to the first point of intersection between MC and MR in Figure 4.4. If the slope of MC is positive, equation (4.23) is negative, and a point of profit maximization is found corresponding to the second point of intersection between MC and MR in Figure 4.4. The minimum point on the profit function represents the maximum loss for the farmer.

The farmer has an option not recognized by the mathematics. Suppose that MC has a positive slope, but $MR = MC$ at a price level so low that it is below AVC. In this instance, the farmer would be better off not to produce, because he or she would lose only fixed costs (FC). This would be less than the loss incurred at the point where $MR = MC$. If, however, $MC = MR$ at a level between AVC and AC, the farmer would be better off to produce. In this instance, the farmer, by producing, would cover all the variable costs plus a portion of the fixed costs. The total loss would be less than if production ceased and all the fixed costs had to be paid. This explains why farmers might continue to produce corn even though the market price is less than the total costs of production. With a high ratio of fixed to variable costs (as would often be the case in grain production), the farmer is better off to produce and incur only the partial loss, at least in the short run.

Of course, in the long run, the farmer can make major adjustments, and all costs should be treated as variable. Farmers can buy and sell land and machinery in the long run, making these costs variable. If the length of run is sufficiently long, a farmer will continue to produce only insofar as all costs are covered. A farmer cannot continue to lose money indefinitely without going bankrupt.

Table 4.1 illustrates some hypothetical total cost data for corn production and shows the corresponding average and marginal costs. Corn is assumed to sell for $4.00 per bushel. The relationships represented in the data contained

Table 4.1 Hypothetical Cost Data for Corn Production

Corn Yield, y	TVC	FC	TC	AVC	AFC	AC	MC	MR
40	90	75	165	2.25	1.88	4.13		
							2.00	4.00
50	110	75	185	2.20	1.50	3.70		
							2.00	4.00
60	130	75	205	2.17	1.25	3.42		
							1.00	4.00
70	140	75	215	2.00	1.07	3.07		
							1.50	4.00
80	155	75	230	1.94	0.94	2.88		
							2.00	4.00
90	175	75	250	1.94	0.83	2.78		
							2.50	4.00
100	200	75	275	2.00	0.75	2.75		
							3.00	4.00
110	230	75	305	2.09	0.68	2.77		
							4.00	4.00
120	270	75	345	2.25	0.63	2.88		
							5.00	4.00
130	320	75	395	2.46	0.58	3.04		
							6.00	4.00
140	380	75	455	2.71	0.54	3.25		

in Table 4.1 are the same as those illustrated in Figure 4.4. Marginal cost (MC) is the change in cost over the 10-bushel increment obtained by calculating the change in TC (or VC) and dividing by the change in output. Marginal cost equals marginal revenue at between 110 and 120 bushels of corn per acre. Profits are maximum at that output level. It is not possible to determine the exact output level without first knowing the exact mathematical function underlying the data contained in Table 4.1.

4.3 The Duality of Cost and Production

The shape of the total variable cost function is closely linked to the shape of the production function that underlies it. If input prices are constant, all the information about the shape of the VC function is contained in the equation for the underlying production function. Moreover, if the VC function and the prices for the inputs are known, so is the shape of the underlying production function. If input prices are constant, all the needed information for determining the shape of the VC is given by the production function, and all the information for determining the shape of the production function is given by the VC function.

In Chapter 2, the law of diminishing returns was stated: "As units of a variable input are added to units of a fixed input, after a point, each additional unit of variable input produces less and less additional output." Another way of stating this law is that after a point, incremental or additional units of input each produce less and less additional output.

The law of diminishing returns might also be interpreted from the output side. From the output side, the law states that as output is increased by 1 unit at a time, after a point, each incremental or additional unit of output requires more and more additional units of one or more variable inputs. Another way of saying this is that if output is increased incrementally, after a point, each incremental or additional unit of output becomes more and more costly with respect to the use of inputs. Another unit of output is produced but only at the expense of using more and more additional input.

The reason the variable-cost function appears to be a mirror-image production function with its axes reversed now becomes clear. The production function reflects the fact that each incremental unit of input produces less and less additional output. The corresponding variable cost function reflects the fact that incremental units of output become more and more costly in terms of input requirements.

The fertilizer response data contained in Table 2.5 are presented in a manner in which this dual relationship can be readily observed (Table 4.2). Compared with Table 2.5, the data appear inverted. In Chapter 2, average physical product was defined as y/x, and marginal physical product was defined as $\Delta Y/\Delta x$. Now x/y and $\Delta x/\Delta y$ have been calculated.

If $y/x = APP$, then x/y must be $1/APP$. The expression x/y represents the average cost for nitrogen to produce the incremental unit of output, but the cost is expressed in terms of physical units of the input, not in dollar terms. This cost is equal to $1/APP$. This cost can be converted to dollar units by multiplying by the price of nitrogen, earlier called $v°$. The result is the average variable cost for nitrogen per unit of output $AVC_n = v°/APP$.

Table 4.2 Corn Response to Nitrogen Fertilizer

Nitrogen, x	Corn, y	Exact MPP	1/MPP	$v°$	$v°/MPP$ (MC)	Exact APP	1/APP	$v°/APP$ (AVC)
0	0	0.75	1.33	0.15	0.200	a	a	a
20	16.496	0.8904	1.12	0.15	0.168	0.8248	1.21	0.182
40	35.248	0.9756	1.03	0.15	0.154	0.8812	1.13	0.170
60	55.152	1.0056	0.99	0.15	0.149	0.9192	1.09	0.163
80	75.104	0.9804	1.02	0.15	0.153	0.9388	1.07	0.160
100	94.000	0.9000	1.11	0.15	0.167	0.9400	1.06	0.160
120	110.736	0.7644	1.31	0.15	0.196	0.9228	1.08	0.163
140	124.208	0.5736	1.74	0.15	0.262	0.8872	1.13	0.169
160	133.312	0.3276	3.05	0.15	0.458	0.8332	1.20	0.180
180	136.944	0.0264	37.88	0.15	5.682	0.7608	1.31	0.197
200	134.000	−0.3300	−3.03	0.15	−0.454	0.6700	1.49	0.224
220	123.376	−0.7416	−1.35	0.15	−0.202	0.5608	1.78	0.267
240	103.968	−1.2084	−0.83	0.15	−0.124	0.4332	2.31	0.346

[a] Undefined. Errors due to rounding.

If $\Delta y/\Delta x = MPP$, then $\Delta x/\Delta y$ must be $1/MPP$. The expression $\Delta x/\Delta y$ represents the marginal cost for nitrogen to produce the incremental unit of output, but again the cost is represented in physical terms, not in dollar terms. This cost is equal to $1/MPP$. This cost can again be converted to dollar units by multiplying by the price of nitrogen or $v°$. The result is the marginal cost for nitrogen per unit of output $MC_n = v°/MPP$.

At a nitrogen application rate of 180 pounds per acre, marginal cost is $5.68 per bushel of corn produced. If corn is selling for $4.00 per bushel, the incremental bushel of corn costs $5.68 but returns only $4.00. However, at a nitrogen application rate of 160 pounds per acre, the marginal cost of the incremental bushel of corn is but $0.458. If corn is selling for $4.00 per bushel, the difference of $3.54 is profit to the farmer. The farmer could increase profits by increasing the use of nitrogen fertilizer until the marginal cost associated with the production of the incremental bushel of corn just equals marginal revenue. This should be at a nitrogen application level of slightly less than 180 pounds per acre—179.322 pounds to be exact. That is exactly the solution found in Chapter 3. It makes no difference whether VMP is equated to MFC or MR is equated to MC. The solution provides the farmer with exactly the same conclusion with regard to how much input should be used. The solution to the profit-maximization problem is the same regardless of whether it is done on the output or input side.

4.4 The Inverse of a Production Function

Any production function has an underlying dual cost function or correspondence (Figure 4.5). The production function has input (nitrogen or x) on the horizontal axis and output (corn or y) on the vertical axis. The corresponding cost function expressed in physical terms is the production function with the axes reversed. The result is the inverse production function, or cost function expressed in physical terms. This cost function is dual to the production function.

Note that this function is in many ways the mirror image of the underlying production function. If the production function is increasing at an increasing

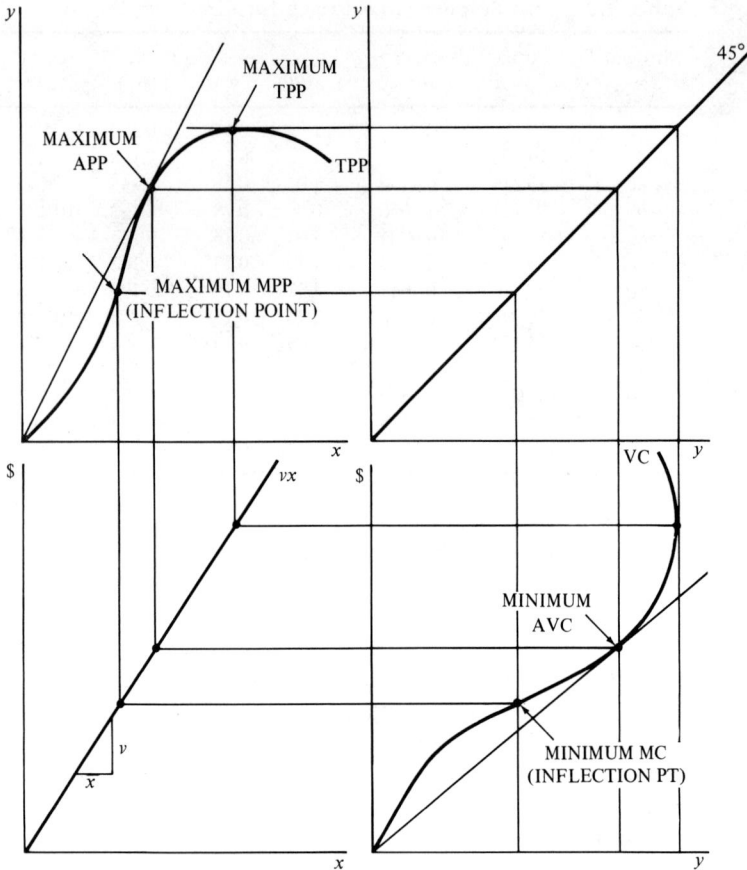

Figure 4.5 Cost Function as the Inverse Production Function

rate, the inverse production function increases at a decreasing rate. If the production function is increasing at a decreasing rate, the inverse production function increases at an increasing rate.

Inverses to production functions for some simple functions might readily be calculated. All that is required is to solve the function in terms of the x instead of y. For example, suppose that the production function is

$$y = 2x \tag{4.24}$$

The corresponding inverse production function is

$$x = y/2 = 0.5y \tag{4.25}$$

If the production function is

$$y = bx \quad \text{where } b \text{ is any number} \tag{4.26}$$

4.4 The Inverse of a Production Function

the corresponding inverse production function is

$$x = y/b. \tag{4.27}$$

Suppose that the production function is

$$y = x^{0.5} \tag{4.28}$$

The corresponding inverse production function is

$$x = y^{1/0.5} = y^2 \tag{4.29}$$

and if the production function is

$$y = x^2 \tag{4.30}$$

the inverse production function is

$$x = y^{1/2} = y^{0.5} \tag{4.31}$$

For the production function

$$y = ax^b \tag{4.32}$$

the corresponding inverse function is

$$x = (y/a)^{1/b} \tag{4.33}$$

In each of these examples, the inverse function contains all the coefficients contained in the original production function and can be converted into true variable cost functions by multiplying by the constant price ($v°$) of the input x. If these functions were drawn, the vertical axis would then be in terms of dollars rather than physical units of the input x.

It is therefore not necessary to know the physical quantities of the inputs that are used in the production process in order to determine the coefficients of the production function. If the cost function is known, it is frequently possible to determine the underlying production function.

A general rule is that if the production function is

$$y = f(x) \tag{4.34}$$

the corresponding inverse production function is

$$x = f^{-1}(y) \tag{4.35}$$

Not all production functions can be inverted into another function to obtain the corresponding dual cost function. Any production function that includes both increasing and decreasing *TPP* will not have a inverse function, but only an inverse correspondence. The neoclassical production function is an example. The inverse in Figure 4.5 is actually a correspondence, but not a function.

The total cost for the input expressed in terms of units of output is obtained by multiplying the inverse function times the input price. Suppose that

$$y = f(x) \tag{4.36}$$

Then

$$x = f^{-1}(y) \tag{4.37}$$

Multiplying by $v°$ results in the total cost (TC_x) for the input (x or nitrogen) from the production function for corn [$y = f(x)$]:

$$v°x = TFC = TC_x = v°f^{-1}(y) \tag{4.38}$$

4.5 Some Further Illustrations of the Linkages between Cost and Production Functions

Suppose that the price of the input is $v°$ and the production function is

$$y = 2x \tag{4.39}$$

Then $MPP = APP = 2$, and $MC_x = AVC_x = v°/2$.
If the production function is

$$y = bx \tag{4.40}$$

then $MPP = APP = b$, and $MC_x = AVC_x = v°/b$.
If the production function is

$$y = x^{0.5} \tag{4.41}$$

then $MPP = 0.5/x^{0.5}$, $APP = x^{0.5}/x = x^{0.5}x^{-1} = x^{-0.5} = 1/x^{0.5}$, $MC_x = (v°x^{0.5})/0.5 = 2v°x^{0.5}$, and $AVC_x = v°x^{0.5}$.

If *MPP* is precisely one-half of *APP*, then MC_x will be precisely twice AVC_x. If the elasticity of production (E_p) is defined as the ratio *MPP/APP*, then $1/E_p$ is the ratio of MC_x/AVC_x.
If the production function is

$$y = ax^b \tag{4.42}$$

then the inverse production function is

$$x = (y/a)^{1/b} \tag{4.43}$$

$$MPP = abx^{b-1} \tag{4.44}$$

$$APP = ax^{b-1} \tag{4.45}$$

$$E_p = b \tag{4.46}$$

$$MC_x = v°/abx^{b-1} \tag{4.47}$$

$$AVC_x = v°/ax^{b-1} \tag{4.48}$$

$$\text{ratio of } MC_x/AVC_x = 1/b \tag{4.49}$$

Some important relationships between APP, MPP, MC, and AVC become clear. In stage I, MPP is greater than APP and E_p is greater than 1. As a result, MC_x must be less than AVC_x in stage 1. The exact proportion is defined by $1/E_p$. In stages II and III, MPP is less than APP, and as a result, E_p is less than 1. Therefore, MC_x must be greater than AVC_x. The exact proportion is again defined by $1/E_p$. At the dividing point between stages I and II, $MPP = APP$ and $E_p = 1$. $1/E_p = 1$ and $MC_x = AC_x$, and at the dividing point between stages II and III, $MPP = 0$, $E_p = 0$, $1/E_p$ is undefined, and MC_x is undefined.

4.6 The Supply Function for the Firm

The profit-maximizing firm will equate marginal cost with marginal revenue. If the firm operates under conditions of pure competition, marginal revenue will be the same as the constant price of the output. If the farmer produces but one output, the marginal cost curve that lies above average variable cost will be the supply curve for the farm. Each point on the marginal cost curve above average variable cost consists of a point of profit maximization if the output sells for the price associated with the point. The supply curve or function for the farm will consist of the series of profit-maximizing points under alternative assumptions with respect to marginal revenue or the price of the product.

Consider, for example, the production function

$$y = ax^b \tag{4.50}$$

The inverse production function is

$$x = (y/a)^{1/b} \tag{4.51}$$

Variable cost is defined as

$$VC = vx = v(y/a)^{1/b} \tag{4.52}$$

Marginal cost can be found by differentiating equation (4.52) with respect to y:

$$MC = d(vx)/dy = (1/b)vy^{(1/b)-1}a^{-1/b} \tag{4.53}$$

$$MC = (1/b)vy^{(1-b)/b}a^{-1/b} \tag{4.54}$$

Costs, Returns, and Profits on the Output Side

Equating marginal cost with marginal revenue or the price (p) of the product yields

$$p = (1/b)vy^{(1-b)/b}a^{-1/b}$$
$$MR = MC \qquad (4.55)$$

Solving equation (4.55) for y yields the supply function for the firm:

$$y = (bp)^{b/(1-b)}v^{-b/(1-b)}a^{(1/b)(b/(1-b))} \qquad (4.56)$$

The elasticity of supply with respect to the product price is

$$(dy/dp)p/y = b/(1-b) \qquad (4.57)$$

The elasticity of supply is positive when b is less than 1.
The elasticity of supply with respect to the input price is

$$(dy/dv)v/y = -b/(1-b) \qquad (4.58)$$

The elasticity of supply with respect to the input price is negative if b is less than 1.
Average (variable) cost is

$$AC = vx/y = [v(y/a)^{1/b}]/y = vy^{(1-b)/b}a^{-1/b} \qquad (4.59)$$

Since marginal cost is

$$MC = (1/b)vy^{(1-b)/b}a^{-1/b} \qquad (4.60)$$

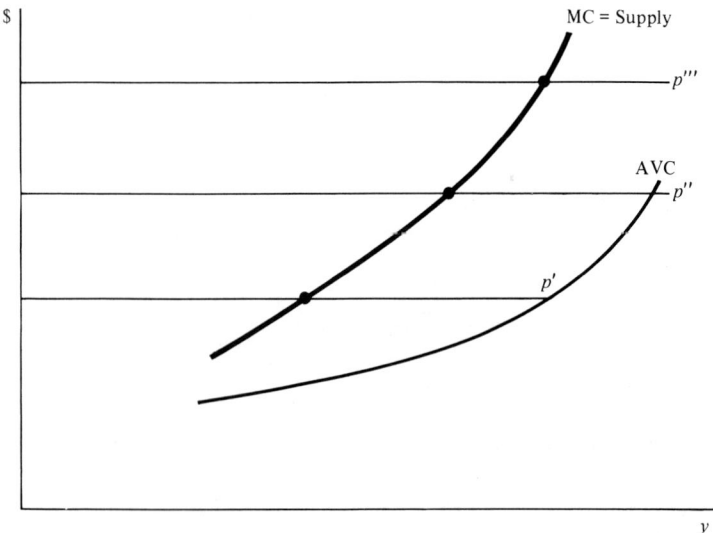

Figure 4.6 Aggregate Supply When the Ratio $MC/AC = 1/b$ and b Is Less Than 1

the ratio of marginal to average cost is

$$MC/AC = 1/b = 1/E_p \qquad (4.61)$$

In this example, the marginal and average cost functions must remain in fixed proportion to each other. The proportion is equal to 1 over the elasticity of production for the production function. Figure 4.6 illustrates the aggregate supply function derived for a production function in which b is less than 1, and the product price is set at alternative levels. The supply function is the portion of the marginal cost function above average variable cost. However, in this example marginal cost lies above average variable cost everywhere and is at the fixed ratio to average variable cost of $1/b$.

4.7 Concluding Comments

Profit-maximizing conditions for the firm have been derived. Profits are maximum when the level of output chosen is where marginal cost equals marginal revenue. The cost function is the inverse of the production function that underlies it multiplied by the price of the input. A close linkage thus exists between the coefficients of the production function and those of the underlying cost function. The firm's supply curve can be derived from the equilibrium $MC = MR$ conditions and is represented by the marginal cost curve above average variable cost. Expressions for elasticities of supply with respect to product and input prices can be obtained from the equilibrium conditions.

Problems and Exercises

1. Explain the difference between total value of the product (*TVP*) and total revenue (*TR*).
2. Explain the difference between total cost (*TC*) and total factor cost (*TFC*).
3. Suppose that the price of the input x is $3. Total fixed costs are $200. Fill in the blanks.

x (Input)	y (Output)	TVC	TC	MC	AVC	AC
0	0	___	___		___	___
10	50	___	___	___	___	___
25	75	___	___	___	___	___
40	80	___	___	___	___	___
50	85	___	___	___	___	___

4. Suppose that the production function is

$$y = 3x^{0.5}$$

The price of the input is $3. per unit, and total fixed costs are $50. Find and graph the functions that represent:

  a. *MPP*
  b. *APP*

c. AVC
   d. AC (or ATC)
   e. MC

Suppose that the output price is $5. Find:

   f. AVP
   g. VMP
   h. MFC

5. Using the data contained in Problem 4, find the profit-maximizing level of input use by equating VMP and MFC.

6. Using the data contained in Problem 4, find the profit-maximizing output level by equating MR and MC. What is the relationship between the profit-maximizing output level and the profit-maximizing input level?

7. Draw a three-stage production function on a sheet of paper. Now turn the paper so that the input x is on the vertical axis and output y is on the horizontal axis. Now turn the sheet of paper over and hold the sheet of paper up to a light. Look at the production function through the back side. What you see is the cost function that underlies the production function, with costs expressed in physical units of input use rather than dollars. If input prices are constant, the vertical axis can be converted to dollars by multiplying the physical units of input by the corresponding input price.

8. Draw a graph of the corresponding total cost correspondence when fixed costs are zero, the input costs $2 per unit, and the production function is given by

$$y = 0.4x + 0.09x^2 - 0.003x^3$$

Reference

Viner, Jacob, "Cost Curves and Supply Curves," *Zeitschrift für Nationalökonomie* III (1931) pp. 23–46. Also in American Economics Association, *Readings in Price Theory*, K. E. Boulding and G. J. Stigler eds. Homewood, Ill.: Richard D. Irwin, 1952.

5
Production with Two Inputs

This chapter introduces the basics of the technical relationships underlying the factor-factor model, in which two inputs are used in the production of a single output. The concept of an isoquant is developed from a simple table containing data similar to that which might be available in a fertilizer response trial. The slope of the isoquant is defined as the marginal rate of substitution. Isoquants with varying shapes and slopes are illustrated. The shape of an isoquant is closely linked to the characteristics of the production function that transforms the two inputs into the output. The linkages between the marginal rate of substitution and the marginal products of each input are derived.

Key Terms and Definitions:

Isoquant
Marginal Rate of Substitution (MRS)
Diminishing Marginal Rate of
 Substitution
Constant Marginal Rate of
 Substitution
Increasing Marginal Rate of
 Substitution
Convex to the Origin
$\Delta x_2/\Delta x_1$
Asymptotic to the Axes
Concentric Rings
Synergistic Effect

Tangency
Infinite Slope
Zero Slope
Ridge Line
Family of Production Functions
Change in Output
Change in Input
Limit
Infinitesimally Small
Partial Derivative
Total Derivative
Total Differential

5.1 Introduction

The discussion in Chapters 2 to 4 centered around the problems faced by a farmer who wishes to determine how much of a single input should be used or how much of a single output should be produced to maximize profits or

Production with Two Inputs

net returns to the farm. The basic assumption of this chapter is that two inputs, not one input, are allowed to vary. As a result, some modifications need to be made in the basic production function. The production function used in Chapters 1 to 4 was

$$y = f(x) \tag{5.1}$$

Suppose instead that two inputs called x_1 and x_2 are allowed to vary. The resulting production function is

$$y = f(x_1, x_2) \tag{5.2}$$

if there are no more inputs to the production process. If there are more than two, or n different inputs, the production function might be written as

$$y = f(x_1, x_2 | x_3, \ldots, x_n) \tag{5.3}$$

The inputs $x_3, \ldots, x_n$ will be treated as fixed and given, with only the first two inputs allowed to vary.

In the single-input case, each level of input used produced a different level of output, as long as inputs were being used below the level resulting in maximum output. In the two-input case, there may be many different combinations of inputs that produce exactly the same amount of output. Table 5.1 illustrates some hypothetical relationships that might exist between phosphate (P_2O_5) application levels, potash (K_2O) application levels, and corn yields. The nitrogen application rate was assumed to be 180 pounds per acre.

The production function from which these data were generated is

$$y = f(x_1, x_2 | x_3) \tag{5.4}$$

where y = corn yield in bushels per acre
x_1 = potash in pounds per acre
x_2 = phosphate in pounds per acre
x_3 = nitrogen in pounds per acre assumed constant at 180

Table 5.1 Hypothetical Corn Response to Phosphate and Potash Fertilizer

Phosphate (lb/acre)	Potash (lb/acre)								
	0	10	20	30	40	50	60	70	80
0	96	98	99	99	98	97	95	92	88
10	98	101	103	104	105	104	103	101	99
20	101	104	106	108	109	110	110	109	106
30	103	107	111	114	117	119	120	121	121
40	104	109	113	117	121	123	126	128	129
50	104	111	116	121	125	127	129	131	133
60	103	112	118	123	126	128	130	131	134
70	102	111	117	123	126	127	131	136	135
80	101	108	114	119	119	125	129	131	134

5.1 Introduction

Notice from Table 5.1 that potash is not very productive without an adequate availability of phosphate. The maximum yield with no phosphate is but 99 bushels per acre and that occurs at comparatively low levels of potash application of 20 to 30 pounds per acre. The production function for potash in the absence of any phosphate is actually decreasing at potash application rates of over 30 pounds per acre. In the absence of phosphate fertilizer, stage III for potash begins quite early.

Phosphate in the absence of potash is more productive, but only slightly so. The maximum yield without any potash is 104 bushels per acre at between 40 and 50 pounds of phosphate. Stage III for phosphate begins at beyond 50 pounds per acre if no potash is applied.

Each of the rows of Table 5.1 represents a production function for potash fertilizer with the assumption that the level of phosphate applied is fixed at the level given by the application rate, which is the first number of the row. As the level of phosphate is increased, the productivity of the potash increases. The marginal product of an additional 10 pounds of potash is usually larger for rows near the bottom of the table than for rows near the top of the table. Moreover, production functions for potash with the larger quantities of phosphate typically achieve their maximum at higher levels of potash use.

Each of the columns of Table 5.1 represents a production function for phosphate fertilizer with the assumption that the level of potash remains constant as defined by the first number in the column. Again the same phenomenon is present. The productivity of phosphate is usually improved with the increased use of potash, and as the assumed fixed level of potash use increases, the maximum of each function with respect to phosphate occurs at larger levels of phosphate use.

These relationships are based on a basic agronomic or biological characteristic of crops. A crop would not be expected to produce high yields if an ample supply of all nutrients were not available. To a degree, phosphate can be substituted for potash, or potash for phosphate. In this example, there are several different combinations of phosphate and potash that will all produce the same yield.

But if the crops are to grow, some of both nutrients must be present, and the highest yields are obtained when both nutrients are in ample supply. This concept in economics is closely linked to Von Liebig's "Law of the Minimum," which states that plant growth is constrained by the most limiting nutrient.

Notice also that it is possible to use too much of both potash and phosphate. Yields using 70 pounds of each are greater than when 80 pounds of each are used. The law of diminishing returns applies to units of phosphate and potash fertilizer taken together when other inputs are held constant, just as it applies to each individual kind of fertilizer.

Table 5.1 contains data from nine production functions for phosphate, under nine different assumptions with regard to potash use. Table 5.1 also contains data from nine production functions for potash, each obtained from a different assumption with regard to the level of phosphate use.

Due to the biology of crop growth, a synergistic effect is present. This means that the presence of ample amounts of phosphate makes the productivity of potash greater. Ample amounts of potash makes the productivity of phosphate greater. The two fertilizers, taken together, result in productivity gains in terms of increased yields greater than would be expected by looking at yields resulting from the application of only one type of fertilizer.

This effect is not limited to crop production. The same phenomenon may be observed if data were collected on the use of the inputs grain (concentrate) and forage used in the production of milk. A cow that is fed all grain and no forage would not be a good milk producer. Similarly, a cow fed all forage and no grain would not produce much milk. Greatest milk production would be achieved with a ration containing a combination of grain and forage.

Each possible ration represents a particular combination or mix of inputs grain and forage. Some of these rations would be better than others in that they would produce more milk. The particular ration chosen by the farmer would depend not only on the amount of milk produced, but also on the relative prices of grain and forage. These ideas are fully developed in Chapter 7.

Data for yet another production function are contained in Table 5.1. From Table 5.1 it is possible to determine what will happen to corn yields if fertilizer application rates for potash and phosphate are increased by the same proportion. Suppose that 1 unit of fertilizer were to consist of 1 pound of phosphate and 1 pound of potash and that this proportion did not change. Table 5.2 was constructed using numbers found on the diagonal of Table 5.1.

These data appear to be very similar to the data in the earlier chapters for single-input production functions, and they are. The only difference here is that two types of fertilizer are assumed be used in fixed proportion to each other. Under this assumption, the amount of fertilizer needed to maximize profits could be found in a manner similar to that used in earlier chapters, but there is uncertainty as to whether or not the 1:1 ratio in the use of phosphate and potash is the correct ratio.

What would happen, for example, if phosphate were very expensive and potash were very cheap? Perhaps the 1:1 ratio should be changed to 1 unit of phosphate and 2 units of potash to represent a unit of fertilizer. Data for a production function with a 1:2 ratio could also be derived in part from Table 5.1. These data are presented in Table 5.3.

Table 5.2 Corn Yield Response to 1:1 Proportionate Changes in Phosphate and Potash

Units of Fertilizer (1 unit = 1 lb phosphate and 1 lb potash)	Corn Yield (bu/acre)
0	96
10	101
20	106
30	114
40	121
50	127
60	130
70	136
80	134

5.2 An Isoquant and the Marginal Rate of Substitution

Table 5.3 Corn Yield Response to 1:2 Proportionate Changes in Phosphate and Potash

Units of Fertilizer (1 unit = 1 lb phosphate and 2 lb potash)	Corn Yield (bu/acre)
10–20	103
20–40	109
30–60	120
40–80	129

Much of the next several chapters is devoted to the basic principles used for determining the combination of two inputs (such as phosphate and potash fertilizer) that represents maximum profit for the producer. Here the proper proportions are closely linked to the relative prices for the two types of fertilizer.

5.2 An Isoquant and the Marginal Rate of Substitution

Many combinations of phosphate and potash all result in exactly the same level of corn production. Despite the fact that Table 5.1 includes only discrete values, a bit of interpolation will result in additional combinations that produce the same corn yield. Take, for example, a corn yield of 121 bushels per acre (Table 5.1). This yield can be produced with the following input combinations: 30 pounds of phosphate and 70 pounds of potash, 30 pounds of phosphate and 80 pounds of potash, 40 pounds of phosphate and 40 pounds of potash, and 50 pounds of phosphate and 30 pounds of potash.

Moreover, there are many more points that might also achieve approximately 121 bushels per acre: 60 pounds of phosphate and approximately 27 pounds of potash, 70 pounds of phosphate and approximately 27 pounds of potash, and 80 pounds of phosphate and approximately 45 pounds of potash to name a few. All these combinations share a common characteristic in that they produce the same yield.

A line can be drawn that connects all points on Table 5.1 representing the same yield. This line is called an *isoquant*. The prefix *iso* comes from the Greek *isos* meaning equal. *Quant* is short for quantity. An isoquant is literally a line representing equal quantities. Every point on the line represents the same yield or output level, but each point on the line also represents a different combination of the two inputs. As one moves along an isoquant, the proportions of the two inputs vary, but output (yield) remains constant.

An isoquant could be drawn for any output or yield that one might choose. If it is possible to draw an isoquant for a yield of 121 bushels per acre, it is also possible to draw one for a yield of 125.891 bushels per acre if the data were sufficiently detailed, or an isoquant could be drawn for a yield of 120.999 bushels per acre, or any other plausible yield.

Production with Two Inputs

If isoquants are drawn on graph paper, the graph is usually drawn with the origin ($0y$, $0x$) in the lower left-hand corner. The isoquants are therefore bowed toward the origin of the graph.

The slope of an isoquant is referred to by some economists as the *marginal rate of substitution* (*MRS*).[1] Other authors refer to it as the rate of technical substitution (RTS) or the marginal rate of technical substitution (*MRTS*). This text uses the terminology *MRS*.

The *MRS* is a measurement of how well one input substitutes for another as one moves along a given isoquant. Suppose that the horizontal axis is labeled x_1, and the vertical axis is labeled x_2. The terminology $MRSx_1x_2$ is used to describe the slope of the isoquant assuming that input x_1 is increasing and x_2 is decreasing. In this example, x_1 is the replacing input and x_2 is the input being replaced, moving down and to the right along the isoquant.

Figure 5.1 illustrates an isoquant exhibiting a diminishing marginal rate of substitution. As one moves farther and farther downward and to the right along the isoquant representing constant output, each incremental unit of x_1 (Δx_1) replaces less and less x_2 (Δx_2). The diminishing marginal rate of substitution between inputs accounts for the usual shape of an isoquant bowed inward, or convex to the origin. The shape is also linked to the synergistic effect of inputs used in combination with each other. An input is normally more productive when used with ample quantities of other inputs.

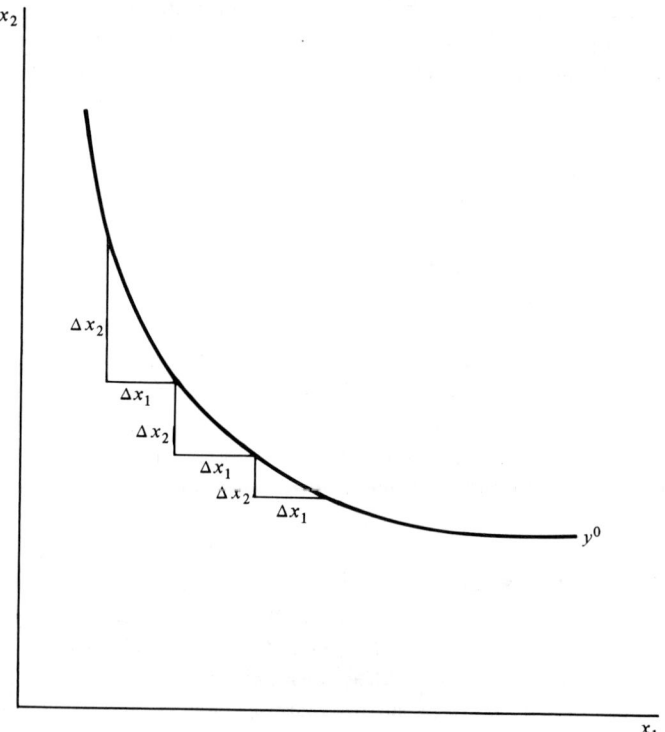

Figure 5.1 Illustration of Diminishing MRS_{x1x2}

5.2 An Isoquant and the Marginal Rate of Substitution

The *MRS* might also measure the inverse slope of the isoquant. Suppose that the use of x_2 is being increased, while the use of x_1 is decreased. The terminology $MRSx_2x_1$ is used to describe the inverse slope of the isoquant. In this example, x_1 is the replacing input, and x_2 is the input being replaced, as one moves up and to the left along the isoquant. The $MRSx_2x_1$ is equal to $1/MRSx_1x_2$.

The slope of an isoquant can also be defined as $\Delta x_2/\Delta x_1$. Then[2]

$$MRSx_1x_2 = \Delta x_2/\Delta x_1 \tag{5.5}$$

and

$$MRSx_2x_1 = \Delta x_1/\Delta x_2 = 1/MRSx_1x_2 \tag{5.6}$$

Isoquants are usually downward sloping, but not always. If the marginal product of both inputs is positive, isoquants will be downward sloping. It is possible for isoquants to slope upward if the marginal product of one of the inputs is negative.

Isoquants are usually bowed inward, convex to the origin, or exhibit diminishing marginal rates of substitution, but not always. The diminishing marginal rate of substitution is normally a direct result of the diminishing marginal product of each input. There are some instances, however, in which the *MPP* for both inputs can be increasing and yet the isoquant remains convex to the origin (see specific cases in Chapter 10).

Figure 5.2 illustrates some possible patterns for isoquant maps. Diagram *A* illustrates isoquants as a series of concentric rings. The center of the series of rings corresponds to the input combination that results in maximum output or product. In Table 5.1, this would correspond with an input combination of 70 pounds of phosphate and 70 pounds of potash, for a yield of 136 bushels per acre. This pattern results when output is actually reduced because too much of both inputs have been used.

Diagram *B* illustrates another common isoquant map. The isoquants are not rings; rather, they approach both axes but never reach them. These isoquants are called asymptotic to the x_1 and x_2 axes, since they approach but do not reach the axes. A diminishing marginal rate of substitution exists everywhere on these isoquants. These isoquants appear to be very similar to the average fixed-cost curve discussed in Chapter 4. However, depending on the relative productivity of the two inputs, these isoquants might be positioned nearer to or farther from one of the two axes. In this example, more of either input, or both inputs taken in combination, will always increase output. There are no maxima for the underlying production functions.

Another possibility is for the isoquants to be bowed outward but not inward (diagram C). This pattern represents an increasing rather than diminishing marginal rate of substitution between input pairs. As the use of x_1 increases and the use of x_2 decreases along the isoquant, less and less additional x_1 is required to replace units of x_2 and maintain output. This shape is not very likely, because

Production with Two Inputs

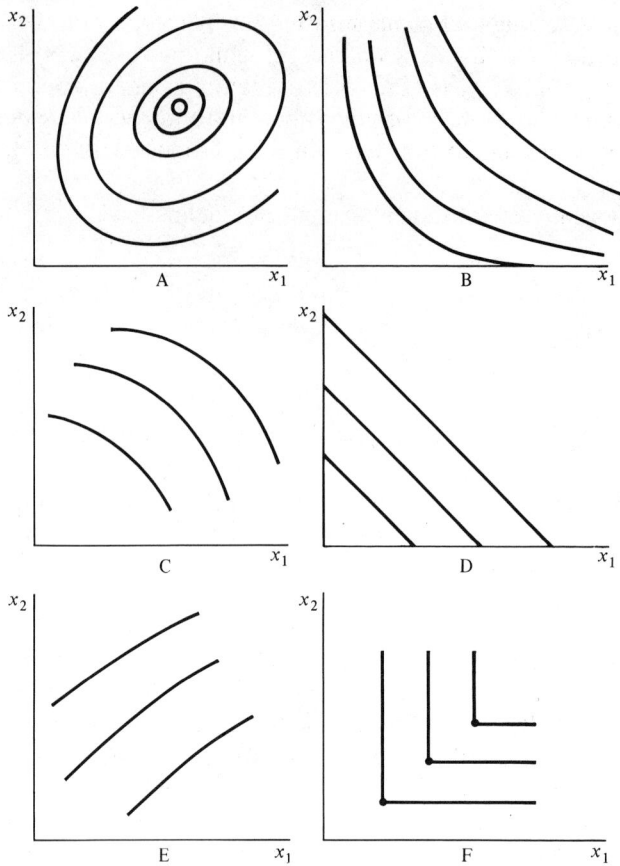

Figure 5.2 Some Possible Isoquant Maps

the pattern would suggest that the two inputs used in combination result in a decrease in relative productivity rather than the synergistic increase that was discussed earlier.

It is possible for isoquants to have a constant slope (diagram D). In this instance, one input or factor of production substitutes for the other in a fixed proportion. Here there is a constant, not a diminishing marginal rate of substitution. For example, if inputs substituted for each other in a fixed proportion of 1 unit x_1 to 2 units of x_2, the following input combinations would all result in exactly the same output—$4x_1$, $0x_2$; $3x_1$, $2x_2$; $2x_1$, $4x_2$; $1x_1$, $6x_2$; $0x_1$, $8x_2$.

It is also possible for isoquants to have a positive slope (diagram E). This can occur in a situation where additional amounts of one of the inputs actually reduces output. Diagram A also includes some points where the isoquants have a positive slope.

Finally, isoquants might be right angles (diagram F). This can occur when two inputs must be used in fixed proportion with each other. The classic example here is tractors and tractor drivers. A tractor without a driver produces no output. A driver without a tractor produces no output. These inputs must be used in a constant fixed proportion to each other: one tractor driver to one tractor.

5.3 Isoquants and Ridge Lines

Two families of production functions underlie every isoquant map. Figure 5.3 illustrates this relationship. Assume x_2 to be fixed at some predetermined level x_2^*. A horizontal line is drawn from x_2^* across the diagram. A production function for x_1 holding x_2 constant at x_2^* can then be drawn by putting x_1 on the horizontal axis, and noting the output obtained from the intersection of the line drawn at x_2^* with each isoquant.

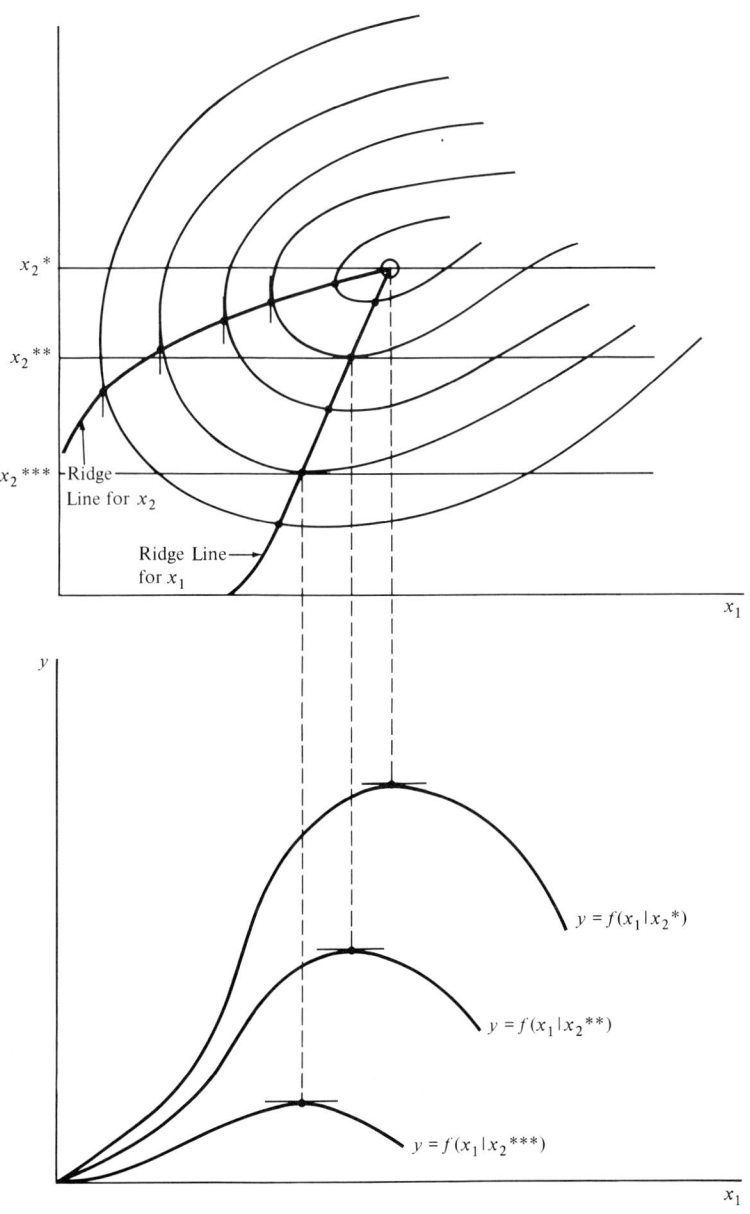

Figure 5.3 Ridge Lines and a Family of Production Functions for Input x_1

Now choose another level of x_2. Call this level x_2^{**}. The process can be repeated over and over again for any level of x_2. Each alternative fixed level for x_2 generates a new production function for x_1 assuming that x_2 is held constant at the predetermined level.

Moreover, the same process can be repeated by holding x_1 constant and tracing out the production functions for x_2. Every time x_1 changes, a new production function is obtained for x_2. As one moves from one production function for x_2 to another, different quantities of output from x_2 are produced, despite the fact that neither the quality or quantity of x_2 has changed. This is because the varying assumptions about the quantity of x_1 either enhance or reduce the productivity of x_2. Another way of saying this is that the marginal productivity (or *MPP*) of x_2 is not independent of the assumption that was made about the availability of x_1, and the *MPP* of x_1 is not independent of the assumption that is made about the availability of x_2.

Now suppose that a level for x_2 is chosen of x_2^* that is just tangent to one of the isoquants. The point of tangency between the line drawn at x_2^* and the isoquant will represent the maximum possible output that can be produced from x_1 holding x_2 constant at x_2^*. The production function derived by holding x_2 constant at x_2^* will achieve its maximum at the point of tangency between the isoquant and the horizontal line drawn at x_2^*. The point of tangency is the point of zero slope on the isoquant and marks the dividing point between stages II and III for the production function

$$y = f(x_1 | x_2 = x_2^*) \tag{5.7}$$

This process could be repeated over and over again by selecting alternative values for x_2 and drawing a horizontal line at the selected level for x_2. Each isoquant represents a different output level, just as each horizontal line represents a different assumption about the magnitude of x_2. An infinite number of isoquants could be drawn, each representing a slightly different output level. An infinite number of horizontal lines could be drawn across the isoquant map, each representing a slightly different assumption about the value for x_2. For each horizontal line, there would be a point of tangency on one (and only one!) of the isoquants. This point of tangency is a point of zero slope on the isoquant. Each isoquant would have a corresponding horizontal line tangent to it. The point of tangency represents the maximum for the underlying production function for x_1 under the predetermined assumption with regard to the fixed level of x_2.

The choice of the input to be labeled x_1 and x_2 is quite arbitrary. However, if x_2 remains on the vertical axis, the same process could be repeated by drawing vertical lines from the value chosen on the x_1 axis (the assumption with respect to the value for x_1) and finding the points of tangency between the vertical line and its corresponding isoquant. In this case however, the point of tangency will occur at the point where the isoquant assumes an infinite slope. Each point of tangency marks the division between stages II and III for the underlying production function for x_2 with x_1 set at some predetermined level x_1^*. The production function is

$$y = f(x_2 | x_1 = x_1^*) \tag{5.8}$$

A line could be drawn that connects all points of zero slope on the isoquant map. This line is called a *ridge line* and marks the division between stages II and III for input x_1, under varying assumptions with regard to the quantity of x_2 that is used. This line is designated as ridge line 1 for x_1.

A second line could be drawn that connects all points of infinite slope on the isoquant map. This is also a ridge line, and marks the division between stages II and III for input x_2, under varying assumptions with regard to the quantity of x_1 that is used. This might be designated as ridge line 2 for x_2.

The two ridge lines intersect at the single point of maximum output. The neoclassical diagram, drawn from an isoquant map that consists of a series of concentric rings, appears not unlike a football. The ridge lines normally assume a positive slope. This is because the level of x_1 that results in maximum output increases as the assumption with regard to the fixed level for x_2 increases. Moreover, the level of x_2 that results in maximum output increases as the assumption with regard to the fixed level for x_1 is increased. The football appearance is the result of the underlying single-input production functions that assume the neoclassical three-stage appearance.

Notice that ridge line 1 connects points where the *MRS* is zero. Ridge line 2 connects points where the *MRS* is infinite. Finally, note that ridge lines can be drawn for only certain types of isoquant patterns or maps. For a ridge line to be drawn, isoquants must assume either a zero or an infinite slope. Look again at Figure 5.2. Ridge lines can be drawn only for isoquants appearing in diagram A. For diagrams B to E, there are no points of zero or infinite slope. This suggests that the ridge lines do not exist. Moreover, this implies that the underlying families of production functions for x_1 and x_2 never achieve their respective maxima. Diagram F presents a unique problem. The right-angle isoquants have either a zero or an infinite slope everywhere on either side of the angle. This would imply "thick" ridge lines. In this example, the underlying production functions for each input are but a series of points that represent the respective maximum output at each level of input use.

5.4 *MRS* and Marginal Product

The slope or *MRS* of an isoquant and the underlying productivity of the two families of production functions used to derive an isoquant map are closely intertwined. An algebraic relationship can be derived between the *MRS* and the marginal products of the underlying production functions.

Suppose that one wished to determine the change in output (called Δy) that would result if the use of x_1 were changed by some small amount (called Δx_1) and the use of x_2 were also changed by some small amount (called Δx_2). To determine the resulting change in output (Δy), two pieces of information would be needed. First, the exact magnitude of the changes in the use of each of the inputs x_1 and x_2. It is not possible to determine the change in output by merely summing the respective change in the use of the two inputs. An additional piece of information would also be needed. That information is the rate at which each input can be transformed into output. This rate is the marginal physical product of each input x_1 and x_2 ($MPPx_1$ and $MPPx_2$).

Production with Two Inputs

The total change in output can be expressed as

$$\Delta y = MPPx_1\, \Delta x_1 + MPPx_2\, \Delta x_2 \tag{5.9}$$

The total change in output resulting from a given change in the use of two inputs is the change in each input multiplied by its respective *MPP*.

By definition, an isoquant is a line connecting points of equal output. Output does not change along an isoquant. The only way that output can change is to move on the isoquant map from one isoquant to another. Along any isoquant, Δy is exactly equal to zero. The equation for an isoquant can then be written as

$$\Delta y = 0 = MPPx_1\, \Delta x_1 + MPPx_2\, \Delta x_2 \tag{5.10}$$

Equation (5.10) can be rearranged such that

$$MPPx_1\, \Delta x_1 + MPPx_2\, \Delta x_2 = 0 \tag{5.11}$$

$$MPPx_2\, \Delta x_2 = -\, MPPx_1\, \Delta x_1 \tag{5.12}$$

Dividing both sides of equation (5.12) by Δx_1 gives us

$$MPPx_2\, \Delta x_2/\Delta x_1 = -MPPx_1 \tag{5.13}$$

Dividing both sides by $MPPx_2$ yields

$$\Delta x_2/\Delta x_1 = -\, MPPx_1/MPPx_2 \tag{5.14}$$

or[3]

$$MRSx_1x_2 = -\, MPPx_1/MPPx_2 \tag{5.15}$$

The marginal rate of substitution between a pair of inputs is equal to the negative ratio of the marginal products. Thus the slope of an isoquant at any point is equal to the negative ratio of the marginal products at that point, and if the marginal products for both inputs are positive at a point, the slope of the isoquant will be negative at that point. The replacing input (in this example, x_1) is the *MPP* on the top of the ratio. The replaced input (in this example, x_2) is the *MPP* on the bottom of the ratio. By again rearranging, we have

$$MRSx_2x_1 = -MPPx_2/MPPx_1 \tag{5.16}$$

The inverse slope of the isoquant is equal to the negative inverse ratio of the marginal products. Thus the slope (or inverse slope) of an isoquant is totally dependent on the *MPP* of each input.

In Section 5.3 a ridge line was defined as a line that connected points of zero or infinite slope on an isoquant map. Consider first a ridge line that connects points of zero slope on an isoquant map. This implies that

$MRSx_1x_2 = 0$. But $MRSx_1x_2 = -MPPx_1/MPPx_2$. The only way for $MRSx_1x_2$ to equal 0 is for $MPPx_1$ to equal zero. If $MPPx_1$ is zero, the $TPPx_1$ (assuming a given value for x_2 again of x_2^*) must be maximum, and thus the underlying production function for x_1 holding x_2 constant at x_2^* must be at its maximum.

Now consider a ridge line that connects points of infinite slope on an isoquant map. This implies that $MRSx_1x_2$ is infinite. Again $MRSx_1x_2 = -MPPx_1/MPPx_2$. $MRSx_1x_2$ will become more and more negative as $MPPx_2$ comes closer and closer to zero. When $MPPx_2$ is exactly equal to zero, the $MRSx_1x_2$ is actually undefined, since any number divided by a zero is undefined. However, note that when $MPPx_2 = 0$, then $MRSx_2x_1 = 0$, since $MPPx_2$ appears on the top, not the bottom of the ratio. A ridge line connecting points of infinite slope on an isoquant map connects points of zero inverse slope where the inverse slope is defined as $\Delta x_1/\Delta x_2$.

5.5 Partial and Total Derivatives and the Marginal Rate of Substitution

Consider again the production function

$$y = f(x_1, x_2) \tag{5.17}$$

For many production functions, the marginal product of x_1 ($MPPx_1$) can be obtained only by making an assumption about the level of x_2. Similarly, the marginal product of x_2 cannot be obtained without making an assumption about the level of x_1. The $MPPx_1$ is defined as

$$MPPx_1 = \partial f/\partial x_1 \mid x_2 = x_2^* \tag{5.18}$$

The expression $\partial y/\partial x_1$ is the partial derivative of the production function $y = f(x_1, x_2)$, assuming x_2 to be constant at x_2^*. It is the MPP function for the member of the family of production functions for x_1, assuming that x_2 is held constant at some predetermined level x_2^*.

Similarly, the $MPPx_2$, under the assumption that x_1 is fixed at some predetermined level x_1^*, can be obtained from the expression

$$MPPx_2 = \partial f/\partial x_2 \mid x_1 = x_1^* \tag{5.19}$$

In both examples the f refers to output or y.

The big difference between dy/dx_1 and $\partial y/\partial x_1$ is that the dy/dx_1 requires that no assumption be made about the quantity of x_2 that is used. dy/dx_1 might be thought of as the total derivative of the production function with respect to x_1, with no assumptions being made about the value of x_2. The expression $\partial y/\partial x_1$ is the partial derivative of the production function, holding x_2 constant at some predetermined level called x_2^*.

A few examples better illustrate these differences. Suppose that the production function is

$$y = x_1^{0.5} x_2^{0.5} \tag{5.20}$$

Then

$$MPPx_1 = \partial y/\partial x_1 = 0.5x_1^{-0.5}x_2^{0.5} \quad (5.21)$$

Since differentiation takes place with respect to x_1, x_2 is treated simply as if it were a constant in the differentiation process, and

$$MPPx_2 = \partial y/\partial x_2 = 0.5x_2^{-0.5}x_1^{0.5} \quad (5.22)$$

Since differentiation takes place with respect to x_2, x_1 is treated as if it were a constant in the differentiation process.

Note that in this example, each marginal product contains the other input. An assumption needs to be made with respect to the amount of the other input that is used in order to calculate the respective *MPP* for the input under consideration. Again, the *MPP* of x_1 is conditional on the assumed level of use of x_2. The *MPP* of x_2 is conditional on the assumed level of use of x_1.

Now consider a slightly different production function,

$$y = x_1^{0.5} + x_2^{0.5} \quad (5.23)$$

In this production function, inputs are additive rather than multiplicative. The corresponding *MPP* for each input is

$$MPPx_1 = \partial y/\partial x_1 = 0.5x_1^{-0.5} \quad (5.24)$$

$$MPPx_2 = \partial y/\partial x_2 = 0.5x_2^{-0.5} \quad (5.25)$$

For this production function, $MPPx_1$ does not contain x_2, and $MPPx_2$ does not contain x_1. No assumption needs to be made with respect to the level of use of the other input in order to calculate the respective *MPP* for each input. Since this is true, this is an example where

$$\partial y/\partial x_1 = dy/dx_1 \quad (5.26)$$

and

$$\partial y/\partial x_2 = dy/dx_2 \quad (5.27)$$

The partial and the total derivatives are exactly the same for this particular production function.

Consider again the expression representing the total change in output

$$\Delta y = MPPx_1 \, \Delta x_1 + MPPx_2 \, \Delta x_2 \quad (5.28)$$

A Δ denotes a finite change, and the respective *MPP*'s for x_1 and x_2 are not exact but rather, merely approximations over the finite range.

Suppose that Δx_1 and Δx_2 become smaller and smaller. At the limit, the changes in x_1 and x_2 become infinitesimally small. If the changes in x_1 and x_2

5.5 Partial and Total Derivatives and the Marginal Rate of Substitution

are no longer assumed to be finite, at the limit, equation (5.28) can be rewritten as

$$dy = MPPx_1\, dx_1 + MPPx_2\, dx_2 \qquad (5.29)$$

or

$$dy = \partial y/\partial x_1\, dx_1 + \partial y/\partial x_2\, dx_2. \qquad (5.30)$$

Equation (5.30) is the total differential for the production function $y = f(x_1, x_2)$.

Along an isoquant, there is no change in y, so $dy = 0$. An isoquant by definition connects points representing the exact same level of output. The total differential is equal to zero. The exact $MRSx_1x_2$ at $x_1 = x_1^*$ and $x^2 = x_2^*$ is

$$MRSx_1x_2 = dx_2/dx_1 = -MPPx_1/MPPx_2 = -(\partial y/\partial x_1)/(\partial y/\partial x_2) \qquad (5.31)$$

Similarly, the exact $MRSx_2x_1$ is defined as

$$MRSx_2x_1 = dx_1/dx_2 = -MPPx_2/MPPx_1 = -(\partial y/\partial x_2)/(\partial y/\partial x_1) \qquad (5.32)$$

The total change in the MPP for x_1 can be obtained by dividing the total differential of the production function by dx_1. The result is

$$dy/dx_1 = \partial y/\partial x_1 + (\partial y/\partial x_2)(dx_2/dx_1) \qquad (5.33)$$

Equation (5.33) is the total derivative of the production function $y = f(x_1, x_2)$. It recognizes specifically that the productivity of x_1 is not independent of the level of x_2 that is used.

The total change in output as a result of a change in the use of x_1 is the sum of two effects. The direct effect $(\partial y/\partial x_1)$ measures the direct impact of the change in the use of x_1 on output. The indirect effect measures the impact of a change in the use of x_1 on the use of $x_2(dx_2/dx_1)$, which in turn affects y (through $\partial y/\partial x_2$).

The shape of the isoquant is closely linked to the production functions that underlie it. In fact, if the underlying production functions are known, it is possible to determine with certainty the exact shape of the isoquant and its slope and curvature at any particular point. The marginal rate of substitution, or slope of the isoquant at any particular point, is equal to the negative ratio of the marginal products of each input at that particular point. If the marginal product of each input is positive but declining, the isoquant normally will be bowed inward or convex to the origin.

The curvature of an isoquant can be determined by again differentiating the marginal rate of substitution with respect to x_1.[4] If the sign on the derivative is positive, the isoquant is bowed inward and exhibits a diminishing marginal rate of substitution. It is also possible for isoquants to be bowed inward in certain instances where the marginal product of both inputs is positive but not declining. Examples of this exception are contained in Chapter 10.

Diagrams B to D of Figure 5.2 all represent isoquants that are downward sloping, and hence dx_2/dx_1 is negative in each case. In diagram B, $d(dx_2/dx_1)/dx_1$ is positive, which is consistent with a diminishing marginal rate of substitution. Diagram C illustrates a case in which $d(dx_2/dx_1)/dx_1$ is negative, resulting in isoquants concave to the origin, while for diagram D, $d(dx_2/dx_1)/dx_1$ is zero, and the isoquants have a constant slope with no diminishing or increasing marginal rates of substitution.

The derivative dx_2/dx_1 is positive in diagram E and undefined in diagram F. In diagram A, the isoquants have both positive and negative slopes, and the sign on dx_2/dx_1 depends on the particular point being evaluated.

Thus the concept of an isoquant with a particular marginal rate of substitution at any particular point and the concept of a production function with marginal products for each input are not separate and unrelated. Rather the slope, curvature, and other characteristics of an isoquant are uniquely determined by the marginal productivity of each input in the underlying production function.

5.6 Concluding Comments

This chapter has been concerned with the physical and technical relationships underlying production in a setting in which two inputs are used in the production of a single output. An isoquant is a line connecting points of equal output on a graph with the axes represented by the two inputs. The slope of an isoquant is referred to as a marginal rate of substitution (*MRS*). The *MRS* indicates the extent to which one input substitutes for another as one moves from one point to another along an isoquant representing constant output. The marginal rate of substitution is usually diminishing. In other words, when output is maintained at the constant level represented by the isoquant, as units of input x_1 used in the production process are added, each additional unit of x_1 that is added replaces a smaller and smaller quantity of x_2.

A diminishing marginal rate of substitution between two inputs normally occurs if the production function exhibits positive but decreasing marginal product with respect to incremental increases in the use of each input, a condition normally found in stage II of production. Thus the marginal rate of substitution is closely linked to the marginal product functions for the inputs. This chapter has illustrated how the marginal rate of substitution can be calculated if the marginal products for the inputs are known.

Notes

1. Not all textbooks define the marginal rate of substitution as the slope of the isoquant. A number of economics texts define the marginal rate of substitution as the *negative* of the slope of the isoquant. That is, $MRSx_1x_2 = -\Delta x_2/\Delta x_1$ (or $-dx_2/dx_1$). Following this definition, a downward-sloping isoquant exibits a positive marginal rate of substitution.
2. Or $-\Delta x_2/\Delta x_1$.
3. If the marginal rate of substitution is defined as the negative of the slope of the isoquant, it is equal to the ratio of the marginal products, not the negative ratio of the marginal products.

5.6 Concluding Comments

4. Let the marginal rate of substitution (MRS) of x_1 for x_2 be defined as dx_2/dx_1. Then the total differential of the MRS is defined as

$$dMRS = (\partial MRS/\partial x_1)dx_1 + (\partial MRS/\partial x_2)dx_2$$

The total derivative with respect to x_1 is

$$dMRS/dx_1 = (\partial MRS/\partial x_1) + (\partial MRS/\partial x_2)(dx_2/dx_1)$$

or

$$dMRS/dx_1 = (\partial MRS/\partial x_1) + (\partial MRS/\partial x_2)MRS$$

As units of x_1 are increased, the total change in the marginal rate of substitution ($dMRS/dx_1$) is the sum of the direct effect of the change in the use of x_1 on the MRS [$(\partial MRS/\partial x_1)$] plus the indirect effect [$(\partial MRS/\partial x_2)MRS$]. The indirect effect occurs because if output is to remain constant on the isoquant, an increase in x_1 must be compensated with a decrease in x_2.

Problems and Exercises

1. The following combinations of x_1 and x_2 all produce 100 bushels of corn. Calculate the $MRSx_1x_2$ and the $MRSx_2x_1$ at each midpoint.

Combination	Units of x_1	Units of x_2	$MRSx_1x_2$	$MRSx_2x_1$
A	10	1		
B	5	2		
C	3	3		
D	2	4		
E	1.5	5		

2. For the production function

$$y = 3x_1 + 2x_2$$

find:

a. The MPP of x_1.
b. The MPP of x_2.
c. The marginal rate of substitution of x_1 for x_2.

3. Draw the isoquants for the production function given in Problem 1.

4. Find those items listed in Problem 2 for a production function given by

$$y = ax_1 + bx_2$$

where a and b are any constants. Is it possible for such a production function to produce isoquants with a positive slope? Explain.

5. Suppose that the production function is given by

$$y = x_1^{0.5} x_2^{0.333}$$

find:
   a. The *MPP* of x_1.
   b. The *MPP* of x_2.
   c. The marginal rate of substitution of x_1 for x_2.
   d. Draw the isoquants for this production function. Do they lie closer to the x_1 or the x_2 axis? Explain. What relationship does the position of the isoquants have relative to the productivity of each input?

6. Suppose that the production function is, instead,

$$y = 2x_1^{0.5}x_2^{0.333}$$

find:
   a. The *MPP* of x_1.
   b. The *MPP* of x_2.
   c. The marginal rate of substitution of x_1 for x_2.
   d. What happens to the position of the isoquants relative to those drawn for Problem 5? Compare your findings with those found for Problem 5.

6 Maximization in the Two-Input Case

This chapter develops the fundamental mathematics for the maximization or minimization of a function with two or more inputs and a single output. The necessary and sufficient conditions for the maximization or minimization of a function are derived in detail. Illustrations are used to show why certain conditions are required if a function is to be maximized or minimized. Examples of functions that fulfill and violate the rules are illustrated. An application of the rules is made using the yield maximization problem.

Key Terms and Definitions:

Maximization
Minimization
First-Order Conditions
Second-Order Conditions
Young's Theorem
Necessary Conditions
Sufficient Conditions
Matrix
Matrix of Partial Derivatives
Principal Minors

Local Maximum
Global Maximum
Saddle Point
Determinant
Critical Value
Unconstrained Maximization and
    Minimization
Constrained Maximization and
    Minimization

6.1 An Introduction to Maximization

An isoquant map might be thought of as a contour map of a hill. The height of the hill at any point is measured by the amount of output that is produced. An *isoquant* connects all points producing the same quantity of output, or having the same elevation on the hill. In general, isoquants consist of concentric rings, just as there are points on all sides of the hill that have the same elevation. Similarly, there are many different combinations of two inputs that would all produce exactly the same amount of output.

An infinite number of isoquants can be drawn. Each isoquant represents a slightly different output level or elevation on the hill. Isoquants never intersect or cross each other, for this would imply that the same combination of two inputs could produce two different levels of output. The quantity of output produced from each combination of the two inputs is unique. If one is standing at a particular point on a side of a hill, that particular point has one and only one elevation.

If the isoquants are concentric rings, any isoquant drawn inside another isoquant will always represent a slightly greater output level than the one on the outside (Figure 5.1, diagram A). If the isoquants are not rings, the greatest output is normally associated with the isoquant at the greatest distance from the origin of the graph. No two isoquants can represent exactly the same level of output. Each isoquant by definition represents a slightly different quantity of output from any other isoquant.

If an isoquant map is drawn as a series of concentric rings, these rings become smaller and smaller as one moves toward the center of the diagram. At comparatively low levels of output, the possible combinations of the two inputs x_1 and x_2 suggest a wide range of options: a large quantity of x_2 and a small quantity of x_1, a small quantity of x_2 and a large quantity of x_1, or something in between. At higher levels of output, the isoquant rings become smaller and smaller, suggesting that the range of options becomes more restricted, but there remains an infinite number of possible combinations on a particular isoquant within the restricted range, each representing a slightly different combination of x_1 and x_2.

The concentric rings finally become a single point. This is the global point of maximum output and would be the position where the farm manager would prefer to operate a farm if inputs were free and there were no other restrictions on the use of the inputs. This single point is the point where the two ridge lines intersect. The *MRS* for an isoquant consisting of a single point is undefined, but this point represents the maximum amount of output that can be produced from any combination of the two inputs x_1 and x_2.

If one were standing on the top of a hill, at the very top, the place where one would be standing would be level. Moreover, regardless of the direction that one looked from the top of a hill, the hill would slope downward from its level top. If one were standing on the hilltop, no other point on the hill would slope upward. If it did, one would not be on the top of the hill. Every other point on the hill would be at a somewhat lower elevation.

The top of the highest hill represents the greatest possible elevation, or global maximum. However, hills that are not as high are also level at the top. The tops of these hills represent local, but not global maxima.

Minimum points can be defined similarly. The bottom of a valley is also level. The bottom of the deepest valley represents a global minimum, while the bottom of other valleys not as deep represent local but not global minima. If one were to draw contour lines for a valley, they would be indistinguishable from the contour lines for a hill.

The slope at both the bottom of a valley and at the top of the hill is zero in all directions. It is not possible to distinguish the bottom of a valley from the top of a hill simply by looking at the slope at that point, because the slope for both is zero. Much of the mathematics of maximization and minimization is concerned with the problem of distinguishing bottoms of valleys from tops of hills based on second-derivative tests or second-order conditions.

6.2 The Maximum of a Function

The problem of finding the combination of inputs x_1 and x_2 that results in the true maximum output from a two-input production function is the mathematical equivalent of finding the top of the hill, or the point on a hill with the greatest elevation. Two conditions need to be checked. First, the point under consideration must be level, or have a zero slope, which is a necessary condition, but level points are found not only at the top of hills but at the bottom of valleys.

The saddle for a horse provides another example and problem for the mathematician. The saddle is level in the middle, but it slopes upward at both ends and downward at both sides. A saddle looks like neither a hill nor a valley, but is a combination of both. So an approach needs to be taken that will separate the true hill from the valley and the saddle point.

Suppose again the general production function

$$y = f(x_1, x_2) \tag{6.1}$$

The first-order or necessary conditions for the maximization of output are

$$\partial y/\partial x_1 = 0 \quad \text{or} \quad f_1 = 0 \tag{6.2}$$

and

$$\partial y/\partial x_2 = 0 \quad \text{or} \quad f_2 = 0 \tag{6.3}$$

Equations (6.2) and (6.3) ensure that the point is level relative to both the x_1 and the x_2 axes.

The second-order conditions for the maximization of output require that the partial derivatives be obtained from the first-order conditions. There are four possible second derivatives obtained by differentiating the first equation with respect to x_1 and then with respect to x_2. The second equation can also be differentiated with respect to both x_1 and x_2.

These four second partial derivatives are

$$\partial(\partial y/\partial x_1)/\partial x_1 = \partial^2 y/\partial x_1^2 = f_{11} \tag{6.4}$$

$$\partial(\partial y/\partial x_1)/\partial x_2 = \partial^2 y/\partial x_1 \partial x_2 = f_{12} \tag{6.5}$$

$$\partial(\partial y/\partial x_2)/\partial x_1 = \partial^2 y/\partial x_2 \partial x_1 = f_{21} \tag{6.6}$$

$$\partial(\partial y/\partial x_2)/\partial x_2 = \partial^2 y/\partial x_2^2 = f_{22} \tag{6.7}$$

Maximization in the Two-Input Case

Young's theorem states that the order of the partial differentiation makes no difference and that $f_{12} = f_{21}$.[1]

The second-order conditions for a maximum require that

$$f_{11} < 0 \tag{6.8}$$

and

$$f_{11}f_{22} > f_{12}f_{21} \tag{6.9}$$

Since $f_{12}f_{21}$ is non-negative, $f_{11}f_{22}$ must be positive for equation (6.9) to hold, and $f_{11}f_{22}$ can be positive only if f_{22} is also negative. Taken together, these first- and second-order conditions provide the necessary and sufficient conditions for the maximization of a two-input production function that has one maximum.

6.3 Some Illustrative Examples

Some specific examples will further illustrate these points. Suppose that the production function is

$$y = 10x_1 + 10x_2 - x_1^2 - x_2^2 \tag{6.10}$$

The first-order or necessary conditions for a maximum are

$$f_1 = 10 - 2x_1 = 0 \tag{6.11}$$

$$x_1 = 5 \tag{6.12}$$

$$f_2 = 10 - 2x_2 = 0 \tag{6.13}$$

$$x_2 = 5 \tag{6.14}$$

The critical values for a function is a point where the slope of the function is equal to zero. The critical values for this function occur at the point where $x_1 = 5$, and $x_2 = 5$. This point could be a maximum, a minimum, or a saddle point.

For a maximum, the second-order conditions require that

$$f_{11} < 0 \quad \text{and} \quad f_{11}f_{22} > f_{12}f_{21} \tag{6.15}$$

For equation (6.10)

$$f_{11} = -2 < 0 \tag{6.16}$$

$$f_{22} = -2 \tag{6.17}$$

$$f_{12} = f_{21} = 0 \text{ since } x_2 \text{ does not appear in } f_1, \text{ nor } x_1 \text{ in } f_2. \tag{6.18}$$

6.3 Some Illustrative Examples

Hence

$$f_{11}f_{22} - f_{12}f_{21} = 4 > 0 \tag{6.19}$$

The necessary and sufficient conditions have been met for the maximization of equation (6.10) at $x_1 = 5, x_2 = 5$. This function is illustrated in diagram A of Figure 6.1.

Now consider a production function

$$y = -10x_1 - 10x_2 + x_1^2 + x_2^2 \tag{6.20}$$

The first-order conditions are

$$f_1 = -10 + 2x_1 = 0 \tag{6.21}$$

$$x_1 = 5 \tag{6.22}$$

$$f_2 = -10 + 2x_2 = 0 \tag{6.23}$$

$$x_2 = 5 \tag{6.24}$$

The second-order conditions for a minimum require that

$$f_{11} > 0 \tag{6.25}$$

$$f_{11}f_{22} > f_{12}f_{21} \tag{6.26}$$

For equation (6.20) the second-order conditions are

$$f_{11} = 2 > 0 \tag{6.27}$$

$$f_{22} = 2 \tag{6.28}$$

Moreover

$$f_{11}f_{22} - f_{12}f_{21} = 4 > 0 \tag{6.29}$$

The necessary and sufficient conditions have been met for the minimization of equation (6.20) at $x_1 = 5, x_2 = 5$. This function is illustrated in diagram B of Figure 6.1.

Now consider a production function

$$y = 10x_1 - 10x_2 - x_1^2 + x_2^2 \tag{6.30}$$

The first-order conditions are

$$f_1 = 10 - 2x_1 = 0 \tag{6.31}$$

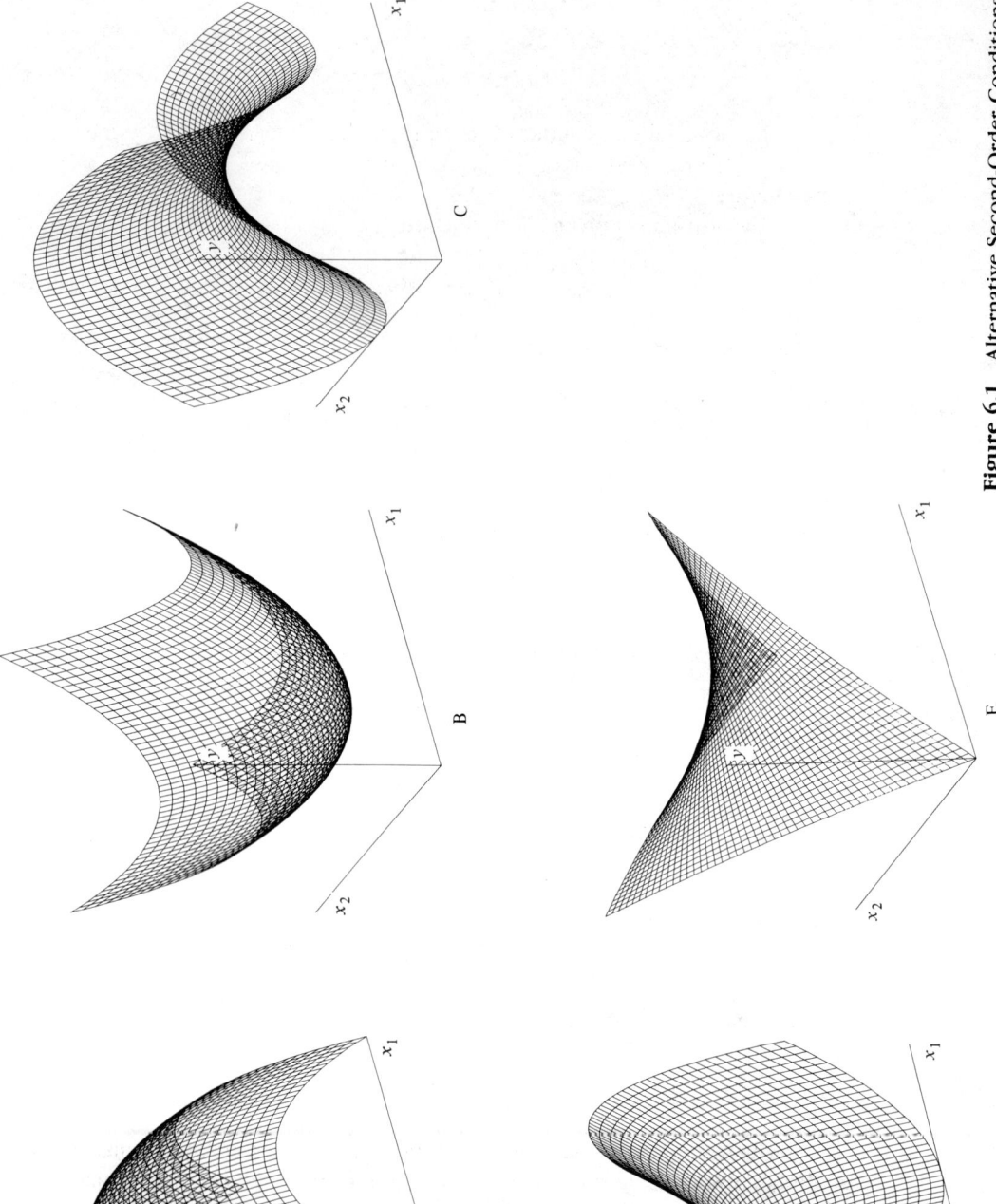

Figure 6.1 Alternative Second-Order Conditions

6.3 Some Illustrative Examples

$$x_1 = 5 \tag{6.32}$$

$$f_2 = -10 + 2x_2 = 0 \tag{6.33}$$

$$x_2 = 5 \tag{6.34}$$

For equation (6.30), the second-order conditions are

$$f_{11} = -2 < 0 \tag{6.35}$$

$$f_{22} = 2 \tag{6.36}$$

Moreover

$$f_{11}f_{22} - f_{12}f_{21} = -4 < 0 \tag{6.37}$$

The necessary and sufficient conditions have not been met for the minimization or maximization of equation (6.30) at $x_1 = 5, x_2 = 5$. This function is the unique saddle point illustrated in diagram C of Figure 6.1 that represents a maximum in the direction parallel to the x_1 axis, but a minimum in the direction parallel to the x_2 axis.

The function

$$y = -10x_1 + 10x_2 + x_1^2 - x_2^2 \tag{6.38}$$

results in a very similar saddle point with the axes reversed. That is, a minimum occurs parallel to the x_1 axis, but a maximum occurs parallel to the x_2 axis. The surface of this function is illustrated in diagram D of Figure 6.1.

Now consider a production function

$$y = -2x_1 - 2x_2 - x_1^2 - x_2^2 + 10x_1x_2 \tag{6.39}$$

The first-order conditions are

$$f_1 = -2 - 2x_1 + 10x_2 = 0 \tag{6.40}$$

$$f_2 = -2 - 2x_2 + 10x_1 = 0 \tag{6.41}$$

Solving for x_2 in equation (6.41) for f_2 gives us

$$-2x_2 = 2 - 10x_1 \tag{6.42}$$

$$x_2 = 5x_1 - 1 \tag{6.43}$$

Inserting equation (6.43) x_2 into equation (6.40) for f_1 results in

$$x_1 = 0.25 \tag{6.44}$$

Maximization in the Two-Input Case

Since $x_2 = 5x_1 - 5$, x_2 also equals 0.25.

In this instance the second-order conditions are

$$f_{11} = -2 < 0 \tag{6.45}$$

$$f_{22} = -2 < 0 \tag{6.46}$$

However,

$$f_{12} = f_{21} = 10 \tag{6.47}$$

Thus

$$f_{11}f_{22} - f_{12}f_{21} = 4 - 100 = -96 < 0 \tag{6.48}$$

Although these conditions may at first appear to be sufficient for a maximum at $x_1 = x_2 = 0.25$, the second-order conditions have not been fully met. In this example, the product of the direct second partial derivatives $f_{11}f_{22}$ is less than the product of the second cross partial derivatives $f_{12}f_{21}$, and therefore $f_{11}f_{22} - f_{12}f_{21}$ is less than zero. In the earlier examples, the second cross partial derivatives were always zero, since an interaction term such as $10x_1x_2$ did not appear in the original production function.

As a result, another type of saddle point occurs, as illustrated in diagram E of Figure 6.1, which appears somewhat like a bird with wings outstretched. Like the earlier saddle points, a minimum exists in one direction and a maximum in another direction at a value for x_1 and x_2 of 0.25, but the saddle no longer is parallel to one of the axes, but rather lies along a line running between the two axes. This is the result of the product of the second cross partials being greater than the second direct partials.

In the preceding examples, care was taken to develop polynomial functions that had potential maxima or minima at levels for x_1 and x_2 at positive but finite amounts. If a true maximum exists, the resultant isoquant map will consist of a series of concentric rings centered on the maximum with ridge lines intersecting at the maximum.

One is sometimes tempted to attempt the same approach for other types of functions. For example, consider a function such as

$$y = 10x_1^{0.5}x_2^{0.5} \tag{6.49}$$

In this instance

$$f_1 = 5x_1^{-0.5}x_2^{0.5} \tag{6.50}$$

and

$$f_2 = 5x_1^{0.5}x_2^{-0.5} \tag{6.51}$$

These first partial derivatives of equation (6.49) could be set equal to zero, but they would each assume a value of zero only at $x_1 = 0$ and $x_2 = 0$. There is no possibility that f_1 and f_2 could be zero for any combination of positive values for x_1 and x_2. Hence the function never achieves a maximum.

6.4 Some Matrix Algebra Principles

Matrix algebra is a useful tool for determining if a function has achieved a maximum or minimum. A *matrix* consists of a series of numbers (also called *values* or *elements*) organized into rows and columns. The matrix

$$\begin{matrix} a_{11} & a_{12} & a_{13} \\ a_{21} & a_{22} & a_{23} \\ a_{31} & a_{32} & a_{33} \end{matrix} \tag{6.52}$$

is a square 3 × 3 matrix, since it has the same number of rows and columns. For each element, the first subscript indicates its row, the second subscript its column. For example a_{23} refers to the element or value located in the second row and third column.

Every square matrix has a number associated with it called its *determinant*. For a 1 × 1 matrix with only one value or element, its determinant is a_{11}. The determinant of a 2 × 2 matrix is $a_{11}a_{22} - a_{12}a_{21}$. The determinant of a 3 × 3 matrix is $a_{11}a_{22}a_{33} + a_{12}a_{23}a_{31} + a_{21}a_{32}a_{13} - a_{31}a_{22}a_{13} - a_{11}a_{32}a_{23} - a_{33}a_{21}a_{12}$. Determinants for matrices larger than 3 × 3 are very difficult to calculate, and a computer routine is usually used to calculate them.

The *principal minors* of a matrix are obtained by deleting first all rows and columns of the matrix except the element located in the first row and column (a_{11}) and finding the resultant determinant. In this example, the first principal minor is a_{11}. Next, all rows and columns except the first two rows and columns are deleted, and the determinant for the remaining 2 × 2 matrix is calculated. In this example, the second principal minor is $a_{11}a_{22} - a_{12}a_{21}$. The third principal minor would be obtained by deleting all rows and columns with row or column subscripts larger than 3, and then again finding the resultant determinant.

The second order conditions can better be explained with the aid of matrix algebra. The second direct and cross partial derivatives of a two input production function could form the square 2 × 2 matrix

$$\begin{matrix} f_{11} & f_{12} \\ f_{21} & f_{22} \end{matrix} \tag{6.53}$$

The principal minors of equation (6.53) are

$$\begin{aligned} H_1 &= f_{11} \\ H_2 &= f_{11}f_{22} - f_{12}f_{21} \end{aligned} \tag{6.54}$$

Assuming that the first-order conditions have been met, The second-order condition for a maximum requires that the principal minors H_1 and H_2 alternate in sign, starting with a negative sign. In other words, $H_1 < 0; H_2 > 0$.

For a minimum, all principal minors must be positive. That is, $H_1, H_2 > 0$.

A saddle point results for either of the remaining conditions

$$H_1 > 0; \quad H_2 < 0$$

or,

$$H_1 < 0; H_2 < 0$$

6.5 A Further Illustration

A further illustration of second-order conditions is obtained from the two input polynomial

$$y = 40x_1 - 12x_1^2 + 1.2x_1^3 - 0.03x_1^4$$
$$+ 40x_2 - 12x_2^2 + 1.2x_2^3 - 0.03x_2^4 \quad (6.55)$$

This function has nine values where the first derivatives are equal to zero. Each of these values, called *critical values,* represents a maximum, a minimum, or a saddle point. Figure 6.2 illustrates the function. Table 6.1 illustrates the corresponding second order conditions. In this example, H_1 is f_{11} and H_2 is $f_{11}f_{22} - f_{12}f_{21}$.

This function differs from the previous functions in that there are several combinations of x_1 and x_2 that generate critical values where the slope of the function is equal to zero. There is but one global maximum for the function, but several local maxima. A global maximum might be thought of as the top of the highest mountain, whereas a local maximum might be considered the top of a nearby hill. There are also numerous saddle points. The second-order conditions can be verified by carefully studying figure 6.2.

Table 6.1 Critical Values for the Polynomial $y = 40x_1 - 12x_1^2 + 1.2x_1^3 - 0.03x_1^4 + 40x_2 - 12x_2^2 + 1.2x_2^3 - 0.03x_2^4$

	x_1		
x_2	2.54	6.93	16.24
16.24	Local maximum: $y = 232.3$ $H_1 < 0$ $H_2 > 0$	Saddle point: $y = 209.5$ $H_1 > 0$ $H_2 < 0$	Global maximum: $y = 379.8$ $H_1 < 0$ $H_2 > 0$
6.93	Saddle point: $y = 61.9$ $H_1 < 0$ $H_2 < 0$	Local minimum: $y = 39.1$ $H_1 > 0$ $H_2 > 0$	Saddle point: $y = 209.5$ $H_1 < 0$ $H_2 < 0$
2.54	Local maximum: $y = 84.8$ $H_1 < 0$ $H_2 > 0$	Saddle point: $y = 61.9$ $H_1 > 0$ $H_2 < 0$	Local maximum: $y = 232.3$ $H_1 < 0$ $H_2 > 0$

6.6 Maximizing a Profit Function with Two Inputs

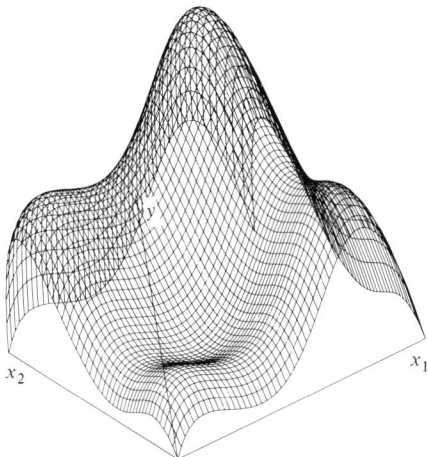

Figure 6.2 The Three-Dimensional Polynomial $y = 40x_1 - 12x_1^2 + 1.2x_1^3 - 0.03x_1^4 + 40x_2 - 12x_2^2 + 1.2x_2^3 - 0.03x_2^4$

6.6 Maximizing a Profit Function with Two Inputs

The usefulness of the criteria for maximizing a function can be further illustrated with an agricultural example using a profit function for corn. Suppose that the production function for corn is given by

$$y = f(x_1, x_2) \tag{6.56}$$

where y = corn yield in bushels per acre
x_1 = pounds of potash applied per acre
x_2 = pounds of phosphate applied per acre

All other inputs are presumed to be fixed and given, or already owned by the farm manager. The decision faced by the farm manager is how much of the two fertilizer inputs or factors of production to apply to maximize profits to the farm firm.

The total revenue or total value of the product from the sale of the corn from 1 acre of land is

$$TVP = py \tag{6.57}$$

where p = price of corn per bushel
y = corn yield in bushels per acre

The total input or factor cost is

$$TFC = v_1 x_1 + v_2 x_2 \tag{6.58}$$

where v_1 and v_2 are the prices on potash and phosphate, respectively, in cents per pound. The profit function is

$$\Pi = TVP - TFC \qquad (6.59)$$

Equation (6.59) can also be expressed as

$$\Pi = py - v_1 x_1 - v_2 x_2 \qquad (6.60)$$

or

$$\Pi = pf(x_1, x_2) - v_1 x_1 - v_2 x_2 \qquad (6.61)$$

The first-order or necessary conditions for a maximum are

$$\Pi_1 = pf_1 - v_1 = 0 \qquad (6.62)$$

$$\Pi_2 = pf_2 - v_2 = 0 \qquad (6.63)$$

Equations (6.62) and (6.63) require that the slope of the *TVP* function with respect to each input equal the slope of the *TFC* function for each input, or that the difference between the slopes of the two functions be zero for both inputs, or as

$$pf_1 = v_1 \qquad (6.64)$$

$$pf_2 = v_2 \qquad (6.65)$$

The value of the marginal product must equal the marginal factor cost for each input. If the farmer is able to purchase as much of each type of fertilizer as he or she wishes at the going market price, the marginal factor cost is the price of the input, v_1 or v_2. This also implies that at the point of profit maximization the ratio of *VMP* to *MFC* for each input is 1. In other words,

$$pf_1/v_1 = pf_2/v_2 = 1 \qquad (6.66)$$

The last dollar spent on each input must return exactly $1, and most if not all previous units will have given back more than a dollar. The accumulation of the excess dollars in returns over costs represents the profits or net revenues accruing to the farm firm.

Moreover, the equations representing the first-order conditions can be divided by each other

$$pf_1/pf_2 = v_1/v_2 \qquad (6.67)$$

Note that the output price cancels in equation (6.67) such that

$$f_1/f_2 = v_1/v_2 \qquad (6.68)$$

Recall from Chapter 5 that f_1 is the *MPP* of x_1 and f_2 is the *MPP* of x_2. The ratio of the respective marginal products is one definition of the marginal rate of substitution of x_1 for x_2 or $MRSx_1x_2$ (see Note 3, Chapter 5). Then at the point of profit maximization,

$$MRSx_1x_2 = v_1/v_2 \qquad (6.69)$$

or

$$dx_2/dx_1 = v_1/v_2 \qquad (6.70)$$

As will be seen later, equation (6.70) holds at other points on the isoquant map in addition to the point of profit maximization.

The second-order conditions also play a role. Assuming fixed input prices (v_1 and v_2), the second-order conditions for the profit function are

$$\Pi_{11} = pf_{11} \qquad (6.71)$$

$$\Pi_{22} = pf_{22} \qquad (6.72)$$

$$\Pi_{12} = \Pi_{21} = pf_{12} = pf_{21} \quad \text{(by Young's theorem)} \qquad (6.73)$$

or in the form of a matrix

$$\begin{matrix} pf_{11} & pf_{12} \\ pf_{21} & pf_{22} \end{matrix} \qquad (6.74)$$

For a maximum,

$$pf_{11} < 0 \qquad (6.75)$$

and

$$pf_{11}pf_{22} - pf_{12}pf_{21} > 0 \qquad (6.76)$$

The principal minors must alternate in sign starting with a minus. Equations (6.75) and (6.76) require that the *VMP* functions for both x_1 and x_2 be downsloping. With fixed input prices, the input cost function will have a constant slope, or the slope of *MFC* will be zero.

The conditions that have been outlined determine a single point of global profit maximization, assuming that the underlying production function itself has but a single maximum. This single profit-maximization point will require less of both x_1 and x_2 than would be required to maximize output, unless one or both of the inputs were free.

6.7 A Comparison with Output- or Yield-Maximization Criteria

A comparison can be made of the criteria for profit maximization versus the criteria for yield maximization. If the production function is

$$y = f(x_1, x_2) \qquad (6.77)$$

maximum yield occurs where

$$f_1 = MPPx_1 = 0 \tag{6.78}$$

$$f_2 = MPPx_2 = 0 \tag{6.79}$$

or

$$f_1 = f_2 = 0 \tag{6.80}$$

The second-order conditions for maximum output require that $f_{11} < 0$ and $f_{11}f_{22} > f_{12}f_{21}$. The *MPP* for both inputs must be downward sloping.

The first- and second-order conditions comprise the necessary and sufficient conditions for the maximization of output or yield and are the mathematical conditions that define the center of an isoquant map that consists of a series of concentric rings.

Since zero can be multiplied or divided by any number other than zero, and zero would still result, when *MPP* for x_1 and x_2 is zero,

$$pf_1/v_1 = pf_2/v_2 = 0 \tag{6.81}$$

To be at maximum output, the last dollar spent on each input must produce no additional output, yield, or revenue.

Recall that the first-order, or necessary conditions for maximum profit occur at the point where

$$pf_1 - v_1 = 0 \tag{6.82}$$

$$pf_2 - v_2 = 0 \tag{6.83}$$

$$pf_1/v_1 = pf_2/v_2 = 1 \tag{6.84}$$

and the corresponding second-order conditions for maximum profit require that

$$pf_{11} < 0 \tag{6.85}$$

$$pf_{11}pf_{22} - pf_{12}pf_{21} > 0. \tag{6.86}$$

$$p^2(f_{11}f_{22} - f_{12}f_{21}) > 0 \tag{6.87}$$

Since p^2 is positive, the required signs on the second-order conditions are the same for both profit and yield maximization.

6.8 Concluding Comments

This chapter has developed some of the fundamental rules for determining if a function is at a maximum or a minimum. The rules developed here are useful in finding a solution to the unconstrained maximization problem. These rules also provide the basis for finding the solution to the problem of constrained maximization or minimization. The constrained maximization or minimization problem makes it possible to determine the combination of inputs that is re-

6.8 Concluding Comments

quired to produce a given level of output for the least cost, or to maximize the level of output for a given cost. The constrained maximization problem is presented in further detail in Chapters 7 and 8.

Notes

1. A simple example can be used to illustrate that Young's theorem does indeed hold in a specific case. Suppose that a production function

$$y = x_1^2 x_2^3$$

Then

$$f_1 = 2x_1 x_2^3$$

$$f_2 = 3x_1^2 x_2^2$$

$$f_{12} = 6x_1 x_2^2$$

$$f_{21} = 6x_1 x_2^2$$

A formal proof of Young's theorem in the general case can be found in most intermediate calculus texts.

Problems and Exercises

1. Does the function $y = x_1 x_2$ ever achieve a maximum? Explain.
2. Does the function $y = x_1^2 - 2x_2^2$ ever achieve a maximum? Explain.
3. Does the function $y = x_1 + 0.1x_1^2 - 0.05x_1^3 + x_2 + 0.1x_2^2 - 0.05x_2^3$ ever achieve a maximum? If so, at what level of input use is output maximized.
4. Suppose that price of the output is $2. For the function given in Problem 3, what level of input use will maximize the total value of the product?
5. Assume that the following conditions exist

$$f_1 = 0$$
$$f_2 = 0$$

Does a maximum, minimum, or saddle point exist in each case?

   a. $f_{11} < 0$
   $f_{11} f_{22} - f_{12} f_{21} < 0$

   b. $f_{11} < 0$
   $f_{11} f_{22} - f_{12} f_{21} > 0$

   c. $f_{11} > 0$
   $f_{11} f_{22} - f_{12} f_{21} > 0$

   d. $f_{11} < 0$
   $f_{11} f_{22} - f_{12} f_{21} < 0$

6. Suppose that the price of the output is $3, the price of the input x_1 is $5, and the price of input x_2 is $4. Is it possible to produce and achieve a profit? Explain. What are the necessary and sufficient conditions for profit maximization?

7 Maximization Subject to Budget Constraints

This chapter presents the factor-factor model by relying primarily on simple algebra and graphics. Here the concept of a constraint to the maximization process is introduced. Points of tangency between the budget constraint and the isoquant are defined. Conditions along the expansion path are outlined, and the least-cost combination of inputs is defined. Pseudo scale lines are developed, and the global point of profit maximization is identified. The chapter concludes with a summary of the fundamental marginal conditions for the factor-factor model. The algebraic and graphical presentation forms the basis for a better understanding of the mathematical presentation contained in Chapter 8.

Key Terms and Definitions:

Constraint
Budget Constraint
Iso-outlay Line
Isoquant Map
Points of Tangency
Isocline
Expansion Path
Least-Cost Combination

Equimarginal Return Principle
Input Bundle
Pseudo Scale Lines
Global Output Maximization
Global Profit Maximization
Marginal Conditions
Decision Rules

7.1 Introduction

Chapter 6 dealt with basic relationships governing the maximization of output or profit without regard for constraints or limitations on the maximization process. However, farmers do not normally operate in an environment where maximization of profit can take place without regard to constraints on the maximization process.

The consumer, seeking to purchase goods and services in such a manner as to maximize utility, must invariably face constraints or limitations imposed

7.2 The Budget Constraint

by the availability of money income. The consumer must operate within these constraints by choosing a mix of goods that requires a total outlay not to exceed income. While the consumer might borrow money to purchase goods and services, eventually loans need to be paid back. Ultimately, the bundle of goods and services purchased by the consumer must be in line with the consumer's money income.

The producer, too, faces constraints. The constraints or limitations imposed on the producer fall into two categories: (1) internal constraints occurring as a result of limitations in the amount of money available for the purchase of inputs, and (2) external constraints imposed by the federal government or other institutions. An example of such a constraint might be an acreage allotment within a government farm program.

This chapter is devoted to a discussion of how constraints internal to a farm firm might limit the farmer's ability to achieve profit maximization. The models developed in this chapter also provide a useful analytical tool for assessing the impact of certain external constraints on the behavior of the farm manager. The application of these models to situations where external constraints are imposed is developed fully in Chapter 8.

7.2 The Budget Constraint

Suppose that a farmer again uses two inputs (x_1 and x_2) to produce an output (y). The farmer can no longer purchase as much of both inputs as is needed to maximize profits. The farmer faces a budget constraint that limits the amount total expenditures on the two inputs to some fixed number of dollars $C°$. The budget constraint faced by the farmer can be written as

$$C° = v_1 x_1 + v_2 x_2 \tag{7.1}$$

where v_1 and v_2 are prices on the inputs x_1 and x_2, respectively. Another way of writing equation (7.1) is

$$C° = \Sigma v_i x_i \quad \text{for } i = 1, 2 \tag{7.2}$$

Now suppose that the farmer has $100 available for the purchase of the two inputs, x_1 and x_2. Suppose also that x_1 costs $5.00 per unit and x_2 costs $3.00 per unit. Table 7.1 illustrates possible combinations of x_1 and x_2 that could be purchased with the $100.

Table 7.1 Alternative Combinations of x_1 and x_2 Purchased with $100

Combination	Units of x_1	Units of x_2	Total Cost, $C°$
A	20.00	0.00	$100
B	15.00	8.33	$100
C	10.00	16.67	$100
D	8.00	20.00	$100
E	5.00	25.00	$100
F	0.00	33.33	$100

Table 7.1 illustrates but a few of the possible combinations of x_1 and x_2 that could be purchased with a total budget outlay ($C°$) of exactly $100. If inputs are assumed to be infinitely divisible, there are an infinite number of alternative combinations that could be purchased for exactly $100. The assumption that inputs are infinitely divisible is not a bad one for certain classes of inputs such as fertilizer or livestock feed. For example, 186.202 pounds of fertilizer or 149.301 bushels of feed could be purchased. For other classes of inputs in agriculture, the assumption is silly. No farmer would purchase 2.09 tractors or 1.57 bulls. However, the basic model has as an underlying assumption that inputs are infinitely divisible.

Now suppose that the budget line or constraint indicated by the tabular data in Table 7.1 is plotted with input x_1 on the horizontal axis and x_2 on the vertical axis. It may seem surprising that a budget line that has dollars as its units can be plotted on a diagram in which the axes are physical quantities of inputs. However, the position of the budget constraint on both the horizontal and vertical axis can be determined. First, suppose that the farmer chooses to purchase with the $100 all x_1 and no x_2. The total amount of x_1 that would be purchased is $100/$5.00 ($C°/v_1$) or 20 units of x_1. The budget constraint therefore intersects the x_1 axis at 20 units.

Tabular data similar to that contained in Table 7.1 can be derived for any chosen budget outlay. The terms *iso-outlay* or *isocost* have frequently been used by economists to refer to the budget constraint or outlay line. The iso-outlay function can be thought of as a line of constant or equal budget outlay.

Suppose instead that the farmer chose to allocate the $100 in such a way that no x_1 was purchased and all of the $100 was used to purchase x_2. The total amount of x_2 that could be purchased is $100/$3.00 ($C°/v_2$) or approximately 33.33 units of x_2. The budget constraint therefore intersects the vertical axis at 33.33 units of x_2.

The final step is to determine the shape of the budget constraint between the points of intersection with the axes. If input prices are constant, the budget constraint will have a constant slope. A line with a constant slope might be drawn between the previously identified points on the two axes to form a triangle. The height of this triangle is $100/$3.00 (33.33 units of x_2). The length of the triangle is $100/$500 (20 units of x_2). The slope of the triangle is height divided by length, or

$$(\$100/\$3.00) \div (\$100/\$5.00) = (\$100/\$3.00)(\$5.00/\$100)$$
$$= \$5.00/\$3.00 = 1.67 \qquad (7.3)$$

In equation (7.3), the budget constraint has a constant slope of 5/3 or 1.67. Under the assumption of fixed input prices, the budget constraint will always have a constant slope of $(C°/v_2)(v_1/C°) = v_1/v_2$, sometimes called the *inverse input price ratio*. The term *inverse* is used because the price for the input appearing on the horizontal axis appears on the top of the fraction, the price for the input on the vertical axis at the bottom of the fraction.

By varying the total amount of the budget constraint or outlay ($C°$), a family of budget constraints can be developed, each representing a slightly different total outlay. Like isoquants, budget constraint lines are everywhere dense. That is, an infinite number of budget constraint lines can be drawn, each with the constant slope v_1/v_2.

The characteristics of an iso-outlay line can be summarized by making use of the total differential. The iso-outlay line is

$$C° = v_1 x_1 + v_2 x_2$$

The input prices are taken as fixed constants. The total differential of the iso-outlay line is

$$dC° = v_1\, dx_1 + v_2\, dx_2 \tag{7.4}$$

The outlay ($C°$) along the iso-outlay line is assumed to be constant. Thus $dC° = 0$. Therefore,

$$0 = v_1\, dx_1 + v_2\, dx_2 \tag{7.5}$$

$$-v_1\, dx_1 = v_2\, dx_2 \tag{7.6}$$

$$dx_2/dx_1 = -v_1/v_2 \tag{7.7}$$

The term dx_2/dx_1 in equation (7.7) is the slope of the iso-outlay or budget constraint line in factor-factor (x_1 on the horizontal axis, x_2 on the vertical axis) space. The slope of the budget line is equal to the negative inverse ratio of input prices. The negative sign indicates that the iso-outlay line is downward sloping when both input prices are positive.

7.3 The Budget Constraint and the Isoquant Map

A diagram showing a series of isoquants is sometimes referred to as an isoquant map. The budget constraint or iso-outlay line developed in Section 7.2 is placed on a diagram with input x_1 on the horizontal axis and x_2 on the vertical axis. This factor-factor space is the same as that used to graph isoquants. Figure 7.1 illustrates an isoquant map superimposed on top of a series of budget constraints. In each case, only selected isoquants and selected iso-outlay lines are shown. An infinite number of either isoquants or iso-outlay lines could be drawn, each representing a slightly different level of output or a slightly different total outlay.

Each isoquant has a corresponding iso-outlay line that comes just tangent to it. Moreover, for each iso-outlay line there is a corresponding isoquant that comes just tangent to it.

Assuming that the isoquant is bowed inward or convex to the origin of the graph, the point of tangency between the isoquant and the iso-outlay line represents the combination of inputs that will produce the greatest quantity of output for the expenditure represented by the iso-outlay line. This is the maximum output given the budgeted dollars $C°$ or subject to the budget constraint.

Another approach is to think of the amount of output represented by a particular isoquant as being fixed. Then the point of tangency between the isoquant and the iso-outlay line represents the minimum-cost, or least-cost com-

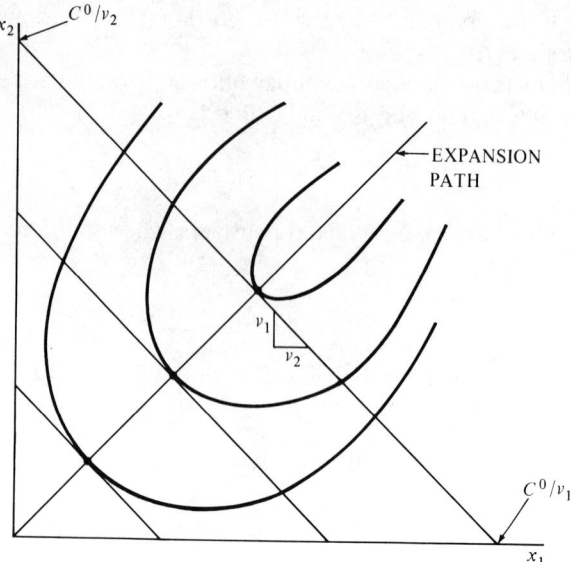

Figure 7.1 Iso-outlay Lines and an Isoquant Map

bination of input x_1 and x_2 that can be used to produce the fixed level of output represented by the isoquant.

Either rationale leads to the same important conclusion. If the farmer faces a budget constraint in the purchase of inputs x_1 and x_2, and as a result is unable to globally maximize profits, the next best alternative is to select a point of least-cost combination where the budget constraint faced by the farmer comes just tangent to the corresponding isoquant.

Any line drawn tangent to an isoquant represents the slope of the isoquant at that point. As indicated earlier, the slope of the isoquant can be represented by dx_2/dx_1. But the slope of the iso-outlay line was also found to be dx_2/dx_1, so the point of least-cost combination is defined as the point where the slope of the iso-outlay line equals the slope of the corresponding isoquant. At the point of least-cost combination, both the isoquant and the iso-outlay line will be downward sloping.

One definition of the slope of the isoquant is $-MRSx_1x_2$ (see Note 1, Chapter 5). The slope of the iso-outlay line is $-v_1/v_2$. Both the isoquant and the iso-outlay line are downward sloping, so the point of tangency between the isoquant and the iso-outlay line can be defined as

$$-MRSx_1x_2 = -v_1/v_2 \qquad (7.8)$$

or

$$MRSx_1x_2 = v_1/v_2 \qquad (7.9)$$

At the point of least-cost combination, the *MRS* of x_1 for x_2 must equal the inverse price ratio (v_1/v_2).

7.4 Isoclines and the Expansion Path

The term *isocline* is used to refer to any line that connects points of the same slope on a series of isoquants. The ridge lines developed in Chapter 5 were examples of isoclines. Ridge line I connected all points of zero slope on the series of isoquants. Ridge line II connected all points of infinite slope on the same series of isoquants. Each are examples of isoclines because each connects points with the same slope.

As outlined in Section 7.3, the inverse ratio of input prices v_1/v_2 is very important in determining where within a series of isoquants a farm manager can operate. To produce a given amount of output at minimum cost for inputs, or to produce the maximum amount of output for a given level of expenditure on x_1 and x_2, the farmer must equate $MRSx_1x_2$ with v_1/v_2. However, if input prices are constant, a key assumption of the model of pure competition outlined in Chapter 1, the slope of the iso-outlay line will be a constant v_1/v_2.

A line connecting all points of constant slope v_1/v_2 on an isoquant map is a very important isocline. This isocline has a special name, the *expansion path* (Figure 7.1). The expansion path is a specialized isocline that connects all points on an isoquant map where the slope of the isoquants is equal to the ratio v_1/v_2, where v_1 and v_2 refer to the prices on the inputs.

The term *expansion path* is used because the line refers to the path on which the farmer would expand or contract the size of the operation with respect to the purchases of x_1 and x_2. A farmer seeking to produce a given amount of output at minimum cost, or seeking to produce maximum output for a given expenditure on x_1 and x_2, would always use inputs x_1 and x_2 in the combinations indicated along the expansion path. The exact point on the expansion path where the farmer would operate would depend on the availability of dollars ($C°$) for the purchase of inputs.

The points of tangency between the iso-outlay lines and the corresponding isoquant on the expansion path thus represent the least-cost combination of inputs that can be used to produce the output level associated with the isoquant. There is no combination of x_1 and x_2 that can produce that specific quantity of output at lower cost. If isoquants are convex to the origin, or bowed inward, all points of tangency represent points of least-cost combination for the output level associated with the particular tangent isoquant. While every point on the expansion path is a point of least-cost combination, there is only one point on the expansion path that represents the global point of profit maximization for the farmer. This particular point is derived in Section 7.7.

The expansion path begins at the origin of the graph ($x_1 = 0, x_2 = 0$) and travels across isoquants until the global point of output maximization in reached, where the MPP of both x_1 and x_2 is zero. Points beyond the global point of output maximization, while having the same constant slope v_1/v_2, would never be chosen by the entrepreneur. Note that at points beyond global output maximization, isoquants are no longer convex to the origin of the graph. Points of tangency occur as a result of the isoquants curving upward from below, not downward from above. These points of tangency represent the maximum expenditure for a given level of output, not the desired minimum expenditure. So these points would never be considered economic for the farmer.

Some widely used agricultural production functions generate expansion paths with a constant slope. The class of production functions that generate linear expansion paths when input prices are constant are referred to as *homothetic production functions*.

The equation for an expansion path can be derived through the use of the general expansion path conditions

$$dx_2/dx_1 = v_1/v_2 \qquad (7.10)$$

But

$$dx_2/dx_1 = -MPPx_1/MPPx_2 \qquad (7.11)$$

The equation for the expansion path can be obtained by solving the expression $MPPx_1/MPPx_2 = v_1/v_2$ for x_2 in terms of x_1. For example, suppose that the production function is

$$y = ax_1^{0.5}x_2^{0.5} \qquad (7.12)$$

The corresponding *MPP*'s are

$$MPPx_1 = 0.5ax_1^{-0.5}x_2^{0.5} \qquad (7.13)$$

$$MPPx_2 = 0.5ax_1^{0.5}x_2^{-0.5} \qquad (7.14)$$

The $MRSx_1x_2$ is

$$(0.5ax_1^{-0.5}x_2^{0.5})/(0.5ax_1^{0.5}x_2^{-0.5}) \qquad (7.15)$$

$$x_2/x_1 = v_1/v_2 \qquad (7.16)$$

Thus, the equation for the expansion path is

$$x_2 = (v_1/v_2)x_1 \qquad (7.17)$$

Since the ratio v_1/v_2 is a constant b, the expansion path [equation (7.17)] in this example is linear

$$x_2 = bx_1 \qquad (7.18)$$

7.5 General Expansion Path Conditions

In Chapter 6 the general conditions for the maximization of profit were defined as

$$VMPx_1/v_1 = VMPx_2/v_2 = 1 \qquad (7.19)$$

There are two parts to the rule in equation (7.19). The first part requires that the ratio of *VMP* to the corresponding input price be the same for both

7.5 General Expansion Path Conditions

(all) inputs. The second part requires that ratio to be equal to 1. The farmer should use inputs up to the point where the last dollar spent on the input returns back a dollar, and most if not all prior units of input returns more than a dollar.

What if the farmer faces a limitation or constraint on the availability of funds for the purchase of inputs x_1 and x_2? The farmer's next best alternative is to apply the *equimarginal return principle*. The equimarginal return principle ensures that if the farmer is not at the point of profit maximization, at least costs are being minimized for the level of output that can be produced. Alternatively, maximum output is being produced for a given budget outlay.

The equimarginal return principle requires the farmer to operate using combinations of inputs such that

$$VMPx_1/v_1 = VMPx_2/v_2 = K \qquad (7.20)$$

Equation (7.20) is only slightly different from the profit maximizing condition outlined in equation (7.19). Instead of requiring that the ratio of the *VMP* to the corresponding input price to be equal to 1, now the ratio of *VMP* to the corresponding input price must be equal to some constant number K, where K can be any number. The ratios of the *VMP* to the input price must be the same for both inputs, and thus the ratio for both inputs must be equal to a number K.

Another way of looking at the expansion path is that it represents the series of points defined by equation (7.20). Any point on the expansion path has a different value for K assigned to it. In general, as one moves outward along the expansion path, the value of K will decline. Points along the expansion path can be identified according to the value of K.

Suppose, for example, that $K = 3$. The last dollar spent on the input returns $3. This is a point on the expansion path that represents a least cost combination of inputs (since the ratio of $VMPx_1/v_1 = VMPx_2/v_2 = 3$). This is not a point of profit maximization. The farmer is constrained by the availability of funds available for the purchase of inputs x_1 and x_2.

Suppose that $K = 1$. This is also a point of least-cost combination on the expansion path, but this is the same as the previously defined point of profit maximization. The point of global profit maximization is a special point along the expansion path where the value of K is equal to 1, indicating that the last dollar spent on each input returns exactly a dollar of revenue. This is probably a point on the expansion path farther out than the point where $K = 3$, where funds for the purchase of input were restricted.

Now suppose that $K = 0$. This is also a point of least-cost combination on the expansion path, but $VMP = pMPP$ where p is the price of the output. If p is positive, the only way that K can be zero is for MPP to be zero. The last dollar spent on each input returns back absolutely nothing in terms of revenue. The point where $VMPx_1/v_1 = VMPx_2/v_2 = 0$ defines the global point of output maximization where the two ridge lines intersect. There is no other point where output is greater. This is a point that normally requires more of both x_1 and x_2 than the global point of profit maximization.

Whenever $0 < K < 1$, the last dollar spent on each input is returning less than its incremental cost. The section of the expansion path between the point of profit maximization and the point of output maximization represents a section where the farmer would never wish to operate. This is despite the fact that the isoquants in this section are curving downward toward the budget or iso-outlay line. For example, a value for K of 0.3 suggests that the last dollar spent on each input returns only 30 cents. The farmer would never wish to use an input at levels beyond the point of profit maximization, despite the fact that funds can be available for the purchase of additional units. Not only is stage III of the production function irrational, but any point that uses more of x_1 and x_2 than the profit-maximizing point in stage II is also irrational.

Finally, suppose that $K < 0$. If input and output prices are positive, this suggests that MPP must be negative. The use of both inputs must exceed the level required to globally maximize output. The last dollar spent on an additional unit of input not only does not return its cost in terms of VMP, but revenues are declining as a result of the incremental use of inputs. A value for K of -0.2 suggests that the last dollar spent on the input results in a reduction in revenue of 20 cents. The total loss from the last dollar spent on the input is $1.00 + $0.20 = $1.20. This is clearly not economic and is stage III for the use of both inputs, since MPP for both inputs is negative. Isoquants are tangent to the iso-outlay line, but are bowed outward (concave to the origin), not inward (convex to the origin). The entrepreneur could increase profit by a reduction in the use of both x_1 and x_2.

7.6 The Production Function for the Bundle

Envision a bundle of the two inputs x_1 and x_2. Suppose that the proportion of each input contained in the bundle is defined by the expansion path. If the expansion path has a constant slope, then as one moves up the expansion path, the proportion of x_1 and x_2 does not change. Suppose that a point on the expansion path requires 2 units of x_1 and 1 unit of x_2. If the expansion path has a constant slope, the point requiring 6 units of x_1 would require 3 units of x_2. The point requiring 8.8 units of x_1 would require 4.4 units of x_2, and so on. The size of the bundle varies, but if the expansion path has a constant slope, the proportion of each input contained in the bundle remains constant. In this example, that constant proportion is 2 units of x_1 to 1 unit of x_2.

Now suppose that a single-input production function is drawn [Figure 7.2(a)]. The difference here is that instead of showing input x_1 on the horizontal axis, the horizontal axis is instead the bundle of x_1 and x_2. Each unit of the bundle consists of 2 units of x_1 and 1 unit of x_2. The production function for the bundle looks very similar to the traditional three stage single-input production function. This production function has a point of output maximization where the MPP of the bundle of x_1 and x_2 is equal to zero. It also has a point of profit maximization, where the VMP of the bundle is exactly equal to the price per unit of the bundle, or the cost of 2 units of x_1 and 1 unit of x_2 taken together.

Now consider a series of isoquants in three dimensions [Figure 7.2(b)]. The input x_1 is on the horizontal axis and x_2 is on the vertical axis. The third dimension is y or output. If one were to look along the expansion path of production surface such as that depicted in Figure 7.2, the shape would correspond exactly to the shape of the production function for the bundle. The

7.6 The Production Function for the Bundle

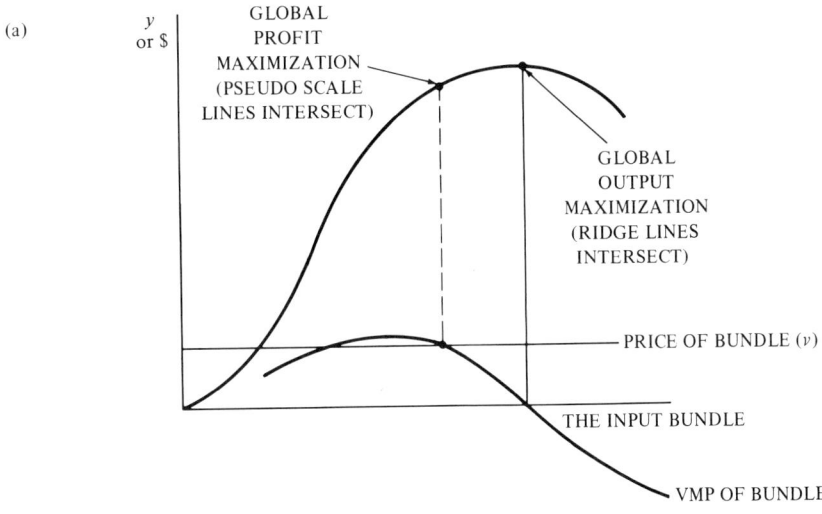

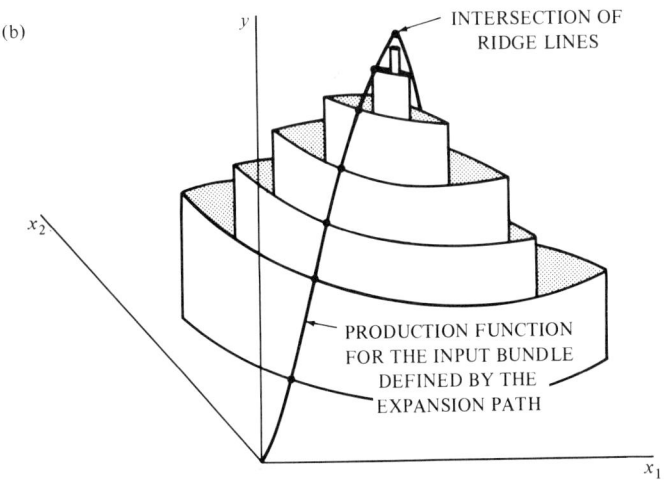

Figure 7.2 Global Output and Profit Maximization for the Bundle

output-maximization point on the production function for the bundle would correspond exactly to the global point of output maximization defined by the center of the series of concentric ring isoquants.

The point of global profit maximization, where the VMP for the bundle equals its cost, would correspond to a point on an isoquant that is on the expansion path but below the point of global output maximization. This is where the farmer would most like to be, in that the point represents the greatest total profits of any possible point. The only reason that a farmer would not operate here would be as the result of a limitation in the availability of dollars needed to purchase such a globally optimal bundle of x_1 and x_2, or some institutional constraint, such as a government farm program, that would prohibit the use of the required amount of one or both of the inputs.

7.7 Pseudo Scale Lines

Recall from Chapter 5 that two families of production functions underlie any series of isoquants. A single-input production function can be obtained for one of the inputs by assuming that the other input is held constant at some fixed level. By making alternative assumptions about the level at which the second input is to be fixed, a series of production functions for the first input can be derived. The family of production functions thus derived each has a maximum. The maximum value for each production function for the first input (x_1) holding the second input (x_2) constant corresponds to a point on ridge line I (where the slope of the isoquant is zero). The maximum value for each production function for the second input (x_2) holding the first input (x_1) constant corresponds to a point on ridge line II (where the slope of the isoquant is infinite).

Now suppose that output has some positive price called p, and the prices for x_1 and x_2 are v_1 and v_2, respectively. Each member of the two families of underlying production functions will have a profit-maximizing level of input use for one input, assuming that the second input is fixed. This is not the global point of profit maximization, since only one input is allowed to vary. For input x_1, this is where $pMPPx_1/v_1 = 1$, assuming that x_2 is fixed at x_2^*. For input x_2, this is where $pMPPx_2/v_2 = 1$, assuming that x_1 is fixed at x_1^*.

If input prices are positive, this profit-maximizing level of input use for each member of the family will require less x_1 or x_2 than did the output-maximizing level of input use. Figure 7.3 illustrates the relationship for input x_1, which is assumed to be on the horizontal axis. A vertical line drawn from the profit-maximizing level of input use to the line that represents the assumed fixed level of the other input (x_2 on the vertical axis) defines also a point on an isoquant. This point will be on an isoquant that lies below the isoquant that defines the ridge line. This isoquant will intersect but not be tangent to the line representing the fixed level of x_2. This is because profit maximization results in less output than does yield maximization.

For input x_1, this point will lie to the left of the ridge line. The greater the price of x_1 (v_1), the farther to the left of the ridge line this point will lie, and the lower the profit-maximizing level of input x_1 and the resulting output from the use of x_1. This procedure can be repeated for each member in the family of the production functions for x_1, by assuming alternative values for the input x_2, which is treated as fixed.

A similar approach can be used for the family of production functions for x_2, assuming that x_1 is held constant at alternative fixed levels. Here the points of profit maximization for x_2 (holding x_1 constant at alternative levels) will occur below the ridge line for the second input along the vertical line defined by the assumption with respect to the quantity of x_1 that is to be used. Again the process can be repeated over and over for varying assumptions this time with regard to the level at which x_1 is to be fixed.

A line connecting all points of profit maximization for one input, assuming the other input to be fixed at some constant level, is called a *pseudo scale line*. Just as there are two ridge lines, so are there two pseudo scale lines, one for each input. If input prices are positive, pseudo scale lines will lie interior to the ridge lines. If inputs were free. the pseudo scale lines would lie on top of

7.7 Pseudo Scale Lines

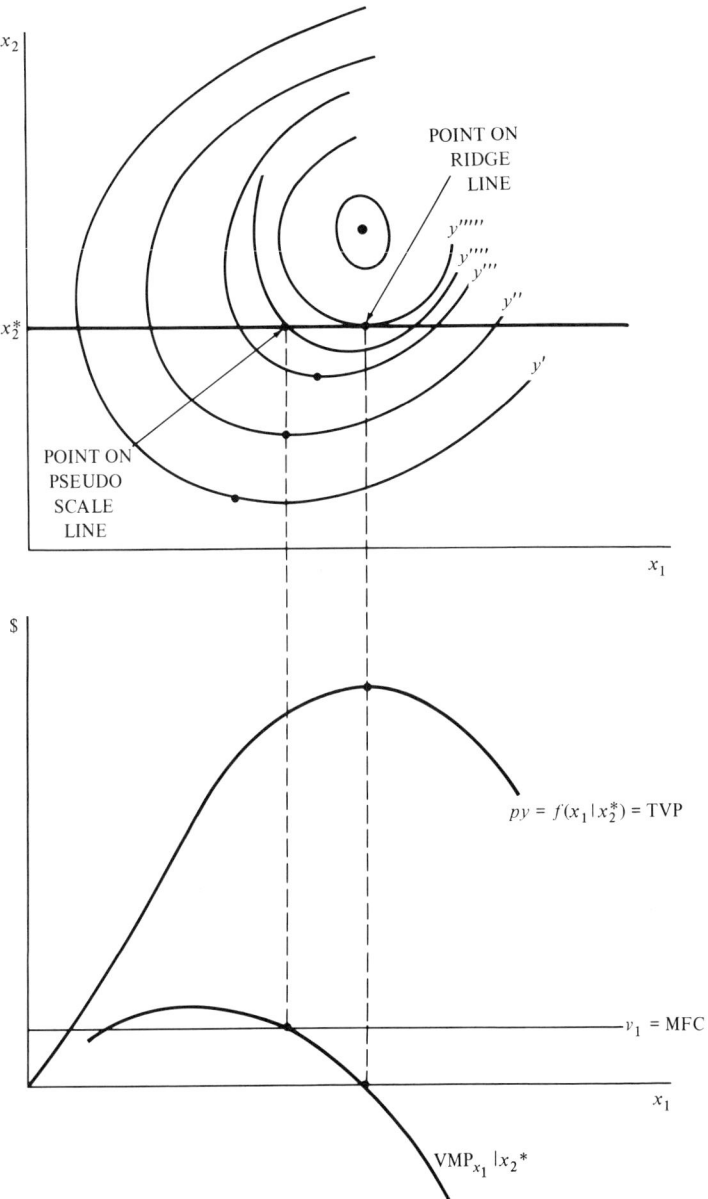

Figure 7.3 Deriving a Point on a Pseudo Scale Line

the ridge lines, just as profits would be maximized by maximizing output. The greater the input price, the farther will be the pseudo scale line for that input from the ridge line for that input.

The most important characteristic of pseudo scale lines is that the two lines intersect at the global point of profit maximization. The intersection of the pseudo scale lines defines precisely the point on the expansion path where profits are greatest. There is no other point more profitable (Figure 7.4).

Maximization Subject to Budget Constraints

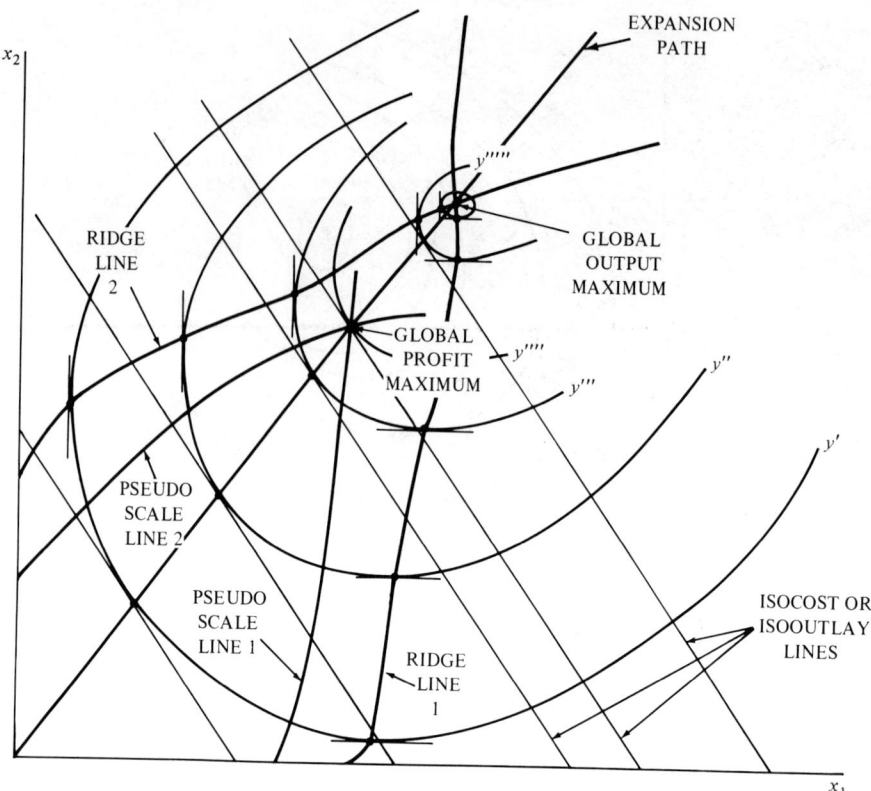

Figure 7.4 Complete Factor-Factor Model

The global point of profit maximization, where profits are greatest when both inputs can be varied, is at once a point on the expansion path, a point of least-cost combination, and a point where the pseudo scale lines intersect. There is no other point where these conditions are met. Any other point on a pseudo scale line is no longer on the expansion path, and the expansion path meets both pseudo scale lines only once.

Another way of looking at the concept of the pseudo scale line is in relation to the equimarginal returns equations. The global point of profit maximization is defined by

$$VMPx_1/v_1 = VMPx_2/v_2 = 1 \qquad (7.21)$$

This is the point where the pseudo scale lines intersect.

Points on the pseudo scale line for input x_1 are defined by

$$VMPx_1/v_1 = 1 \qquad VMPx_2/v_2 \geq 1 \qquad (7.22)$$

If

$$VMPx_1/v_1 = 1 \quad \text{and} \quad VMPx_2/v_2 > 1 \qquad (7.23)$$

the farmer could increase profit by increasing the use of x_2. This could be accomplished either by increasing total outlay for x_2 until the global profit-maximizing condition was met for both inputs, or by a reduction in the use of x_1 until the expansion path condition that

$$VMPx_1/v_1 = VMPx_2/v_2 = K \qquad (7.24)$$

is met. The closer K could be brought to 1, the closer the farmer would be to maximum global profit.

Points on the pseudo scale line for input x_2 are defined by

$$VMPx_1/v_1 \geq 1 \qquad VMPx_2/v_2 = 1 \qquad (7.25)$$

If $VMPx_1/v_1 > 1$, profits could be increased by increasing the use of x_1 such that the expansion path condition is again met. Again, the closer K is brought to 1, the closer the farmer would be to maximum profit.

7.8 Summary of Marginal Conditions and Concluding Comments

Table 7.2 summarizes the marginal conditions associated with the ridge lines, expansion path, and pseudo scale lines. These marginal conditions comprise the decision rules for the farmer in choosing the amount and combination of inputs to be used in a two input, single-output, factor-factor setting.

Table 7.2 Marginal Conditions for Ridge Lines, the Expansion Path, and Pseudo Scale Lines

Condition	Comment
On the expansion path	
$VMPx_1/v_1 = VMPx_2/v_2 = 0$	Global output maximization
$VMPx_1/v_1 = VMPx_2/v_2 < 0$	Stage III for both inputs; the profit-maximizing farmer would not operate here
$VMPx_1/v_1 = VMPx_2/v_2 = 0 < K < 1$	Between profit and output maximum; farmer would not operate here
$VMPx_1/v_1 = VMPx_2/v_2 = 1$	Global profit maximization; point of least-cost combination
$VMPx_1/v_1 = VMPx_2/v_2 > 1$	Point of least-cost combination; not global profit maximization
On pseudo scale lines	
$VMPx_1/v_1 = 1 \; VMPx_2/v_2 > 1$	Point on pseudo scale line for input x_1; not global profit maximization
$VMPx_1/v_1 > 1 \; VMPx_2/v_2 = 1$	Point on pseudo scale line for input x_2; not global profit maximization
$VMPx_1/v_1 = 1 \; VMPx_2/v_2 = 1$	Global profit maximization and on the expansion path.
On the ridge lines	
$VMPx_1/v_1 = 0 \; VMPx_2/v_2 = 0$	Global output maximization and on the expansion path
$VMPx_1/v_1 = 0 \; VMPx_2/v_2 \neq 0$	On ridge line I for input x_1
$VMPx_1/v_1 \neq 0 \; VMPx_2/v_2 = 0$	On ridge line II for input x_2

This chapter has developed graphically and algebraically the fundamental conditions for the least-cost combination of inputs with the factor-factor model. The expansion path along which a farmer would expand or contract the scale of operation was derived. All points along the expansion path represent points of least-cost combination for the farmer. Both the global point of output maximization and the global point of profit maximization are on the expansion path. All points on the expansion path are points of least-cost combination of inputs as long as isoquants are convex to the origin. However, there is but a single point of global profit maximization for the farmer, as defined by the point where the pseudo scale lines intersect the expansion path.

If the farmer were given a choice, he or she would prefer to operate on the expansion path, for it is here that a given level of output can be produced at the lowest possible cost. A point on the expansion path is sometimes referred to as a point of least-cost combination. If the farmer were on the expansion path and a sufficient number of dollars were available for the purchase of x_1 and x_2, the farmer would prefer to be at the point of profit maximization where the pseudo scale lines intersect.

The farmer would never choose a level of input use on the expansion path beyond the point of profit maximization, for at any point on the expansion path beyond the point of profit maximization, the last dollar spent on inputs returns less than a dollar. The condition is analogous to using an input at a level beyond the point of profit maximization in the single-input factor-product model. In both instances, the last dollar spent on the input (or inputs) returns less than a dollar. Only if there is a limitation on the availability of dollars for the purchase of the two inputs would the farmer choose to operate on the expansion path but with an operation smaller than that needed to achieve global profit maximization.

Chapter 8 will develop the same set of decision rules for points of least-cost combination and profit maximization. However, rather using primarily graphics and algebra as a vehicle for presentation, Chapter 8 uses basic calculus and relies heavily on the maximization and minimization principles presented in Chapter 6.

Problems and Exercises

1. Consider the following table, given in Problem 1, Chapter 5:

Combination	Units of x_1	Units of x_2	$MRSx_1x_2$	$MRSx_2x_1$
A	10	1		
B	5	2		
C	3	3		
D	2	4		
E	1.5	5		

a. Suppose that the price of x_1 and x_2 is each a dollar. What combination of x_1 and x_2 would be used to achieve the least-cost combination of inputs needed to produce 100 bushels of corn?

7.8 Summary of Marginal Conditions and Concluding Comments

b. Suppose that the price of x_2 increased to $2. What combination of x_1 and x_2 would be used to produce 100 bushels of corn?

c. If the farmer was capable of producing 100 bushels of corn when the price of x_1 and x_2 were both $1, would he or she necessarily also be able to produce 100 bushels of corn when the price of x_2 increases to $2? Explain.

2. Assume that a farmer has available $200. What is the slope of the isocost line when:

a. $v_1 = \$1;\ v_2 = \$2.00$?
b. $v_1 = \$3;\ v_2 = \$1.75$?

3. Assume that the following conditions hold. What action should the farmer take in each instance?

a. $VMPx_1/v_1 = VMPx_2/v_2 = 3$
b. $VMPx_1/v_1 = VMPx_2/v_2 = 5$
c. $VMPx_1/v_1 = VMPx_2/v_2 = 1$
d. $VMPx_1/v_1 = VMPx_2/v_2 = 0.2$
e. $VMPx_1/v_1 = VMPx_2/v_2 = 0$
f. $VMPx_1/v_1 = VMPx_2/v_2 = -0.15$
g. $VMPx_1/v_1 = 9;\ VMPx_2/v_2 = 5$
h. $VMPx_1/v_1 = -2;\ VMPx_2/v_2 = 5$
i. $VMPx_1/v_1 = 2;\ VMPx_2/v_2 = 1$
j. $VMPx_1/v_1 = 1;\ VMPx_2/v_2 = 0$
k. $VMPx_1/v_1 = -1;\ VMPx_2/v_2 = 1$

8
Further Topics in Constrained Maximization and Minimization

This chapter presents the factor-factor model with the use of the maximization and minimization mathematics developed in Chapter 6. In many respects, this chapter is very similar to Chapter 7. The same fundamental conclusions with respect to the correct allocation of inputs are developed. However, the presentation here relies primarily on mathematics rather than the graphical and algebraic presentation of Chapter 7. The basic similarity between this chapter and Chapter 7 with regard to conclusions is reassuring. The use of mathematics as a tool for presenting production theory does not mean that the marginal principles change. Rather, the mathematics provides further insight as to why the rules developed in Section 7.8 work the way they do. The chapter provides some applications of the factor-factor model to problems in designing a landlord–tenant lease arrangement, and to a problem involving maximization when the government imposes an acreage allotment.

Key Terms and Definitions:

Constrained Optimization
Classical Optimization Technique
Objective Function
Constraint
Joseph-Louis Lagrange
Lagrange's Function
Lagrangian Multiplier
Implicit (Imputed) Value
Shadow Price

Corner Solution
First-Order Conditions
Second-Order Conditions
Constrained Revenue Maximization
Constrained Output Maximization
Constrained Cost Minimization
Lease Arrangement
Acreage Allotment

8.1 Simple Mathematics of Global Profit Maximization

Assume that a farmer is searching to operate at the global point of profit maximization. The farmer would prefer to use the amounts and combination of inputs where total profits (revenue less costs) are greatest. Diagrammatically,

8.1 Simple Mathematics of Global Profit Maximization

the farmer would like to operate at the point on the expansion path where the pseudo scale lines intersect. Revenue from the sale of an output (y) such as corn can be defined as

$$R = py \tag{8.1}$$

where R = revenue from the sale of the corn
p = output price
y = quantity of corn produced

Suppose also that the production function for corn is

$$y = f(x_1, x_2) \tag{8.2}$$

For the moment, assume that only two inputs are used in the production of corn, or that all other inputs are taken as already owned by the entrepreneur.
Another way of writing the revenue function is

$$R = pf(x_1, x_2), \tag{8.3}$$

since

$$y = f(x_1, x_2). \tag{8.4}$$

Now suppose that each input can be purchased at the going market prices (v_1 for x_1; v_2 for x_2), and the farmer can purchase as much or as little as desired. Therefore, the cost function is

$$C = v_1x_1 + v_2x_2 \tag{8.5}$$

The problem faced by a farmer interested in globally maximizing profits, or finding the point where the pseudo scale lines intersect, could be expressed as a profit function

$$\Pi = R - C \tag{8.6}$$

$$\Pi = py - v_1x_1 - v_2x_2 \tag{8.7}$$

$$\Pi = pf(x_1, x_2) - v_1x_1 - v_2x_2 \tag{8.8}$$

$$\partial\Pi/\partial x_1 = pf_1 - v_1 = 0 \tag{8.9}$$

$$\partial\Pi/\partial x_2 = pf_2 - v_2 = 0 \tag{8.10}$$

$$pf_1/v_1 = pf_2/v_2 = 1 \tag{8.11}$$

The farmer interested in maximizing profit would equate the VMP (pf_1 or pf_2) divided by the price of the input. To maximize profits, this equality should be equal to 1.

8.2 Constrained Revenue Maximization

If the farmer is unable to globally maximize profits, the next best alternative is to find a point of least-cost combination. The least-cost combination of inputs represents a point of revenue maximization subject to the constraint imposed by the availability of dollars for the purchase of inputs. The graphical presentation in Chapter 7 revealed that points of least-cost combination were found on the expansion path. Here the same points of least-cost combination are found with the aid of mathematics.

Any problem involving maximization or minimization subject to constraints can be termed a *constrained optimization problem*. The constrained optimization problem consists of two component parts: (1) the objective function to be maximized or minimized, and (2) the function representing the constraints on the objective function. Suppose that the objective function faced by a farmer is to maximize revenue from the sale of corn. The objective function to be maximized is

$$R = py \tag{8.12}$$

or

$$R = pf(x_1, x_2) \tag{8.13}$$

The limitation or restriction in the availability of dollars for the purchase of inputs x_1 and x_2 is represented by the expression

$$C^\circ = v_1 x_1 + v_2 x_2 \tag{8.14}$$

where C° is some fixed number of dollars that the farmer has available for the purchase of inputs x_1 and x_2.

The approach used here is sometimes referred to as the *classical optimization technique*. This approach uses Lagrange's function to solve problems involving the maximization or minimization of a function subject to constraints. Joseph-Louis Lagrange was a French mathematician and astronomer who lived from 1736 to 1813. *Lagrange's function* consists of an objective function and a constraint. A new variable is also added. This variable is called *Lagrange's multiplier*. A Greek letter such as λ or μ is often used to represent Lagrange's multiplier.

A general expression for Lagrange's function L is

$$L = \text{(objective function to be maximized or minimized)} \\ + \lambda(\text{constraint on the objective function}) \tag{8.15}$$

The Lagrangian representing revenue from farmer's production of corn (y) subject to the constraint imposed by the availability of inputs (x_1 and x_2) used in the production of corn is

$$L = py + \lambda(C^\circ - v_1 x_1 - v_2 x_2) \tag{8.16}$$

8.2 Constrained Revenue Maximization

or

$$L = pf(x_1, x_2) + \lambda(C° - v_1x_1 - v_2x_2) \tag{8.17}$$

The necessary conditions for the maximization or minimization of the objective function subject to the constraints are the first-order conditions. These conditions require that the first derivatives of L with respect to x_1, x_2, and λ be found and then be set equal to zero. Thus the necessary conditions are

$$\partial L/\partial x_1 = pf_1 - \lambda v_1 = 0 \tag{8.18}$$

$$\partial L/\partial x_1 = pf_2 - \lambda v_2 = 0 \tag{8.19}$$

$$\partial L/\partial \lambda = C° - v_1x_1 - v_2x_2 = 0 \tag{8.20}$$

where $f_1 = \partial y/\partial x_1 = MPPx_1$, the marginal product of x_1 holding x_2 constant
$f_2 = \partial y/\partial x_2 = MPPx_2$, the marginal product of x_2 holding x_1 constant
pf_1 and pf_2 can be interpreted as the VMP of x_1 and x_2, respectively
v_1 and v_2 are input prices or the marginal factor costs (MFC) for x_1 and x_2

Equations (8.18) and (8.19) appear to be very similar to the profit-maximizing conditions developed in Section 8.1, but the newly added Lagrangian multiplier now enters. The third equation indicates that when the objective function has been maximized, all dollars available for the purchase of x_1 and x_2 will have been spent. Lagrange's method requires that all dollars available for the purchase of the inputs be spent on the inputs. The farmer therefore does not have the option of not spending some of the budgeted amount.

Equations (8.18) and (8.19) can be rearranged such that

$$pf_1/v_1 = \lambda \tag{8.21}$$

and

$$pf_2/v_2 = \lambda \tag{8.22}$$

Equations (8.18) and (8.19) might also be divided by each other such that

$$pf_1/pf_2 = \lambda v_1/\lambda v_2 \tag{8.23}$$

or

$$pMPPx_1/pMPPx_2 = \lambda v_1/\lambda v_2 \tag{8.24}$$

or

$$f_1/f_2 = v_1/v_2 \tag{8.25}$$

or

$$MPPx_1/MPPx_2 = v_1/v_2 \tag{8.26}$$

or

$$dx_2/dx_1 = v_1/v_2 \tag{8.27}$$

Equations (8.23) to (8.27) precisely define a point of tangency between the isoquant and the budget constraint. The first-order conditions presented here represent a single point on the expansion path. This point is the tangency between a specific isoquant and the iso-outlay line associated with an expenditure on inputs of exactly $C°$ dollars.

The Lagrangian multiplier λ is a number, and equations (8.18) and (8.19) can also be set equal to each other such that

$$pf_1/v_1 = pf_2/v_2 = \lambda \tag{8.28}$$

The meaning of λ suddenly becomes clear, for λ is the constant K as developed in Chapter 7. The term pf_1 is the *VMP* of input x_1, or the value of output from the incremental unit of x_1. The term pf_2 is the *VMP* or value of output from the incremental unit of input x_2. The v_1 and v_2 represent costs of the incremental units of x_1 and x_2. The Lagrangian multiplier represents the ratio of the marginal value of the input in terms of its contribution to revenue on the farm (*VMP*) relative to its marginal cost (*MFC*), when the inputs are allocated as indicated by the conditions that exist along the expansion path.

In this example, the Lagrangian multiplier can be interpreted as the imputed or implicit value of last dollar spent on the input. It represents the worth of the incremental dollar spent on inputs to the firm if the inputs are allocated according to the expansion path conditions.

The Lagrangian multiplier can also be thought of as a shadow price. The cost of the last dollar spent on an input is $1.00. The value of that dollar is the *VMP* of the dollar spent on the purchase of the input. The shadow price may or may not be the same as the price of the input. If $VMPx_1$ and v_1 are equal, the last dollar spent returns precisely a dollar to the firm. If this is also true for input x_2, Lagrange's method yields exactly the same result as the profit-maximization solution presented in Section 8.1.

As was also true for the value of K, a value for the Lagrangian multiplier of 1 defines the point where the pseudo scale lines intersect. If this were to be the case, the farmer would need to have precisely the correct total number of dollars ($C°$) available for the purchase of x_1 and x_2 that would result in a Lagrangian multiplier of 1, since Lagranges method requires that all dollars available for the purchase of the inputs be spent. A farmer would not necessarily know how many total dollars would be needed.

8.2 Constrained Revenue Maximization

Lagrange's method tells the farmer nothing about how much should be spent in total on inputs. Lagrange's method merely assumes that some given fixed amount of funds in total are available for the purchase of inputs. Lagrange's method then provides the decision rule with respect to how the available funds should be allocated in the purchase of the two inputs. Lagrange's method provides a formal derivation of the equimarginal return principle. The decision rule developed with the aid of Lagrange's method states that the farmer should allocate dollars available for the purchase of the two inputs such that the last dollar spent on each input returns the same amount (λ) for both inputs. This rule might also be represented as

$$VMPx_1/MFCx_1 = VMPx_2/MFCx_2 = \lambda \qquad (8.29)$$

where $VMPx_1$ and $VMPx_2$ are the values of the marginal product of x_1 and x_2, and $MFCx_1$ and $MFCx_2$ are the respective marginal factor costs. In a purely competitive environment, the respective marginal factor costs are the input prices.

Another way of defining the Lagrangian multiplier in this example is that it is the change in revenue associated with an additional dollar added to the budget outlay C. In other words, λ is dR/dC, where R is revenue. The Lagrangian is the revenue function for values that satisfy the cost constraint. Therefore, $dR/dC = dL/dC = \lambda$.

There is absolutely nothing built into Lagrange's method that ensures a λ of 1, greater that 1, or any other value. Lagrange's method merely requires the ratios of VMP to MFC to be the same for all inputs. This is equivalent to finding a point on the expansion path associated with the budgeted outlay represented by the constraint.

Diagrammatically, if one input were cheap enough relative to the other input, it might be possible to find a point of least-cost combination that uses only the cheaper input and requires none of the more expensive input. (Isoquants would also have to intersect the axis for the cheaper input if this were to be possible.) However, Lagrange's method rules out the possibility of a corner solution in which production can take place in the absence of one of the inputs.

The mathematical reason for this is that the derivatives are not defined on the axes. Figure 8.1 illustrates the problem. If isoquants intersect the axes and if certain relative price ratios between v_1 and v_2 prevail, it might be optimal to use none of the relatively high priced input. The budget line depicting the corner solution may or may not be tangent to the isoquant, and thus may or may not have a slope equal to the slope of the isoquant.

The solution to Lagrange's method assumes that the budget constraint is tangent to the isoquant and that both inputs must be used in strictly positive amounts. This assumption is consistent with an underlying production function that is multiplicative (such as $y = ax_1^{0.5}x_2^{0.5}$) but not additive (such as $y = ax_1 + bx_1^2 + cx_2 + dx_2^2$), since an additive function can produce positive quantities of output even in the absence of one of the inputs.

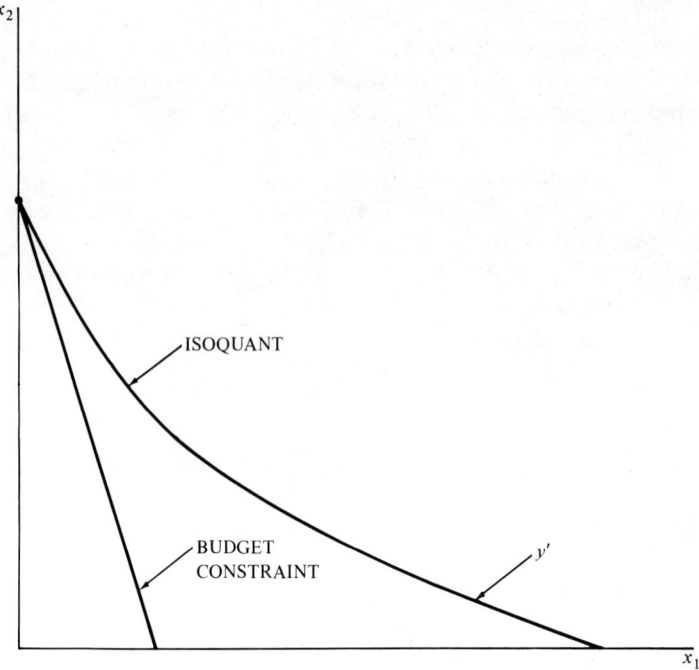

Figure 8.1 Corner Solution

8.3 Second-Order Conditions

The first derivatives of the Lagrangian are the necessary but not sufficient conditions needed to maximize revenue subject to a cost constraint. These conditions are

$$pf_1 - \lambda v_1 = 0 \tag{8.30}$$

$$pf_2 - \lambda v_2 = 0 \tag{8.31}$$

$$C^\circ - v_1 x_1 - v_2 x_2 = 0 \tag{8.32}$$

These first-order conditions define the points of tangency between the isoquant and the budget constraint. However, it is possible on the basis of these conditions for revenue to be minimum, not maximum. Consider a point of tangency between an isoquant and a budget constraint that occurs at a level of input use beyond the point of global output maximization. This point represents minimum, not maximum, revenue from the outlay represented by the budget constraint. To ensure that revenue is maximum, rather than minimum, the second-order conditions are needed. Equations (8.30), (8.31), and (8.32) are each differentiated with respect to x_1, x_2 and λ. Define

$$\partial f_i / \partial x_j = f_{ij} \qquad i, j = 1, 2 \tag{8.33}$$

Then

$$\partial(8.30)/\partial x_1 = pf_{11}$$
$$\partial(8.30)/\partial x_2 = pf_{12}$$
$$\partial(8.30)/\partial \lambda = -v_1$$

$$\partial(8.31)/\partial x_1 = pf_{21} = pf_{12} \text{ (by Young's theorem)}$$
$$\partial(8.31)/\partial x_2 = pf_{22}$$
$$\partial(8.31)/\partial \lambda = -v_2$$

$$\partial(8.32)/\partial x_1 = -v_1$$
$$\partial(8.32)/\partial x_2 = -v_2$$
$$\partial(8.32)/\partial \lambda = 0$$

Form the matrix

$$\begin{matrix} pf_{11} & pf_{12} & -v_1 \\ pf_{12} & pf_{22} & -v_2 \\ -v_1 & -v_2 & 0 \end{matrix} \tag{8.34}$$

The determinant of the matrix (8.34) is

$$pf_{11}pf_{22} \cdot 0 + pf_{12}(-v_2)(-v_1) + pf_{12}(-v_2)(-v_1) \\ - [(-v_1)pf_{22}(-v_1) + (-v_2)(-v_2)pf_{11} + pf_{12}pf_{12} \cdot 0] \tag{8.35}$$

$$= 2pf_{12}v_1v_2 - pf_{22}v_1^2 - pf_{11}v_2^2 \tag{8.36}$$

$$= p[2f_{12}v_1v_2 - f_{22}v_1^2 - f_{11}v_2^2] \tag{8.37}$$

If the farmer is using only two inputs, equation (8.37) must be positive to ensure that revenue has been maximized subject to the budget constraint. The first- and second-order conditions when taken together are the necessary and sufficient conditions for the maximization of revenue subject to the budget constraint. The first-order conditions position the farmer on the expansion path. The second-order conditions assure a maximum rather than a minimum or a saddle point.

8.4 Interpretation of the Lagrangian Multiplier

The interpretation of the Lagrangian multiplier is much the same as the interpretation of the value for K developed in Chapter 7. Economics rules out some potential points on the expansion path. For example, suppose that the farmer were operating in a position where

$$VMPx_1/v_1 = VMPx_2/v_2 = \lambda = -2.8 \tag{8.38}$$

Equation (8.38) is beyond the point of output maximization for both inputs, since λ is negative. This possibility is ruled out on the basis of the economic logic outlined in Chapter 7. Lagranges method will not find an optimal solution with a negative λ, on the expansion path, but beyond the point of output maximization.

As suggested in Chapter 7, if λ were exactly zero, the farmer would be operating at precisely the global point of output maximization with respect to both inputs. Unless both inputs were free, a farmer interested in maximizing profits would never operate here either, despite the fact that this solution is permitted by the mathematics of the Lagrangian method.

As also was indicated in Chapter 7, a λ of precisely 1 would coincide exactly with the global point of profit maximization where the pseudo scale lines intersect on the expansion path. For Lagrange's constrained optimization problem to lead to this solution, the farmer would need a priori to have precisely the amount of dollars allocated for the purchase of x_1 and x_2 that would correspond to the budget outlay line that cuts through this point, and this would be highly unlikely.

If a farmer is interested in maximizing profits, he or she need only maximize the profit function, or the difference between revenue and costs. The solution provides both the total outlay that should be made for both x_1 and x_2 as well as indicating how these expenditures should be allocated between the two inputs. The constrained revenue maximization problem takes the total outlay to be spent on both inputs as fixed and given, and determines how this outlay should be allocated between the two inputs.

Values for λ between zero and 1 are points on the expansion path between the point where the pseudo scale lines intersect (and profits are maximum) and the point where the ridge lines intersect (and output is maximum). Except perhaps at very low levels of input use, λ exceeds one at any point on the expansion path inside the point of global profit maximization. The Lagrangian multiplier represents the ratio of *VMP* to *MFC* for the input bundle as defined by the proportions along the expansion path. This means that at any point on the expansion path that requires less x_1 and x_2 than the profit-maximizing point, the contribution of each input to revenue exceeds the cost. In general, the value of λ declines as one moves outward along the expansion path and as the budgeted outlay for the purchase of x_1 and x_2 is increased. This is because x_1 and x_2 become less and less productive as more and more units are used (Figure 7.2).

8.5 Constrained Output Maximization

The problem of finding the least-cost combination of inputs can also be set up as a problem with the objective of maximizing output (not revenue) subject to the same budget constraint. The solution is very similar to the constrained revenue maximization problem, but the interpretation of the Lagrangian multiplier differs.

Suppose that the objective is to maximize output y. Output is generated by the production function

$$y = f(x_1, x_2) \tag{8.39}$$

8.5 Constrained Output Maximization

The constraint is again

$$C^\circ = v_1x_1 + v_2x_2. \tag{8.40}$$

The new Lagrangian is

$$L = f(x_1, x_2) + \theta(C^\circ - v_1x_1 - v_2x_2) \tag{8.41}$$

where θ is the new Lagrangian multiplier. The corresponding first-order conditions are

$$f_1 - \theta v_1 = 0 \tag{8.42}$$

$$f_2 - \theta v_2 = 0 \tag{8.43}$$

$$C^\circ - v_1x_1 - v_2x_2 = 0 \tag{8.44}$$

By dividing equation (8.42) by equation (8.43), the familiar result that

$$f_1/f_2 = MRSx_1x_2 = v_1/v_2 \tag{8.45}$$

is obtained. Equation (8.45) is the same as for the revenue-maximization problem. However, by rearranging equations (8.42) and (8.43), we obtain

$$f_1/v_1 = f_2/v_2 = \theta \tag{8.46}$$

$$MPPx_1/v_1 = MPPx_2/v_2 = \theta \tag{8.47}$$

Maximization of output subject to the budget constraint requires that the *MPP* for both inputs divided by the respective input prices be equal to θ, the Lagrangian multiplier. In this case, θ represents the physical quantity of output, not revenue, arising from the last dollar spent on each input. The interpretation of a particular value for θ is not as clear for the output-maximization problem as for the revenue maximization problem. For example, a θ of 1 indicates that the last dollar spent on each input returns 1 physical unit of output.

For example, suppose the output is corn that sells for $4.00 per bushel. Then the last dollar spent returns $4.00. To correctly interpret the Lagrangian multiplier, it is necessary to know the price of the output. The optimal value for the Lagrangian multiplier θ at the global point of profit maximization is $1/p$, where p is the price of the output. Or, more generally, θ from the constrained output-maximization problem equals λ/p from the constrained revenue maximization problem.

The equation

$$MPPx_1/v_1 = MPPx_2/v_2 = \theta \tag{8.48}$$

can be multiplied by the price of the output, which results in

$$pMPPx_1/v_1 = pMPPx_2/v_2 = p\theta \tag{8.49}$$

Clearly, $p\theta = \lambda$ from the constrained revenue-maximization problem.

The second-order conditions for the constrained output-maximization problem are no different from the second-order conditions for the constrained revenue-maximization problem, since dividing by a positive output price will not change the required sign. The second-order conditions for the revenue-maximization problem [equation (8.37)] required that

$$p[2f_{12}v_1v_2 - f_{22}v_1^2 - f_{11}v_2^2] > 0 \qquad (8.50)$$

The constrained output-maximization problem requires that

$$2f_{12}v_1v_2 - f_{22}v_1^2 - f_{11}v_2^2 > 0 \qquad (8.51)$$

8.6 Cost-Minimization Subject to a Revenue Constraint

The problem of finding a point on the expansion path representing the least-cost combination of inputs can also be constructed as a problem of minimizing cost subject to a revenue constraint.

The objective function is to minimize cost:

$$C^\circ = v_1 x_1 + v_2 x_2 \qquad (8.52)$$

subject to the constraint that revenue be some fixed amount R°:

$$R^\circ = py \qquad (8.53)$$

or

$$R^\circ = pf(x_1, x_2) \qquad (8.55)$$

The Lagrangian is

$$L = v_1 x_1 + v_2 x_2 + \mu[R^\circ - pf(x_1, x_2)] \qquad (8.55)$$

The first-order conditions are

$$v_1 - \mu p f_1 = 0 \qquad (8.56)$$

$$v_2 - \mu p f_2 = 0 \qquad (8.57)$$

$$R^\circ - pf(x_1, x_2) = 0 \qquad (8.58)$$

or

$$v_1 = \mu p f_1 \qquad (8.59)$$

$$v_2 = \mu p f_2 \qquad (8.60)$$

8.6 Cost-Minimization Subject to a Revenue Constraint

or

$$v_1/pf_1 = v_2/pf_2 = \mu \tag{8.61}$$

or

$$v_1/pMPPx_1 = v_2/pMPPx_2 = \mu \tag{8.62}$$

Compared with the constrained revenue-maximization problem, the first-order conditions appear to be inverted. In this instance, the Lagrangian multiplier is the increase in cost associated with the incremental unit of output. A value for the Lagrangian multiplier of 1 would again indicate the profit-maximizing position, in that the last dollar of revenue cost the farm firm exactly $1. Points of least-cost combination inside the profit-maximizing position now imply a Lagrangian multiplier of less than 1, and a Lagrangian multiplier of greater than 1 implies that inputs have been used beyond the point of profit maximization but less than output maximization. The Lagrangian multiplier approaches infinity as output maximization is achieved, but assumes negative values of less than infinity beyond the point of output maximization. Lagrange's method will not generate a solution calling for negative values of the Lagrangian multiplier, and at precisely the point of output maximization, the Lagrangian multiplier is undefined, since the MPP for both inputs is zero.

It is clear that μ from the constrained cost-minimization problem is $1/\lambda$ from the constrained revenue-maximization problem. Moreover, λ from the constrained revenue-maximization problem is $1/\mu$ from the constrained cost-minimization problem.

The second-order conditions differ in that they must assure a minimum rather than a maximum. Again, each of the first-order conditions are differentiated with respect to x_1, x_2, and μ, and a matrix is formed:

$$\begin{matrix} -\mu p f_{11} & -\mu p f_{12} & -p f_1 \\ -\mu p f_{12} & -\mu p f_{22} & -p f_2 \\ -p f_1 & -p f_2 & 0 \end{matrix} \tag{8.63}$$

The second-order conditions require that

$$\mu p^3 f_1 f_1 f_{22} + \mu p^3 f_2 f_2 f_{11} - 2\mu p^3 f_2 f_1 f_{12} < 0 \tag{8.64}$$

By substituting $f_1 = v_1/\mu p$ and $f_2 = v_2/\mu p$, the result is

$$(p/\mu)(f_{22}v_1^2 + f_{11}v_2^2 - 2f_{12}v_1v_2) < 0 \tag{8.65}$$

or

$$(p/\mu)(2f_{12}v_1v_2 - f_{22}v_1^2 - f_{11}v_2^2) > 0 \tag{8.66}$$

If $\mu > 0$, the required signs on the second-order conditions are the same as those needed for the constrained revenue-maximization problem.

8.7 An Application in the Design of a Lease

Heady proposed a model designed to determine a lease arrangement for a farm that would be optimal from the standpoint of both the landlord and the tenant. This section is an adaptation of that model and illustrates an application of the factor-factor model in the design of contractual arrangements between landlords and tenants. Landlords can elect to charge a cash rent for the use of the land by the tenant, or they might elect a lease arrangement in which returns and costs are shared by the tenant and the landlord.

8.7.1 Cash rent

Consider first the case in which the landlord charges a fixed cash rent per acre to the tenant. The landlord is no longer concerned with the success or failure of the tenant in growing crops, except to the extent that a crop failure might jeopardize the tenant's ability to cover the cash rent. The landlord has broader concerns of a longer-run nature than does the tenant, relating to the tenant's interest in and ability to keeping up the productivity of the land through activities such as maintenance of soil fertility.

Assume that the tenant is interested in a least-cost combination solution in factor-factor space. If the cash rent were free, the tenant would be found on the expansion path. With the imposition of a positive cash rent, the tenant would still be found on the expansion path. However, in a constrained optimization framework, since the cash rent is paid, the availability of dollars for the purchase of other variable inputs has declined. In other words, the value of constraint ($C°$ in the Lagrangian formulation of the factor-factor model) for the tenant has declined. This means that less money will be available for the purchase of inputs such as fertilizer that might be needed to maintain soil fertility.

The cash rent lease has the desirable feature of not altering the usual first-order conditions for constrained revenue maximization in terms of the mix of inputs to be used in the short-run or single-season planning horizon. Landlords must be concerned that the availability of dollars for the purchase of inputs will be more restricted and the variable input bundle X used on the farm will become smaller as the cash rent increases. Renters under a cash rent arrangement will probably underutilize inputs that have no immediate effect on output but which would affect output over a long planning horizon, such as soil conservation measures designed to improve the long-run productivity of the soil. The implementation of such measures by the tenant depends in large measure on the tenant's expectations with regard to how many years the farm will be available for rent, as well as the specific obligations cited in the lease agreement.

8.7.2 Shared rental arrangements

For purposes of exposition, the analysis is presented assuming that the farmer utilizes only two inputs, but the same analysis could be applied to a case with more than two inputs. In the absence of the shared rental arrangement, the profit function is

$$\Pi = pf(x_1, x_2) - v_1 x_1 - v_2 x_2 \tag{8.67}$$

8.7 An Application in the Design of a Lease

The corresponding first-order conditions require that

$$pf_1 = v_1 \tag{8.68}$$

$$pf_2 = v_2 \tag{8.69}$$

where p = price of the output
x_1, x_2 = inputs
v_1, v_2 = prices for x_1 and x_2, respectively
f_1, f_2 = marginal products of x_1 and x_2, respectively

First-order conditions require that the *VMP*'s for each input be equal to the corresponding factor price.

Consider first a lease arrangement in which the landlord gets back a share of gross revenues from the farm but pays none of the expenses. A shared rental arrangement might be one in which the landlord gets one-fourth of the crop, with the tenant getting three-fourths. Assume that both the landlord and tenant are interested in maximizing profits. The landlord's profit function is

$$\Pi = \tfrac{1}{4} p f(x_1, x_2) \tag{8.70}$$

where $f(x_1, x_2) = y$, the output of the crop, p is the price of y, and x_1 and x_2 are two inputs. The landlord gets one-fourth of the revenue but pays no costs.

The tenant's profit function is

$$\Pi = \tfrac{3}{4} p f(x_1, x_2) - v_1 x_1 - v_2 x_2 \tag{8.71}$$

where v_1 and v_2 are the prices on inputs x_1 and x_2, respectively.

The landlord prefers that the inputs be used until the point where

$$\tfrac{1}{4} p f_1 = 0 \tag{8.72}$$

$$\tfrac{1}{4} p f_2 = 0 \tag{8.73}$$

where f_1 and f_2 are the marginal products of x_1 and x_2, respectively.

The landlord is interested in making the marginal product of x_1 and x_2 zero (or $f_1 = f_2 = 0$), or making the tenant maximize output or *TPP* on the farm, rather than profits. The landlord's share under this arrangement is greatest if output is maximized. However, the point is on the expansion path.

The tenant prefers that inputs be used until the point where

$$\tfrac{3}{4} p f_1 = v_1 \tag{8.74}$$

$$\tfrac{3}{4} p f_2 = v_2 \tag{8.75}$$

The usual first-order conditions for profit maximization are

$$pf_1 = v_1 \tag{8.76}$$

Further Topics in Constrained Maximization and Minimization

$$pf_2 = v_2 \tag{8.77}$$

The tenant acts as if the price for x_1 and x_2 were actually $\frac{4}{3}$ of the market price. Under this lease arrangement, the tenant would not only underutilize inputs relative to what the landlord wanted, but would underutilize inputs relative to what should be used for global profit maximization if there were not a landlord–tenant relationship. This point is also on the expansion path.

Lease arrangements in which the landlord receives a share of the crop but pays none of the cost can result in substantial conflict between the landlord and tenant with regard to the proper quantities of each input to be used. Given these results, conflict between the landlord and tenant with respect to the proper level of input use is not at all unexpected. A better arrangement might be for the landlord and tenant to share in both the returns and the expenses.

Suppose that the landlord and the tenant agree to a lease arrangement in which the landlord gets r percent of the revenue and pays s percent of the costs. Therefore, the tenant gets $1 - r$ percent of the revenue and pays $1 - s$ percent of the costs. The values of r and s are negotiated. The value of r may not be the same as s, but could be. The landlord's profit equation is

$$\Pi = rpf(x_1, x_2) - s(v_1 x_1 + v_2 x_2) \tag{8.78}$$

The tenant's profit equation is

$$\Pi = (1 - r)pf(x_1, x_2) - (1 - s)(v_1 x_1 + v_2 x_2) \tag{8.79}$$

The landlord's first-order conditions for profit maximization are

$$rpf_1 = sv_1 \tag{8.80}$$

$$rpf_2 = sv_2 \tag{8.81}$$

or

$$pf_1 = (s/r)v_1 \tag{8.82}$$

$$pf_2 = (s/r)v_2 \tag{8.83}$$

The tenant's first-order conditions for profit maximization are

$$(1 - r)pf_1 = (1 - s)v_1 \tag{8.84}$$

$$(1 - r)pf_2 = (1 - s)v_2 \tag{8.85}$$

or

$$pf_1 = [(1 - s)/(1 - r)]v_1 \tag{8.86}$$

$$pf_2 = [(1 - s)/(1 - r)]v_2 \tag{8.87}$$

Both the landlord and tenant prefer to be on the expansion path, but conflict may exist with regard to where each would like to be on the expansion path.

Suppose that r is greater than s. Then the ratio of s/r is smaller than 1. The landlord would prefer that the tenant overutilize inputs relative to the global profit-maximizing condition. Similarly, if r is greater than s, then $(1 - s)/(1 - r)$ is greater than 1. The tenant will underutilize inputs relative to the profit maximizing solution.

If r is less then s, the ratio of s/r is greater than 1. The landlord would prefer that the tenant use less of the inputs than would be the case for the global profit-maximizing solution. From the tenant's perspective, $(1 - s)/(1 - r)$ is smaller than 1, and the inputs appear to be cheaper to the tenant than the market prices would indicate. The tenant will overutilize inputs relative to the global profit-maximizing solution.

Only if r is equal to s and the landlord and tenant agree that costs and returns should be shared in the same percentage, whatever that percentage might be, will the first-order conditions for the landlord and the tenant be the same as the global profit-maximizing conditions in the absence of the landlord–tenant relationship. If the landlord agrees to pay the full cost of any particular input, the tenant will overutilize that input relative to the profit-maximizing solution. It the tenant agrees to pay the full cost of an input, the tenant will underutilize that input. Tenants usually supply all the labor. Landlords often feel that tenants do not work as hard as they would if they were on their own farm. If the tenant only receives $\frac{3}{4}$ of the revenue, it is if the imputed wage for labor to the tenant is multiplied by $\frac{4}{3}$. Tenants will use less of the input labor as a result. The landlord is correct, but the tenant is also behaving consistent with a profit maximizing objective.

8.8 An Application to an Acreage Allotment Problem

The factor-factor model can be used for analyzing the behavior of a farmer faced with an acreage allotment imposed by the federal government. Consider a farmer who uses two categories of inputs to produce a commodity such as wheat. The two categories of inputs are land and a bundle of all other inputs. Figure 8.2 illustrates a series of isoquants for this farmer, with the vertical axis represented by land and the horizontal axis represented by all other inputs.

In the absence of any government program, the farmer is assumed to operate on a point on the expansion path. Points on the expansion path are defined by

$$VMP_L/V_L = VMP_X/V_X = \lambda \qquad (8.88)$$

where VMP_L = value of the marginal product of an additional acre of land in the production of wheat
V_L = rental price of the land per acre, or the opportunity cost per acre of the farmer's funds tied up in the land
V_X = weighted price of the input bundle X
VMP_X = value of the marginal product of the input bundle consisting of the remaining inputs

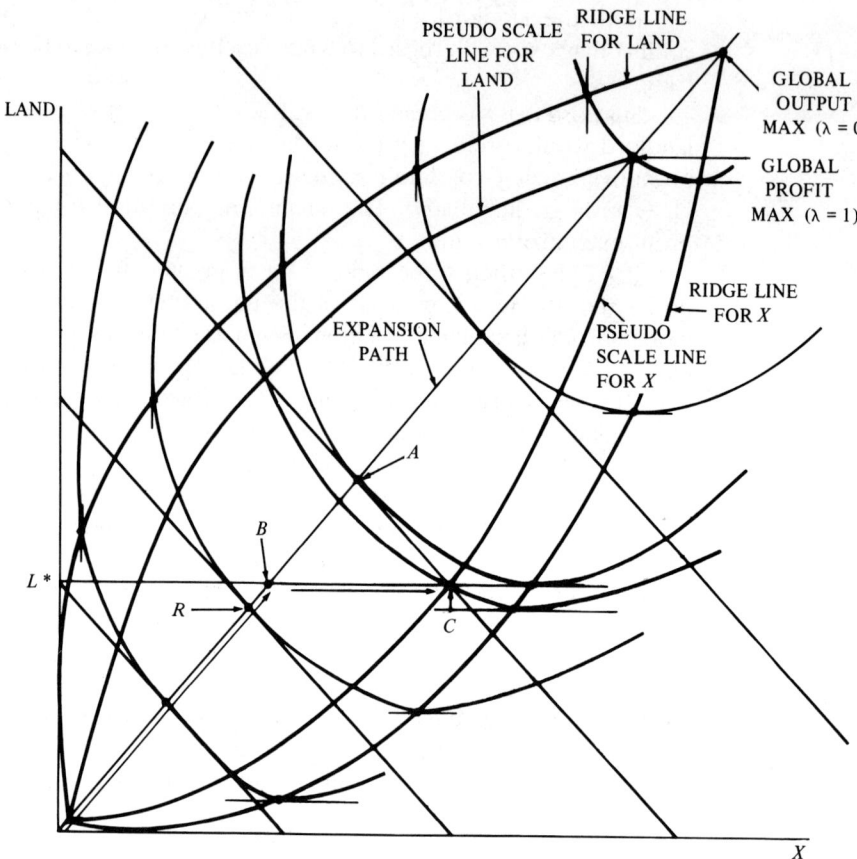

Figure 8.2 Acreage Allotment

The combination of individual inputs in the bundle is considered to be in the proportion defined by the equation

$$VMPx_1/v_1 = VMPx_2/v_2 = \cdots = VMPx_n/v_n = \lambda \qquad (8.89)$$

where terms are as previously defined, and λ is a Lagrangian multiplier equal to a constant.

If a wheat acreage allotment did not exist and the farmer were not constrained by the availability of funds for the purchase or rental of land and other inputs, the farmer would find the global point of profit maximization on the expansion path, and the value of the Lagrangian multiplier for the farmer would be 1 in all cases for all inputs.

Now suppose that the farmer faced a restriction placed by the government on the acreage of wheat that can be grown. A wheat acreage allotment is the same as a restriction on the availability of land. Let the land acreage restriction be represented by the horizontal line L^* in Figure 8.2. If the farmer was initially producing fewer acres of wheat than is allowed under the acreage restriction, the acreage allotment will have no impact on the farmer's input allocation. For

8.8 An Application to an Acreage Allotment Problem

example, if the farmer was initially at point R, the acreage allotment would have no impact.

Assume that the farmer initially was producing more wheat than the acreage restriction allowed. In the face of such a restriction, the farmer must move back down the expansion path to a point on the expansion path that lies on the constraint L^*. Let point A in Figure 8.2 represent the initial production level. In the face of the acreage allotment, the farmer must move back to point B. Both point A and point B are points of least-cost combination, but point B differs from point A in that at point B, the value for the Lagrangian multiplier is larger. For example, point A might represent a point where

$$VMP_L/V_L = VMP_X/V_X = 2 \qquad (8.90)$$

Point B might represent a point where

$$VMP_L/V_L = VMP_X/V_X = 4 \qquad (8.91)$$

Despite the fact that point B is now consistent with all constraints and is also a point of least-cost combination, the farmer will probably not wish to stay there. The farmer, having previously achieved point A, clearly has more money available for the purchase of other inputs than is being used at point B. Once reaching the land constraint L^*, the farmer moves off the expansion path to the right along the constraint. Movement to the right involves the purchase of additional units of the input bundle X. How far the farmer can move to the right depends on the availability of funds for the purchase of the input bundle X, but limits on the movement can be determined.

At the ridge line for the input bundle X, the marginal product of the input bundle X is zero. The farmer would clearly not want to move that far to the right, for units of the input bundle surely cost something ($V_X > 0$). The point where the farmer will try to move is represented by the intersection of the constraint L^* and the pseudo scale line for the input bundle X. Point C is the profit-maximizing level of input use for the bundle X, and is on an isoquant representing a larger output that was point B on the expansion path.

In the absence of a wheat acreage allotment, the farmer's only constraint is the availability of dollars for the purchase of other inputs, and the farmer will find a point on the expansion path where

$$VMP_L/V_L = VMP_X/V_X = \lambda \qquad (8.92)$$

With the acreage allotment, the farmer will move back along the expansion path to a point on the wheat allotment constraint. If the farmer moves back along the expansion path, the ratio VMP_L/V_L will almost certainly be larger than before. However, the farmer will not maintain this new ratio with respect to the bundle of other inputs. The farmer would increase profitability to the farm by attempting to make the ratio VMP_X/V_X as near to 1 as possible. (The ratio VMP_X/V_X is 1 at point C.) This entails using more of the inputs other than land per acre in order to achieve wheat production that exceeds the level that would have occurred at the intersection of the expansion path and the land constraint.

Since the amount of land used is restricted by the acreage allotment, the land input is treated as a fixed resource, and profit maximization for the bundle of variable inputs X is the same as for the single-factor solution outlined in Chapter 3. If the input bundle is divided into its component inputs and a limitation is placed on the amount of money available for the purchase of inputs in X, the equimarginal return rule for each input in the bundle applies. In other words, if the ratio of VMP_X to V is 1, the ratio of VMP to its price for every input in the bundle should also be 1.

If money for the purchase of each x_i in the bundle is constrained, the ratio of $VMPx_i$ to v_i will be the same for all inputs but be some number larger than 1, and the farmer will be found at a point between the pseudo scale line and the expansion path (between B and C) along the line representing the acreage allotment constraint. The equimarginal return rule still applies to units of each variable input in the bundle.

When a wheat acreage restriction is imposed, the total production of wheat normally does not decline by the full amount calculated by subtracting the allotment from the acreage without the restriction and multiplying by the yield per acre. In the face of an acreage restriction, the least productive farmland goes out of production first, and farmers attempt to improve yields on the remaining acres by using more fertilizer, better seed, and improved pest management, represented in this model by the bundle of inputs X. The limited dollars available for the purchase of these inputs is now spread over a smaller acreage, resulting in a higher yield per acre. This model explained why the imposition of a wheat acreage allotment improves wheat yields, and these improved yields are consistent with the goal of profit maximization and the equimarginal return rule.

8.9 Concluding Comments

Despite the fact that the presentation of the factor-factor model in this chapter made use of calculus, the conclusions that have been reached should be reassuringly familiar. The basic equimarginal return rule still applies, which requires that the last dollar spent for each input must produce the same amount in terms of revenue for the least-cost combination of inputs. Moreover, the last dollar spent on each input must return exactly $1 for profit maximization. In addition, the factor-factor model can be applied to problems in agriculture such as the design of lease arrangements and acreage allotment restrictions, if minor modifications to the basic model are made.

The mathematical presentation contained in this chapter presents a formal proof of the equimarginal return rules in the two-factor setting. These rules can also be extended to a case in which more than two factors are used. Of course, the diagrammatic presentation cannot be used in instances where there are more than two inputs and a single output, for it is not possible to draw in more than three dimensions. Here the mathematics must be used, and a detailed presentation in the many-factor case is given in Section 18.2.

8.9 Concluding Comments

Problems and Exercises

1. Suppose that total revenue is maximized subject to the cost or budget constraint. Interpret the following values for the Lagrangian multiplier.

   a. 10
   b. 5
   c. 3
   d. 1
   e. 0
   f. −2

2. Assume that profit or total value of the product minus total factor cost is maximized subject to the budget or cost constraint. Interpret the following values for the Lagrangian multiplier.

   a. 10
   b. 5
   c. 3
   d. 1
   e. 0
   f. −2

3. Assume that the objective function is cost minimization subject to a total revenue constraint. Interpret the following values for the Lagrangian multiplier.

   a. Infinity
   b. 999
   c. 5
   d. 2
   e. 1
   f. 0.8
   g. 0.3
   h. 0
   i. −1

4. Suppose that the objective function is cost minimization subject to a profit constraint. Interpret the following values for the Lagrangian multiplier.

   a. Infinity
   b. 999
   c. 5
   d. 2
   e. 1
   f. 0.8
   g. 0.3
   h. 0
   i. −1

5. Consumers are interested in maximizing utility subject to the constraint imposed by the availability of money income. Show that:

   a. The Lagrangian multiplier in such a constrained optimization problem can be interpreted as the marginal utility of money.
   b. If the producer is interested in maximizing revenue subject to the constraint imposed by the availability of dollars for the purchase of inputs x_1 and x_2, what is the comparable definition for the corresponding Lagrangian multiplier?

6. Suppose that the production function is given by

$$y = x_1^{0.5} x_2^{0.3}$$

   a. Set up a Lagrangian optimization problem using this production function. Derive first-order conditions.

   b. Suppose that the output, y, sells for $4.00 per unit and that x_1 and x_2 both sell for $0.10 per unit? How much x_1 and x_2 would the farmer purchase in order to maximize profit?

Hint: Set up a profit function for the farmer and derive first-order conditions. You now have two equations in two unknowns. Solve this the second equation for x_2 in terms of x_1. Then substitute x_2 in terms of x_1 into the first equation. Once you have found the value for x_1, insert it into the second equation and solve for x_2. Part (b) of this problem will require a calculator that can raise a number to a fractional power.

7. Is a cash rent lease always more desirable than a crop share lease? Explain.

8. Are both the landlord and tenant better off when they agree to share expenses and revenues using the same percentages for both revenues and expenses (for example, a 0.6:0.4 split of revenues and expenses between the landlord and the tenant)? Explain.

9. Under what conditions would an acreage allotment have no impact whatsoever on the output of a commodity?

10. What possible impacts might an acreage allotment have on a farmer's demand for fertilizer? Will the demand for fertilizer in total always decline as the result of an acreage allotment?

11. Will a farmer be at a point of least-cost combination ($MRSx_1x_2 = v_1/v_2$) when an acreage allotment exists? Explain.

Reference

Heady, Earl O. "Optimal Sizes of Farms Under Varying Tenure Forms, Including Renting, Ownership, State and Collective Structures." *American Journal of Agricultural Economics* 53:1 (1971) pp. 17–25.

9
Returns to Scale, Homogeneous Production Functions, and Euler's Theorem

This chapter examines the relationships that exist between the concept of size and the concept of scale. The terms *size* and *scale* have been widely misused in relation to adjustment processes in the use of inputs by farmers. The linkages between scale economies and diseconomies and the homogeneity of production functions are outlined. The cost function can be derived from the production function for the bundle of inputs defined by the expansion path conditions. The relationship between homogeneous production functions and Euler's theorem is presented.

Key Terms and Definitions:

Economies of Size
Diseconomies of Size
Pecuniary Economies
Economies of Scale
Diseconomies of Scale
Homogeneous Production Function
Homogeneous of Degree n
Production Function Not
 Homogeneous
Returns to Scale Parameter
Function Coefficient
Production Function for the Input
 Bundle
Inverse Production Function
Cost Elasticity
Leonhard Euler
Euler's Theorem

9.1 Economies and Diseconomies of Size

The term *economies of size* is used to describe a situation in which as the farm expands output, the cost per unit of output decreases. There are a number of reasons why costs per unit of output might decrease as output levels increase.

The farm may be able to spread its fixed costs over a larger amount of output as the size of the operation increases. It may be possible to do more field work with the same set of machinery and equipment. A building designed for housing cattle might be used to house more animals than before, lowering the depreciation costs per unit of livestock produced.

An expansion in output may reduce some variable costs. A farmer who previously relied on bagged fertilizer may be able to justify the additional equipment needed to handle anhydrous ammonia or nitrogen solutions if the size of the operation is expanded. While fixed costs for machinery may increase slightly, these increases may be more than offset by a reduction in the cost per unit of fertilizer.

The larger producer may be able to take advantage of pecuniary economies. As the size of the operation increases, the farmer might pay less per unit of variable input because inputs can be bought in larger quantities. Such pecuniary economies might be possible for inputs such as seed, feeds, fertilizers, herbicides, and insecticides.

The term *diseconomies of size* is used to refer to increases in the per unit cost of production arising from an increase in output. There exist two major reasons why diseconomies of size might occur as the farm is expanded.

First, as output increases, the manager's skills must be spread over the larger farm. A farmer who is successful in managing a 500-acre farm in which most of the labor is supplied by the farm family may not be equally adept at managing a 2000-acre farm that includes five salaried employees. The skills of the salaried employees will not necessarily be equivalent to the skills of the farm manager. A firm with many employees may not necessarily be as efficient as a firm with only one or two employees.

The farm may become so large that the assumptions of the purely competitive model are no longer met. This could result in the large firm to a degree determining the price paid for certain inputs or factors of production. The farm may no longer be able to sell all its output at the going market price. Although this may seem unlikely for a commodity such as wheat, it is quite possible for a commodity such as broilers.

The long-run average cost curve represents a planning curve for the farmer as he or she increases or decreases the size of the operation by expanding or contracting output over a long period of time. Each of the short-run average cost curves represents possible changes in output that could occur within a much shorter period of time. The possible changes in output associated with each short-run average cost curve are a result of varying some, but not all, of the inputs. Thus the respective short-run average cost curves each represent possible levels of output during a period long enough so that some inputs can be varied, but short enough so that all inputs cannot be varied.

The term *economies of size* is also used to refer to something other than economies associated with an increase in the physical quantity of output that is produced. The United States Bureau of the Census categorizes farms by size according to the value, not quantity, of output that is produced. Their measure of size makes possible comparisons between farms that produce widely varying products as well as makes possible measurement of the size of a farm that produces many different products.

The census definition is based on total revenue from the sale of agricultural products (py), not output (y). It is not the economist's definition of size, for an increase in the price of a particular agricultural commodity will cause the size of the farm producing the commodity to increase. Inflation that results in a general increase in the prices for all agricultural commodities will cause this measure of farm size to increase, despite the fact that the physical quantity of output may not have increased.

The term *economies of size* is sometimes used in conjunction with economies associated with an increase in one or more (but not all) major input categories, either inputs normally thought of as fixed or inputs normally thought of as variable. A common measure is the acreage of land in the farm, an input that might change only over the long run. A commercial grain producer may think of increasing the size of the operation by expanding the amount of the planted acres. But a broiler operation may increase in size not by acquiring additional land, but by adding a building and additional chickens.

So the definition of farm size is a troublesome one. Because there exist many possible interpretations of the term "size" in relation to economies or diseconomies, great care should be taken in the use of the term. An additional explanation is usually warranted with respect to exactly which measure or interpretation should be made of the term *size*.

9.2 Economies and Diseconomies of Scale

The term *scale of farm* is a good deal more restrictive than the term *size of farm*. There is widespread agreement as to the meaning of the term *scale*. If the scale of a farm is to increase, each input must also increase proportionately. Included are inputs commonly thought of as fixed, as well as variable, inputs.

The term *economy* or *diseconomy of scale* refers to what happens when all input categories are increased proportionately. Assume that all input categories are doubled. If output doubles, neither economies or diseconomies of scale are said to exist. If output more than doubles, economies of scale exist. If output does not double, diseconomies of scale exist.

For economies or diseconomies of size to take place, all that is required is that the output level change. All inputs need not change proportionately. However, if economies or diseconomies of scale are to take place, not only must output change but each of the inputs must change in a fixed proportion to the others. For example, the term *economies* or *diseconomies of scale* could be used to describe what happens to per unit costs of production when all inputs are doubled, tripled, quadrupled, or halved. The term *economies* or *diseconomies of size* could be used to describe what happens to per unit costs of production when output is doubled, tripled, quadrupled, or halved but input levels do not necessarily increase in the same proportionate amounts.

The term *scale* is also closely intertwined with the length of time involved. One interpretation of the envelope long-run average cost curve developed in Chapter 4 (Figure 4.1) is that it represents the possible per unit costs associated with each possible scale of operation. It is very difficult to increase or decrease the quantity of all inputs proportionately within a short period. It might be a simple matter for a farmer to increase proportionately the use of inputs normally thought of as variable within a production season. These inputs include feed, fertilizer, chemicals, and the like.

As indicated, the term *scale* implies a proportionate increase in all inputs, not just those treated as variable over a production season, and in agriculture inputs include categories such as land, tractors, and other farm machinery. Moreover, many of these inputs can be increased or decreased only in discrete amounts. For example, a farmer might readily increase the use of fertilizer by 57 percent, but not increase the use of tractors by the exact same 57 percent. A change in the scale of an operation thus represents an economic concept seldom achieved in the real world.

A farm uses land, labor, capital, and management as inputs to the production process. If the scale of the farm is to increase by a factor of 2, each input category must also increase by a factor of 2. It is very difficult for a farmer to truly expand the scale of the operation. If a farmer has 100 acres, 1 worker-year of labor, and one tractor, then to expand the scale of the operation by a factor of 2 would require that the farmer purchase an additional 100 acres, an additional tractor, and hire another laborer with exactly the same skills. The correct definition of *scale* would imply that the level of management should also double.

The term *scale* can be misused. The most common misuse is with reference to an increase in one or more of the input categories (such as land) without a corresponding increase in all other input categories. This violates the economist's definition of the term *scale*.

If production of a commodity takes place with only two inputs, movement along a line of constant slope out of the origin of a graph of a factor-factor model represents a proportionate change in the use of both inputs (Figure 9.1). In Figure 9.1, each successive isoquant represents a doubling of output. Diagram A illustrates a case in which output was doubled with less than a doubling of inputs, so economies of scale exist. Diagram B illustrates a case in which the doubling of output required more than a doubling of input, so diseconomies of scale exist. Diagram C illustrates a case where the doubling of output required that the size of the input bundle also be doubled, so constant returns to scale exist.

However, production within an agricultural setting normally takes place with many more than two inputs. Each of the inputs in the production process may differ with respect to whether or not the amount that is used can be changed within a specific period. Thus an illustration such as Figure 9.1 as a representation of scale economies or diseconomies can be highly misleading, in that the production process is oversimplified and the all-important time element required for the adjustment process is ignored.

Economies and diseconomies of scale, which produce a long-run envelope curve that is U shaped, have long fascinated economists. Despite the fact that it is possible for diseconomies of scale to occur, empirical studies conducted for various agricultural enterprises have revealed very little hard evidence supporting the existence of significant diseconomies of scale within agriculture. Rather, the per unit costs of production usually form an L-shaped curve. However, it is very difficult to verify as that true change in scale has taken place as the output of each farm increases or decreases.

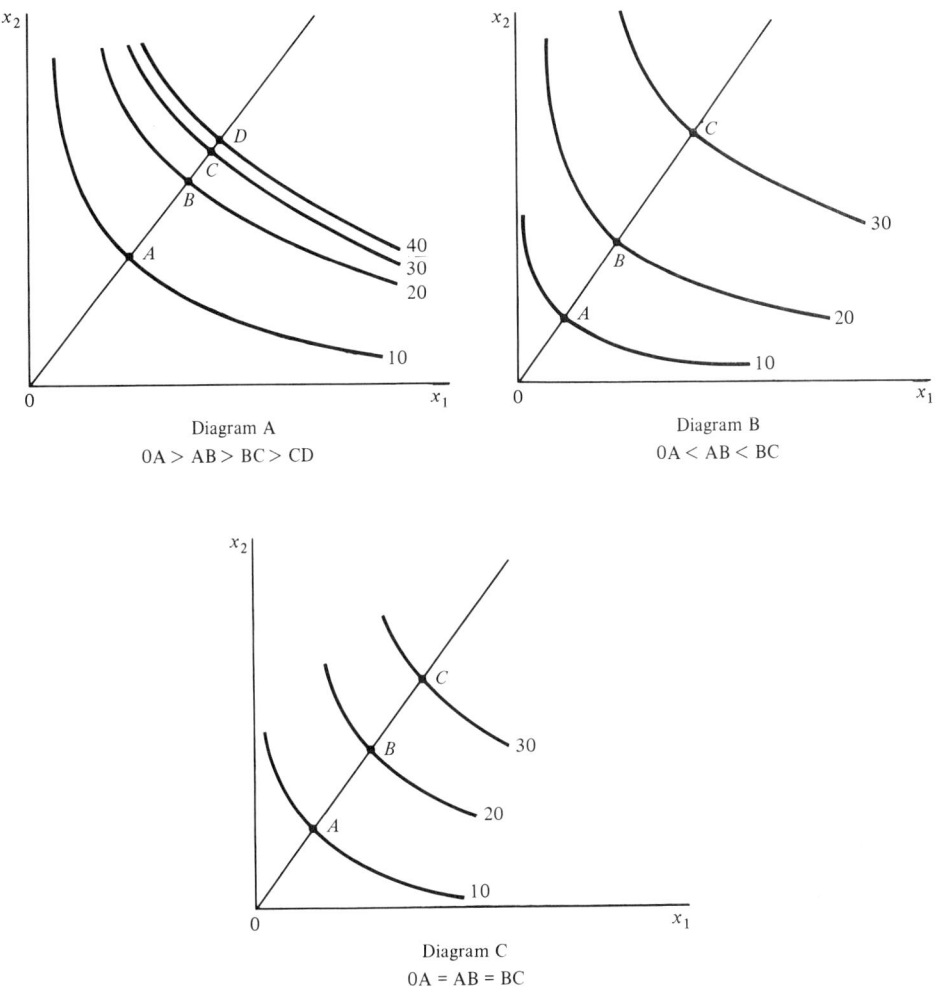

Figure 9.1 Economies, Diseconomies, and Constant Returns to Scale for a Production Function with Only Two Inputs

9.3 Homogeneous Production Functions

The terms *economy* or *diseconomy of scale* can be confusing to interpret. Some economists define the terms with reference to a particular class of production functions, known as homogeneous production functions.

Homogeneous production functions consist of a broad array of functions with a special characteristic. A production function is said to be homogeneous of degree n if when each input is multiplied by some number t, output increases by the factor t^n. Assuming that the time period is sufficiently long such that all inputs can be treated as variables and are included in the production function, n, the degree of homogeneity refers to the returns to scale. Homogeneous production functions are frequently used by agricultural economists to represent a variety of transformations between agricultural inputs and products.

A function homogeneous of degree 1 is said to have constant returns to scale, or neither economies or diseconomies of scale. A function homogeneous of a degree greater than 1 is said to have increasing returns to scale or economies of scale. A function homogeneous of degree less than 1 is said to have diminishing returns to scale or diseconomies of scale.

While there are many different production functions, only certain kinds of production functions are homogeneous. In general, they are multiplicative rather than additive although a few exceptions exist.

The production function

$$y = ax_1^{0.5}x_2^{0.5} \tag{9.1}$$

is homogeneous of degree 1. Multiply x_1 and x_2 by t to get

$$\begin{aligned}a(tx_1)^{0.5}(tx_2)^{0.5} &= tax_1^{0.5}x_2^{0.5}\\ &= t^1 y\end{aligned} \tag{9.2}$$

Thus the function in equation (9.1) exhibits constant returns to scale without any economies or diseconomies.

The production function

$$y = ax_1^{0.5}x_2^{0.8} \tag{9.3}$$

is homogeneous of degree 1.3. Multiply x_1 and x_2 by t to get

$$\begin{aligned}a(tx_1)^{0.5}(tx_2)^{0.8} &= t^{1.3}ax_1^{0.5}x_2^{0.8}\\ &= t^{1.3} y\end{aligned} \tag{9.4}$$

Thus increasing returns to scale and economies of scale exist.

The production function

$$y = ax_1^{0.5}x_2^{0.3} \tag{9.5}$$

is homogeneous of degree 0.8. Multiply x_1 and x_2 by t to get

$$\begin{aligned}a(tx_1)^{0.5}(tx_2)^{0.3} &= t^{0.8}ax_1^{0.5}x_2^{0.3}\\ &= t^{0.8} y\end{aligned} \tag{9.6}$$

Thus decreasing returns to scale and diseconomies of scale exist. For multiplicative functions of the general form

$$y = ax_1^{\alpha}x_2^{\beta} \tag{9.7}$$

the degree of homogeneity can be determined by summing the parameters α and β.

An example of a function that is not homogeneous is

$$y = ax_1 + bx_1^2 + cx_2 + dx_2^2 \tag{9.8}$$

Each input can be increased by the factor t, but it is not possible to factor t out of the equation. As the use of x_1 and x_2 increases proportionately along the expansion path, a function such as this may exhibit points of increasing, constant, and diminishing returns to scale.

Homogeneous production functions possess a unique characteristic. A line of constant slope drawn in factor-factor space will represent a proportionate change in the use of the inputs represented on the axes. For homogeneous functions, any line of constant slope drawn from the origin will connect all points on the isoquant map with equal slopes. In other words, any isocline has a constant slope for a homogeneous function.

Since an expansion path is a specific isocline with a slope $-v_1/v_2$, any homogeneous function will have an expansion path with a constant slope. (This characteristic is also true of a broader class of production functions, called *homothetic production functions,* which include homogeneous production functions as a special case.) For a homogeneous production function and fixed factor prices, movement along an expansion path or, for that matter, movement along any isocline represents a proportionate change in the use of the inputs. For homogeneous production functions, if all inputs are included, movement along any isocline represents a change in the scale of an operation.

9.4 Returns to Scale and Individual Production Elasticities

Assume that only a single input is required to produce an output. The production process is described by the function

$$y = ax_1^\beta \tag{9.9}$$

In this example, the elasticity of production is equal to the percentage change in output divided by the percentage change in the input. The elasticity of production is also equal to $MPPx_1/APPx_1$, and the elasticity of production is equal to β.

The production function described by equation (9.9) is homogeneous of degree β. The returns to scale in this case are determined by the value of β, the *returns-to-scale parameter*. If there is only one input to the production process, diminishing returns to scale is equivalent to diminishing returns to the variable input. Constant returns to scale is equivalent to constant returns to the variable input. Increasing returns to scale is equivalent to increasing returns to the variable input.

Now assume that the production function contains two inputs, x_1 and x_2. The production function is

$$y = ax_1^{\beta_1}x_2^{\beta_2} \tag{9.10}$$

$$MPPx_1 = \beta_1 ax_1^{\beta_1-1}x_2^{\beta_2} \tag{9.11}$$

$$APPx_1 = ax_1^{\beta_1-1}x_2^{\beta_2} \tag{9.12}$$

$$MPPx_2 = \beta_2 a x_1^{\beta_1} x_2^{\beta_2 - 1} \qquad (9.13)$$

$$APPx_2 = a x_1^{\beta_1} x_2^{\beta_2 - 1} \qquad (9.14)$$

$$MPPx_1/APPx_1 = \varepsilon_1 = \beta_1 \qquad (9.15)$$

$$MPPx_2/APPx_2 = \varepsilon_2 = \beta_2 \qquad (9.16)$$

The returns-to-scale parameter, sometimes called the *function coefficient*, is

$$\begin{aligned} E &= \varepsilon_1 + \varepsilon_2 \\ &= \beta_1 + \beta_2 \\ &= MPPx_1/APPx_1 + MPPx_2/APPx_2 \end{aligned} \qquad (9.17)$$

If the production function is homogeneous of degree n, and all inputs are represented in the production function, the parameter representing the returns to scale is the degree of homogeneity. For a multiplicative power production function with g inputs, the degree of homogeneity and the returns to scale is determined by summing the g respective β coefficients which are the elasticities of production for the individual inputs.

If the production function is not homogeneous, the returns to scale can still be determined by summing the respective ratios of marginal to average product (MPP/APP). These ratios will not be constants but rather will be a function of the quantities of inputs that are being used. An assumption will need to be made with regard to the scale of the firm (the quantities of each individual input) before the returns-to-scale parameter can be determined.

Consider the production function for the input bundle developed in Chapter 7. Assuming that the underlying production function has a linear expansion path, and there are but two inputs to the production process, the function coefficient or the returns-to-scale parameter is the ratio of *MPP* to *APP* for the bundle.

The returns-to-scale parameter may be constant for all possible sizes of the input bundle, or it may vary. A production function homogeneous of degree n will yield a returns-to-scale parameter of a constant value n. This suggests that the ratio of *MPP* to *APP* for the bundle is also equal to n. The degree of homogeneity n is the sum of the production elasticities for the individual inputs. If the returns-to-scale parameter varies as all inputs are increased proportionately, the production function cannot be homogeneous.

9.5 Duality of Production and Cost for the Input Bundle

If all input prices are fixed, and therefore there are no pecuniary economies or diseconomies, the returns-to-scale parameter indicates what is happening to average cost as all inputs are increased proportionately. To see this, assume

9.5 Duality of Production and Cost of the Input Bundle

that the production function for the input bundle ($\otimes$) defined by a linear expansion path characteristic of a homogeneous production function is

$$y = f(\otimes) \tag{9.18}$$

where $\otimes = w_1 x_1 + w_2 x_2$. The weights w_1 and w_2 are the proportions of x_1 and x_2 contained in the input bundle. For example, if each unit of the bundle consists of 2 units of x_1 and 1 unit of x_2, then w_1 is 2, and w_2 is 1. The cost of 1 unit of the input bundle is

$$v_1 w_1 + v_2 w_2 = V \tag{9.19}$$

The inverse production function is

$$\otimes = f^{-1}(y) \tag{9.20}$$

where f^{-1} is obtained by solving the original production for the input in terms of the output.

The total cost function that is dual to the production function for the input bundle is obtained by multiplying the inverse production function by V, the price of 1 unit of the bundle. Therefore,

$$V\otimes = Vf^{-1}(y) \tag{9.21}$$

$$TC = Vf^{-1}(y) \tag{9.22}$$

$$AC = Vf^{-1}(y)/y \tag{9.23}$$

$$MC = V d[f^{-1}(y)]/dy \tag{9.24}$$

Notice that if the price of the input bundle V is known, all the information needed to derive the dual total cost function can be obtained from the corresponding production function for the bundle.

The production function for the input bundle is unique in that each and every point on it represents a point of least-cost combination of inputs for a given outlay. In this sense, the entire production function for the bundle represents the series of solutions to an infinite number of optimization problems that lie on the expansion path; and the dual total cost function represents a series of minimum-cost points for a given total output or product y.

A numerical example can be used to further illustrate the point. Assume that the production function is

$$y = 1 x_1^{0.3} x_2^{0.6} \tag{9.25}$$

$$dy/dx_1 = 0.3 x_1^{-0.7} x_2^{0.6} \tag{9.26}$$

$$dy/dx_2 = 0.6 x_1^{0.3} x_2^{-0.4} \tag{9.27}$$

The *MRS* of x_1 for x_2 is $-MPPx_1/MPPx_2$ or

$$-(0.3x_1^{-0.7}x_2^{0.6})/(0.6x_1^{0.3}x_2^{-0.4}) = -(\tfrac{1}{2})(x_2/x_1) \tag{9.28}$$

Assume that the price of x_1 (v_1) is $1 and the price of x_2 (v_2) is $3. Then the slope of the budget constraint, or iso-outlay line is $-\tfrac{1}{3}$.

Now equate the $MRSx_1x_2$ with the inverse price ratio v_1/v_2, and multiply both sides of the equation by -1. The result is

$$(\tfrac{1}{2})(x_2/x_1) = \tfrac{1}{3} \tag{9.29}$$

Equation (9.29) provides information with respect to the slope of the expansion path as well as the relative proportion of x_1 and x_2 contained in the bundle of inputs as defined by the expansion path. Solving equation (9.29) for x_2 results in

$$x_2 = (\tfrac{2}{3})x_1 \tag{9.30}$$

The slope of the isocline representing the expansion path is a constant $\tfrac{2}{3}$. One unit of the bundle of inputs consists of 1 unit of x_1 and $\tfrac{2}{3}$ unit of x_2. The cost of 1 unit of this bundle is $1(1) + $3(\tfrac{2}{3}) = $3.

The production function that was used in this example was homogeneous of degree 0.9. The individual production elasticities when summed resulted in a returns-to-scale parameter or function coefficient of 0.9. The production function for the bundle can be written as

$$y = \otimes^{0.9} \tag{9.31}$$

This production function can be inverted or solved for the bundle in terms of y to obtain the dual cost curve expressed in physical terms

$$\otimes^{0.9} = y \tag{9.32}$$

$$\otimes = y^{1/0.9} \tag{9.33}$$

$$\otimes = y^{1.11} \tag{9.34}$$

The inverse production function equation (9.34) can be multiplied by the price of the input bundle V, which was determined to be $3. The result is the dual total cost function expressed in terms of dollars and units of y

$$\$3 \cdot \otimes = \$3y^{1.11} \tag{9.35}$$

$$TC = \$3y^{1.11} \tag{9.36}$$

$$AC = \$3y^{1.11}/y = \$3y^{0.11} \tag{9.37}$$

$$MC = (1.11)\$3y^{0.11} \tag{9.38}$$

9.5 Duality of Production and Cost of the Input Bundle

The returns-to-scale parameter, or function coefficient of 0.9 indicated diseconomies of scale. If this were the case, AC should be increasing. Therefore, the slope of AC should be increasing and dAC/dy should be positive. In this example

$$dAC/dy = (0.11)(\$3)y^{-0.89} > 0 \quad \text{(since } y \text{ is greater than 0)} \quad (9.39)$$

Therefore, AC is increasing. The slope of MC is dMC/dy

$$dMC/dy = (0.11)(1.11)\$3y^{-0.89} > 0 \quad (9.40)$$

Therefore, MC is increasing and TC must be increasing at an increasing rate. MC is 1.11 or 1/0.9 times AC.

The cost elasticity (ψ) can be defined as the percentage change in total cost divided by the percentage change in output. If this elasticity is greater than 1, diseconomies of scale exist. An elasticity equal to 1 suggests neither economies nor diseconomies of scale, and a cost elasticity of less than 1 indicates that economies of scale exist. The cost elasticity is easily calculated, for it is the ratio of MC to AC:

$$\psi = MC/AC \quad (9.41)$$

Note that for homogeneous production functions and constant input prices (no pecuniary economies), the cost elasticity is the inverse of the function coefficient, or the inverse of the returns-to-scale parameter ($1/E$). Thus the cost elasticity for the dual cost function is one over the function coefficient of the production function for the bundle. For a homogeneous production function, the information required to obtain the cost elasticity for the dual cost function is available from the production function for the bundle. Furthermore, if the cost elasticity is known, the function coefficient that applies to the bundle can be readily calculated, assuming that the production function is homogeneous. Table 9.1 summarizes these relationships for several homogeneous production functions.

Table 9.1 Relationships Between the Function Coefficient, the Dual Cost Elasticity, and Returns to Scale

Degree of Homogeneity, n	Function Coefficient, E	Cost Elasticity, ψ	Input Prices	Returns to Scale
0	0	Infinite	Constant	???
0.1	0.1	10	Constant	Diseconomies
0.5	0.5	2	Constant	Diseconomies
1	1	1	Constant	Constant
2	2	0.5	Constant	Economies
10	10	0.1	Constant	Economies

9.6 Euler's Theorem

Leonhard Euler (pronounced "oiler") was a Swiss mathematician who lived from 1707 to 1783. *Euler's theorem* is a mathematical relationship that applies to any homogeneous function. It has implications for agricultural economists who make use of homogeneous production functions. Euler's theorem states that if a function is homogeneous of degree n, the following relationship holds

$$(\partial y/\partial x_1)x_1 + (\partial y/\partial x_2)x_2 = ny \qquad (9.42)$$

where n is the degree of homogeneity. If the function is a production function, then

$$MPPx_1 x_1 + MPPx_2 x_2 = ny \qquad (9.43)$$

or

$$MPPx_1 x_1 + MPPx_2 x_2 = Ey \qquad (9.44)$$

where E is the returns-to-scale parameter or function coefficient.

The equation can be multiplied by the price of the output p, with the result

$$pMPPx_1 x_1 + pMPPx_2 x_2 = npy \qquad (9.45)$$

Since total revenue (*TR*) is py, and $pMPP$ is *VMP*, equation (9.45) can be rewritten as

$$VMPx_1 x_1 + VMPx_2 x_2 = nTR \qquad (9.46)$$

Euler was a mathematician and not an economist. Euler's theorem is a mathematical relationship that applies to all homogeneous functions, whether or not they represent production relationships. Euler's theorem has sometimes been interpreted as a rule to follow not only with respect to how the individual farm or nonfarm manager should reward factors of production, but also a rule to be followed with regard to how labor and capital should be rewarded within a society.

The *VMP* of a factor of production represents the return from the use of the incremental unit of the factor. First consider the case in which the production function is homogeneous of degree 1, or constant returns to scale exist for the firm. Assume that the only two inputs used on the farm are labor and capital. Following Euler's theorem, the wage rate for each unit of labor on the farm would be equal to its *VMP*.

Assuming that the farmer owned the capital, the return to each unit of owned capital would be the *VMP* of the last unit multiplied by the quantity that is used. Laborers would receive a wage rate equal to their *VMP*. There seems something "correct" and "decent" about the notion that laborers "ought" to receive a wage payment equal to their *VMP* or contribution to revenues to the firm. Moreover, such payments would just exhaust the total revenue produced by the firm, such that there would be no pure or economic profit that would suggest an exploitation of labor on the part of the manager.

Now consider a similar case in which a society pays a wage rate to each laborer according to the respective *VMP*. Some have argued that such a society would be very good indeed in that labor would receive its just reward and therefore not be exploited.

Consider a case in which the farmer has a production function homogeneous of a degree greater than 1. This would be considered to be a very desirable and productive production function in that a doubling of all inputs would result in a greater than doubling of output. If the degree of homogeneity of the function were 3, then if each factor of production were paid according to its *VMP*, total revenue would be more than exhausted (three times to be exact). The farmer would not have sufficient revenue to do this because the *VMP*'s paid to each input or factor would be so very large. The society faced with a very desirable production function would be in the same predicament if it followed this rule.

A final case is a relatively unproductive production function with a degree of homogeneity of less than 1. If the degree of homogeneity were 0.5, then paying each factor of production according to its *VMP* would exhaust only half the revenue that was produced. The rest would remain as a pure or economic profit. Society, too, would exhaust only half the revenue produced in a case such as this.

Euler's theorem might have applicability only in an instance where the underlying production function was known to be homogeneous of degree 1. Even if this were the case, there is no built-in assurance that a society would be better off, that there would be less poverty among laborers, or that the distribution of incomes would be more equal in the society that followed the rule than in a society that did not.

The people who contributed very little to society in terms of *VMP* would be in poverty. The star professional basketball player, TV newscaster, or talk-show host, despite a salary in the millions of dollars, can be underpaid relative to the contribution to revenue to the firm. If each laborer in a society truly earned its *VMP*, income distribution might be less equal than in a society that did not follow this rule.

Euler's theorem should be regarded as a mathematical relationship that holds for homogeneous functions. It should not be interpreted as a simple rule that, if followed, would make laborers, or perhaps even an entire society, better off.

9.7 Concluding Comments

The term *economy (diseconomy) of size* and the term *economy (diseconomy) of scale* are not the same thing. An economy of size occurs if, by increasing output, the per unit costs of production are lowered. Conversely, a diseconomy of size occurs if per unit costs of production increase as output increases.

The terms *economy* and *diseconomy of scale* refer to what happens to output when all input are increased or decreased proportionately, including those normally regarded as fixed in the short run. If output increases in exact proportion to the increase in the scale of the operation, neither economies nor diseconomies of scale are said to exist. If output increases by a greater proportion than the proportionate increase in the scale of the operation, economies of scale exist. If output increases by a smaller proportion than the proportionate increase in the scale, diseconomies of scale are said to exist. Scale economies and diseconomies are inherently long-run phenomena, in that all inputs must be allowed to vary.

If all inputs are included in the production function and the underlying production function is homogeneous, the degree of homogeneity indicates the scale economies or diseconomies. The degree of homogeneity can also be referred to as the function coefficient. It represents the percentage change in output divided by the percentage change in all inputs, where the percentage change is the same for each input.

The dual cost function can be derived from the production function for the input bundle if the production function is homogeneous. The production function for the input bundle is the function defined by the points along the expansion path. Each point on the production function is optimal in the sense that it represents the least-cost input mix for the specific output level represented by that point.

Euler's theorem describes a unique property of homogeneous functions. If a production function is homogeneous of degree 1, and each factor of production earns its marginal product, revenue will exactly be exhausted. If the production function is homogeneous of a degree greater than 1, revenue will be more than exhausted if each factor is paid its value of marginal product. Revenue will be less than exhausted if the production function is homogeneous of degree less than 1 and if each factor is paid its value of marginal product.

Problems and Exercises

1. Distinguish between the term *economies of size* and the term *economies of scale*.

2. If a production function is homogeneous of degree 1, what happens to output when all inputs are tripled?

3. What happens to output when all inputs are doubled if the production function is homogeneous of degree 0.9?

4. Assume that Euler's theorem is used to reward or pay factors of production. What happens when the production function is homogeneous of degree:

    a. 1.9?
    b. 1.0?
    c. 0.2?
    d. 0?

5. Consumer demand functions are frequently assumed to be homogeneous of degree zero in all prices and income. Why? If this assumption is met, what happens to the demand for each good when all prices and income doubles? Explain.

6. Fill in the following table. Assume constant input prices.

Homogeneity of Production	Function Coefficient	Cost Elasticity	Returns to Scale
5	___	___	___
2	___	___	___
1	___	___	___
0.3	___	___	___
0	___	___	___

7. Discuss the linkages between the production function for the input bundle and the underlying cost function.

8. Is the production function $y = x_1^2 + x_2^2 + x_1 x_2$ homogeneous? Explain.

10 The Cobb–Douglas Production Function

This chapter describes in detail the most famous of all production functions used to represent production processes both in and out of agriculture. First used in 1928 in an empirical study dealing with the productivity of capital and labor in the United States, the function has been widely used in agricultural studies because of its simplicity. However, the function is not an adequate numerical representation of the neoclassical three-stage production function. One of the key characteristics of a Cobb–Douglas type of production function is that the specific corresponding dual cost function can be derived by making use of the first-order optimization conditions along the expansion path. Examples of constrained output or revenue-maximization problems using a Cobb–Douglas type of function are included.

Key Terms and Definitions:

Cobb–Douglas Production Function
True Cobb–Douglas
Base 10 Logarithm
Base e Logarithm
Cobb–Douglas Type of Function
Technology and the Parameter A
Homogeneity
Partial Elasticities of Production
Function Coefficient
Total Elasticity of Production
Asymptotic Isoquants
Three-Dimensional Surface
Duality of Cost and Production
Cost Elasticity
Finite Solution

10.1 Introduction

The paper describing the Cobb–Douglas production function was published in the journal *American Economic Review* in 1928. The original article dealt with an early empirical effort to estimate the comparative productivity of capital versus labor within the United States.

Since the publication of the article in 1928, the term *Cobb–Douglas production function* has been used to refer to nearly any simple multiplicative production function. The original production function contained only two inputs, capital (K) and labor (L). Moreover, the function was assumed to be homogeneous of degree 1 in capital and labor, or constant returns to scale.

Economists of this period, while recognizing that the law of diminishing returns (or the law of variable proportions) applied when units of a variable factor were added to units of a fixed factor, were fascinated with the possibility of constant returns to scale, when all factors of production were increased or decreased proportionately. They probably believed that as the scale of the operation changed, it was no longer possible to divide inputs into the categories fixed and variable. In the long run, the marginal product of the bundle of inputs that comprise the resources or factors of production for the society should be proportionate to the change in the size of the bundle, or the amount of resources available to the society.

There were other constraints in 1928. Econometrics, the science of estimating economic relationships using statistics, was only in its infancy. The function had to be very simple to estimate. The lack of computers and even pocket calculators meant that at most, statistical work had to be done on a mechanical calculator. Estimates of parameters of the function derived from the data had to be possible within the constraints imposed by the calculation tools of the 1920s.

10.2 The Original Cobb–Douglas Function

The function proposed in the 1928 article was

$$y = A x_1^{\alpha} x_2^{1-\alpha} \qquad (10.1)$$

where x_1 = labor
x_2 = capital

The function had three characteristics viewed at that time as desirable:

1. It was homogeneous of degree 1 with respect to the input bundle, which was consistent with the economics of the day that stressed that production functions for a society should have constant returns to scale.
2. The function exhibited diminishing marginal returns to either capital or labor, when the other was treated as the fixed input, so the law of variable proportions held. The parameter A was thought to represent the technology of the society that generated the observations upon which the parameters of the function were to be estimated.
3. The function was easily estimated with the tools of the day. Both sides

of the function could be transformed to logarithms in base 10 or natural logarithms in base $e(2.71828...)$

$$\log y = \log A + \alpha \log x_1 + (1 - \alpha) \log x_2 \qquad (10.2)$$

The resulting equation is referred to as *linear in the parameters* or *linear in the coefficients*. In other words, $\log y$ is a linear function of $\log x_1$ and $\log x_2$. The transformed function is the equation for a simple two-variable regression line in which all observations in the data set used for estimating the regression line have been transformed into base 10 or natural logs:

$$\log y = b_0 + b_1 \log x_1 + b_2 \log x_2 + \varepsilon \qquad (10.3)$$

where $A = e^{b_0}$ if the transformation is to natural logarithms, or 10^{b_0} if the transformation is to base 10 logs
$b_1 = \alpha$
$b_2 = 1 - \alpha$
ε = regression error term

There was no point in empirically estimating b_2 if the assumption was made that the parameters on capital and labor summed to 1. The function could be estimated with only one input or independent variable. Cobb and Douglas estimated the parameter on labor using regression analysis and saved their statistical clerks a lot of work on the mechanical calculator.

It is important to recognize that the Cobb–Douglas production function, when originally proposed, was not intended to be a perfect representation for the United States of the technical relationships governing the transformation of labor and capital into output. Rather, it was chosen because it retained the two key economic assumptions of the day (diminishing returns to each input and constant returns to scale) and because its parameters were easy to obtain from actual data.

The Cobb–Douglas function had economic properties clearly superior to what was the probable alternative of the day, a simple linear function with constant marginal products for both inputs

$$y = ax_1 + bx_2 \qquad (10.4)$$

As will be seen shortly, the Cobb–Douglas function lacked many features characteristic of the three-stage production function proposed by the neoclassical economists, which was graphically developed earlier. Had Cobb and Douglas perceived the massive impact of their early work on both economists and agricultural economists, they perhaps would have come up with something more complicated and sophisticated. Part of the appeal of the function rested with its utter simplicity in estimation. Agricultural economists today use only slightly modified versions of the Cobb–Douglas production function for much the same reasons that the function was originally developed—it is simple to estimate but allows for diminishing marginal returns to each input.

10.3 Early Generalizations

The first generalization of the Cobb–Douglas production function was to allow the parameters on the inputs to sum to a number other than 1, allowing for returns to scale of something other than 1. The function

$$y = Ax_1^{\beta_1}x_2^{\beta_2} \tag{10.5}$$

where $\beta_1 + \beta_2$ sum to any number, is sometimes referred to as a Cobb–Douglas type of production function, but it is not the true Cobb–Douglas function. This function was also readily transformed to logs. Parameters could still be estimated by least-squares regression with two inputs or explanatory variables, and with the advent of the computer, this could be done very easily.

As the use of the function moved from the problem of estimating the relationships between capital, labor, and output at the society level to problems of representing production processes at the individual farm level, the interpretation of some of the parameters changed. Cobb and Douglas assumed that output could be produced with only capital and labor. At the farm firm level, x_1 and x_2 more likely represent two variable inputs that are under the control of the manager. The remaining inputs are treated as fixed. The parameter A might be thought of as the combined impact of these fixed factors on the production function. In this context

$$A = \Sigma x_i^{\beta_i} \quad \text{for all } i = 3, \ldots, n \tag{10.6}$$

In equation (10.6), there are n inputs, with all but $n - 2$ being treated as fixed. Technology could have an impact on the magnitude of the β_i themselves. The parameters β_1 and β_2 might be expected to sum to a number substantially less than 1, particularly if there are a large number of fixed inputs contained in the parameter A. Thus, a restriction that forced the coefficients on the variable inputs to sum to 1 would be silly.

The second generalization was to expand the function in terms of the number of inputs. The four-input expansion is

$$y = Ax_1^{\beta_1}x_2^{\beta_2}x_3^{\beta_3}x_4^{\beta_4} \tag{10.7}$$

A function of the general form of equation (10.7) with any number of inputs was readily transformed to logs, and the parameters were empirically estimated from appropriate data using ordinary least-squares regression techniques. As the number of inputs treated as variable expanded, the sum of the parameters on the variable inputs should also increase, assuming that each variable input has a positive marginal product.

In this text, the term *Cobb–Douglas function* or *true Cobb–Douglas function* is used only in reference to the two-input multiplicative function in which the sum of the individual production elasticities is equal to 1. The term *Cobb–Douglas type of function* is used in reference to a multiplicative function where the elasticities of production sum to a number other than 1, or in a case where there are more than two inputs or factors of production.

10.4 Some Characteristics of the Cobb–Douglas Type of Function

The Cobb–Douglas type of function is homogeneous of degree $\Sigma \beta_i$. The returns-to-scale parameter or function coefficient is equal to the sum of the β values on the individual inputs, assuming that all inputs are treated explicitly as variable. The β values represents the elasticity of production with respect to the corresponding input and are constants.

The partial elasticities of production for each input are simply the β parameters for the input. This can easily be shown. The partial elasticity of production for input x_i is the ratio of *MPP* to *APP* for that input. The *MPP* for input x_i is

$$MPPx_i = \beta_i A x_i^{\beta_i - 1} \Sigma x_j^{\beta_j} \tag{10.8}$$

for all $j \neq i = 1, \ldots, n$ where n is the number of inputs. The *APP* for input x_i is

$$APPx_i = A x_i^{\beta_i - 1} \Sigma x_j^{\beta_j} \tag{10.9}$$

The ratio of *MPP* to *APP* for the *i*th input is b_i. Hence the elasticities of production for the Cobb–Douglas type of production function are constant irrespective of the amounts of each input that are used. The ratio of *MPP* to *APP* is constant, which is very unlike the neoclassical three-stage production function.

Moreover, MPP and APP for each input never intersect, but stay at the fixed ratio relative to each other as determined by the partial elasticity of production. The only exception is an instance where the partial production elasticity is exactly equal to 1 for one of the inputs. If this were the case, the *MPP* and the *APP* for that input would be the same everywhere irrespective of how much of that input were used.

All inputs must be used for output to be produced. Since the Cobb–Douglas function is multiplicative, the absence of any one input will result in no total output, even if other inputs are readily available. This characteristic may not be extremely important when there are but a few categories of highly aggregated inputs, but if there are a large number of input categories, this characteristic may be of some concern, since it is unlikely that every input would be used in the production of each commodity.

There is no finite output maximum at a finite level of input use. The function increases up the expansion path at a rate that corresponds to the value of the function coefficient. If the function coefficient is 1, the function increases at a constant rate up the expansion path. If the function coefficient is greater than 1, the function increases at an increasing rate. If the function coefficient is less than 1, the function increases at a decreasing rate. Agricultural production functions of the Cobb–Douglas type when estimated usually have function coefficients of less than 1.

For a given set of parameters, the function can represent only one stage of production for each input, and ridge lines do not exist. If the elasticities of production are for each input less than 1, the function will depict stage II everywhere.

If the function coefficient is less than 1, there will normally be a point of global profit maximization at a finite level of input use. Pseudo scale lines exist and will intersect on the expansion path at this finite level.

10.5 Isoquants for the Cobb–Douglas Type of Function

The Cobb–Douglas type of production function, as given by

$$y = A x_1^{\beta_1} x_2^{\beta_2} \tag{10.10}$$

has the corresponding marginal products

$$MPPx_1 = \partial y/\partial x_1 = \beta_1 x_1^{\beta_1-1} x_2^{\beta_2} \tag{10.11}$$

$$MPPx_2 = \partial y/\partial x_2 = \beta_2 x_1^{\beta_1} x_2^{\beta_2-1} \tag{10.12}$$

The $MRSx_1x_2$ is obtained by finding the negative ratio of $MPPx_1/MPPx_2$.

$$MRSx_1x_2 = -(\beta_1 x_2)/(\beta_2 x_1) \tag{10.13}$$

The MRS is a linear function of the input ratio x_2/x_1

The equation for an isoquant is obtained by fixing the output of y at some constant level $y°$ and solving for x_2 in terms of x_1

$$y° = A x_1^{\beta_1} x_2^{\beta_2} \tag{10.14}$$

$$x_2^{\beta_2} = y°/(A x_1^{\beta_1}) \tag{10.15}$$

$$x_2 = [y°/(A x_1^{\beta_1})]^{1/\beta_2} \tag{10.16}$$

$$x_2 = y^{°(1/\beta_2)} A^{-1/\beta_2} x^{-\beta_1/\beta_2} \tag{10.17}$$

$$dx_2/dx_1 = -(\beta_1/\beta_2) y^{°(1/\beta_2)} A^{-1/\beta_2} x_1^{(-\beta_1/\beta_2)-1} < 0 \tag{10.18}$$

The isoquants for a Cobb–Douglas type of production function have a downward slope as long as the individual production elasticities are positive. This is true irrespective of the values of β_1 and β_2.

Moreover,

$$d^2x_2/dx_1^2 = [(-\beta_1/\beta_2) - 1][-\beta_1/\beta_2] y^{°(1/\beta_2)} A^{-1/\beta_2} x_1^{(-\beta_1/\beta_2)-2}$$
$$> 0 \quad \text{if the individual production elasticities are positive.} \tag{10.19}$$

The sign on equation (10.19) indicates that the isoquants for the Cobb–Douglas type of production function are asymptotic to the x_1 and x_2 axes irrespective of

The Cobb–Douglas Production Function

the values of the partial production elasticities, as long as the partial production elasticities are positive. Isoquants for a Cobb–Douglas type of function are illustrated in Figure 10.1. Although these isoquants appear to be rectangular hyperbolas, their position relative to the x_1 and x_2 axes will depend on the relative magnitudes of β_1 and β_2. The isoquant will be positioned closer to the axis of the input with the larger elasticity of production.

To reemphasize, the general shape of the isoquants for a Cobb–Douglas type of function are not conditional on the values of the individual production elasticities. As long as the individual production elasticities are greater than zero, the isoquants will always be downward sloping, convex to the origin of the graph, and asymptotic to the axes. The convexity of the isoquants for the function occurs because of the diminishing marginal rate of substitution and because the function is multiplicative, not additive, resulting in a synergistic influence on output when inputs are used in combination with each other. That is, output is the product of that attributed to each input, not the sum of that attributed to each input.

The expansion path generated by a Cobb–Douglas function in the x_1 and x_2 plane has a constant slope equal to $(v_2/v_1)(\beta_1/\beta_2)$. The expansion path is obtained by setting the $MRSx_1x_2$ equal to the inverse price ratio

$$MRSx_1x_2 = (\beta_1 x_2)/(\beta_2 x_1) = v_1/v_2 \qquad (10.20)$$

$$\beta_2 x_1 v_1 = \beta_1 x_2 v_2 \qquad (10.21)$$

$$\beta_2 x_1 v_1 - \beta_1 x_2 v_2 = 0 \qquad (10.22)$$

$$x_2 = (v_2/v_1)(\beta_1/\beta_2) x_1 \qquad (10.23)$$

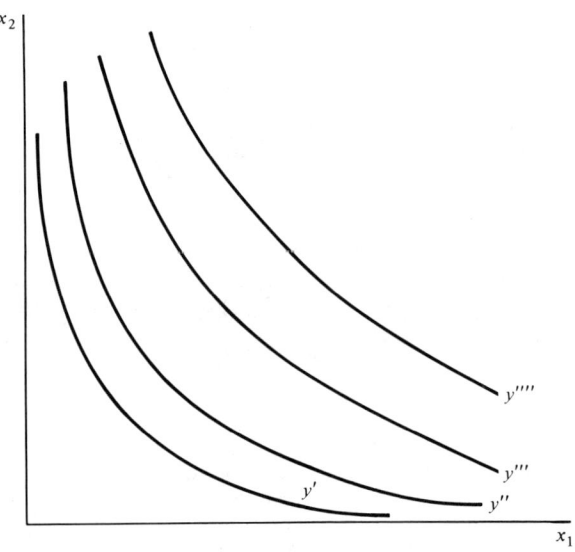

Figure 10.1 Isoquants for a Cobb–Douglas Type of Function

10.6 The Production Surface of the Cobb–Douglas Production Function

Figure 10.2 illustrates the three-dimensional surface of the Cobb–Douglas type of production function with two inputs, under varying assumptions with respect to the values of the β coefficients. Depending on the specific coefficients, the production surface for the Cobb–Douglas type of function can vary rather dramatically. Diagram A illustrates the case in which the parameters on the two inputs sum to 1. In this illustration, $β_1$ is 0.4 and $β_2$ is 0.6. Each line on the diagram represents a production function for one of the inputs, holding the other input constant. Production functions for x_2 begin at the x_1 axis. Production functions for x_1 begin at the x_2 axis. Since x_2 is the more productive input, production functions for x_2 have a steeper slope than do the production functions for x_1. Now move along an imaginary diagonal line midway between the x_1 and x_2 axes. The production surface directly above this imaginary diagonal line has a constant slope. The slope of the surface above this line represents the function coefficient or returns-to-scale parameter of 1 for this two-input Cobb–Douglas production function which has constant returns to scale.

Diagram B illustrates a Cobb–Douglas type of production function in which the elasticities of production sum to a number smaller than 1. In this example, $β_1$ is 0.1 and $β_2$ is 0.2. The function is homogeneous of degree 0.3 and has a function coefficient of 0.3. Again, x_2 is the more productive input, as verified by its larger elasticity of production. Production functions for x_2 are found by starting upward at the x_1 axis, and production functions for x_1 are found by following a line upward from the x_2 axis. Input x_2 has the production functions with the steepest slope. The marginal product of each input appears to be very great at small values for x_1 and x_2, but drops off rapidly as input use is increased. The output (y) produced by the function for a specific quantity of x_1 and x_2 is much smaller than for the function illustrated in diagram A. The production surface above the imaginary diagonal line is concave from below. The function coefficient of 0.3 indicates that the marginal product of incremental units of a bundle of x_1 and x_2 is declining.

Diagram C illustrates a Cobb–Douglas type of production function in which the individual elasticities of production for each input are less than 1 but the elasticities of production sum to a number greater than 1. In this example, $β_1$ is 0.6 and $β_2$ is 0.8, yielding a function coefficient of 1.4. The marginal product for individual production functions is declining, but the marginal product for the bundle along the imaginary diagonal line is increasing. This implies that the production surface above this imaginary scale line is convex, not concave from below.

Diagram D illustrates a Cobb–Douglas type of production function in which one input has an elasticity of production greater than 1, but the elasticity of production for the other input is less than 1. In this example, $β_1$ is 0.4 and $β_2$ is 1.5. Starting at the x_1 axis, follow a line representing the production function for x_2. Note that this production function is curving upward, or increasing at an increasing rate, and the marginal product of input x_2 is increasing as the level of x_2 is increased. But the production functions for x_1, which start at the x_2 axis, have a declining marginal product, as evidenced by the fact that they

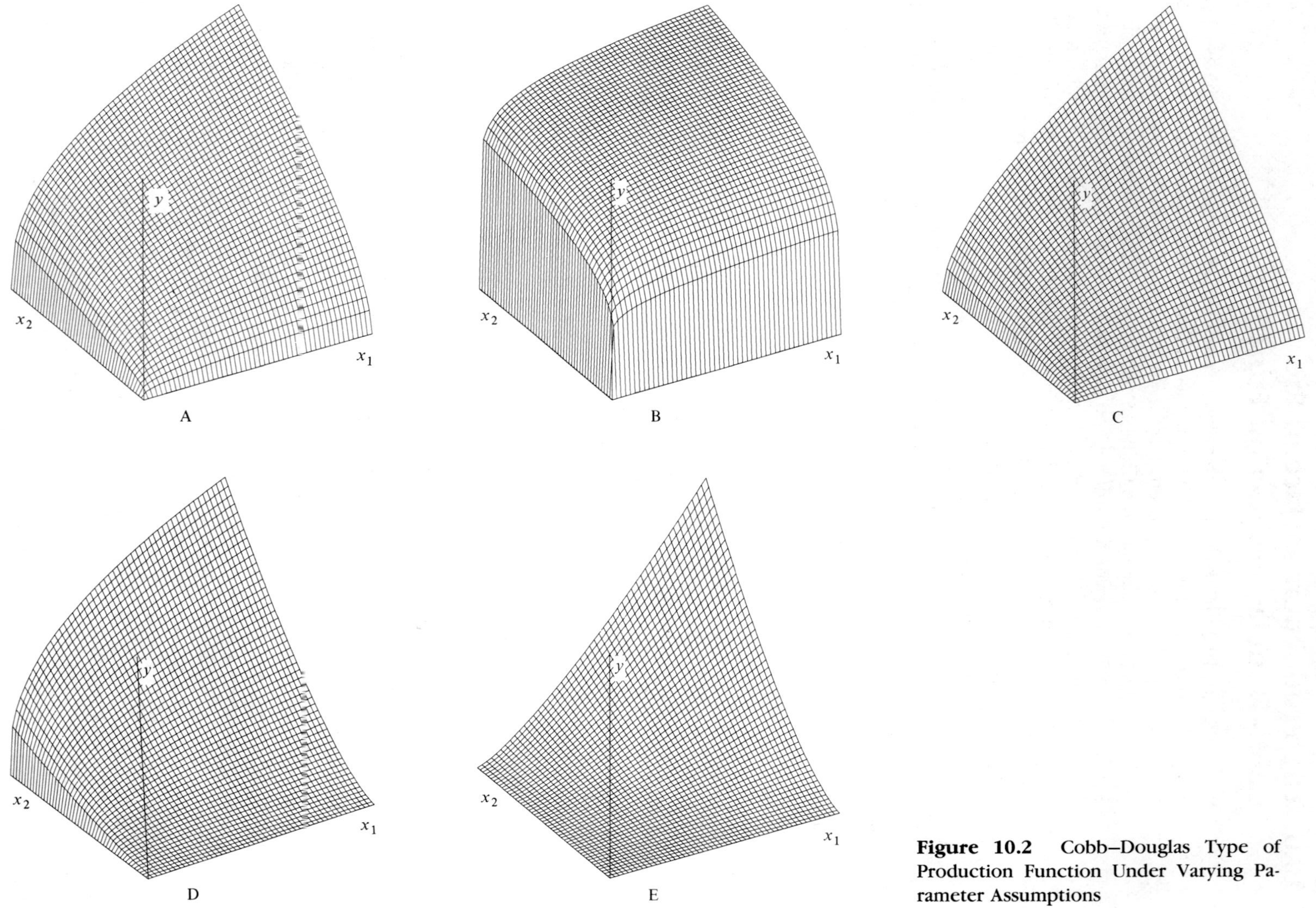

Figure 10.2 Cobb–Douglas Type of Production Function Under Varying Parameter Assumptions

increase at a decreasing rate. The production surface above the imaginary diagonal line is convex from below. The marginal product of the input bundle defined by the diagonal line increases as the size of the bundle increases, and the function coefficient is 1.9.

Diagram E illustrates a Cobb–Douglas type of production function in which both inputs have elasticities of production of greater than 1. In this example, β_1 is 1.3 and β_2 is 1.5, yielding a total elasticity of production or function coefficient of 2.8. That the marginal product of both x_1 and x_2 is increasing is clearly evident from a careful examination of individual production functions in diagram E. The production surface above the imaginary diagonal line representing the input bundle is clearly convex from below.

10.7 Profit Maximization with the Cobb–Douglas Function

Regardless of the values for the elasticities of production, a multiplicative production function of the Cobb–Douglas type never achieves an output maximum for a finite level of x_1 and x_2. Upon learning that the first-order conditions of a maximum are achieved by setting the first partial derivatives of a function equal to zero, students are sometimes tempted to try this with a Cobb–Douglas type of function. Unless the elasticities of production for each input are zero (in which case, increases in each input produce no additional output, since any number raised to the zero power is 1), the only way for these first-order conitions to hold is for no input to be used, and if that were the case, there would also be no output. A Cobb–Douglas type of function has no finite maximum where the ridge lines would intersect. This is not surprising, since the ridge lines do not exist, and any point on any isoquant for a Cobb–Douglas type of function, irrespective of the parameter values, will have a negative slope.

Profit maximization is possible only if the function coefficient is less than 1, assuming that the purely competitive model holds, with constant input and output prices. In the purely competitive model, the price of the output is a constant p, total revenue is py and the total value of the product (TVP) is

$$TVP = px_1^{\beta_1}x_1^{\beta_2} \qquad (10.24)$$

The function coefficient or total elasticity of production for the production function indicates the responsiveness of output to changes in the size of the input bundle. It is the percentage change in output divided by the percentage change in the size of the input bundle. Assuming a constant output price, the function coefficient also represents the responsiveness of total value of the product to changes in the size of the input bundle. It is the percentage change in the total value of the product or output divided by the percentage change in the input bundle.

With constant input prices, the marginal cost of acquiring an additional unit of the input bundle along the expansion path is also constant, not decreasing or increasing. If the function coefficient is greater than 1, each additional unit of the bundle produces more and additional output and total value of the product. Incremental units of the bundle can be obtained at a fixed constant price per unit. The manager would be better off in terms of increased revenue by acquiring more and more additional units of the bundle. This process could occur indefinitely, and both input use and output would be expanded up to the point where the purely competitive assumptions with regard to both input and output prices are no longer met. Either the manager is producing so much output that it can no longer be sold at the going market price, or so much input is being purchased that more cannot be bought without causing the price of the input bundle to increase.

Now consider a case in which each input has a production elasticity of less than 1 but the total elasticity of production or function coefficient is exactly 1. If this case, a 1 percent increase in the size of the bundle is accompanied by a 1 percent rise in revenue. The marginal cost of an additional unit of the bundle is a constant V. The revenue from the use of an additional unit of the bundle is the revenue generated from an additional unit of output, or p. The manager would attempt to equate the marginal cost of the bundle (V) with the marginal revenue from the additional unit of output (p). Both numbers are constants. If $p > V$, the manager could make additional profits by expanding use of the input bundle indefinitely, which is the same solution as the first case. Total profit is $(p - V)y$ where y is the number of units of output produced. If p were less than V, the manager should shut down since each and all incremental units of output cost more than they generated in additional revenue. The total loss is $(p - V)y$, where y is the number of units of output produced. Only if p were equal to V would the manager be indifferent to producing or shutting down. Each incremental unit of output cost exactly what it returned, so there would be zero profit everywhere.

Finally, consider a case in which the sum of the individual elasticities of production is less than 1. Again the price of the input bundle is treated as a constant, but in this case the value of the marginal product is declining. Profits can be maximized at some finite level of use of the input bundle, assuming that for certain levels of input use, *TVP* does exceed the cost of the bundle.

Another way of looking at the profit-maximization conditions for the Cobb–Douglas type of function is with the aid of the pseudo scale lines developed earlier. Assume constant input and output prices. If the function coefficient is less than 1, the pseudo scale lines exist and converge at some finite level of input use along the expansion path. The convergence of the pseudo scale lines represents the global point of profit maximization. If the function coefficient is equal to 1, the pseudo scale lines exist but are parallel to each other, so that they do not intersect for any finite level of use of the input bundle along the expansion path. If the function coefficient is greater than 1 but the individual elasticities of production are less than 1, the pseudo scale line exist but diverge, going farther and farther apart as the use of the bundle is expanded. A pseudo scale line for an individual input does not exist if the elasticity of production for that input is greater than or equal to 1.

10.8 Duality and the Cobb–Douglas Function

The Cobb–Douglas type of function is homogeneous, and its corresponding dual cost function exists. It is possible to derive the specific cost function in

10.8 Duality and the Cobb–Douglas Function

terms of output for a Cobb–Douglas type of production function. Assume the production function

$$y = A x_1^{\beta_1} x_2^{\beta_2} \qquad (10.25)$$

The input cost function is

$$C = v_1 x_1 + v_2 x_2 \qquad (10.26)$$

The dual cost function for a Cobb–Douglas type of production function is found using the following procedure. First, the equation for the expansion path is found by partially differentiating the production function with respect to x_1 and x_2, to find the marginal products. The negative ratio of the marginal products is the $MRSx_1x_2$. This is equated to the inverse input price ratio. The result can be written as

$$\beta_2 v_1 x_1 = \beta_1 v_2 x_2 \qquad (10.27)$$

Equation (10.27) defines the points of least-cost combination along the expansion path.

Equation (10.27) is solved for x_1 to yield

$$x_1 = \beta_1 v_2 x_2 \beta_2^{-1} v_1^{-1} \qquad (10.28)$$

Equation (10.28) is inserted into equation (10.26) and x_2 is factored out:

$$C = x_2(\beta_1 v_2 \beta_2^{-1} + v_2) \qquad (10.29)$$

Equation (10.29) defines the quantity of x_2 that is used in terms of cost (C) and the parameters of the production function

$$x_2 = C/(\beta_1 v_2 \beta_2^{-1} + v_2) \qquad (10.30)$$

Similarly, for input x_1,

$$x_1 = C/(\beta_2 v_1 \beta_1^{-1} + v_1) \qquad (10.31)$$

Inputs x_1 and x_2 are now defined totally in terms of cost C, the input prices (v_1 and v_2), and the parameters of the production function. Inserting equations (10.30) and (10.31) into the original production function [equation (10.25)] and rearranging, results in

$$y = C^{\beta_1+\beta_2} A (\beta_2 v_1 \beta_1^{-1} + v_1)^{-\beta_1} (\beta_1 v_2 \beta_2^{-1} + v_2)^{-\beta_2} \qquad (10.32)$$

Solving equation (10.32) for C in terms of y, the production function parameters and the input prices yields

$$C = y^{1/(\beta_1+\beta_2)} A^{-1/(\beta_1+\beta_2)} (\beta_1^{-1} \beta_2 v_1 + v_1)^{\beta_1/(\beta_1+\beta_2)} (\beta_2^{-1} \beta_1 v_2 + v_2)^{\beta_2/(\beta_1+\beta_2)}$$

or

$$C = y^{1/(\beta_1+\beta_2)}Z \tag{10.33}$$

where

$$Z = A^{-1/(\beta_1+\beta_2)}(\beta_1^{-1}\beta_2 v_1 + v_1)^{\beta_1/(\beta_1+\beta_2)}(\beta_2^{-1}\beta_1 v_2 + v_2)^{\beta_2/(\beta_1+\beta_2)}$$

Notice that y is raised to the power 1 over the degree of homogeneity of the original production function. The value of Z is a constant, since it is dependent only on the assumed constant prices of the inputs and the assumed constant parameters of the production function. Notice that prices for inputs are available, all the information needed to obtain the corresponding dual cost function can be obtained from the production function. The coefficients or parameters of a Cobb–Douglas type of production function uniquely define a corresponding dual cost function. C is cost in terms of output.

Marginal cost is

$$MC = dC/dy = [1/(\beta_1+\beta_2)]y^{1/(\beta_1+\beta_2)-1}Z \tag{10.34}$$

The slope of MC is positive if the sum of the individual partial production elasticities or function coefficient is less than 1. If the individual production elasticities sum to a number greater than 1, MC is declining. MC has a zero slope when the production elasticities sum exactly to 1. The supply function for a firm with a Cobb–Douglas type of production function can be found by equating marginal cost [equation (10.34)] with marginal revenue or the price of the product and solving the resultant equation for y.

Average cost is

$$AC = TC/y = y^{1/(\beta_1+\beta_2)-1}Z \tag{10.35}$$

Since Z is positive, average cost decreases when the partial production elasticities sum to a number greater than 1. Average cost increases if the partial production elasticities sum to a number less than 1. If the production function is a true Cobb–Douglas, total cost is given by

$$TC = yZ \tag{10.36}$$

Both marginal and average cost are given by the constant Z, and therefore both MC and AC have a zero slope. For a Cobb–Douglas type of production function, MC and AC never intersect, except in the instance where the function coefficient (or the cost elasticity) is 1, in which case MC and AC are the same everywhere.

The ratio of marginal to average cost or the cost elasticity (ψ) is

$$\begin{aligned}(\psi) &= 1/(\beta_1+\beta_2) \\ &= 1/E \end{aligned} \tag{10.37}$$

where E is the returns-to-scale parameter or function coefficient.

If total product along the expansion path is increasing at a decreasing rate, costs are increasing at an increasing rate. If total product along the expansion path is increasing at an increasing rate, costs are increasing at a decreasing rate. If total product along the expansion path is increasing at a constant rate (the true Cobb–Douglas function), costs are also increasing at a constant rate. If the product sells for a fixed price, that price is a constant marginal revenue (MR). Marginal revenue [MR can be equated to marginal cost (MC) only if MC is increasing]. With fixed input prices and elasticities of production, this can happen only if the cost elasticity is greater than 1, which means that the function coefficient for the underlying production function is strictly less than 1.

The profit function can be written as:

$$\Pi = TR - TC \quad (10.38)$$

$$\Pi = py - Zy^{1/E} \quad (10.39)$$

where E is the function coefficient.

Maximum profits occur if

$$d\Pi/dy = p - (1/E)y^{(1/E)-1} = 0$$
$$MR - MC = 0 \quad (10.40)$$

and

$$d^2\Pi/dy^2 = -(1/E)[(1/E)-1]y^{(1/E)-2} < 0 \quad (10.41)$$

E is positive. The only way the second derivative can be negative is for E to be smaller than 1. This implies that MC is increasing. If E is equal to 1, the second derivative of the profit function is zero, and MC is constant. If E is greater than 1, the second derivative of the profit function is positive, and MC is decreasing.

10.9 Constrained Output or Revenue Maximization

A finite solution to the problem of globally maximizing profits could be found only in those instances where the production function had a function coefficient of less than 1. The same conditions do not hold for the problem of finding the least-cost combination of inputs required to produce a particular level of output or revenue. The isoquants generated by a Cobb–Douglas type of production function are convex to the origin if the partial elasticities of production are positive, and as a result, points of tangency that meet second-order conditions are easy to find. For example, suppose that the production function is

$$y = x_1 x_2 \quad (10.42)$$

The individual partial elasticities of production for each input is 1, and the function coefficient is 2. Despite its strange appearance, this is a production function of the Cobb–Douglas type.

Suppose that the price of both x_1 and x_2 is \$1 per unit. The Lagrangian would be

$$L = x_1 x_2 + \lambda(C^\circ - 1x_1 - 1x_2) \quad (10.43)$$

With the corresponding first-order conditions

$$\partial L / \partial x_1 = x_2 - 1\lambda = 0 \quad (10.44)$$

$$\partial L / \partial x_2 = x_1 - 1\lambda = 0 \quad (10.45)$$

$$\partial / \partial \lambda = C^\circ - 1x_1 - 1x_2 = 0 \quad (10.46)$$

The second-order conditions require that the determinant of the following matrix be positive

$$\begin{vmatrix} 0 & 1 & -1 \\ 1 & 0 & -1 \\ -1 & -1 & 0 \end{vmatrix} \quad (10.47)$$

The determinant of equation (10.47) is 2, which is clearly positive, thus meeting the second-order conditions for a constrained output maximization. Despite the fact that the production function in equation (10.42) meets both first- and second-order conditions for a constrained revenue maximization, there is no assurance that revenue less costs will be positive when the point of least-cost combination is found.

10.10 Concluding Comments

The Cobb–Douglas type of production function has been estimated by agricultural economists for virtually any production process involving the transformation of inputs into outputs in an agricultural setting. Economists have used a Cobb–Douglas type of specification for virtually every conceivable type of production process. To review specific applications of the Cobb–Douglas type of function would be to review a large share of the literature in which empirical attempts have been made to estimate production functions. Some of this literature is cited in the reading list.

The appeal of the Cobb–Douglas type of function rests largely with its simplicity. Even when the Cobb–Douglas form is not used as the final form of the function, it is often used as a benchmark specification for comparison with other functional forms. The null research hypothesis might be that the production function is of the Cobb–Douglas type. The alternative hypothesis is that another specification provides a better fit to the data.

Cobb and Douglas never intended that the Cobb–Douglas production function represent the subtle details of the three-stage production function of the neoclassical economists. However, the elegant simplicity of the algebra surrounding the Cobb–Douglas type of production function seems to appeal to economists and agricultural economists alike. Never mind that the relationships were not always as the neoclassical economists had proposed.

The neoclassical three-stage production function was a marvelous invention. However, as subsequent chapters will show, the three-stage production function as originally conceived is not always the easiest thing to represent with mathematics. The problem becomes especially difficult as extensions are made to multiple-input categories. Agricultural economists use the Cobb–Douglas specification for no better reason than that the algebra is simplified.

Problems and Exercises

1. For a Cobb–Douglas type of function

$$y = Ax_1^a x_2^b$$

for each case, does there exist the following?

a. A global point of output maximization.
b. A global point of profit maximization (assume constant input and output prices).
c. A series of points of constrained output maximization.

Case	Value for A	Value for a	Value for b
(1)	1	0.2	0.3
(2)	1	0.4	0.6
(3)	1	0.6	0.8
(4)	1	1	1
(5)	1	2	2
(6)	1	−0.3	0.5
(7)	−1	0.4	0.6

2. For each case outlined above, find *MPP* and *APP* for each input, holding the other input constant at some predetermined level. What is the relationship between *MPP* and *APP* in each case?

3. Suppose that the production function is

$$y = x_1 x_2$$

The input x_1 sells for $1 per unit and input x_2 sells for $2 per unit. The farmer has $200 to spend on x_1 and x_2. How much of each input will the farmer purchase in order to be at a point of constrained output maximization?

4. Making certain that the scale on both the x_1 and the x_2 axes is the same, draw a graph for an isoquant generated by the function

$$y = x_1^{0.5} x_2^{0.33}$$

Assume that the length of each axis represents 10 units of input use. Is the isoquant closer to the x_1 axis or the x_2 axis? Why?

5. Assume that the production function is

$$y = x_1^{0.5} x_2^{0.33}$$

x_1 costs \$1 per unit; x_2 costs \$2 per unit. Find the corresponding total cost function with total cost expressed as a function of output (y), the input prices, and the production function parameters.

Reference

Cobb, Charles W., and Paul H. Douglas. "A Theory of Production." *American Economic Review* 18:(Suppl.(1928) pp 139–156.

11 Other Agricultural Production Functions

In addition to the Cobb–Douglas, agricultural economists have made use of a diverse array of other functional forms. The earliest efforts to develop production functions from agricultural data predate the Cobb–Douglas work, using a production function developed by Spillman. The transcendental production function represented an attempt conducted in the 1950s to develop a specification closely tied to the characteristics of the neoclassical three-stage production function. Production functions with variable rather than constant input elasticities represented a development during the 1960s. In the early 1970s de Janvry showed that the Cobb–Douglas function with either fixed or variable input elasticities and the transcendental production functions were all members of a family of production functions called generalized power production functions. All of these production functions have been used as a basis for estimating relationships within agriculture. This chapter will be of primary interest to students interested in doing research in agricultural economics.

Key Terms and Definitions:

Spillman Production Function
Transcendental Production Function
Cobb–Douglas Function with
    Variable Elasticities
Generalized Power Production
    Function
Polynomial Forms

11.1 Introduction

Despite the widespread use of the Cobb–Douglas production function, it was not the first or the only production function to be used by agricultural economists for representing production relationships. Agricultural economics as a formal discipline is relatively new, having had its start as a separate discipline in the first decade of the twentieth century. The first work in agricultural economics was conducted by biological scientists who were interested in providing farmers with useful information with regard to designing plans for feeding livestock or fertilizing crops. Even these early efforts, conducted by biological scientists with little or no training in economics, had a central focus in obtaining estimates of parameters of agricultural production functions as a basis for the development of recommendations to farmers.

11.2 The Spillman Production Function

One of the earliest efforts to estimate a production function in agriculture was conducted by Spillman and was published in the newly created *Journal of Farm Economics* (later to become the *American Journal of Agricultural Economics*) in two articles in 1923 and 1924. The first article was titled "Application of the Law of Diminishing Returns to Some Fertilizer and Feed Data." The second was "Law of the Diminishing Increment in the Fattening of Steers and Hogs." It is not surprising that Spillman was interested in determining whether or not the law of diminishing returns had empirical support within some rather basic agricultural production processes.

The empirical efforts by Spillman were published prior to the work by Cobb and Douglas in 1928, and the form of the production functions used by Spillman differed slightly. The Spillman function was

$$y = A(1 - R_1^{x_1})(1 - R_2^{x_2}) \tag{11.1}$$

where A, R_1 and R_2 are parameters to be estimated. The parameters R_1 and R_2 would normally be expected to fall between zero and 1. The sum of $R_1 + R_2$ would normally be less than or equal to 1.

An example of the Spillman function is

$$y = 1(1 - 0.3^{x_1})(1 - 0.4^{x_2}) \tag{11.2}$$

In equation (11.2), if one of the inputs is increased, output increases, but at a decreasing rate. The marginal products of x_1 or x_2 are positive but decreasing.

The marginal product of input x_1 ($MPPx_1$) is

$$\partial y / \partial x_1 = -\ln R_1 (1 - R_2^{x_2}) A R_1^{x_1} > 0 \tag{11.3}$$

Since $A, R_1 > 0$,

$$(1 - R_2^{x_2}) \ln R_1 < 0 \tag{11.4}$$

Like the Cobb–Douglas function, the marginal product is positive for any level of input use.

Moreover,

$$\partial^2 y / \partial x_1^2 = -\ln^2 R_1 (1 - R_2^{x_2}) A R_1 x_1 < 0 \tag{11.5}$$

MPP is declining for any level of input use.

The production surface of the Spillman function is somewhat different from the Cobb–Douglas. Figure 11.1 illustrates the surface under the assumption that $R_1 = 0.4$ and $R_2 = 0.6$ and $A = 10$. Compared with a Cobb–Douglas with similar parameters (diagram A, Figure 10.1), the function appears to initially increase at a much more rapid rate, and then increase very slowly.

Since the advent of the Cobb–Douglas, the Spillman has seldom been used by agricultural economists. It is primarily of historical interest because the Spillman research represented one of the first efforts to estimate parameters of a production function for some basic agricultural processes.

11.3 The Transcendental Production Function

By the mid-1950s, both economists and agricultural economists were very much aware of many of the limitations of the Cobb–Douglas production function. They recognized that although parameters of the function were very easy to estimate from data, the function did not very well represent the neoclassical three-stage production function. The problem of greatest concern at that time was the fixed production elasticities, which require that APP and MPP be at a fixed proportion to each other. This issue was not unrelated to the fact that the Cobb–Douglas could represent only one stage of production at a time, very much unlike the neoclassical presentation.

Halter, Carter, and Hocking were very concerned with the lack of compatibility between the Cobb–Douglas and the neoclassical three-stage production function. The researchers sought to make modifications in the Cobb–Douglas to allow for the three stages of production and variable production elasticities, yet at the same time retain a function that was clearly related to the Cobb–Douglas and was easy to estimate from agricultural data.

The function that Halter et al. introduced in 1957 looked like a slightly modified version of the Cobb–Douglas. The base of the natural logarithm, e was added and raised to a power that was a function of the amount of input that was used.

The two-input function was

$$y = A x_1^{\alpha_1} x_2^{\alpha_2} e^{\gamma_1 x_1 + \gamma_2 x_2} \tag{11.6}$$

The corresponding single-input function was

$$y = A x^{\alpha} e^{\gamma x} \tag{11.7}$$

The MPP for the single-input version, using the composite function rule, was

$$\begin{aligned} dy/dx &= \alpha A x^{\alpha-1} e^{\gamma x} + \gamma e^{\gamma x} A x^{\alpha} \\ &= (\alpha/x + \gamma) y \end{aligned} \tag{11.8}$$

Since APP is y/x and the elasticity of production is MPP/APP, the elasticity of production for the single-input transcendental is

$$\begin{aligned} \varepsilon &= (\alpha/x + \gamma) y (x/y) \\ &= \alpha + \gamma x \end{aligned} \tag{11.9}$$

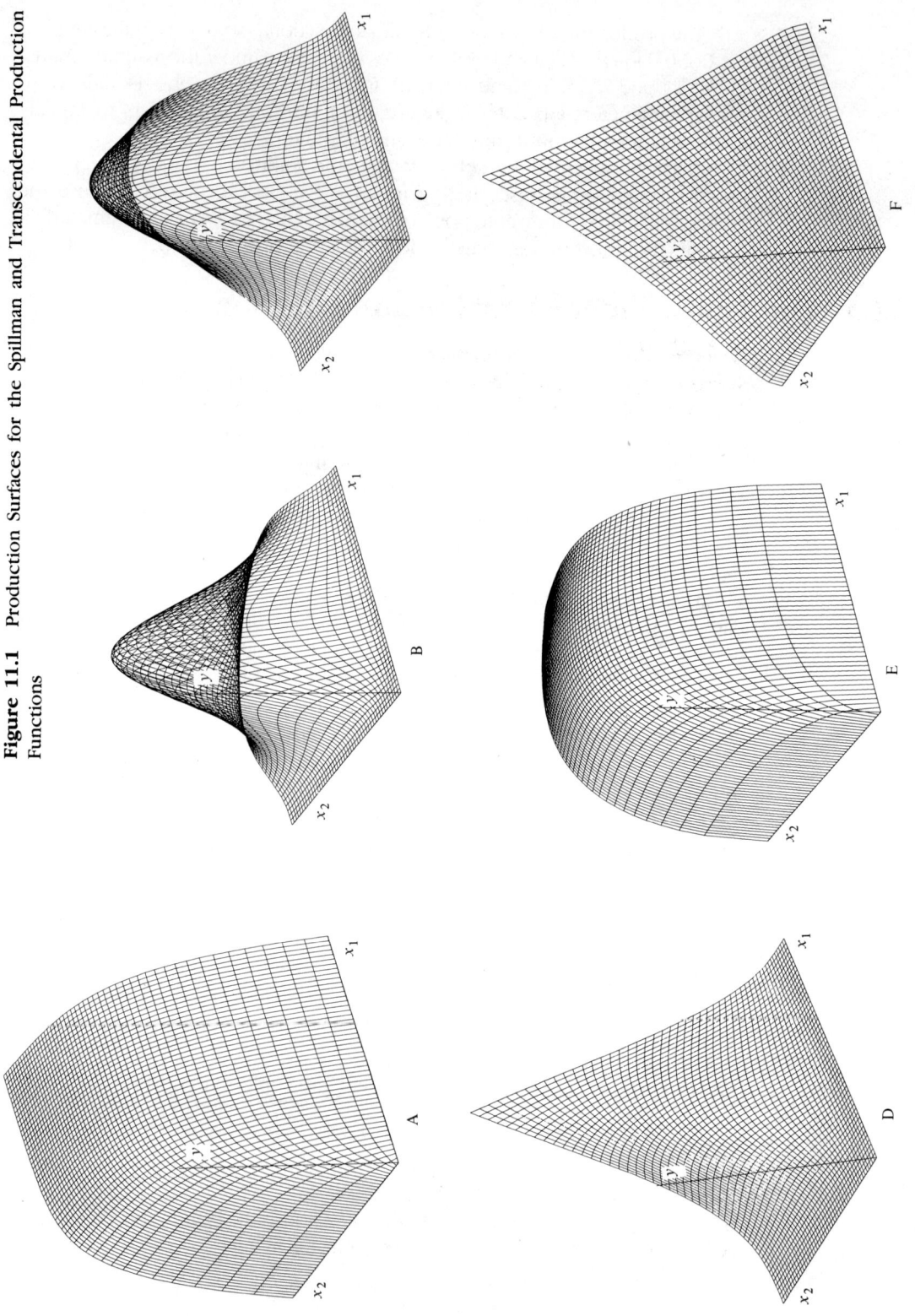

Figure 11.1 Production Surfaces for the Spillman and Transcendental Production Functions

11.4 The Two-Input Transcendental

Table 11.1 Properties of the Single-Input Transcendental Under Varying Assumptions with Respect to Parameters α and γ

Value of α	Value of γ	What Happens to y and ε
$0 < \alpha \leq 1$	<0	y increases at a decreasing rate until $x = -\alpha/\gamma$, then decreases; as x increases, ε is declining.
>1	<0	The neoclassical case: y increases at an increasing rate until $x = (-\alpha + \sqrt{\alpha})/\gamma$, increases at a decreasing rate until $x = -\alpha/\gamma$, then decreases; as x increases, ε is declining
$0 < \alpha < 1$	0	y increases at a decreasing rate; ε is constant equal to α
1	0	y increases at a constant rate; ε is 1; *MPP* and *APP* are the same everywhere
>1	0	y increases at an increasing rate; ε is constant equal to α
$0 < \alpha < 1$	>0	y increases at a decreasing rate until $x = (-\alpha + \sqrt{\alpha})/\gamma$, then increases at increasing rate; ε is increasing
≥ 1	>0	y increases at an increasing rate; ε is increasing

Source: Adapted from Halter et al.

The elasticity of production, and hence the ratio of *MPP* to *APP*, is clearly dependent on the amount of input that is used. The change in the elasticity of production (ε) with respect to a change in the use of x ($d\varepsilon/dx$) is equal to the parameter γ. In other words, the size of γ indicates how rapidly the elasticity of production is declining. In the case of a single-input power production function such as $y = Ax^b$, the elasticity of production is a constant b, and hence $d\varepsilon/dx$ is 0. This function is a special case of the single input transcendental with the parameter γ equal to zero. Since illustrations of the neoclassical production function show a declining elasticity of production as the use of the input increases, the transcendental production functions of greatest interest are those in which γ is negative.

Halter et al. worked out the properties of the transcendental production function for the single-input case under varying assumptions with respect to the values of α and γ. Table 11.1 summarizes their findings.

11.4 The Two-Input Transcendental

Halter et al. proposed an extension of the single-input transcendental to two inputs

$$y = Ax_1^{\alpha_1} x_2^{\alpha_2} e^{\gamma_1 x_1 + \gamma_2 x_2} \tag{11.10}$$

The *MPP* of x_1 is

$$\partial y/\partial x_1 = (\alpha_1/x_1 + \gamma_1)y \tag{11.11}$$

The *MPP* of x_2 is

$$\partial y/\partial x_2 = (\alpha_2/x_2 + \gamma_2)y \tag{11.12}$$

$APPx_1$ is y/x_1 and $APPx_2$ is y/x_2. Therefore, the partial elasticity of production with respect to x_1 is

$$\varepsilon_1 = \alpha_1 + \gamma_1 x_1 \tag{11.13}$$

and with respect to x_2 is

$$\varepsilon_2 = \alpha_2 + \gamma_2 x_2 \tag{11.14}$$

Each production elasticity is dependent on the quantity of that input being used but not on the quantity of the other input. If a measurement of returns to scale is the sum of the individual production elasticities, the returns to scale are not constant but are dependent on the amount of x_1 and x_2 that is used. The two-input transcendental is not homogeneous of any degree.

$$\partial \varepsilon_1 / \partial x_1 = \gamma_1 \qquad \partial \varepsilon_1 / \partial x_2 = 0 \tag{11.15}$$

$$\partial \varepsilon_2 / \partial x_1 = 0 \qquad \partial \varepsilon_2 / \partial x_2 = \gamma_2 \tag{11.16}$$

The marginal rate of substitution of x_1 for x_2 is equal to the negative ratio of the marginal products:

$$\begin{aligned} MRSx_1 x_2 = dx_2/dx_1 &= -[(\alpha_1/x_1 + \gamma_1)y]/[(\alpha_2/x_2 + \gamma_2)y] \\ &= -(\alpha_1/x_1 + \gamma_1)/(\alpha_2/x_2 + \gamma_2) \\ &= -[x_2(\alpha_1 + \gamma_1 x_1)]/[x_1(\alpha_2 + \gamma_2 x_2)] \end{aligned} \tag{11.17}$$

The isoquants for the transcendental when α_1 and $\alpha_2 > 0$ and γ_1 and $\gamma_2 < 0$ consist of a series of concentric rings or lopsided ovals centered at the global output maximum for the function (Figure 11.2). The exact shape of the rings is determined by the value of the parameters for the function. The exact center of the rings occurs at $x_1 = -\alpha_1/\gamma_1$, $x_2 = -\alpha_2/\gamma_2$.

The first-order conditions for profit maximization can be derived by setting the marginal rate of substitution equal to the negative ratio of the input prices ($-v_1/v_2$). The resultant equation defines the expansion path along which the farmer would move as output is expanded. The first-order conditions are defined by

$$(\alpha_1/x_1 + \gamma_1)/(\alpha_2/x_2 + \gamma_2) = v_1/v_2 \tag{11.18}$$

The expansion path equation is defined by

$$x_2 v_2 (\alpha_1 + \gamma_1 x_1) = x_1 v_1 (\alpha_2 + \gamma_2 x_2) \tag{11.19}$$

$$x_2 = v_1 x_1 \alpha_2 / (v_2 \alpha_1 + v_2 \gamma_1 x_1 - v_1 x_1 \gamma_2) \tag{11.20}$$

The expansion path for the transcendental production function is clearly nonlinear unless γ_1 and γ_2 are zero.

11.4 The Two-Input Transcendental

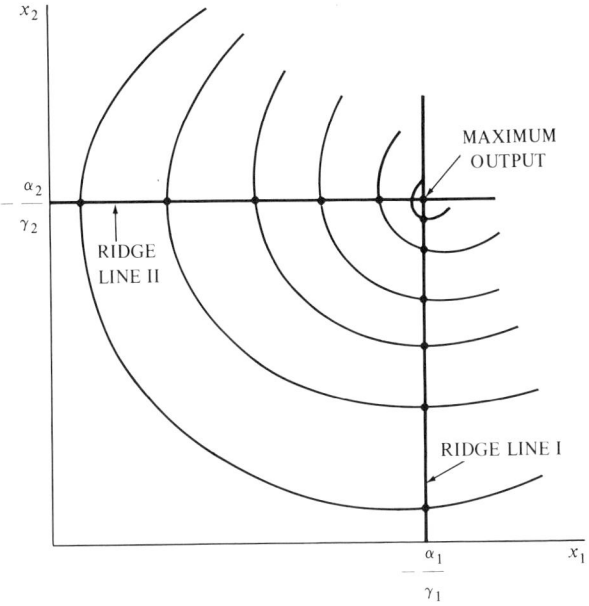

Figure 11.2 Isoquants and Ridge Lines for the Basic Transcendental (No Interaction Term). $y = Ax_1^{\alpha_1} X_2^{\alpha_2} e^{\gamma_1 x_1 + \gamma_2 x_2}$

The ridge lines for the transcendental are present only when γ_1 and γ_2 are negative, and are straight lines that form a right angle at the point of maximum output, where $x_1 = -\alpha_1/\gamma_1$. The position of the ridge line for x_1 in the horizontal axis is determined by the value of α_1 and γ_1. Similarly, the position of the ridge line on the x_2 axis corresponds to the point where $x_2 = \alpha_2/\gamma_2$. (The slope of this ridge line dx_2/dx_1 is clearly zero.)

The resultant square is very much unlike the football shape defined by the ridge lines for the neoclassical case. This ridge line pattern suggests that the maximum output for the family of production functions for the input x_1 occurs at the same level of use for input x_1, regardless of how much of the second input is used. The same holds for input x_2. This is not consistent with the neoclassical case in which an increase in the use of x_2 pushes the maximum of the production function for x_1 farther and farther to the right.

A modification of the transcendental suggested by this author to make the function more closely correspond to the neoclassical diagram would be to include an interaction term in the power of e. The function is

$$y = Ax_1^{\alpha_1} x_2^{\alpha_2} e^{(\gamma_1 x_1 + \gamma_2 x_2 + \gamma_3 x_1 x_2)} \tag{11.21}$$

the corresponding *MPP* for x_1 is $(\alpha_1/x_1 + \gamma_1 + \gamma_3 x_2)y$. *APP* is y/x_1, so the corresponding partial elasticity of production for input x_1 is

$$\varepsilon_1 = \alpha_1 + \gamma_1 x_1 + \gamma_3 x_2 x_1 \tag{11.22}$$

Along the ridge line for x_1, the production elasticity for x_1 is zero. This implies that

$$\alpha_1 + \gamma_1 x_1 + \gamma_3 x_2 x_1 = 0 \tag{11.23}$$

or

$$x_1(\gamma_1 + \gamma_3 x_2) = -\alpha_1 \tag{11.24}$$

$$x_1 = -\alpha_1/(\gamma_1 + \gamma_3 x_2) \tag{11.25}$$

The amount of x_1 required to maximize output is clearly a function of the quantity of x_2 that is available. Ridge lines no longer form right angles with each other parallel to the x_1 and x_2 axes. If γ_3 is positive, ridge lines will slope upward and to the right. Moreover, ε_1 and ε_2 are functions of the amount of both inputs that are used.

11.5 Illustrations and Applications of the Transcendental

Figure 11.1 also illustrates production surfaces under varying assumptions with respect to the parameters of the two-input transcendental. Diagram B illustrates the original two-input transcendental with $\alpha_1 = \alpha_2 = 4$ and $\gamma_1 = \gamma_2 = -2$.

The three stages of production are clearly visible, as is the fact that the maximum for each single input production function for x_1 generated by assuming x_2 held fixed at a varying level occurs at the same level of input use for x_1. Diagrams C and D illustrate what happens as an interaction term with the parameter γ_3 is added. Diagram C assumes that γ_3 is 0.2, whereas diagram D assumes that γ_3 is 0.3. Each successive production function for x_1 has a maximum to the right of the one below it. The same holds for input x_2. The shape of the production surface is highly sensitive to changes in the value of the parameter γ_3.

Diagram E illustrates the surface when α_1 and α_2 are positive but less than 1 (0.5), γ_1 and γ_2 are negative (-2), and γ_3 is zero. The function increases at a decreasing rate, and then decreases at $x_1 = -\alpha_1/\gamma_1, x_2 = -\alpha_2/\gamma_2$.

Diagram F illustrates what happens when γ_1 and γ_2 are positive (1.0) and α_1 and α_2 are positive (0.5). The surface looks not unlike a total cost function in three dimensions, first increasing at an increasing rate, and then increasing at a decreasing rate.

The transcendental production function can be viewed as a generalization of the Cobb–Douglas production function that can depict the three stages of production and has variable production elasticities. The transcendental is easily transformed to natural logs to yield

$$\ln y = \ln A + \alpha_1 \ln x_1 + \alpha_2 \ln x_2 + \gamma_1 x_1 + \gamma_2 x_2 + \gamma_3 x_1 x_2 \tag{11.26}$$

This function is linear in the parameters, and is again easily estimated via ordinary least-squares regression techniques.

The first attempt to estimate parameters of a transcendental production function was published by Halter and Bradford in 1959. They estimated a *TVP* function with gross farm income as the dependent variable and dollar values for owned and purchased inputs as x variables. The dependent variable was adjusted by a weather measure based on the number of drought-free days during the growing season. Data were collected from 153 individual farms in 1952 and 1956.

The function was estimated both as a Cobb–Douglas specification and as a transcendental specification. Based on the statistical results, including a comparison of actual values for the dependent variable with those predicted by the equation, the transcendental specification did give slightly improved results than the Cobb–Douglas specification.

11.6 Cobb–Douglas with Variable Input Elasticities

Another approach was to develop a Cobb–Douglas type of function in which the powers on each input were assumed to vary. The function was

$$y = Ax_1^{\beta_1(X)} x_2^{\beta_2(X)} \tag{11.27}$$

The β_i are functions of one or more inputs represented by X. These inputs may include x_1 and x_2, but they also may include inputs not incorporated in the function directly. One proposal suggested that X should incorporate the skills of the manager, and that production functions for skilled managers should have greater partial elasticities of production than production functions for unskilled managers.

11.7 de Janvry Modifications

de Janvry recognized the linkages between the Cobb–Douglas production function with variable input elasticities and the two-input transcendental. He proposed the generalized power production function (GPPF), which had as special cases the Cobb–Douglas, the Cobb–Douglas with variable input elasticities, and the transcendental.

The general form of the GPPF is

$$y = x_1^{g(x_1,x_2)} x_2^{h(x_1,x_2)} e^{j(x_1,x_2)} \tag{11.28}$$

where g, h and j are each functions of the inputs. If $j = 0$; $g = \alpha_1$; and $h = \alpha_2$, the function is the traditional Cobb–Douglas type. If g and h are constants and j is nonzero, the function is a general two-input transcendental, without any particular restriction of the form of j. If $j = \gamma_1 x_1 + \gamma_2 x_2$, the function is the standard transcendental. The Cobb–Douglas function with variable input elasticities results where j is zero but g and h vary according to x_1 and x_2.

The major contribution of de Janvry was to develop a general functional form that included as special cases many of the other production functions used by agricultural economists.

11.8 Polynomial Forms

The production functions described so far in Chapters 10 and 11 require that a positive amount of each input be present for output to be produced. Isoquants come asymptotic to, but do not intersect, the axes. When isoquants intersect an axis, output is possible even in the absence of the input represented by the other axis.

A polynomial form is inherently additive rather than multiplicative. if interaction terms are not included, there will be an additive but not synergistic impact on output as a result of an increase in the level of input use.

Consider the polynomial

$$y = a + bx_1 + cx_1^2 + dx_2 + ex_2^2 \qquad (11.29)$$

where a, b, c, d, and e are constant parameters. The marginal product of x_1 is $b + 2cx_1$. The marginal product of x_2 is $d + 2ex_2$. The marginal product of x_1 is not linked to the quantity of x_2 that is present. The marginal product of x_2 is not linked to the quantity of x_1 that is present. The function achieves a maximum (or possibly minimum) when $b + 2cx_1 = 0$ and $d + 2ex_2 = 0$. Ridge lines again form right angles that intersect at the global output maximum. Second-order conditions for a maximum require that c be negative and ce be positive. (The proof is left with the reader.) This implies that both c and e must be negative or that the *MPP* with respect to both inputs must slope downward to the right. The parameters b and d must be positive, or there will be no point at which an increase in the use of the input will produce a positive marginal product.

Now consider the polynomial

$$y = A + bx_1 + cx_1^2 + dx_2 + ex_2^2 + fx_1x_2 \qquad (11.30)$$

The marginal product of x_1 is $b + 2cx_1 + fx_2$. The marginal product of x_2 is $d + 2ex_2 + fx_1$. The marginal product of each input is linked to the quantity of the other input that is present, as long as f is nonzero. The first-order conditions for maximum output require that each marginal product be zero. Ridge lines no longer intersect at right angles, but if f is positive, each successive single-input production function achieves its maximum to the right of the one below it. Second-order conditions for a maximum require that $2c$ be negative and $2c \cdot 2e - f^2$ be positive. These polynomials and any other polynomial that is linear in its parameters could be estimated via ordinary least squares.

Figure 11.3 illustrates the polynomial

$$y = x_1 + x_1^2 - 0.05x_1^3 + x_2 + x_2^2 - 0.05x_2^3 + 0.4x_1x_2 \qquad (11.31)$$

The three stages of production are clearly evident, and output is possible even in the absence of one of the two inputs. Note the white area between each axis and the production surface, indicating that the isoquants intersect both axes.

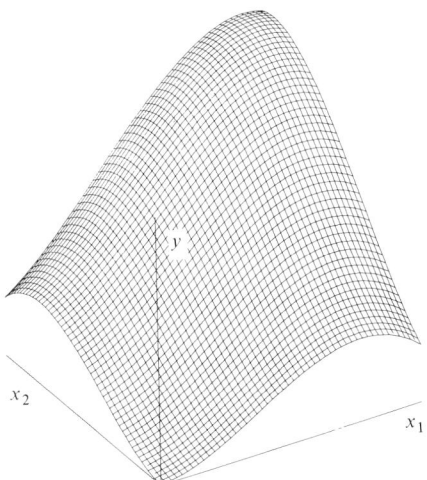

Figure 11.3 The Polynomial $y = x_1 + x_1^2 - 0.05x_1^3 + x_2 + x_2^2 - 0.05x_2^3 + 0.4x_1x_2$

11.9 Concluding Comments

Agricultural economists have made use of a wide array of production functions over the last 50 years and more. Some of these efforts have represented attempts to make explicit linkages between the mathematical specification and the traditional neoclassical three-stage production function. The effort conducted by Halter and his colleagues was clearly aimed at that objective, as have been the attempts to estimate polynomial forms.

Other agricultural economists saw the problem somewhat differently. Efforts in the early 1970s by de Janvry and others focused on the development of general functional forms that would encompass a number of explicit specifications as special cases.

In the 1960s and 1970s, the direction of research both in general and in agricultural economics increasingly turned to the problem of determining the extent to which inputs to a production process substituted for each other. This led to the development of functional forms that are not necessarily linked to the neoclassical three-stage form, but rather were useful in estimating elasticities of substitution between input pairs. Chapter 12 discusses some of these functional forms.

Problems and Exercises

1. For input levels between zero and 10 units, graph the following production functions and compare their shape.

   a. Single-input power (Cobb–Douglas-like):

   $$y = x^{0.5}$$

b. Single-input (Spillman-like):

$$y = (1 - 0.5^x)$$

c. Single-input transcendental:

$$y = x^4 e^{-2x}$$

where e it the base of the natural log 2.71828 ...

2. For part (c) in Problem 1, find the level of x corresponding to:

a. The inflection point.
b. Maximum *MPP*.
c. Maximum *APP*.
d. Maximum *TPP*.

3. If the production function is a polynomial consistent with the neoclassical three-stage production function (see Problem 5, Chapter 2), show that the level of x that maximizes *MPP* will be two-thirds of the level that maximizes *APP*.

References

de Janvry, Alain. "The Class of Generalized Power Production Functions." *American Journal of Agricultural Economics* 54 (1972) pp. 234–237.

Halter, A. N. and G. L. Bradford. "Changes in Production Functions with Weather Adjustments on Western Kentucky Farms," *Progress Report 84,* Kentucky Agricultural Experiment Station, 1959.

Halter, A. N., H. O. Carter, and J. G. Hocking. "A Note on the Transcendental Production Function." *Journal of Farm Economics* 39 (1957), pp. 966–974.

Spillman, W. J. "Application of the Law of Diminishing Returns to Some Fertilizer and Feed Data," *Journal of Farm Economics* 5 (1923), pp. 36–52.

Spillman, W. J. "Law of the Diminishing Increment in the Fattening of Steers and Hogs." *Journal of Farm Economics* 6 (1924) pp. 166–178.

12 The Elasticity of Substitution

This chapter develops the concept of an elasticity of substitution. An elasticity of substitution is a measure of the extent to which one input substitutes for another input along an isoquant. To the extent inputs substitute for each other, a farmer can respond to changing relative input prices by adjusting the combination or mix of inputs that are used. The constant elasticity of substitution, or CES production function, is used as a means for illustrating how the shape of isoquants change as the input mix changes. Examples of research using a translog production function to estimate elasticities of substitution for agricultural inputs are cited.

Key Terms and Definitions:

Isoquant Pattern
Right-Angle Isoquant
Diagonal Isoquant
Elasticity of Substitution
Zero Elasticity of Substitution
Infinite Elasticity of Substitution
Constant Elasticity of Substitution
    (CES) Production Function
Translog Production Function
Translog Cost Function
Shephard's Lemma
Cost-Share Equations

12.1 An Introduction to the Concept

Isoquants can vary widely in their patterns. Isoquants might form a series of right angles, or they might have constant slopes and look like iso-outlay lines. Isoquants for the Cobb–Douglas production function appear to be hyperbolic. Isoquants for the transcendental production function under certain parameter assumptions appear to be a series of concentric rings, ovals, or lopsided ovals. The shape of the isoquants can tell a good deal about the nature of the production functions that underlie them.

The shape of an isoquant depends on the extent to which the two inputs being pictured substitute for each other, as changes in the mix or proportions of the two inputs are made. A specific isoquant produces a fixed amount of output (y). Along an isoquant, a diminishing marginal rate of substitution is usually a result of the law of diminishing returns that applies to the underlying production functions for each input.

Consider a production function

$$y = ax_1 + bx_2 \qquad (12.1)$$

The marginal product of x_1 is a, and the marginal product of x_2 is b. Since both marginal products are constant, the slopes of each member of the family of single-input production functions for x_1 and x_2 are also constant. The marginal rate of substitution of x_1 for $x_2 = -MPPx_1/MPPx_2$, or $-a/b$. The slope of each isoquant is everywhere $-a/b$. Inputs are perfect substitutes for each other at the rate given by the marginal rate of substitution. An example is a production function for steers. Assume that x_1 is corn the farmer grew and x_2 is corn purchased from a neighbor. If the corn is of comparable quality, or have constant MPP's, corn grown at home and corn grown by the neighbor should be perfect substitutes for each other.

The production function in equation (12.1) indicates a constant marginal product of beef from incremental units of corn. Such a super steer has not yet been developed, and it is easy to see why such a production function is seldom used by agricultural economists. The expansion path conditions for such a production function can be derived by the reader.

Now consider a production function in which the two inputs must be used in a fixed proportion, such as tractors and tractor drivers. Two tractor drivers and one tractor produce no more output than one tractor and one driver. Two tractors and one driver produce no more output than do one tractor and one driver. Isoquants are right angles, and inputs can be thought of as not substituting with each other at all, or zero substitutability between inputs.

Between these extreme cases lie a myriad of other possible isoquant patterns or maps. Isoquants might be bowed in only slightly toward the origin, or they might look very nearly like, but not quite be, right angles. The hyperbolic isoquants for the Cobb–Douglas production function that asymptotically approach each axis appear to be in between these extreme cases.

The need exists for a simple measure linked to the shape of the isoquants that would make it possible to determine the extent to which one input substitutes for another. The ideal measure would be a pure or unitless number that could assume values between zero and infinity. The number should be unitless to make possible comparisons between isoquant maps representing widely varying pairs of inputs. Any elasticity is a unitless or pure number in that it represents the ratio of two percentages, and thus the units cancel. The ideal measure would assume a value of zero if inputs do not substitute for each other, but approach infinity as the inputs became perfect substitutes for each other.

Thus the concept of the elasticity of substitution came into being. Actually,

12.1 An Introduction to the Concept

several formulas were developed. For example, Heady proposed that the elasticity of substitution (e_{sh}) should be equal to the percentage change in the use of x_2 divided by the percentage change in the use of x_1:

$$e_{sh} = (\Delta x_2/x_2)/(\Delta x_1/x_1) \qquad (12.2)$$

Assuming that the change in x_2 and x_1 is sufficiently small

$$e_{sh} = (dx_2/dx_1)(x_1/x_2) \qquad (12.3)$$

or

$$e_{sh} = MRSx_1x_2(x_1/x_2) \qquad (12.4)$$

This elasticity of substitution is the slope of the isoquant at a particular point multiplied by the inverse ratio of input use defined by that point.

For a Cobb–Douglas type of production function, $MRSx_1x_2 = \alpha_1 x_2/\alpha_2 x_1$, and therefore the elasticity of substitution between the input pairs is α_1/α_2, the ratio of the partial elasticities of production. Moreover, this elasticity of substitution for a Cobb–Douglas type of function could vary widely even though the isoquant map for any Cobb–Douglas type function looks very similar in terms of the shape of the isoquants. So if being able to broadly determine the shape of the isoquant map on the basis of the elasticity of substitution was important, this measure failed.

The more generally accepted algebraic definition of the elasticity of substitution is somewhat more complicated, but the interpretation of the calculated values relative to the shape of the underlying isoquant map is clear. In the two-input setting, the elasticity of substitution is defined as the percentage change in the input ratio divided by the percentage change in the marginal rate of substitution:

$$\begin{aligned} e_s &= [\% \text{ change in } (x_2/x_1)]/(\% \text{ change in } MRSx_1x_2) \\ &= [\Delta(x_2/x_1)/(x_2/x_1)]/(\Delta MRSx_1x_2/MRSx_1x_2) \end{aligned} \qquad (12.5)$$

If the change is sufficiently small, the formula becomes

$$\begin{aligned} e_s &= [d(x_2/x_1)/(x_2/x_1)]/(dMRSx_1x_2/MRSx_1x_2) \\ &= [d(x_2/x_1)/(x_2/x_1)]/[d(dx_2/dx_1)/(dx_2/dx_1)] \end{aligned} \qquad (12.6)$$

Equation (12.6) can be rearranged as

$$e_s = [d(x_2/x_1)/(dx_2/dx_1)][(dx_2/dx_1)/(x_2/x_1)] \qquad (12.7)$$

The expression contained within the first pair of brackets represents the rate of change in the proportions of the two inputs being used as the marginal rate of substitution changes. The expression in the second pair of brackets is the marginal rate of substitution divided by the proportions of the two inputs.

The Elasticity of Substitution

This second definition for the elasticity of substitution can be presented graphically and is illustrated in Figure 12.1. Suppose that the elasticity of substitution is to be calculated over the finite range from point P_1 to point P_2. First calculate the percentage change in the input ratio. The input ratio at point P_1 is equal to OB/OA. The input ratio at point P_2 is equal to OD/OC. The input ratio at some average point between P_1 and P_2 is OK/OJ. The percentage change in the input ratio is $(OB/OA - OD/OC)/(OK/OJ)$.

Now calculate the percentage change in the marginal rate of substitution, or the percentage change in the slope of the isoquant. The slope of the isoquant at point P_1 is OH/OG. The slope of the isoquant at point P_2 is OF/OE. The slope of the isoquant at a point midway between P_1 and P_2 is OM/OL. So the percentage change in the marginal rate of substitution is $(OH/OG - OF/OE)/(OM/OL)$.

The elasticity of substitution is the percentage change in the input ratio divided by the percentage change in the marginal rate of substitution. So the formula for the elasticity of substitution is

$$[(OB/OA - OD/OC)/(OK/OJ)]/[(OH/OG - OF/OE)/(OM/OL)] \quad (12.8)$$

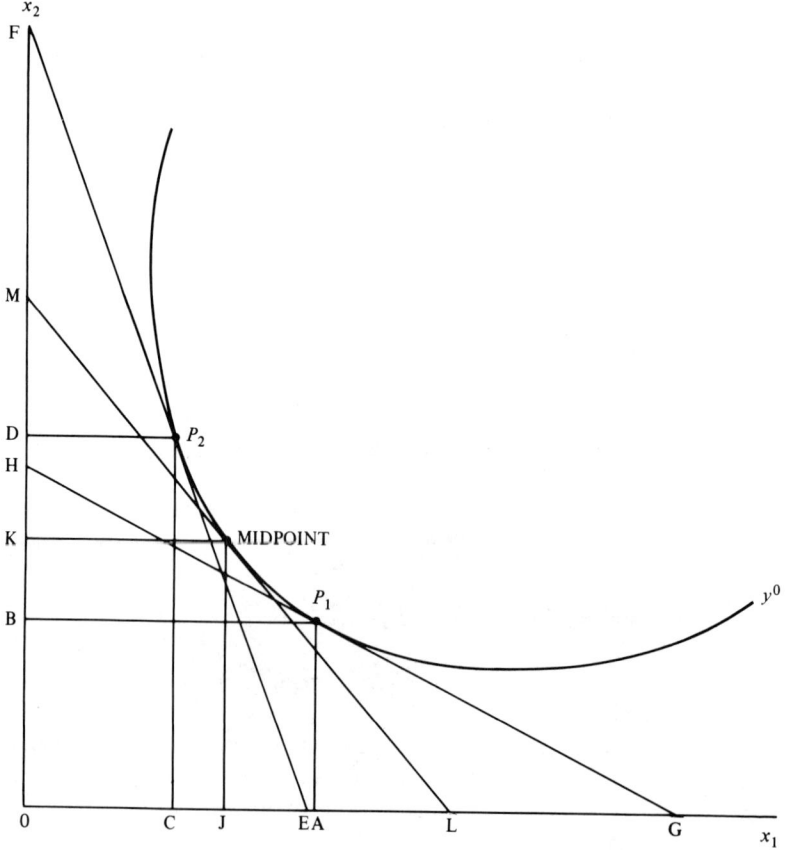

Figure 12.1 Arc Elasticity of Substitution over the Finite Range P_1 to P_2

12.1 An Introduction to the Concept

Assume that the isoquant is very nearly a line with a constant downward slope. As a result, the percentage change in the marginal rate of substitution between point P_1 and P_2 is very near zero. But the percentage change in the input ratio is a comparatively large number. A very small number will be divided into a large number and the result will be a very large elasticity of substitution.

Now suppose that the isoquant is a right angle, with P_1 on the horizontal portion of the angle and P_2 on the vertical portion of the right angle. The slope at P_1 is zero, the slope at P_2 is infinite. The percentage change in the *MRS* between P_1 and P_2 is infinite as well. The percentage change in the input ratio between P_1 and P_2 can be calculated as a very ordinary number, neither very large nor very small. As the percentage change in the *MRS* approaches infinity, a very ordinary number is divided by a very large number, which results in an elasticity of substitution that approaches zero.

In the two-input case, the values for the elasticity of substitution lie between zero and infinity. Inputs that do not substitute at all with each other have a zero elasticity of substitution, while inputs that substitute for each other in fixed proportions at any point along an isoquant have an infinite elasticity of substitution. Values near zero indicate little potential input substitution. Very large values indicate a great potential of substituting one input for another within the production process.

Figure 12.1 illustrates what could be called an "arc" elasticity of substitution, since the difference between P_1 and P_2 is assumed to be finite. The point elasticity of substitution can be calculated with the aid of the calculus.

Henderson and Quandt provide a formula for calculating elasticities of substitution based solely on first and second derivatives of the production function. (See Henderson and Quandt for a detailed derivation of the formula.) Define

$$f_1 = \partial y / \partial x_1 = MPPx_1 \quad (12.9)$$

$$f_2 = \partial y / \partial x_2 = MPPx_2 \quad (12.10)$$

$$f_{11} = \partial^2 y / \partial x_1^2 = \text{slope of } MPPx_1 \quad (12.11)$$

$$f_{22} = \partial^2 y / \partial x_2^2 = \text{slope of } MPPx_2 \quad (12.12)$$

$$f_{12} = f_{21} \text{ (by Young's theorem)} = \partial^2 y / \partial x_1 \partial x_2 \quad (12.13)$$

Equation (12.13) is the change in the slope of $MPPx_1$ with respect to a change in the use of $x_2 = \partial^2 y / \partial x_2 \partial x_1$, or the change in the slope of $MPPx_2$ with respect to a change in the use of x_1.

Then the formula for calculating the elasticity of substitution is

$$e_s = [f_1 f_2 (f_1 x_1 + f_2 x_2)] / [x_1 x_2 (2 f_{12} f_1 f_2 - f_1^2 f_{22} - f_2^2 f_{11})] \quad (12.14)$$

Equation (12.14) makes it possible to calculate the elasticity of substitution at a particular point on an isoquant for any production function for which the first and second derivatives exist.

Still other formulas for elasticities of substitution have been proposed by other authors. These include a definition called the Allen (or AES) measure, found in his 1938 book. McFadden proposed a definition which he called the shadow elasticity of substitution. Yet another definition is called the Morishima measure, and is given in a paper by Koizumi. All these definitions are the same as equation (12.14) when there are but two inputs, but each measure differs slightly from the others when more than two inputs are used in the production process. A detailed discussion and comparison of the alternative measures can be found in the McFadden reference.

12.2 Elasticities of Substitution and the Cobb–Douglas Function

Any Cobb–Douglas type of production function will have an elasticity of substitution according to equation (12.14) of exactly 1. This means that as the percentage change in the ratio of the use of inputs x_1 and x_2 is changed along a specific isoquant, there will be the exact same percentage change in the marginal rate of substitution. The conclusion is not dependent on the magnitude of the individual production elasticities and occurs even if the elasticities do not sum to 1. The result holds for any production function in which the marginal rate of substitution is a linear function of the input ratio.

The proof need not rely on the Henderson and quandt formula. The marginal rate of substitution for a Cobb–Douglas type of function is

$$MRSx_1x_2 = -(\beta_1/\beta_2)(x_2/x_1) \qquad (12.15)$$

Now let b equal the negative ratio of the elasticities of production $(-\beta_1/\beta_2)$. Since β_1 and β_2 are constant, so is b. Let $x = x_1/x_2$. Therefore, the marginal rate of substitution is a linear function of the input ratio:

$$MRSx_1x_2 = bx \qquad (12.16)$$

or

$$x = (1/b)MRSx_1x_2 \qquad (12.17)$$

Therefore,

$dx/dMRSx_1x_2$ (the change in the input ratio with respect to a change in the marginal rate of substitution) $= 1/b$ \qquad (12.18)

$$(MRSx_1x_2)/(x_2/x_1) = bx/x \qquad (12.19)$$

Hence, the elasticity of substitution for a Cobb–Douglas type of function is

$$[d(x_2/x_1)/dMRSx_1x_2][MRSx_1x_2/(x_2/x_1)] = (1/b)(bx/x) = 1! \qquad (12.20)$$

To reiterate, equation (12.20) holds for any two-input multiplicative production function of the Cobb–Douglas type and does not depend on the magnitude or the sum of the individual production elasticities.

12.3 Policy Applications of the Elasticity of Substitution

The elasticity-of-substitution concept has important applications to key issues linked to agricultural production. The recent liquid fuels energy crisis provides an illustration of the importance of the concept. Of concern is the extent to which other inputs can be substituted for liquid fuels energy in agricultural production. An example might be the potential substitutability between farm labor, farm tractors, and machinery and liquid fuels.

Agriculture in the United States as well as in most foreign countries has become increasingly mechanized. Hence tractors and machinery can and do substitute for farm labor. The reduction in the farm population that has taken place in the United States over the past century and more indicates that farm tractors and machinery can substitute for human labor, and this substitution can take place, at least in the aggregate, relatively easily. This suggests that the elasticity of substitution is comparatively high between human labor and farm tractors and machinery.

Massive changes in the mix of inputs required to produce agricultural products would not have taken place without clear economic signals. These economic signals are the relative prices for tractors and machinery and the fuel required to run versus farm labor. Farmers often complain about the prices for tractors and other farm machinery, but changes in the mix of inputs toward tractors and farm machinery would not have taken had it not been economic. Farmers look for the point of least-cost combination today, much as they always have.

If the relative proportions of each input do not change, or change very little in the face of changing relative input prices, there is evidence to suggest that the elasticity of substitution between the inputs is nearly zero. However, when relative prices change and are accompanied by a change in the input mix, there is evidence in support of a positive elasticity of substitution.

Liquid fuel prices increased very rapidly during the 1970s and the early 1980s. Since the price of fuel was increasing relative to other input costs, there again was concern with respect to whether there existed a positive elasticity of substitution between liquid fuels and other agricultural inputs. Some even argued that rising fuel prices would eventually lead back to a labor-oriented agriculture more broadly consistent with agriculture in the nineteenth century, but the mix of inputs used in agriculture changed very little as a result of the increased fuel prices.

There are some hypotheses as to why the input mix did not change significantly in response to increases in liquid fuel prices relative to other inputs. One possibility is that the elasticity of substitution between liquid fuels and other agricultural inputs is nearly zero. This would imply that there would be little if any changes in the input mix even in the face of changing relative prices.

Farm tractors and the fuel to run them may be inputs that are required in nearly fixed proportions. Clearly, a tractor cannot run without fuel. Another possibility is that substitution is possible, but that it takes time, more time than a few years. A farmer cannot dramatically change the approach to the production of crops and livestock overnight. Elasticities of substitution may not remain forever constant, but change over time.

The economic motives for the replacement of a tractor might be examined. A farmer might replace an old tractor with a new one that is more fuel efficient per unit of output produced, thus substituting the new tractor (a form of capital) for liquid fuel energy. The replacement suggests a positive elasticity of substitution between a new tractor and liquid fuels. Rising relative labor costs (wage rates) and declining real fuel prices provided the economic signals that led to the substitution of tractors and machinery for labor during much of the twentieth century.

Consumers replaced their aging and fuel-wasting fleet of automobiles with a newer, more expensive, but energy-conserving fleet as a result of increasing real fuel prices during much of the last decade and a half. The result was a significant reduction in the demand for gasoline. The elasticity of substitution between the capital embodied in a new automobile and gasoline was clearly positive.

The elasticity of substitution between input pairs may differ significantly among various farm enterprises. There still appear to be few substitutes for human labor in tobacco production. Dairy remains labor intensive, but possibilities are increasing for the substitution of capital for labor. Wheat, corn, and soybean production are capital (tractors and machinery) intensive, and the possibility of substituting labor for capital are limited without a drastic reduction in output. A reduction in output suggests a movement across isoquants rather than along an isoquant. The extent to which labor, capital, and energy can be substituted in the production of horticultural crops varies with the specific type of crop. Some crops lend themselves to mechanization, but others remain labor intensive but liquid fuels conserving.

Agricultural economists in developing countries need to be vitally concerned with respect to the elasticities of substitution for the major agricultural commodities being produced. For example, the extent to which labor is free to move out of agriculture and into other sectors of the economy may be dependent on the elasticity of substitution between labor and the other inputs, given the resources and technology within the developing country.

12.4 The CES Production Function

Since the Cobb–Douglas type of production function imposes an elasticity of substitution between input pairs of exactly 1, then if a Cobb–Douglas type of production function were estimated, the elasticity of substitution between input pairs would be an assumption underlying the research rather than a result based on the evidence contained in the data. The problem with the Cobb–Douglas type of production function is widely known and is of particular interest to economists engaged in macro-oriented issues, such as the extent to which capital could substitute for labor within an economy.

12.4 The CES Production Function

The study published by Arrow, Chenery, Menhas, and Solow, "Capital Labor Substitution and Economic Efficiency," in 1961 was a landmark. The study might also be considered a remake of the 1928 effort by Cobb and Douglas without the assumption that the elasticity of substitution between capital and labor was 1. In the study the authors first introduced the constant elasticity of substitution (CES) production function. The CES production function had two principal features. First, the elasticity of substitution between the two inputs could be any number between zero and infinity. Second, for a given set of parameters, the elasticity of substitution was the same on any point along the isoquant, regardless of the ratio of input use at the point: hence the name *constant elasticity of substitution production function*.

The CES production function is

$$y = A[\lambda x_1^{-\rho} + (1 - \lambda)x_2^{-\rho}]^{-1/\rho} \qquad (12.21)$$

The CES appears to be a very complicated function. The developers of the CES no doubt started with the result that they wished to obtain, a constant elasticity of substitution that could assume any value between zero and infinity, and worked toward a functional form that was consistent with this result. The elasticity of substitution (e_s) and the parameter ρ are closely related

$$e_s = 1/(1 + \rho) \qquad (12.22)$$

$$\rho = (1 - e_s)/e_s \qquad (12.23)$$

The authors retained the Cobb–Douglas assumption of constant returns to scale in that $\lambda + (1 - \lambda) = 1$, but this assumption is not required.

In addition to having research application, the CES is a useful pedagogical tool in that it can be used to illustrate what happens to the shape of a series of isoquants as the elasticity of substitution changes. Henderson and Quandt suggest five possible cases. Figure 12.2 illustrates the production surfaces and corresponding isoquants generated under each of these cases.

Case 1: $\rho \to$ infinity, $e_s \to 0$. At the limit, substitution between input pairs is impossible and isoquants form a right angle. Diagram A illustrates what happens as ρ becomes a rather large number. The shape of the production surface becomes like a pyramid. The production surface illustrated in diagram A was drawn with the assumption that $\rho = 10$.

Case 2: $0 < e_s < 1; \rho > 0$. Inputs substitute for each other, but not very easily. The isoquants are asymptotic to some value for x_1 and x_2 rather than the axes. The vertical line is at $x_1 = (k/\lambda)^{-1/\rho}$, and the horizontal line is at $x_2 = (k/(1 - \lambda))^{-1/\rho}$. The number $k = (y/A)^{-\rho}$. The isoquants can be thought of as something in between the right angles in case 1 and those for a Cobb–Douglas type of function. Diagram B illustrates the production surface when $\rho = 0.5$. The production surface is undistinguished and looks similar to that for the Cobb–Douglas.

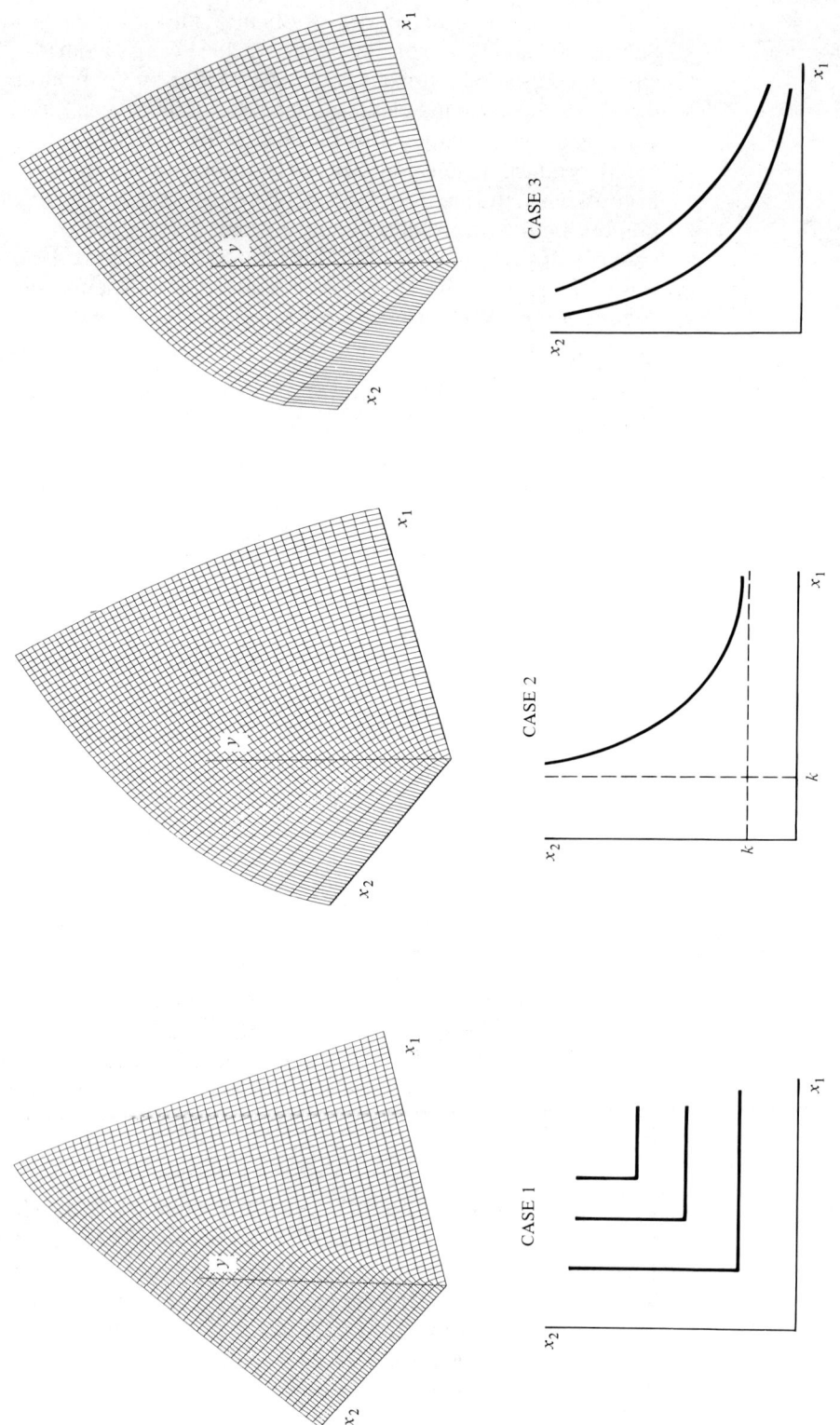

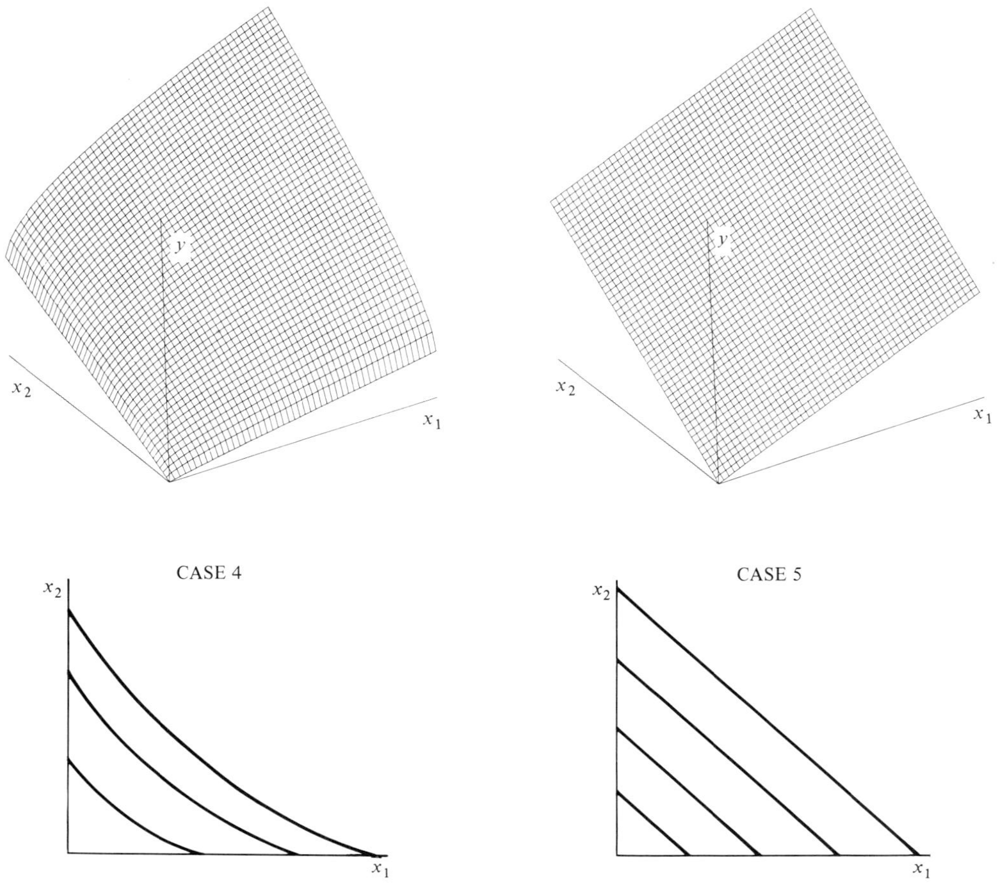

CASE 5

CASE 4

Figure 12.2 Production Surfaces and Isoquants for the CES Production Function

The Elasticity of Substitution

Case 3: $e_s = 1$; $\rho = 0$. The CES becomes the Cobb–Douglas illustrated in diagram C. The proof of this requires the use of L'Hopital's rule and can be found in Henderson and Quandt.

Case 4: $e_s > 1$; $-1 < \rho < 0$. Isoquants cut both axes. In diagram D, for $\rho = -0.5$, $e_s = 2$, note the white area directly above the x_1 and x_2 axes. This suggests that output is possible in the absence of one of the two inputs.

Case 5: As $e_s \to$ infinity, $\rho \to 0$. At the limit the isoquants consist of lines of constant slope (with no curvature), and the production surface is illustrated in diagram E. The CES reduces to the production function $y = \lambda x_1 + (1 - \lambda)x_2$, and inputs substitute for each other in the fixed proportion $\lambda/(1 - \lambda)$.

The CES had some important advantages over the Cobb–Douglas production function in that the same general functional form could be used to represent a variety of substitution possibilities and corresponding isoquant patterns, but the function had two important disadvantages. Like the Cobb–Douglas, for a given set of parameter values, only one stage of production could be represented, usually stage II for both inputs. This problem was not unrelated to the fact that the elasticity of substitution was the same everywhere along the isoquant. Isoquant patterns consisting of concentric rings or ovals were not allowed.

The CES can be extended to allow for more than two inputs. However, there is but one parameter ρ in the multiple-input extensions. Thus only one elasticity of substitution value can be obtained from the production function, and this same value applies to all input pairs. For example, in agriculture, one might expect that the elasticity of substitution between chemicals and labor would differ markedly from the elasticity of substitution between fuel and tractors. But the CES would estimate the same elasticity of substitution between both input pairs. Despite its pedagogical charm for understanding the effects of changing elasticities of substitution on the shape of isoquants, the usefulness of the CES production function for serious research in agricultural economics in which more than two inputs were involved was limited.

12.5 Elasticities of Substitution and the Translog Production Function

Unlike the Cobb–Douglas and the CES, most production functions do not have constant elasticities of substitution. The percentage change in the input ratio divided by the percentage change in the marginal rate of substitution is not constant all along the isoquant but varies from one point to another. To determine the elasticity of substitution for production functions such as these, it is necessary not only to know the parameters of the production function, but also to be aware of the precise point on the isoquant for which the elasticity of substitution is to be estimated and the input ratio (x_2/x_1) for that point.

12.5 Elasticities of Substitution and the Translog Production Function

Application of the Henderson and Quandt formula for calculating the elasticity of substitution can then be made. The elasticity of substitution as based on this formula for most production functions will contain the parameters of the function as well as x_1 and x_2.

If a production function has more than two inputs, partial elasticities of substitution for each pair of inputs can be calculated, but the algebra for doing this quickly becomes quite complicated. In the two-input setting, the elasticity of substitution will always be greater than zero. However, in the multiple-input setting, it is possible for some pairs of inputs to be substitutes and others complements. For the complement pairs, the elasticity of substitution will be negative. An example of a pair of inputs that are complements might be a tractor and the fuel required to run it.

A production function that has recently become popular with agricultural economists interested in estimating elasticities of substitution between input pairs is called the *translog production function*. A specification for the translog production function is

$$\ln y = \ln \alpha + \beta_1 \ln x_1 + \beta_2 \ln x_2 + \tfrac{1}{2}\gamma \ln x_1 \ln x_2 \quad (12.24)$$

Sometimes squared terms are also included (Christensen, Jorgenson, and Lau).

$$y = \ln \alpha + \beta_1 \ln x_1 + \beta_2 \ln x_2 + (\tfrac{1}{2})\gamma \ln x_1 \ln x_2 \\ + \tfrac{1}{2}\phi_1 (\ln x_1)^2 + \tfrac{1}{2}\phi_2 (\ln x_2)^2 \quad (12.25)$$

The translog production function is a member of de Janvry's generalized power production function family. Equation (12.24) written as its antilog is

$$y = \alpha x_1^{\beta_1} x_2^{\beta_2} e^{(\gamma/2)(\ln x_1)(\ln x_2)} \quad (12.26)$$

Notice how similar the appearance of the translog production function is to the transcendental developed by Halter, Carter, and Hocking. Moreover, the Cobb–Douglas is a special case of the translog when γ equals zero.[1]

Equation (12.26) differs from the transcendental in that the parameter γ is usually assumed to be positive. The function is similar to the Cobb–Douglas in that for most possible positive parameter values for γ, the function never achieves a maximum if the level of input use for x_1 and x_2 is finite. However, unlike the Cobb–Douglas, the translog function does not always generate elasticities of substitution of 1. The translog function is easily generalized to problems involving more than two inputs.

The translog production function can be generalized to include any number of input categories, and each pair of inputs may have a different elasticity of substitution. The shape of the isoquants for the translog depend heavily on the parameter γ. If γ were zero, the function would generate isoquants like those for the Cobb–Douglas. The marginal rate of substitution would be a linear function of the input ratio, and the elasticity of substitution would be 1 everywhere along each isoquant.

As the value of γ increases, output increases markedly when both inputs are used in similar proportions to each other. As γ becomes larger and larger, the isoquants bow inward, become more nearly a right angle, and the elasticity of substitution becomes smaller and smaller.

The *MPP* of x_1 for equation (12.26) is

$$\partial y/\partial x_1 = [\beta_1/x_1 + \gamma/2 \ln x_2(1/x_1)]y \qquad (12.27)$$

The *MPP* can be set equal to zero and solved for x_2 in terms of x_1 is the equation for the ridge line for x_1.

The marginal rate of substitution for equation (12.26) is

$$dx_2/dx_1 = -[\beta_1/x_1 + \gamma/2 \ln x_2(1/x_1)]/[\beta_2/x_2 + \gamma/2 \ln x_1(1/x_2)] \qquad (12.28)$$

While parameters of the translog production function can be estimated using physical data on agricultural inputs, cost data on agricultural inputs are generally more readily available than are physical input data. Parameters of the production function are estimated indirectly from the cost function data. Thus a more common research approach is to rely on duality to estimate important parameters of the underlying production function by working with a cost function having a translog form

$$\ln C = \ln \phi + \theta_1 \ln v_1 + \theta_2 \ln v_2 + \tfrac{1}{2}\theta_3 \ln v_1 \ln v_2 \qquad (12.29)$$

where C = total cost
v_1, v_2 = input prices
$\phi, \theta_1, \theta_2, \theta_3$ = parameters or coefficients
ln = natural logarithm of

Partially differentiating the natural logarithm of equation (12.29) with respect to the natural logarithm of v_1 and v_2 results in

$$\partial \ln C/\partial \ln v_1 = \theta_1 \ln v_1 + \tfrac{1}{2}\theta_3 \ln v_2 \qquad (12.30)$$

$$\partial \ln C/\partial \ln v_2 = \theta_2 \ln v_2 + \tfrac{1}{2}\theta_3 \ln v_1 \qquad (12.31)$$

Notice that[2]

$$\partial \ln C/\partial \ln v_1 = (\partial C/\partial v_1)v_1/C \qquad (12.32)$$

$$\partial \ln C/\partial \ln v_2 = (\partial C/\partial v_2)v_1/C \qquad (12.33)$$

Shephard's lemma can be used to convert equations (12.30) and (12.31) into cost-share equations. Shephard's lemma states that

$$\partial C/\partial v_1 = x_1^* \qquad (12.34)$$

$$\partial C/\partial v_2 = x_2^* \qquad (12.35)$$

where x_1^* and x_2^* are the amounts of x_1 and x_2 defined by the points of least-cost combination on the expansion path. Along the expansion path, the change in the cost function with respect to each input price is equal to the quantity of input that is used. Therefore,

$$\partial \ln C / \partial \ln v_1 = v_1 x_1^* / C = S_1 \qquad (12.36)$$

or the share or proportion of total cost for input x_1.

$$\partial \ln C / \partial \ln v_2 = v_2 x_2^* / C = S_2 \qquad (12.37)$$

or the share or proportion of total cost for input x_2. Substitution (12.36) and (12.37) into equations (12.30) and (12.31) gives us

$$S_1 = \theta_1 \ln v_1 + \tfrac{1}{2}\theta_3 \ln v_2 \qquad (12.38)$$

$$S_2 = \theta_2 \ln v_2 + \tfrac{1}{2}\theta_3 \ln v_1 \qquad (12.39)$$

Equations (12.38) and (12.39) are the cost-share equations for inputs x_1 and x_2. Estimates of θ_1, θ_2, and θ_3 can be used as the basis for deriving the elasticities of substitution and other parameters or coefficients for the underlying production function.[3]

Economists and agricultural economists have attempted to determine the elasticities of substitution for major input categories using the cost-share approach outlined above. The focus of economists such as Berndt and Wood has recently been to determine whether capital and energy complement or substitute for each other. Some studies by economists have concluded on the basis of the estimates of the translog production function parameters that energy and capital are complements, whereas others have concluded that they are substitutes.

Webb and Duncan, Brown and Christensen, and Aoun all estimated elasticities of substitution for major input categories in U.S. agriculture using the translog production function as a basis. Aoun estimated partial elasticities of substitution between the input category energy and the input category tractors and machinery. In the 1950s and 1960s, tractors and machinery were complements, as indicated by a positive partial elasticity of substitution, but by the late 1970s, these two input categories had become substitutes. This provides evidence that farmers can now substitute improved tractors and machinery (that produce greater output per unit of fuel burned) for fuel. The belief that improvements in tractors and machinery can come only with increased fuel use may not now hold true.

12.6 Concluding Comments

The elasticity of substitution between pairs of inputs is among the most important concept in all of economics. Increasingly, production research both in and out of agriculture has focused on the estimation of elasticities of substitution between input pairs.

The CES production function is a useful teaching tool for uncovering the linkage between the elasticity of substitution and the shape of the isoquants. Despite its usefulness as a teaching tool, because it could generate only a single estimate of an elasticity of substitution in the multiple-input case, its application to agriculture was limited.

The development of the translog production and cost functions in the early 1970s represented a major step forward in production theory. The translog form was not nearly as restrictive as the Cobb–Douglas and CES forms that preceded it. The translog production and cost functions could be inverted, and recent theoretical developments related to the duality of cost and production could have application both in and out of agriculture. The application of translog cost functions using the cost-share approach for estimating elasticities of substitution between inputs will have applications to many different agricultural sectors in the coming years.

Notes

1. One way of looking at production functions is in terms of Taylor's series expansions. The Cobb–Douglas production function is a first-order Taylor's series expansion of $\ln y$ in $\ln x_1$ and $\ln x_2$, and the translog is a second-order expansion of the same terms. The CES is a first order expansion of y^ρ in x_1^ρ and x_2^ρ. If the translog production function is treated as a Taylor's series expansion, squared terms are included:

$$\ln y = \ln \alpha + \beta_1 \ln x_1 + \beta_2 \ln x_2 + \tfrac{1}{2}\gamma \ln x_1 \ln x_2 + \tfrac{1}{2}\phi_1(\ln x_1)^2 + \tfrac{1}{2}\phi_2(\ln x_2)^2$$

Squared terms can also be added to the translog cost function [equation (12.29)].
2. A detailed proof can be found in Section 13.3.
3. A detailed derivation of the linkage between the parameters of the cost-share equations and the elasticity of substitution can be found in the Brown and Christensen reference.

Problems and Exercises

1. Explain what is meant by the term *elasticity of substitution*. How does the elasticity of substitution differ from the marginal rate of substitution? How does the elasticity of substitution differ from the elasticity of production? Why is the elasticity of substitution between input pairs important in agriculture?

2. For the following production functions, what is the elasticity of substitution?
   a. $y = ax_1 + bx_2$
   b. $y = x_1^{0.33} x_2^{0.5}$
   c. $y = A[bx_1^{-2} + (1-b)x_2^{-2}]^{-1/2}$

3. Draw the isoquants associated with each production function listed in Problem 2.

4. The elasticity of substitution is closely linked to both the marginal rate of substitution and the input ratio (x_2/x_1). Suppose that the marginal rate of substitution is given by the formula

$$MRSx_1x_2 = (x_2/x_1)^b$$

a. What is the corresponding elasticity of substitution?
b. What is known about the production function that produced such a marginal rate of substitution?

References

Allen, R. G. D. *Mathematical Analysis for Economists,* New York: Macmillan, 1956.

Aoun, Abdessalem, "An Econometric Analysis of Factor Substitution in U.S. Agriculture: 1950–80." Unpublished Ph.D. dissertation, Department of Agricultural Economics, University of Kentucky, Lexington, Ky., 1983.

Arrow, Kenneth, H. B. Chenery, B. Menhas, and R. M. Solow. "Capital Labor Substitution and Economic Efficiency." *Review of Economics and Statistics* 43 (1961) pp. 228–232.

Berndt, E. R., and David O. Wood. "Technology, Prices and the Derived Demand for Energy." *Review of Economics and Statistics.* 57:3 (1975) pp. 259–268.

Brown, R. S. and L. R. Christensen. "Estimating Elasticities of Substitution in a Model of Partial Static Equilibrium: An Application to U.S. Agriculture 1947 to 1974," in *Modeling and Measuring Natural Resource Substitution,* E. R. Berndt and B. C. Field, eds. Cambridge, Mass.: MIT Press, 1981.

Christensen, L. R., D. W. Jorgenson, and L. J. Lau., "Transcendental Logarithmic Production Frontiers." *Review of Economics and Statistics* 55:1 (1973) pp. 28–45.

Heady, Earl O. *Economics of Agricultural Production and Resource Use,* Englewood Cliffs, N.J.: Prentice-Hall, 1952, pp. 144–145.

Henderson, James M., and Richard E. Quandt, *Microeconomic Theory: A Mathematical Approach,* 3rd ed. New York: McGraw-Hill, 1971.

Koizumi, T. "A Further Note on the Definition of Elasticity of Substitution in the Many Input Case." *Metroeconomica* 28 (1976) pp. 152–155.

McFadden, Daniel. "Cost, Revenue and Profit Functions" *Production Economics: A Dual Approach to Theory and Application,* Vol 1. M. Fuss and D. McFadden eds. Amsterdam: North-Holland, 1978.

Webb, Kerry, and Marvin Duncan. "Energy Alternatives in U.S. Crop Production." Research Working Paper, Federal Reserve Bank of Kansas City, May 1979, pp. 1–14.

13
The Demand for Inputs to the Production Process

The demand for inputs to a production process within agriculture is dependent on a number of factors: (1) the price of the output being produced, (2) the price of the input, (3) the price of other substitute or complement inputs that are also in the production function, and (4) the technical coefficients or parameters of the production function itself, particularly production elasticities for each input. Under certain conditions, the quantity as well as the price of other inputs, and the availability of dollars for the purchase of inputs may affect the input demand function. This chapter shows how specific input demand functions can be derived that explicitly link the demand by a farmer for an input to the prices of other inputs and the technical parameters of the underlying production function.

Key Terms and Definitions:

Derived Demand
Input Demand Function
Elasticity of Input Demand
Logarithmic Differentiation
Output-Price Input Demand
    Elasticity

Own-Price Input Demand Elasticity
Cross-Price Input Demand Elasticity
Technical Complement
Technical Competitiveness
Technical Independence

13.1 Introduction

The demand for inputs to the agricultural production process is a derived demand. That is, the input demand function is derived from the demand by buyers of the output from the farm. In general, the demand for an input or factor of production depends on (1) the price of the output or outputs being produced, (2) the price of the input, (3) the prices of other inputs that substitute for or complement the input, and (4) the parameters of the production function that describes the technical transformation of the input into an output. In some instances, the demand for an input might also depend on the availability of dollars needed to purchase the input.

For example, the demand by a farmer for seed, fertilizer, machinery, chemicals, and other inputs is derived from the demand by users for the corn produced by the farmer. The demand for each of these inputs is a function not only of their respective prices, but also the price of corn in the marketplace. The demand by a dairy farmer for grain and forage is dependent not only on the respective prices of grain and forage, but also on the price of the milk being produced.

13.2 A Single-Input Setting

In a single-input setting, the derivation of a demand function for an input x makes use of (1) the production function that transforms the input x into the product y; (2) the price of the output y, called p; and (3) the own price of the input, called v. Since there are no other inputs, in a single-input setting prices of other inputs do not enter.

A general statement of the problem is as follows. Given a production function $y = f(x, \alpha)$, where x is the quantity of input used and α represents the coefficients or parameters of the production function, a constant product price (p) and a constant input price (v), the corresponding input demand function can be written as $x = g(\alpha, p, v)$. Notice that the function g, the input demand function, is a different function from f, the production function. The derivation of the input demand function for a specific production function and set of prices makes use of the firm's first-order conditions for profit maximization.

Assume that the farm manager uses only one input in the production of a single output. The farmer is operating in a purely competitive environment, and the price of the input and the output is assumed to be fixed and given. The farmer is interested in maximizing profits. The first-order conditions for maximum profit require that the farmer equate

$$pMPP_x = VMP_x = v \tag{13.1}$$

where p is the output price and v is the input price.

Now suppose that the price of the input (v) varies. Figure 13.1 illustrates what happens. The intersection between VMP_x and v represents the demand for the input at that particular input price, which, in turn, traces out the demand curve or input demand function for the input x under a series of alternative input prices. If the price of the output increases, the VMP curve will shift upward, increasing the demand for x at any positive input price. Conversely, a decrease in the price of the output will reduce the demand for the input x at any given input price. The input demand function normally begins at the start of stage II and ends at the start of stage III.

As the productivity of the underlying production function increases, the MPP_x will increase. This, in turn, will increase the demand by farmers for input x. Conversely, a decrease in the productivity of the underlying production func-

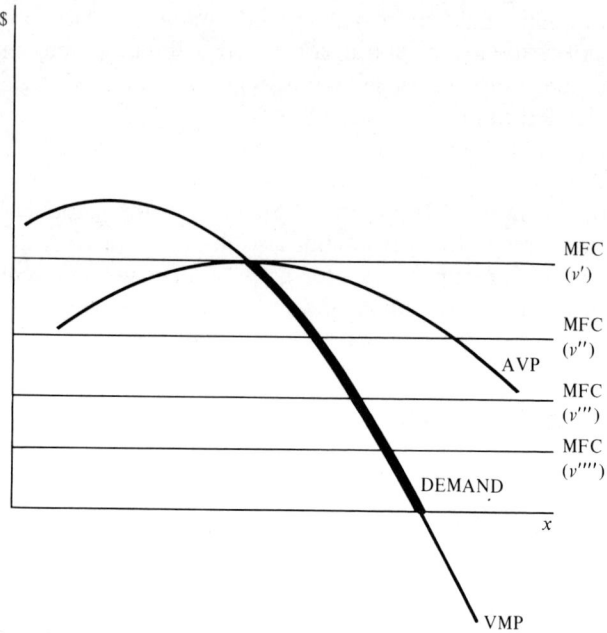

Figure 13.1 The Demand Function for Input x (No Other Inputs)

tion will cause a reduction in the demand for x for a given input and output price.

Assume that the production function is

$$y = Ax^b \tag{13.2}$$

where A is a positive number and b is assumed to be greater than zero but less than 1.

The corresponding MPP of x is

$$MPP_x = dy/dx = bAx^{b-1} \tag{13.3}$$

The first-order conditions for maximum profit require that

$$pMPP_x = pbAx^{b-1} = v \tag{13.4}$$

The demand for the input can be found by solving the first-order conditions for x

$$x^{b-1} = v/pbA \tag{13.5}$$

$$x = (v/pbA)^{1/(b-1)} = v^{1/(b-1)}p^{-1/(b-1)}(bA)^{-1/(b-1)} \tag{13.6}$$

Notice here that the demand for x is a function only of the price of the input (v), the price of the product (p), and the coefficient or parameter of the underlying production function (b) as suggested in the general case.

13.3 The Elasticity of Input Demand

Table 13.1 Demand for Units of Input x Under Various Assumptions About the Output Price, p

Price of $x(v)$ (dollars)	Price of y (dollars)			
	2	4	6	8
1	1	4	9	16
2	0.25	1	2.25	4
3	0.11	0.44	1	1.78
4	0.0625	0.25	0.5625	1
5	0.04	0.16	0.36	0.64

A numerical example is used to further illustrate these relationships. Assume that A is 1 and b is 0.5. Then

$$x = 0.25v^{-2}p^2 = 0.25p^2/v^2 \tag{13.7}$$

Table 13.1 provides four demand schedules for input x, when A is 1 and b is 0.5, and assuming output prices of \$2, \$4, \$6, and \$8. Each column represents a different demand function. As the price of x increases, the quantity demanded declines. An increase in the price of the output (y) causes a shift upward in the entire demand schedule or function.

13.3 The Elasticity of Input Demand

In consumer demand, the elasticity of demand is defined as the percentage change in quantity of a good taken from the market divided by the percentage change in the price of that good. Using calculus, the point elasticity of demand is defined as

$$(dQ/dP)(P/Q) \tag{13.8}$$

where P is the price of the good being demanded by the consumer, and Q is the quantity of the good

Now suppose that the specific demand function is

$$Q = P^a \tag{13.9}$$

Taking natural logarithms of both sides of equation (13.1), we have

$$\ln Q = a \ln P \tag{13.10}$$

Now let r equal $\ln Q$ and s equal $\ln P$; equation (13.10) may be rewritten as

$$r = as \tag{13.11}$$

Now differentiate equation (13.11):

$$dr/ds = a \tag{13.12}$$

But notice that

$$d \ln Q / d \ln P = a \quad (13.13)$$

The elasticity of demand for Q can be shown to be equal to the coefficient or parameter a. In this example

$$dQ/dP = aP^{a-1} \quad (13.14)$$

$$(dQ/dP)(P/Q) = (aP^{a-1})(P/Q) = (aP^{a-1})(P/P^a) = a \quad (13.15)$$

which is the same result as that obtained in equation (13.13). In general, any elasticity can be expressed as the derivative of the logarithm of one of the variables with respect to the derivative of the logarithm of the other variable.

Parallel formulas for input demand elasticities exist. The own-price elasticity of demand for an input is defined as the percentage change in the quantity of the input taken from the market divided by the percentage change in the price of that input. Using calculus, the own-price input demand elasticity is

$$(dx/dv)(v/x) \quad (13.16)$$

or

$$d \ln x / d \ln v \quad (13.17)$$

The output-price elasticity can be similarly defined as the percentage change in the quantity of the input taken from the market divided by the percentage change in the price of the output. Using calculus, the output-price demand elasticity is defined either as

$$(dx/dp)(p/x) \quad (13.18)$$

or as

$$d \ln x / d \ln p \quad (13.19)$$

If there were more inputs to the production process than one, both own-price and cross-price elasticities can be defined. The own-price elasticity is the same as is the single-input case, that is, the percentage change in the quantity of the input x_i taken from the market divided by the percentage change in the price of that input (v_i). The subscript i indicates that the price and quantity are for the same input. The formula using calculus would be either

$$(dx_i/dv_i)(v_i/x_i) \quad (13.20)$$

or as

$$d \ln x_i / d \ln v_i \quad (13.21)$$

13.3 The Elasticity of Input Demand

The cross-price elasticity is defined as the percentage change in the quantity of input x_i taken from the market divided by the percentage change in the price of input x_j (v_j). The subscript i is not the same as j. Using calculus, the formula is

$$(dx_i/dv_j)(v_j/x_i) \quad \text{for all } i \neq j \quad (13.22)$$

or

$$d \ln x_i / d \ln v_j \quad (13.23)$$

Now consider a production function

$$y = Ax^b \quad (13.24)$$

The input price (v) and the output price (p) are assumed constant and the farmer is assumed to maximize profits. The input demand function is

$$x = (v/pbA)^{1/(b-1)} = v^{1/(b-1)} p^{-1/(b-1)} (bA)^{-1/(b-1)} \quad (13.25)$$

The own-price elasticity of input demand is derived as follows:

$$dx/dv = [1/(b-1)/v]x = [1/(b-1)](x/v) \quad (13.26)$$

$$(dx/dv)(v/x) = [1/(b-1)](x/v)(v/x) = 1/(b-1) \quad (13.27)$$

The own-price elasticity could be obtained by taking natural logarithms of the input demand function and then finding the derivative

$$d \ln x / d \ln v = 1/(b-1) \quad (13.28)$$

The own-price elasticity of demand for the input depends entirely on the parameter b from the underlying power production function. Given information about the elasticity of production for the input, the corresponding input demand elasticity can be calculated. For example, if b were 0.5, the own-price elasticity of demand for x is $1/(0.5 - 1) = -2$. There exists a close association between the elasticity of demand for an input and the underlying elasticity of production for that input. This analysis breaks down if b is greater than or equal to 1. If b is greater than 1, VMP cuts MFC (v) from below, and the second-order conditions for profit maximization do not hold for any finite level of use of x. If b is equal to 1, VMP = MFC everywhere and there is no demand function based on the profit-maximization assumption.

A similar analysis can be made for the output-price elasticity

$$dx/dp = [-1/(b-1)](x/p) = -x/[p(b-1)] \quad (13.29)$$

$$(dx/dp)p/x = -px/[px(b-1)] = -1/(b-1) \quad (13.30)$$

or

$$d \ln x / d \ln p = -1/(b-1) \qquad (13.31)$$

In the single-input case, the output-price elasticity of demand for input x is equal to the negative of the own-price elasticity of demand. In this case, the output-price elasticity of demand is 2. This suggests that a 1 percent increase in the price of the output will be accompanied by a 2 percent increase in the demand for the input x. Again, the output-price elasticity of demand is a function solely of the elasticity of production of the underlying production function.

13.4 Technical Complements, Competitiveness, and Independence

An input (x_2) can be defined as a technical complement for another input (x_1) if an increase in the use of x_2 causes the marginal product of x_1 to increase. Most inputs are technical complements of each other. Notice that inputs can be technical complements and still substitute for each other along a downward-sloping isoquant.[1]

A simple example of technical complements in agriculture would be two different kinds of fertilizer nutrients in corn production. For example, the presence of adequate quantities of phosphate may make the productivity of nitrogen fertilizer greater.

Technical complements can also be defined by

$$d(MPPx_1)/dx_2 > 0 \qquad (13.32)$$

Consider a production function given by

$$y = Ax_1^a x_2^b \qquad (13.33)$$

$MPPx_1$ is

$$dy/dx_1 = aAx_1^{a-1} x_2^b \qquad (13.34)$$

$$d(dy/dx_1)/dx_2 = baAx_1^{a-1} x_2^{b-1} > 0 \qquad (13.35)$$

By this definition, inputs are technical complements for a broad class of Cobb–Douglas type of production functions. An increase in the use of x_2 causes the $MPPx_1$ to shift upward.

An input (x_2) is said to be technically independent of another input if when the use of x_2 is increased, the marginal product of x_1 ($MPPx_1$) does not change. This requires that

$$d(MPPx_1)/dx_2 = 0 \qquad (13.36)$$

Consider a production function given by

$$y = ax_1 + bx_1^2 + cx_2 + dx_2^2 \tag{13.37}$$

$$dy/dx_1 = a + 2bx_1 \tag{13.38}$$

$$d(dy/dx_1)/dx_2 = 0 \tag{13.39}$$

For additive production functions without interaction terms, inputs are technically independent.

Examples of technically independent inputs to a production process within agriculture are difficult to find. Even the marginal product of a laborer may be affected by the availability of other inputs such as seed and chemicals.

An input (x_2) is said to be technically competitive with another input (x_1) if when the use of x_2 is increased, the marginal product of x_1 ($MPPx_1$) decreases. This requires that

$$d(MPPx_1)/dx_2 < 0 \tag{13.40}$$

An example of a production function in which this might occur is an additive function with a negative interaction term. Consider a production function given by

$$y = ax_1 + bx_1x_2 + cx_2 \tag{13.41}$$

$$dy/dx_1 = a + bx_2 \tag{13.42}$$

$$d(dy/dx_1)/dx_2 = b \tag{13.43}$$

If b were negative, the inputs would be technically competitive.

Examples of inputs that are technical substitutes for each other would include inputs that are very similar to each other. For example, suppose that x_1 represented nitrogen applied as ammonium nitrate and x_2 represented nitrogen applied as anhydrous ammonia. The presence of ample quantities of x_1 would reduce the marginal product of x_2.

13.5 Input Demand Functions in a Two-Input Setting

Input demand functions in a two-input setting can also be derived. Suppose that the farmer is again interested in maximizing profits, and that output and input prices are given. The production function is

$$y = Ax_1^a x_2^b \tag{13.44}$$

The profit function corresponding to equation (13.44) is

$$\begin{aligned}\Pi &= py - v_1x_1 - v_2x_2 \\ &= pAx_1^a x_2^b - v_1x_1 - v_2x_2\end{aligned} \tag{13.45}$$

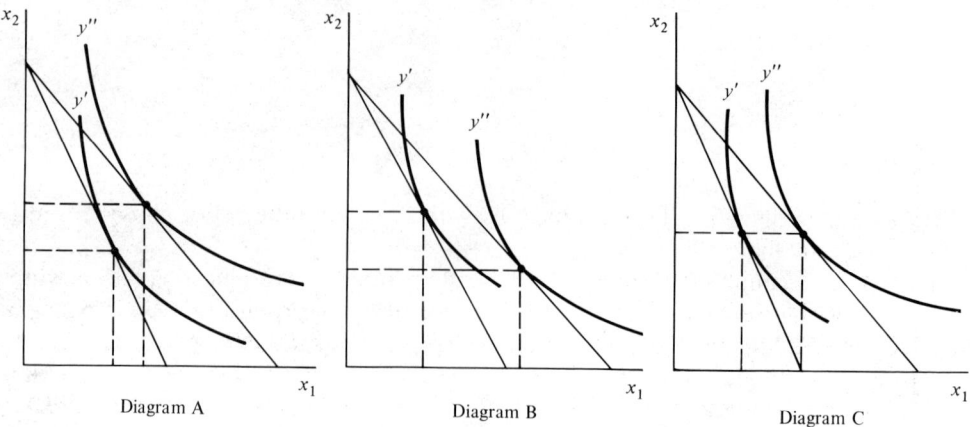

Figure 13.2 Possible Impacts of an Increase in the Price of x_1 on the Use of x_2

Suppose also that $a + b < 0$ (decreasing returns to scale). Then the first order conditions for profit maximization are

$$\partial \Pi / \partial x_1 = apAx_1^{a-1}x_2^b - v_1 = 0 \qquad (13.46)$$

$$\partial \Pi / \partial x_2 = bpAx_1^a x_2^{b-1} - v_2 = 0 \qquad (13.47)$$

One approach for finding the input demand function for x_1 would be to solve the first-order condition equation (13.46) for x_1 in terms of the remaining variables. This yields

$$x_1^{a-1} = v_1(apA)^{-1}x_2^{-b} \qquad (13.48)$$

$$x_1 = v_1^{1/(a-1)}(apA)^{-1/(a-1)}x_2^{-b/(a-1)} \qquad (13.49)$$

Equation (13.49) expresses the demand for x_1 in terms of its own price (v_1), the price of the output (p), and the quantity of the other input (x_2). This approach leads to a demand function made up of points of intersection between a single VMP function (that assumes a constant x_2) and the price of x_1 (v_1). But the quantity of x_2 used will probably change if the price of x_1 changes, so the assumption that x_2 can be assumed constant is untenable.

Figure 13.2 illustrates three cases. Diagram A illustrates the common case in which an increase in the price of x_1 causes the quantity of x_2 that is used to decrease. Diagram B illustrates a case in which the use of x_2 increases as a result of an increase in the price of x_1. Diagram C illustrates a special case in which the use of x_2 remains constant when the price of x_1 increases. Diagram C illustrates the only case in which this approach would yield the correct input demand function.

Only if inputs are technically independent will the marginal product and VMP of one input be unaffected by the quantity of the other input(s) that is(are) available. In other words, it is highly unlikely that the VMP for x_1 would be unaffected by the availability of x_2. As a result, the input demand function speci-

13.5 Input Demand Functions in a Two-Input Setting

fied in equation (13.49) will probably make the demand function for the input x_1 appear less elastic than it really is.

As the price of input x_1 increases, the farmer will use less of it, because the level of x_1 that maximizes profits will shift to the left. This effect is captured by the own-price elasticity in equation (13.49). However, the farmer might also respond to the increased price for x_1 by substituting x_2 for x_1, and equation (13.49) ignores this substitution possibility. The quantity of x_2 used by the farmer is treated as fixed.

Another approach is clearly needed that will explicitly take into account the possibility of substitution x_2 for x_1 as the price of x_1 rises. The use of x_1 should be a function not of the quantity of x_2 but rather of the price of x_2. Such an approach would allow the farmer to move from one *VMP* function to another as the price of x_1 (v_1) changes. A change in the price of x_1 causes the use of x_2 to change, which in turn, results in a new *VMP* function for x_1 (Figure 13.3).

The new approach makes use of the same first-order conditions [equations (13.46) and (13.47)] as those used in the first example. Prices and production function parameters are treated as knowns, the quantities of x_1 and x_2 are unknowns. Equations (13.46) and (13.47) thus represent two equations in two unknowns that are solved as a system. To solve the system, first-order condition (13.46) is divided by first-order condition (13.47) to yield

$$ax_2/bx_1 = v_1/v_2 \tag{13.50}$$

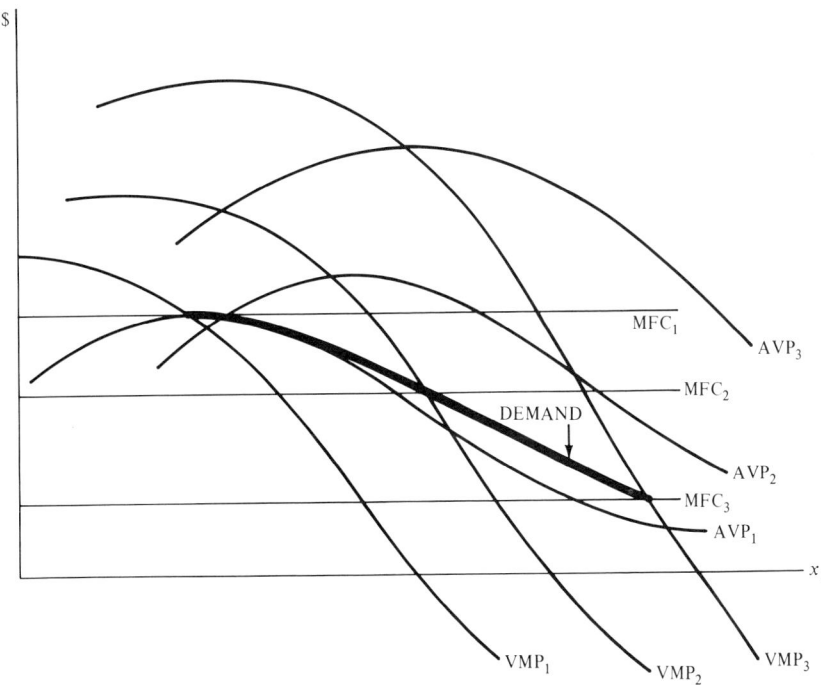

Figure 13.3 Demand for Input x_1 When a Decrease in the Price of x_1 Increases the Use of x_2

or

$$x_2 = v_1 b x_1 / a v_2 \tag{13.51}$$

Equation (13.51) is then substituted into first-order condition (13.46) and solved for x_1

$$apAx_1^{a+b-1} v_1^b v_2^{-b} b^b a^{-b} = v_1 \tag{13.52}$$

$$x_1^{a+b-1} = v_1^{1-b} v_2^b (pA)^{-1} a^{b-1} b^{-b} \tag{13.53}$$

$$x_1 = v_1^{(1-b)/(a+b-1)} v_2^{b/(a+b-1)} (pA)^{-1/(a+b-1)} a^{(b-1)/(a+b-1)} b^{-b/(a+b-1)} \tag{13.54}$$

For equation (13.54), the input own-price demand elasticity is

$$(dx_1/dv_1)(v_1/x_1) = (1 - b)/(a + b - 1) < 0 \tag{13.55}$$

$$d \ln x_1 / d \ln v_1 = (1 - b)/(a + b - 1) < 0 \tag{13.56}$$

If $a + b < 1$, the input own-price demand elasticity is negative. For any specific set of values for a and b, the input own-price demand elasticity may be calculated.

The cross-price demand elasticity between input x_1 and x_2 may be defined from equation (13.54) as

$$(dx_1/dv_2)(v_2/x_1) = b/(a + b - 1) < 0 \tag{13.57}$$

$$d \ln x_1 / d \ln v_2 = b/(a + b - 1) < 0 \tag{13.58}$$

This elasticity is also negative when $a + b < 1$. As the price of x_2 increases, less of x_1 will be used.

The output price elasticity is

$$(dx_1/dp)(p/x_1) = -1/(a + b - 1) > 0 \tag{13.59}$$

$$d \ln x_1 / d \ln p = -1/(a + b - 1) > 0 \tag{13.60}$$

This elasticity is positive when $a + b < 1$. This suggests that the demand for x_1 increases as the output price increases.

Notice also that the sum of the input own-price and cross-price elasticities equals the negative of the output price elasticity

$$(1 - b)/(a + b - 1) + b/(a + b - 1) = -1[-1/(a + b - 1)] \tag{13.61}$$

The relationship defined in equation (13.61) between elasticities holds for production functions with decreasing returns to scale. This relationship would also hold in instances where there are more than two inputs. In general, the sum of the own-price and cross-price input demand elasticities equals the negative of the output-price input demand elasticity.

The own-price and product-price elasticities obtained from the second approach will in general be more strongly negative or elastic than those obtained from the first approach (see Figure 13.3). However, the exact relationship between elasticities will depend on the extent to which the farmer substitutes x_2 for x_1 in the face of rising prices and the impact that this substitution has on the *VMP* function for x_1. Estimates of elasticities from the second approach normally should more accurately portray the extent of the adjustment process by the farmer in response to changing input prices than those estimates obtained from the first approach.

13.6 Input Demand Functions Under Constrained Maximization

Ordinarily, no attempt would be made to derive individual input demand functions for production functions that have constant or increasing returns to scale. If there were increasing returns to scale and input prices were constant (not a function of the demand for the input), profits to the farmer could be maximized by securing as much of both (or all) inputs as possible. Here, no demand function as such could exist. If there were constant returns to scale, the farmer would shut down if the cost of the inputs per unit of output exceeded the output price. If the cost of the inputs per unit of output was less than the product price, the farmer would again attempt to secure as much of each input as possible, and no demand function for the input would exist.

However, if the farmer has a constraint or limitation in the availability of dollars for the purchase of inputs, it may be possible to derive input demand functions even when the underlying production function has no global profit-maximizing solution, or in other situations where a constraint exists in the availability of dollars for the purchase of inputs. Such demand functions are sometimes referred to as *conditional demand functions* in that they assume that the specific budget constraint is met. The conditional demand function specifies the quantity of x_1 and x_2 that will be demanded by the farmer for a series of input prices v_1 and v_2, and assuming that $C°$ total dollars are spent on inputs.

Consider the production function

$$y = x_1 x_2 \qquad (13.62)$$

The function coefficient for this production function is 2. Now suppose that the farmer faces a budget constraint $C°$

$$C° = v_1 x_1 + v_2 x_2 \qquad (13.63)$$

At the budget level defined by equation (13.63), output $y°$ can be produced.

The Lagrangian representing the constrained maximization problem is

$$L = x_1 x_2 + \lambda(C^\circ - v_1 x_1 - v_2 x_2) \tag{13.64}$$

A key assumption of Lagrange's formulation is that the farmer must spend exactly C° dollars on x_1 and x_2. The corresponding first-order conditions are

$$\partial L/\partial x_1 = x_2 - \lambda v_1 = 0 \tag{13.65}$$

$$\partial L/\partial x_2 = x_1 - \lambda v_2 = 0 \tag{13.66}$$

$$\partial L/\partial \lambda = C^\circ - v_1 x_1 - v_2 x_2 = 0 \tag{13.67}$$

Dividing equation (13.65) by equation (13.66) and rearranging gives us

$$x_2 = (v_1/v_2)x_1 \tag{13.68}$$

Inserting equation (13.68) into equation (13.63) yields

$$C^\circ - v_1 x_1 - v_1 x_1 = 0 \tag{13.69}$$

$$C^\circ - 2v_1 x_1 = 0 \tag{13.70}$$

$$2v_1 x_1 = C^\circ \tag{13.71}$$

$$x_1 = C^\circ/2v_1 \tag{13.72}$$

In this example, the demand for input x_1 is a function only of its own price and the dollars available for the purchase of x_1. However, this conclusion is a result of the particular set of coefficients or parameters chosen for the production function and does not hold in the general case.

The input demand function for x_2 could be derived analogously. The price of x_2 (v_2) would have appeared in the input demand function if both x_1 and x_2 appear in each *MPP*. The price of the output does not enter. The constrained maximization problem assumes that the output level defined by the isoquant tangent to the budget constraint will be produced regardless of the output price. The possibility that the farmer may wish to instead shut down is not recognized by the calculus.

13.7 Concluding Comments

This chapter has shown how demand functions for inputs or factors of production can be obtained from the production function for a product. A key assumption of the model of pure competition, that the prices for both inputs and outputs be constant and known with certainty, was made throughout the analysis. The demand for an input is then determined only by the input and output prices and the coefficients or parameters of the underlying production function.

Notes

1. The definitions for technical complements, technical substitutes, and technical independence proposed here are quite different from those suggested in Doll and Orazem (pp. 106–107). Doll and Orazem argue that technical complements must be used in fixed proportion to each other, resulting in isoquants consisting of single points or possibly right angles. Downward-sloping isoquants indicate that inputs are technical substitutes. By the Doll and Orazem definition, most inputs are technical substitutes, not complements. In all three cases specified in this text, isoquants can be downward sloping.

Problems and Exercises

1. Assume that the production function is $y = x^{0.5}$. The price of the input is $2, and the price of the output is $5. What is the profit-maximizing level of use of x? What is the own-price elasticity of demand for input x? What is the output-price elasticity of demand for input x?

2. Find the demand function for input x under an alternative set of prices for x. Graph the function. Now increase the price of y to $7 per unit. Graph the function again. Now decrease the price of y to $3 per unit. Again graph the function.

3. Suppose that the production function is given as $y = 0.3x$. Is there a demand function for input x? Explain.

4. Suppose that the production function is given as $y = x^2$. Is there a demand function for input x? Explain.

5. Suppose that the production function is given as

$$y = x_1^{0.3} x_2^{0.9}$$

Find the input demand function for x_1 assuming that input x_2 is allowed to vary. What happens to the demand for x_1 when the price of x_2 declines? What is the own-price elasticity of demand for input x_1? What is the cross-price elasticity of demand for x_1 (the elasticity of demand for input x_1 when the price of input x_2 changes)? What is the output or product-price elasticity of demand for input x_1?

6. Assume that the production function is

$$y = x_1^{0.5} x_2^{0.5}$$

The price of y is $10 per unit, and the price of x_1 and x_2 are each $2 per unit. How much of each of x_1 and x_2 would the manager demand if he or she had but $100 to spend on x_1 and x_2? Now suppose that the price of x_1 increases to $10 per unit, and the manager has the same $100 to spend. How much of x_1 and x_2 would the manager demand?

Reference

Doll, John P., and Frank Orazem. *Production Economics: Theory with Applications,* 2nd ed. New York: John Wiley, 1984.

14
Variable Product and Input Prices

This chapter relaxes the fixed input and product price assumptions of the purely competitive model and derives the marginal conditions for profit maximization, allowing for the possibility of variable input and product prices. The possibility exists that input or product prices may vary according to how much product is produced or input is used. For a single farmer to affect the price of a product, he or she must control a significant share of the output for the product. The farmer may be able to buy inputs in volume at discount, thus affecting the constant input price assumption.

Key Terms and Definitions:

Price Variation
Downward-sloping Demand Curve
Volume Discounts
Price Flexibility
Function of a Function Rule
Composite Function Rule
Total Value of the Product (TVP)
General Profit-Maximization
    Conditions

14.1 Relaxing the Assumptions of Pure Competition

Until now, two key assumptions of the purely competitive model have been carefully followed. These assumptions were (1) that the farmer can produce and sell as much output as desired at the going, fixed market price, and (2) that the farmer can purchase as much of any input as needed at the going market price. But what if one or both of these assumptions about the real world no longer hold? There are several possible instances in which one or both of these assumptions might not hold.

It is not easy to see how the individual North Dakota wheat producer, by his or her output decision, could possibly influence the market price for wheat, but what about the broiler producer large enough to produce 10 percent of the available broilers for sale in U.S. markets? Surely his or her output decisions could have an influence on broiler prices in the United States. What about a single producer who dominates a small market such as the parsley market? His or her decision not to produce would have an impact on the price of parsley. Control of the market price for an agricultural commodity requires a degree of size on the part of the individual firm.

For certain agricultural commodities, such as broilers, the firm must be rather large in terms of the dollar volume of sales relative to total production of the agricultural commodity to have an impact on prices. For other commodities, such as parsley, where the total market is small, all that is required is that the firm control a significant share of the total output. The percent of the total market that a single farm firm must control in order to have an impact on the price of the commodity varies from commodity to commodity. For a product with a highly inelastic demand curve by consumers in the aggregate, control of but 1 percent of the total output may be sufficient for the individual firm to exert an influence on the market price.

There are two possible rationale for variation in input prices in response to changes in the demand for an input by a farmer. A farmer might be so large as to be the dominant buyer of a particular input in the local market. The farm is large enough such that additional units of the input cannot be purchased without incurring a higher price. It is difficult to see how a market for feed grain or fertilizer could be dominated by a single producer such that the price of feed grains or fertilizer for all producers would be influenced. More likely, market domination in the purchase of inputs might occur for a highly specialized input required solely by the producers of the single commodity which the farm firm dominates, and in a situation for which there may be but a few producers of the input.

The second rationale for variation in input prices is as a result of quantity or volume discounts by input suppliers. Fertilizer purchased by the ton is often cheaper than fertilizer purchased by the pound in a bag, but the crop does not care if the fertilizer was bagged or not. What is required here is that the farm merely be of sufficient size such that the quantities of inputs required to take advantage of the volume discount can be used.

14.2 Variation in Output Prices from the Output Side

If output prices vary with the output level for the farm, the farm must have a degree of monopoly power over the market. The farm need not be the sole producer of the commodity in order to have monopoly power. All that is required is that the output level by the farmer be sufficiently large such that if the level of output from the farm is changed, the market price level will also change.

The example used here relies on some of the characteristics of the model of pure monopoly that are a usual part of introductory economics courses. An important characteristic of a model of a monopoly is a down-sloping demand curve for the product. A down-sloping demand curve, in turn, results in marginal revenue no longer the same as the price of the product. The producer can sell additional units of output only by accepting a lower price for each incremental unit.

In the model of pure competition, with fixed output prices, total revenue is price times output ($TR = py$). Thus the total revenue function under pure competition is a line with a constant positive slope p. Now suppose that price is a function of output, $p = p(y)$ (this notation is read p equals p of y, not p equals p times y). Then total revenue is defined as

$$TR = p(y)y \tag{14.1}$$

Marginal revenue can be obtained by differentiating total revenue with respect to output using the composite function rule

$$MR = dTR/dy = p\, dy/dy + y\, dp/dy \tag{14.2}$$

$$MR = p + y\, dp/dy \tag{14.3}$$

The derivative dp/dy represents the slope of the demand function by consumers for y. The new marginal revenue is equal to marginal revenue under constant product prices plus an expression that explicitly takes into account the slope of the demand function for the output.

Now divide and multiply MR by the output price p

$$MR = p[1 + (y/p)(dp/dy)] \tag{14.4}$$

The expression $(dy/dp)(p/y)$ is the elasticity of demand for the output y or E_d. Marginal revenue under variable output prices is

$$MR = p(1 + 1/E_d) \tag{14.5}$$

The term *price flexibility* is sometimes used as the expression for 1 over an elasticity of demand. A price flexibility represents the percentage change in output price divided by a percentage change in quantity.

The elasticity of demand will be negative if the demand function is downward sloping. As the elasticity of demand for y becomes larger and larger in absolute value (approaching negative infinity), 1 over the elasticity of demand becomes smaller and smaller. At the limit, when the elasticity of demand becomes infinite, marginal revenue is the price of the product and the pure competition assumption is met. If the industry contains monopoly elements, the demand curve will slope downward to a degree and the price of the product will not be equal to marginal revenue.

In other words, if the elasticity of demand lies between zero and $-\infty$, marginal revenue will not be the same as the price of the product. If the elasticity of demand falls in the range ($-\infty < E_d < -1$), marginal revenue will

14.2 Variation in Output Prices from the Output Side

be positive, but less than the product price. If the elasticity of demand falls in the range ($-1 < E_d < 0$), marginal revenue will be negative. If the elasticity of demand equals -1, marginal revenue is zero. The gain in revenue from an increase in the physical quantity of output is just offset by the reduction in revenue attributable to the decrease in the product price.

When marginal revenue is positive, total revenue increases as output is increased. Total revenue is increasing if the elasticity of demand for the product is between $-\infty$ and -1. When marginal revenue is zero, total revenue is constant or perhaps at its maximum. Total revenue is constant when the elasticity of demand for the product exactly -1 (sometimes called *unitary elasticity*). When marginal revenue is negative, total revenue is declining as output is increased. The decrease in revenue from the price reduction more than offsets the increase in revenue from the additional physical quantity of output. Total revenue is decreasing when elasticities of demand for the product lie between 0 and -1 (Figure 14.1).

Now suppose that the demand function for the output is

$$p = a - by \tag{14.6}$$

where a and b are constants. Total revenue is

$$TR = py = (a - by)y = ay - by^2 \tag{14.7}$$

Marginal revenue is

$$MR = dTR/dy = a - 2by \tag{14.8}$$

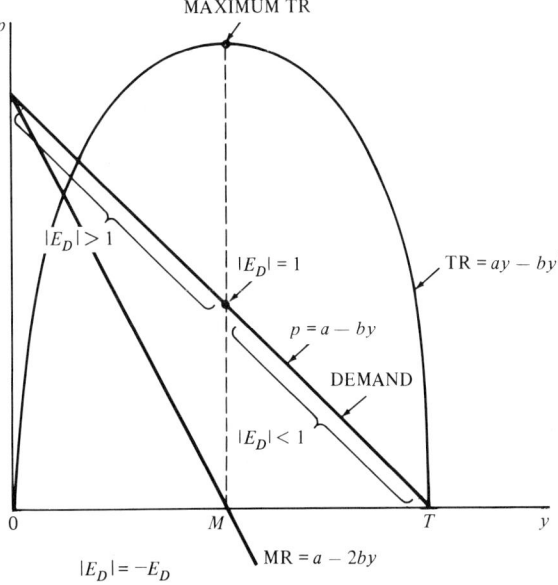

Figure 14.1 Total Revenue, Marginal Revenue, and the Elasticity of Demand

Variable Product and Input Prices

Marginal revenue descends at a rate twice as fast as the demand curve. Hence, for a linear demand function, marginal revenue cuts the horizontal axis at a point exactly one-half the distance from the origin to where the demand function cuts the horizontal axis (Figure 14.1).

The slope of the demand function for y is

$$dp/dy = -b \tag{14.9}$$

The price flexibility of demand for y is

$$(dp/dy)y/p = -b(y/p) \tag{14.10}$$

The elasticity of demand (E_d) for y is

$$E_d = (-1/b)p/y \tag{14.11}$$

For a linear demand function, the elasticity of demand will vary along the demand function. The elasticity of demand at a particular point on the demand function can be determined if the corresponding p and y is known.

Marginal revenue is

$$\begin{aligned} MR &= p[1 + (-b)(y/p)] \\ &= p - (bp)(y/p) \end{aligned} \tag{14.12}$$

14.3 Variation in Output Prices from the Input Side

The farmer controls the level of output that is produced by adjusting the quantity of input that is used. A change in the amount of input that is used will, in turn, affect the amount of output produced. If the market price changes as a result of a change in output, the change in the amount of input that is used can also indirectly affect output prices.

Suppose that the production function is given by

$$y = y(x) \tag{14.13}$$

Equation (14.13) should be read y equals y of x, not y equals y times x. The function $y(x)$ is the same old production function as $f(x)$, but the new notation will simplify the economic interpretation of some of the derivatives.

The product price is again given by

$$p = p(y) \tag{14.14}$$

The price of the product is a function of y, or some p of y, not p times y.

Equations (14.13) and (14.14), when taken together mean that

$$p = p[y(x)] \tag{14.15}$$

14.3 Variation in Output Prices from the Input Side

Output price is equal to p of y of x, not p times y times x. In this example the output price is determined by the quantity of output that is produced. The quantity of output that is produced in turn is a function of the quantity of input that is used. This model suggests that the price of the output is indirectly determined by the quantity of the input that is used.

The equation

$$p = p[y(x)] \quad (14.16)$$

is known as a *function of a function*. Such an equation can be differentiated using the simple *function-of-a-function rule*, which states that the function should be differentiated from the outside in and the result multiplied together

$$dp/dx = (dp/dy)(dy/dx) \quad (14.17)$$

The change in the product price with respect to the change in the quantity of the input used is the product of two slopes. The first (dp/dy) is the slope of the demand function and represents the rate of change in product price as a result of a change in output. The second slope (dy/dx) is our old friend MPP_x and indicates how fast output changes in response to an increase in the use of the input x. The derivatives dp/dy and dy/dx might be constants but they need not be constant. If dp/dy is constant and negative, the demand function has a constant negative slope. If dy/dx is constant, MPP is constant.

The rule is readily extended for a production function with more than one input. Recognize that a change in the use of x_1 also affects the use of x_2. The partial notation for $MPPx_1$ and $MPPx_2$ is used, and the products are summed for each input:

$$y = y(x_1, x_2) \quad (14.18)$$

$$p = p(y) \quad (14.19)$$

$$p = p[y(x_1, x_2)] \quad (14.20)$$

$$dp/dx_1 = (dp/dy)(\partial y/\partial x_1) + (dp/dy)(\partial y/\partial x_2)(dx_2/dx_1) \quad (14.21)$$

$$dp/dx_2 = (dp/dy)(\partial y/\partial x_2) + (dp/dy)(\partial y/\partial x_1)(dx_1/dx_2) \quad (14.22)$$

The expressions to the far right of the equalities in equations (14.21) and (14.22) link explicitly the use of x_1 to x_2 and the use of x_2 to x_1. If the slope of the demand function (dp/dy) is nonzero and $MPPx_1$ and $MPPx_2$ are nonzero, the expressions on the far right will be zero only if a change in the use of one of the two inputs is not accompanied by a change in the use of the other input. This would be highly unlikely.

Suppose again the single-input production function

$$y = y(x) \quad (14.23)$$

Variable Product and Input Prices

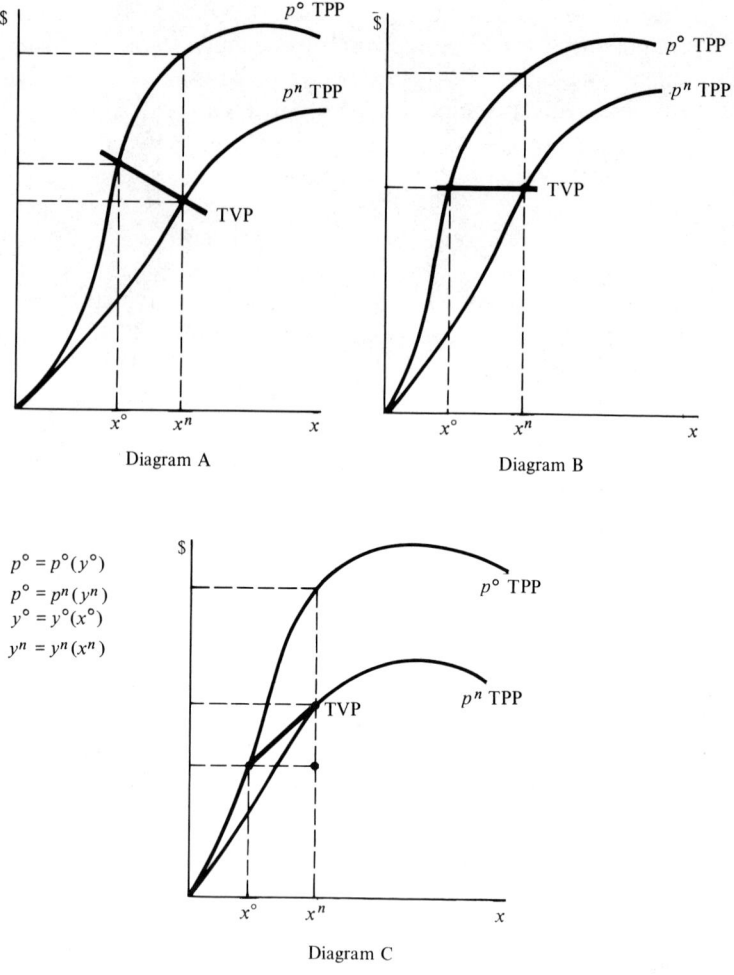

Figure 14.2 Possible *TVP* Functions Under Variable Product Prices

The total value of the product (*TVP*) is given by

$$TVP = p[y(x)][y(x)] \tag{14.24}$$

Figure 14.2 illustrates the relationship between total value of the product under fixed product prices and under variable product prices. There is no assurance that when output increases, total value of the product will also increase if product prices decline in the face on the increase in the output level. Diagram A illustrates a case where the new *TVP* actually declines. In diagram B, the new *TVP* remains constant. In diagram C, both the old and new *TVP* increase, but the *TVP* with decreasing product prices at a slower rate than *TVP* with constant product prices.

To calculate the marginal value of the product (*MVP*), both the composite function rule and the function of a function rule are needed:

14.4 Variable Input Prices

$$\begin{aligned}MVP &= dTVP/dx = p\, dy/dx + y[(dp/dy)(dy/dx)] \\ &= dy/dx(p + y\, dp/dy) \\ &= MPP_x[p + y(\text{the slope of the demand function})] \\ &= pMPP_x(1 + 1/E_d) \\ &= VMP_x(1 + 1/E_d) \\ &= VMP_x + VMP_x/E_d \end{aligned} \quad (14.25)$$

The marginal value of the product (*MVP*) under variable product prices equals the old value of the marginal product (VMP_x) under constant market prices plus the value of the marginal product under constant market prices divided by the price elasticity of demand. Since the price elasticity of demand for the output is usually negative, *MVP* will usually be less than *VMP* under constant product prices. Moreover, the slope of *MVP* will usually be more strongly negative than the slope of *VMP*. The slope of *VMP* is influenced only by the declining marginal product of the underlying production function, The slope of *MVP* is influenced both by the declining *MPP* of the production function and the decrease in price associated with the downward-sloping demand function.

14.4 Variable Input Prices

Two possibilities arise. Increasing input prices in response to increased demand could occur if the individual producer were large enough to influence the market. This would imply $dv/dx > 0$, where v is the price of x. The other possibility is $dv/dx < 0$. This would imply quantity discounts, which result in a lower price per unit of input in response to an increase in demand for the input. If $dv/dx = 0$, input prices are constant and the pure competition assumption with regard to input prices is met.

The variable input price could be defined as

$$v = v(x) \quad (14.26)$$

The input price v is a function of x and equal to v of x (not v times x).
The total factor cost (*TFC*) is

$$TFC = v(x)x \quad (14.27)$$

The total factor cost is v of x times x.
Marginal factor cost (*MFC*) can be found with the aid of the composite function rule

$$\begin{aligned}MFC &= dTFC/dx = v\, dx/dx + x\, dv/dx \\ &= v + x\, dv/dx \\ &= v[1 + (x/v)(dv/dx)] \\ &= v(1 + 1/E_x)\end{aligned} \quad (14.28)$$

where

$$E_x = (dx/dv)(v/x)$$

The elasticity E_x may be positive, negative, or zero. If v is constant, then $dx/dv = 0$, the assumption of pure competition is met and $MFC = v$. If dx/dv is positive, the farmer can obtain additional units of x but only at an increasing price. This condition is consistent with the dominant input buyer case. If dx/dv is negative, additional units of the input can be purchased at a decreasing incremental cost per unit. This condition is broadly consistent with the quantity or volume discounts case.

14.5 A General Profit-Maximization Statement

The general conditions for profit-maximization on the input side can be derived. These conditions allow for variable product and input prices, but include fixed product and input prices as a special case.

Suppose that revenue (R) is a function of output (y)

$$R = r(y) \tag{14.29}$$

Output is a function of input use:

$$y = y(x) \tag{14.30}$$

Cost (C) is a function of input use:

$$C = c(x) \tag{14.31}$$

Profit (Π) is revenue minus cost:

$$\Pi = r[y(x)] - c(x) \tag{14.32}$$

The first-order conditions for the maximization of profit in equation (14.32) require that

$$d\Pi/dx = (dr/dy)(dy/dx) - dc/dx = 0 \tag{14.33}$$

$$MVP - MFC = 0 \tag{14.34}$$

$$MVP = MFC \tag{14.35}$$

The first-order or necessary conditions require that the marginal value of the product (MVP) equal marginal resource cost (MFC), and this occurs at the point where the profit function has a slope of zero. This rule must be followed irrespective of whether or not the input prices are fixed or variable.

The second-order conditions require that

$$d^2\Pi/dx^2 = dMVP/dx - dMFC/dx < 0 \tag{14.36}$$

$$dMVP/dx < dMFC/dx \tag{14.37}$$

14.5 A General Profit-Maximization Statement

The slope of MVP must be steeper or more negative than the slope of MFC. If MVP is downward sloping and MFC is constant or sloping upward, the second-order condition is always satisfied at the intersection. A downward-sloping demand curve for the output leads to an MVP function with a more strongly negative slope than would be the case under constant output prices. But if MVP is downward sloping and so is MFC, the MVP function must cut the MFC function from above. This condition is ordinarily met, but if the farmer were receiving huge discounts for volume purchase of x, it might be possible for the slope of MFC to be more strongly negative than the slope of MVP, and profits would not be maximum.

In the two-input case, the production function is defined as

$$y = y(x_1, x_2) \tag{14.38}$$

The revenue function is

$$R = r(y) \tag{14.39}$$

Thus

$$R = r[y(x_1, x_2)] \tag{14.40}$$

The cost function is

$$C = c(x_1, x_2) \tag{14.41}$$

Profit is

$$\Pi = r[y(x_1, x_2)] - c(x_1, x_2) \tag{14.42}$$

First-order (necessary) conditions for maximum profit in equation (14.42) require that

$$\Pi = (dr/dy)\partial y/\partial x_1 - \partial c/\partial x_1 = 0 \tag{14.43}$$

$$\Pi = (dr/dy)\partial y/\partial x_2 - \partial c/\partial x_2 = 0 \tag{14.44}$$

The slope of the profit function equals zero with respect to both inputs. Moreover,

$$MVPx_1 = MFCx_1 \tag{14.45}$$

$$MVPx_2 = MFCx_2 \tag{14.46}$$

and

$$MVPx_1/MFCx_1 = MVPx_2/MFCx_2 = 1 \tag{14.47}$$

Second-order conditions require that

$$\{\partial[(dr/dy)(\partial y/\partial x_1)]/\partial x_1 - \partial(\partial c/\partial x_1)/\partial x_1\}\{\partial[(dr/dy)(\partial y/\partial x_2)]/\partial x_2$$
$$- \partial(\partial c/\partial x_2)/\partial x_2\} > \{\partial[(dr/dy)(\partial y/\partial x_1)]/\partial x_2 - \partial(\partial c/\partial x_1)/\partial x_2\}$$
$$\{\partial[(dr/dy)(\partial y/\partial x_2)]/\partial x_1 - \partial(\partial c/\partial x_2)/\partial x_1\} \tag{14.48}$$

One implication of these second-order conditions is that if profit maximization is to take place, the *MVP* curve must intersect the *MFC* curve from above. This condition holds irrespective of whether the *MVP* curve or the *MFC* curve has a positive or a negative slope. These first- and second-order conditions could be extended to any number of inputs.

14.6 Concluding Comments

This chapter has provided a set of general profit-maximization conditions that are no longer linked to the pure competition assumption of constant input and product prices. These conditions allow for the possibility of downward-sloping demand curves for the product and volume discounts for input purchases. However, the marginal rules developed in Chapter 7 have not been significantly altered. The value of the incremental unit of the input in terms of its worth in the production process is still equated to the cost of the incremental unit. This rule applies irrespective of whether product and factor prices are allowed to vary.

Problems and Exercises

1. For the following, indicate if a point of profit maximization exists. Explain your answer for each case.

   a. *VMP* cuts *MFC* from above.
   b. *VMP* cuts *MFC* from below.
   c. *VMP* and *MFC* are parallel.
   d. *VMP* and *MFC* diverge.
   e. *VMP* = $3 everywhere; *MFC* = $3 everywhere.
   f. *MFC* and *VMP* intersect, but *MFC* has a more strongly negative slope than *VMP*.

2. Assume the following values. In each case find marginal revenue.

   a. Total revenue (*TR*) = $3y$
   b. $y = 50 - 2p$
   c. $p = 10 - y$
   d. $p = (10 - y)^{0.5}$

3. Find the relationship between *VMP* and *MVP* for the following elasticities of demand for product *y*.

   a. -0.001
   b. -0.2
   c. -1

14.6 Concluding Comments

   d. -5
   e. -1000

4. Suppose that the revenue (R) and cost (C) functions are given by

$$R = 6y^{0.5}$$
$$C = 3y^2$$

Find the first- and second-order conditions for profit maximization.

15 Production of More Than One Product

This chapter introduces the product-product model, in which a single input is used in the production of two products. The basic production possibilities model familiar to students in introductory microeconomics courses is reviewed. The linkages between the production possibilities curve and the product transformation curve for the product-product model are developed. The rate of product transformation represents the slope of the product transformation function. Examples of competitive, complementary supplementary, and joint enterprises are given. Product transformation functions are derived from single-input production functions. An elasticity of substitution on the product side is defined.

Key Terms and Definitions:

Production Possibilities Curve
Concave to the Origin
Bowed Outward
Product-Product Model
Product Transformation Function
Total Differential
Rate of Product Transformation
Competitive Products
Complementary
Supplementary Products
Joint Products
Elasticity of Substitution on the Product Side

15.1 Production Possibilities for a Society

The concept of a production possibilities curve is familiar to students in introductory economics courses. A production possibilities curve represents the range of options open to a society given the resources that are available to the society. The appearance of a production possibilities curve differs from an isoquant in important ways. For example, alternative outputs, not inputs, appear on the axes.

15.1 Production Possibilities for a Society

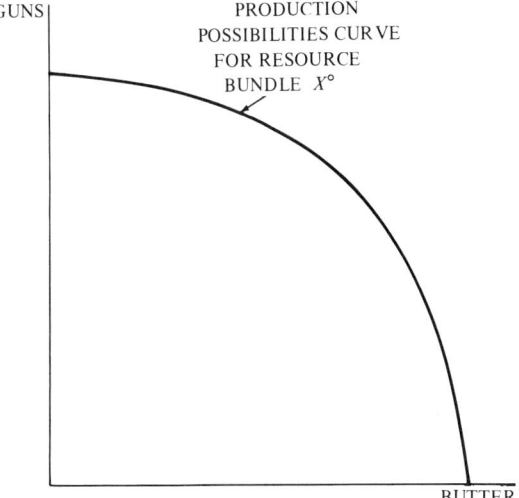

Figure 15.1 Classic Production Possibilities Curve

The production possibilities curve represents the amount of each output that can be produced given that the available resources or inputs are taken as fixed and given. The production possibilities curve is usually drawn bowed outward, or concave to the origin of the graph, rather than convex to the origin of the graph. Figure 15.1 illustrates the classical production possibilities curve.

The classical example of a production possibilities curve for a society has but two goods, butter and guns. Butter represents consumer goods that a society might be able to produce with its resources. Guns represent military weapons. A society might choose any point on its production possibilities curve. For example, the Soviet Union has chosen to invest heavily in defense.

The position of the Soviet Union would be near the guns axis on its production possibilities curve. The United States has chosen to produce some guns and some butter, with a somewhat greater emphasis on butter than guns. The United States would be nearer the butter axis of its curve than would the Soviet Union. A society such as Japan, which invests nearly everything in goods for consumers and virtually nothing on defense, would be found very near the butter axis of its curve.

No two societies have the exact same set of resources available for the production of butter and guns. Therefore, no two societies would have the same production possibilities curve. A society could choose to produce at a point interior to its production possibilities curve, but this would mean that some of the resources available to the society would be wasted. A society could not operate on a point outside its production possibilities curve in that this would require more resources than are available to the society.

A production possibilities curve thus represents the possible alternative efficient sets of outputs from a given set of resources. A simple equation for a production possibilities curve is

$$X° = g(B, G) \tag{15.1}$$

where X° = fixed quantity of resources available to the society
B = amount of butter that is produced
G = amount of guns that are produced

A series of production possibilities curves could be drawn, each representing a slightly different value for the resource bundle X. Production possibilities curves representing smaller resource bundles would lie inside, or interior to, production possibilities curves representing larger resource bundles. Like isoquants, production possibilities curves representing different size input bundles would never touch each other.

15.2 Production Possibilities at the Farm Level

The product-product model of agricultural production is a firm-level version of the production possibilities curve. The production possibilities curve at the firm level is called a *product transformation curve*. The resource base for the farm is a bundle of inputs that could be used to produce either of two outputs. The farmer must chose to allocate the available bundle of inputs between the alternative outputs.

A society faces a problem in attempting to determine how best to allocate its resource bundle between guns and butter, for it cannot rely entirely on market signals. Consumers as individuals would each demand all consumer goods and no defense. But in the aggregate, the society may need protection from other warring nations, so market signals are useless in determining how much of a society's resources should be allocated to the production of guns or butter.

The farmer, or for that matter, any firm, faces a much simpler problem. Firm owners can rely on the market to provide an indication of the proportions of the input bundle that should be allocated to each alternative use. The market provides these signals through the price system. The relative prices, or price ratios, provide important information to the farm firm with respect to how much of each output should be produced.

The other piece of information that a farmer needs to know is the technical coefficients that underlie the production function transforming the input bundle into each alternative output. Just as a family of production functions underlie an isoquant map, so do they underlie a series of product transformation curves or functions. And the law of diminishing returns has as much to do with the outward bow of the product transformation curve as it did with the inward bow of the isoquants.

Consider a farmer who has available 10 units of an input bundle x. Each unit of the input bundle consists of the variable inputs required to produce either corn or soybeans. The proportions of each input in the bundle are equivalent to the proportions defined by the expansion path for the commodity. Since the two commodities require very nearly the same set of inputs, suppose that each unit of the bundle is exactly the same regardless of whether it is being used in the production of corn or soybeans. (This is a bit of a simplification in that no two commodities do require exactly the same inputs in the same proportion. Corn requires nitrogen and seed corn. Soybeans require little if any nitrogen and seed soybeans. Overlook this problem for the moment.)

15.2 Production Possibilities at the Farm Level

Table 15.1 Production Function for Corn and Soybeans from a Variable Input Bundle x

Units of x Applied to Corn	Yield on an Acre (bushels)	Units of x Applied to Soybeans	Yield on an Acre (bushels)	Point
0	0	10	55	A
1	45	9	54	B
2	62	8	52	C
3	87	7	49	D
4	100	6	45	E
5	111	5	40	F
6	120	4	34	G
7	127	3	27	H
8	132	2	19	I
9	135	1	10	J
10	136	0	0	K

The farmer is faced with hypothetical production function data (Table 15.1). The farmer faces a constraint that no more than 10 units of the input bundle x be used. The data for the soybean production function are presented starting with the greatest amount of input first. Each row of Table 15.1 may thus be looked upon as the quantity of each output produced from a total of 10 units of the input bundle. The production function for both corn and soybeans is subject to the law of diminishing returns. Each additional unit of the input bundle produces less and less additional output. The farmer cannot circumvent the law of diminishing returns in the production of either corn or soybeans.

The greatest yields result when the farmer allocates all of the input bundle to the production of one of the possible outputs, but then none of the alternative output is produced. Suppose that the farmer initially allocates all 10 units of x to the production of corn and receives 136 bushels per acre. This point is depicted at A on Figure 15.2. By allocating, instead, 1 of the 10 units of x to the production of soybeans instead of corn, the farmer gives up but 1 bushel of corn. In return, 10 bushels of soybeans are received. What is happening is that the unit of the input bundle is being taken away from corn production in a very nonproductive region of the corn production function, where the MPP of x for corn is very low. The unit of the bundle is applied to the production function for soybeans in a very productive region of the soybean production function, where the MPP of x for soybeans is very high.

Figure 15.2 illustrates some of the other options represented by the tabular data. Each additional unit of x taken from corn production results in a greater and greater loss in yield. As these additional units of x taken from corn production are applied to soybeans, each additional unit of x produces fewer and fewer additional soybeans. If a line is drawn that connects each of these points, the product transformation curve of function for the farmer results. The bowed-out shape of the production possibilities curve is a direct result of the law of diminishing returns, as evidenced by the declining marginal productivity of x in the production of each output.

If the production functions for both outputs do not have diminishing marginal returns, the product transformation curve would not be bowed outward but would have a constant downward slope. The product transformation curve

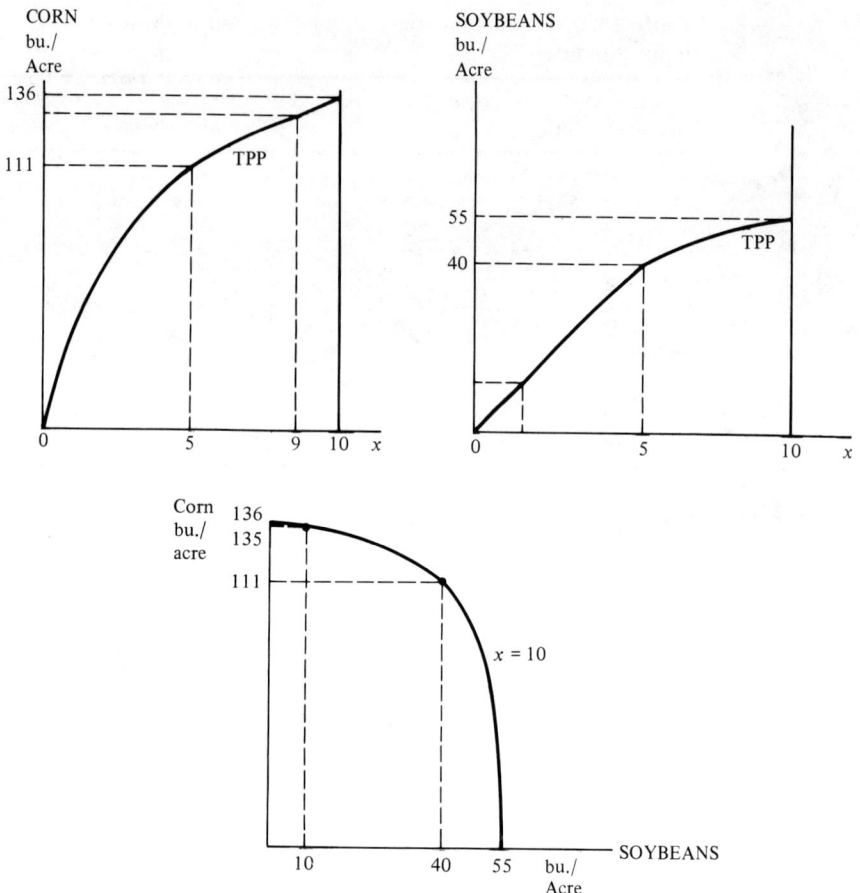

Figure 15.2 Deriving a Product Transformation Function from Two Production Functions

would be bowed inward if both underlying production functions had increasing marginal returns, or increased at an increasing rate.

15.3 General Relationships

There exists a close association between the shape of a product transformation function and the two underlying production functions. Suppose that the equation for the product transformation curve is given by

$$x = g(y_1, y_2) \tag{15.2}$$

where x is the input bundle and y_1 and y_2 are alternative outputs, such as corn and soybeans in the earlier example.

This is clearly not a production function, for it tells the amount of the input bundle that will be used as a result of varying the quantity of y_1 and y_2 that are produced. Note how similar this function is to the earlier function representing

15.3 General Relationships

a product transformation curve for a society, but the function g is clearly not the same as the now familiar production function f.

Following the procedure outlined earlier for taking the total differential of a function, we have

$$dx = (\partial g/\partial y_1)dy_1 + (\partial g/\partial y_2)dy_2 \qquad (15.3)$$

The partial derivatives $\partial g/\partial y_1$ and $\partial g/\partial y_2$ can readily be interpreted. The function g is actually x, and the equation could have been written as $x = x(y_1, y_2)$. (Again, x equals x of y_1 and y_2, not x equals $\dot{x}$ times y_1 and y_2.) Each partial derivative represents the change in the use of the input bundle x that arises from a change in the production of one of the outputs and is an inverse marginal product. The partial derivative $\partial g/\partial y_1$ is $1/MPPx$ in the production of y_1, assuming that y_2 is constant. This might be called $1/MPPx_{y1}$. The partial derivative $\partial g/\partial y_2$ is $1/MPPx$ in the production of y_2, assuming that y_1 is held constant. This might be called $1/MPPx_{y2}$. The equation for the total differential could then be rewritten as

$$dx = (1/MPPx_{y1})dy_1 + (1/MPPx_{y2})dy_2 \qquad (15.4)$$

The basic assumption underlying a specific product transformation function is that the quantity of the input bundle x does not change. The product transformation function thus provides the alternative quantities of y_1 and y_2 that can be produced from a fixed amount of x. Hence dx, the change in x along a product transformation function, is zero. The total differential may then be rewritten as

$$0 = (1/MPPx_{y1})\, dy_1 + (1/MPPx_{y2})\, dy_2 \qquad (15.5)$$

$$-(1/MPPx_{y1})\, dy_1 = (1/MPPx_{y2})\, dy_2 \qquad (15.6)$$

$$-(1/MPPx_{y1}) = (1/MPPx_{y2})(dy_2/dy_1) \qquad (15.7)$$

$$-(1/MPPx_{y1})/(1/MPPx_{y2}) = dy_2/dy_1 \qquad (15.8)$$

$$-MPPx_{y2}/MPPx_{y1} = dy_2/dy_1 \qquad (15.9)$$

The expression dy_2/dy_1 represents the slope of the product transformation curve at a particular point. (The slope between a pair of points could be called $\Delta y_2/\Delta y_1$.) The slope of a product transformation function has been called different things by various economists. The term most often used is the *rate of product transformation* (*RPT*). The *RPT* is the slope (or in some textbooks, the negative slope) of the product transformation function and indicates the rate at which one output can be substituted for or transformed to the production of the other output as the input bundle is reallocated.

For the derivative dy_2/dy_1, y_1 is substituting and y_2 is being substituted. The derivative dy_2/dy_1 is the rate of product transformation of y_1 for y_2, or $RPTy_1y_2$. Some textbooks define the $RPTy_2y_1$ as the negative of dy_2/dy_1, so that

Table 15.2. Rate of Product Transformation of Corn for Soybeans from a Variable Input Bundle x.

Units of x Applied to Corn	Yield per Acre (bushels)	MPP of x in Corn Production	Units of x Applied to Soybeans	Yield per Acre (bushels)	MPP of x in Bean Production	RPT of Corn for Soybeans
0	0		10	55		
1	45	45	9	54	1	1/45 = 0.022
2	62	17	8	52	2	2/17 = 0.118
3	87	15	7	49	3	3/15 = 0.200
4	100	13	6	45	4	4/13 = 0.308
5	111	11	5	40	5	5/11 = 0.455
6	120	9	4	34	6	6/9 = 0.667
7	127	7	3	27	7	7/7 = 1.00
8	132	5	2	19	8	8/5 = 1.60
9	135	3	1	10	9	9/3 = 3.00
10	136	1	0	0	10	10/1 = 10.0

the rate of product transformation is positive when the product transformation function is downward sloping. The derivative dy_1/dy_2 is $RPTy_2y_1$.

Along a product transformation function, the $RPTy_1y_2$ is equal to the negative ratio of individual marginal products

$$RPTy_1y_2 = -MPPx_{y2}/MPPx_{y1} \tag{15.10}$$

(If the rate of product transformation is defined as $-dy_2/dy_1$, it is equal to $MPPx_{y2}/MPPx_{y1}$.) The rate of product transformation for each point in the tabular data can be calculated with this rule (Table 15.2).

15.4 Competitive, Supplementary, Complementary, and Joint Products

Given a fixed amount of the resource bundle x, one output must be forgone in order to produce more of the other output. Therefore, under ordinary circumstances, the $RPTy_1y_2$ will be negative. Hence the two outputs are competitive with each other. Two outputs are said to be *competitive* when the product transformation function is downward sloping.

$$dy_2/dy_1 < 0 \text{ implies competitive products.} \tag{15.11}$$

An output y_1 is said to be *supplementary*, if some positive level of production of the output y_1 is possible without any reduction in the output of y_2. Supplementary outputs imply either a zero or infinite rate of product transformation, depending on which output appears on the horizontal axis. This suggests that

$$dy_2/dy_1 = 0 \text{ or } dy_2/dy_1 = \text{infinity} \tag{15.12}$$

15.4 Competitive, Supplementary, Complementary, and Joint Products

An example of a supplementary enterprise sometimes cited is a farm flock of chickens. The farm wife's labor would be wasted were it not for the chicken flock. The chicken flock does not reduce the output from remaining enterprises on the farm. This example is not very popular with women's groups. Neither is it a very good example. Even if the farm wife's labor were wasted, chickens take other inputs, such as feed, that would reduce the output from the other enterprises. A good example of a supplementary enterprise is difficult to find. Usually, the enterprise is supplementary only with respect to certain types of inputs contained within the input bundle, in this example, the housewife's labor.

An output y_1 is said to be *complementary* if production of y_1 causes the output of y_2 to increase. The rate of product transformation is positive at least for certain combinations of y_1 and y_2. In other words,

$$dy_2/dy_1 > 0 \quad \text{for certain production levels for } y_1 \text{ and } y_2 \quad (15.13)$$

An often cited example of a complementary enterprise is a legume in a rotation. The legume increases production of grain crops in alternate years. But it is not entirely clear that such a rotation would necessarily increase the total

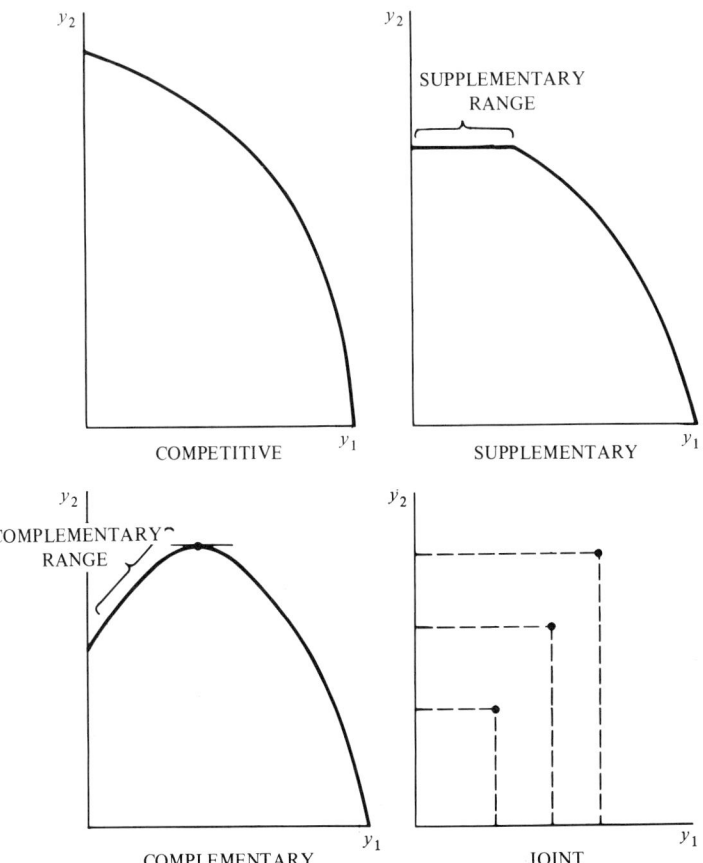

Figure 15.3 Competitive, Supplementary, Complementary, and Joint Products

output of crops over a horizon of several years, and the farmer may produce more output by using chemical fertilizers instead of the legume. Good examples of complementary farm enterprises are difficult to find. Again, these examples are usually called complementary only with respect to a few of the inputs contained in the bundle needed for production.

Joint products, narrowly defined, are those that must be produced in a fixed ratio to each other. As a result, the product transformation function will either be a single point or a right angle. The classical example is the production of beef and hides. Only one hide can be produced per beef animal, no more and no less. The elasticity of product substitution between beef and hides is zero.

Another example is the production of wool and lamb. Although these may appear to be joint products, much like beef and hides, some sheep tend to produce more wool, whereas others are favored for the production of meat. Over time a farmer might substitute a wool breed for a meat breed and produce more wool but less lamb. Or the meat breed might be substituted for the wool breed to produce more meat and less wool. So substitution could take place over time but within a narrow range of possibilities. It would not be possible to raise a sheep that produced all lamb and no wool, or all wool but no lamb.

Figure 15.3 illustrates some possible product transformation functions representing competitive, supplementary, and complementary products. Two outputs are normally competitive everywhere on the product transformation function. It is possible for two outputs to be supplementary or complementary over only a portion of the transformation function.

15.5 Product Transformations from Single-Input Production Functions

It is often possible to develop a specific transformation relationship between two products by working with the underlying single-input production functions. Suppose that the two single-input production functions are given by

$$y_1 = 2x_{y1} \tag{15.14}$$

$$y_2 = 3x_{y2} \tag{15.15}$$

$$x_{y1} + x_{y2} = x \tag{15.16}$$

where y_1 and y_2 are alternative outputs and x_{y1} x_{y2} represent the quantities of x used in the production of y_1 and y_2, respectively. The sum of these quantities must be equal to x, the total amount available. Solving the first and second equations for x_{y1} and x_{y2} and substitution into the third equation yields

$$x_{y1} = y_1/2 \tag{15.17}$$

$$x_{y2} = y_2/3 \tag{15.18}$$

15.5 Product Transformations from Single-Input Production Functions

Therefore,

$$y_1/2 + y_2/3 = x \tag{15.19}$$

If x is fixed at a particular value, this becomes an equation for the product transformation curve. The total differential of equation (15.19) is

$$dx = \tfrac{1}{2}dy_1 + \tfrac{1}{3}dy_2 \tag{15.20}$$

Along a product transformation function, there is no change in x, and dx is zero:

$$dy_2/dy_1 = RPTy_1y_2 = (-\tfrac{1}{2})/(\tfrac{1}{3}) = -\tfrac{3}{2} \tag{15.21}$$

The product transformation function has a constant downward slope of $-\tfrac{3}{2}$. The slope arises directly from the fact that the underlying single-input function exhibit constant marginal returns to the input bundle x.

Now consider a slightly more general form for the underlying production functions:

$$y_1 = bx_{y1} \tag{15.22}$$

$$y_2 = cx_{y2} \tag{15.23}$$

$$x_{y1} + x_{y2} = x \tag{15.24}$$

where b and c are positive constants and other terms are as previously defined. Solving equations (15.22) and (15.23) for x_{y1} and x_{y2} and substituting into equation (15.24) results in

$$(1/b)y_1 + (1/c)y_2 = x \tag{15.25}$$

The total differential of equation (15.25) is

$$dx = (1/b)dy_1 + (1/c)dy_2 = 0 \tag{15.26}$$

Rearranging yields

$$dy_2/dy_1 = RPTy_1y_2 = -c/b \tag{15.27}$$

Again the rate of product transformation is constant and equal to the negative ratio of the marginal products for the two underlying production functions.

Now consider the case where the underlying production functions are

$$y_1 = x_{y1}^{0.5} \tag{15.28}$$

$$y_2 = x_{y2}^{0.33} \tag{15.29}$$

Production of More Than One Product

$$x_{y1} + x_{y2} = x \tag{15.30}$$

Solving equations (15.28) and (15.29) for x_{y1} and x_{y2} yields

$$x_{y1} = y_1^{1/0.5} = y_1^2 \tag{15.31}$$

$$x_{y2} = y_2^{1/0.33} = y_2^3 \tag{15.32}$$

The equation for the underlying product transformation function is

$$y_1^2 + y_2^3 = x \tag{15.33}$$

The rate of product transformation of y_1 for y_2 ($RPTy_1y_2$) can be derived by taking the total differential of equation (15.33):

$$dx = 2y_1\, dy_1 + 3y_2^2\, dy_2 = 0 \tag{15.34}$$

$$dy_2/dy_1 = -2y_1/3y_2^2 \tag{15.35}$$

The slope of the product transformation curve will vary and depend on the specific values of y_1 and y_2 as well as the parameters of the underlying production functions for y_1 and y_2.

A still more general formulation assumes that a general multiplicative production function exists for the production of both outputs

$$y_1 = Ax_{y1}^a \tag{15.36}$$

$$y_2 = Bx_{y2}^b \tag{15.37}$$

$$x = x_{y1} + x_{y2} \tag{15.38}$$

Solving equations (15.36) and (15.37) for x_{y1} and x_{y2} and inserting into equation (15.38) yields

$$x_{y1}^a = y_1/A = y_1 A^{-1} \tag{15.39}$$

$$x_{y1} = y_1^{1/a} A^{-1/a} \tag{15.40}$$

$$x_{y2}^b = y_2/B = y_2 B^{-1} \tag{15.41}$$

$$x_{y2} = y_2^{1/b} B^{-1/b} \tag{15.42}$$

Substitute equations (15.40) and (15.42) into equation (15.38). The equation for the resultant product transformation function is

$$x = y_1^{1/a} A^{-1/a} + y_2^{1/b} B^{-1/b} \tag{15.43}$$

The total differential of equation (15.43) is

$$dx = A^{-1/a}(1/a)y_1^{(1-a)/a} dy_1 \\ + B^{(-1/b)}(1/b)y_2^{(1-b)/b} dy_2 = 0 \qquad (15.44)$$

A general expression for the $RPT y_1 y_2$ is obtained by setting dx in equation (15.44) equal to zero and solving for dy_2/dy_1:

$$\begin{aligned} dy_2/dy_1 &= -[A^{-1/a}(1/a)y_1^{(1-a)/a}]/[B^{-1/b}(1/b)y_2^{(1-b)/b}] \\ &= -[B^{1/b} b y_1^{(1-a)/a}]/[A^{1/a} a y_2^{(1-b)/b}] \end{aligned} \qquad (15.45)$$

The rate of product transformation is explicitly linked to the parameters of the two underlying production functions.

The process of solving the production function for y_1 and y_2 in terms of x involves inversion of the production function. The production function for each output must be solved for x in terms of the output. The production functions used here were chosen primarily because they could easily be inverted. Suppose that the production functions for y_1 and y_2 were

$$y_1 = ax + bx^2 \qquad (15.46)$$

$$y_2 = bx + dx^2 \qquad (15.47)$$

Such functions are not easily inverted. For certain values of the parameters a, b, and d, the inverse functions do not exist. It is difficult to solve for the product transformation function in any instance where the underlying production functions exhibit negative marginal product for certain values of x. The inverse is a correspondence but not a function.

15.6 Product Transformation and the Output Elasticity of Substitution

An output elasticity of substitution could be defined analogous to an elasticity of substitution on the input side. The definition of the output elasticity of substitution is the percentage change in the output ratio divided by the percentage change in the rate of product transformation. The value for the elasticity of product transformation would provide a clue as to the shape of the product transformation function, just as an elasticity of substitution on the input side provides an indication of the shape of an isoquant.

Products that could be substituted for each other without incurring the law of diminishing marginal returns would have a product transformation function with a constant negative slope. This would result in an infinite elasticity of substitution on the product side. Products that could be produced only in fixed proportions would have a right-angle product transformation function and a zero elasticity of substitution on the product side.

The common cases would lie between these two extremes, and elasticities of product substitution in the two-output case would normally lie between zero and infinity. Some formulas for the elasticity of product substitution (e_{ps}) are

$$\begin{aligned} e_{ps} &= \text{percentage change in the output ratio } (y_2/y_1) \text{ divided} \\ &\quad \text{by the percentage change in the rate of product trans-} \\ &\quad \text{formation} \\ &= [\Delta(y_2/y_1)/y_2/y_1]/(\Delta RPTy_1y_2/RPTy_1y_2) \end{aligned} \quad (15.48)$$

At the limit, when $\Delta = d$

$$\begin{aligned} e_{ps} &= [d(y_2/y_1)/y_2/y_1]/dRPTy_1y_2/RPTy_1y_2 \\ &= [d(y_2/y_1)/d(RPTy_1y_2)][RPTy_1y_2/(y_2/y_1)] \end{aligned} \quad (15.49)$$

The development of algebraic formulas representing the product transformation relationship has not taken place to the extent that two-input production functions have been developed. Klein proposed a function

$$x = Ay_1^a y_2^b \quad (15.50)$$

where A, a, and b are parameters. The function looks very similar to a Cobb–Douglas type of production function. Just, Zilberman, and Hockman presented a CES type of function for the output side:

$$x = B[\psi y_1^{-\nu} + (1 - \psi y_2)^{-\nu}]^{-1/\nu} \quad (15.51)$$

However, under the usual parameter assumptions, neither equations (15.50) or (15.51) would generate product transformation functions concave to the origin, consistent with neoclassical theory. Equation (15.51) will generate product transformation functions if $\nu < -1$.

15.7 Concluding Comments

This chapter has developed the physical relationships underlying the product-product model. The product transformation curve is the production possibilities curve on a firm, rather than society level. The slope of the product transformation function is closely tied to the marginal products of the single-input production functions that underlie the transformation of input into outputs. An expression for an output elasticity of substitution can be derived, but specific equations representing input use in the production of alternative outputs have not been developed to the extent that single-output production functions using alternative inputs have been developed by economists and agricultural economists.

Problems and Exercises

1. Assume the following production function data:

15.7 Concluding Comments

Units of x Applied to y_1	Output of y_1	Units of x Applied to y_2	Output of y_2
0	0	10	50
1	20	9	49
2	30	8	47
3	38	7	44
4	45	6	40
5	51	5	35
6	56	4	29
7	60	3	22
8	63	2	14
9	64	1	5
10	64.5	0	0

If only 10 units of input x are available, graph the production possibilities (product transformation) curve from this production function data.

2. Suppose that at a particular point, the *MPP* of x in the production of y_1 is positive but the *MPP* of x in the production of y_2 is negative (stage III of production). What would be the slope of the product transformation function? Explain.

3. Assume the following production functions for x in the production of y_1 and y_2. Find the rate of product transformation of y_1 for y_2.

$$y_1 = x^{0.25}$$
$$y_2 = x^{0.33}$$

4. What do competitive, supplementary, complementary, and joint enterprises each imply about the shape of the production functions that underlie the product transformation functions?

References

Just, Richard E., David Zilberman, and Eithan Hockman."Estimation of Multicrop Production Functions." *American Journal of Agricultural Economics* 65 (1983) pp. 770–780.

Klein, L. R. "The Use of Cross Section Data in Econometrics with Application to a Study of Production of Railroad Services in the United States." Mimeo, National Bureau of Economic Research, Washington, D.C., 1947.

16 Maximization in a Two-Output Setting

This chapter presents the marginal allocation conditions for a single input in the production of two outputs. First, a graphical and tabular presentation is used. Then the fundamental constrained maximization conditions on the output side are derived. Comparisons are made of solutions when the constraint is the physical quantity of the input versus dollars available for the purchase of the input. Global profit maximization conditions on the output side are outlined. Starting with the individual production functions for the two products, the product transformation and input demand functions are derived. The product-product model is applied to an output restriction problem.

Key Terms and Definitions:

Family of Product Transformation Functions
Output Maximization on the Product Side
Isorevenue Line
Constrained Revenue Maximization on the Product Side
Output Expansion Path
Output Pseudo Scale Line
Marginal Cost in Physical Terms
Output Restriction

16.1 The Family of Product Transformation Functions

A family of product transformation functions can be created by varying the assumptions with respect to the availability of the resource or input bundle x. Along each product transformation function, the amount of the resource or input bundle remains constant. Figure 16.1 illustrates a family of product transformation functions. Like isoquant families, an infinite number of product trans-

16.2 Maximization of Output

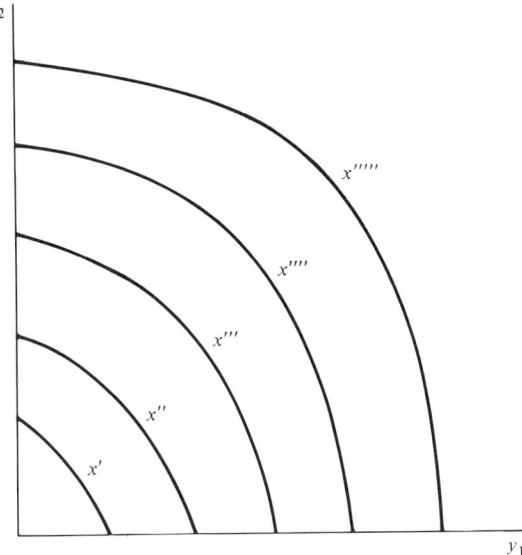

Figure 16.1 Family of Product Transformation Functions

formation functions can be drawn. No two product transformation functions will touch each other or intersect. Each successive product transformation function assumes a slightly different level of use of the input bundle.

16.2 Maximization of Output

Assume that there is no limitation on the availability of the input bundle x. The equation describing the family of product transformation functions is

$$x = g(y_1, y_2) \tag{16.1}$$

Suppose that the farm manager wishes to determine the amount of the input x that would be required such that the output of both y_1 and y_2 is at its maximum. The farm manager has available any amount of the input bundle x, and, at least for the moment, the cost of the input bundle is of no consequence.

One way is to look at the first derivatives of the product transformation equation dx/dy_1 and dx/y_2. The expression dx/dy_1 is $1/(dy_1/dx)$ or $1/MPPx_{y1}$. The expression dx/dy_2 is $1/(dy_1/dx)$ or $1/MPPx_{y2}$. These expressions represent the marginal cost of producing an additional unit of y_1 or y_2, expressed in terms of physical quantities of the input bundle. If the farm manager is interested in maximizing the production of both y_1 and y_2, a level of input use where both y_1 and y_2 are at their respective maxima must be found.

If the amount of both outputs are at a global maximum, an additional unit of the input bundle will produce no additional output of either y_1 or y_2. In other words, the marginal product of x in the production of y_1 ($MPPx_{y1}$) and the marginal product of x in the production of y_2 will be zero. As $MPPx_{y1}$ and

$MPPx_{y2}$ approach zero, $1/MPPx_{y1}$ and $1/MPPx_{y2}$ become very large, and approach infinity. If $MPPx_{y1}$ and $MPPx_{y2}$ were exactly zero, $1/MPPx_{y1}$ and $1/MPPx_{y2}$ are undefined, although economists frequently treat them as infinite.

What happens to the appearance of an isoquant map as output approaches a maximum is clear. Isoquants become smaller and smaller concentric rings until the point of output maximum is achieved and the single point represents the isoquant for maximum output.

What happens to the appearance of a product transformation function as a global maximum for both outputs is approached is less clear. As more y_1 and y_2 is produced, each successive product transformation function becomes larger and larger and is drawn farther and farther from the origin of the graph. Exactly what happens to the shape of the product transformation function as the level of use of the input bundle x becomes large enough to achieve maximum output is not obvious, since at the point of output maximization for x in the production of both y_1 and y_2, the $1/MPPx$ in the production of either output is undefined.

When confronted with a problem such as this, economists frequently make assumptions such that they need not worry about the problem. Some arguments used to avoid thinking about such issues do make sense.

The assumption usually made to get around the problem is that the size of the resource or input bundle will always be constrained by something. Farmers nearly always face limitations in their ability to produce more because of the unavailability of land. An unlimited input bundle would imply that a single farmer owned all the farmland in the United States, not to mention all foreign countries. Then the constraint becomes the size of the earth. (Moreover, if a single farmer were to acquire all the world's farmland, the purely competitive assumptions would no longer hold!)

Every farmer faces capital constraints limiting the ability to borrow money for the purchase of more inputs. Perhaps the fact that a truly global point of output maximization cannot be achieved with the product-product model may not be such a serious problem after all. Important conclusions can be reached without the looking at the case in which output is maximized without constraints.

16.3 The Isorevenue Line

The revenue function (R) for the farmer who produces two outputs is

$$R = p_1 y_1 + p_2 y_2 \tag{16.2}$$

Assume that a farmer needs $1000 of revenue. The price of y_1 is $5 and the price of y_2 is $2. The farmer might choose to generate $1000 by producing all y_1, in which case he or she would need to produce 200 units (1000/5). Or the farmer might choose to produce all y_2, and 500 units of output (1000/2) would be required. Perhaps some combination of the two outputs might be produced. The procedure for creating an isorevenue line is exactly the same as the procedure for creating an isocost line, with the following exceptions. Revenue replaces cost in the equation. Prices are now output prices rather than input prices. Table 16.1 illustrates some combinations of y_1 and y_2 that would yield $1000 of revenue.

16.4 Constrained Revenue Maximization

Table 16.1 Alternative Combinations of y_1 and y_2 That Result in $1000 of Revenue ($p_1 = \$5, p_2 = \$3$)

Combination	Units of y_1	Units of y_2	Revenue
A	200	0	$1000
B	150	125	1000
C	100	250	1000
D	50	375	1000
E	0	500	1000

There are many more (in fact, an infinite number) of combinations of y_1 and y_2 that would yield $1000 in revenue. The isorevenue line can be drawn on a graph with y_1 on the horizontal axis and y_2 on the vertical axis. The position where the isorevenue line cuts the horizontal axis can be found by assuming that the production of y_2 is zero, and solving the revenue function representing a fixed amount of revenue ($R°$) for y_1

$$R° = p_1 y_1 + 0 p_2 \tag{16.3}$$

$$R° = p_1 y_1 \tag{16.4}$$

$$y_1 = R°/p_1 = 1000/5 = 200 \tag{16.5}$$

where p_1 and p_2 are prices for y_1 and y_2, respectively.

A similar procedure can be used to find the point where the isorevenue line cuts the y_2 axis

$$y_2 = R°/p_2 = 1000/2 = 500 \tag{16.6}$$

The slope of an isorevenue line is $-y_2/y_1$, or

$$(R°/p_2)/(R°/p_1) = -p_1/p_2 = (1000/2)/(1000/5) = -5/2. \tag{16.7}$$

The slope of an isorevenue line is a constant ratio of the two output prices. If y_2 appears on the vertical axis and y_1 on the horizontal axis, the slope of the isorevenue line is the negative inverse output price ratio, $-p_1/p_2$.

The term *isorevenue* means equal revenue. At any point on an isorevenue line, total revenue is the same, but if total revenue is allowed to vary, a new isorevenue line can be drawn. The greater the total revenue, the farther the isorevenue line will be from the origin of the graph. If output prices are constant, the slope over every isorevenue line will be the same. No two isorevenue lines will ever touch or intersect. Families of isorevenue lines are drawn with each isorevenue line representing a slightly different revenue level.

16.4 Constrained Revenue Maximization

A family of isorevenue lines can be superimposed on a family of product transformation functions (Figure 16.2). Each isorevenue line has its own product transformation function that comes just tangent to it. The point of tangency represents the maximum revenue attainable from a given product transformation function. It is the point where the slope of the isorevenue line just equals the rate of product transformation. This point represents the position where the farmer would most like to be among the series of points along a product transformation function, for it represents maximum revenue from the given level of inputs that defines that particular product transformation function. The assumption is that the amount of the input bundle is fixed and given. These points of tangency can be defined by the following equations

$$-RPTy_1y_2 = -dy_2/dy_1 = (1/MPPx_{y1})/(1/MPPx_{y2})$$
$$= MPPx_{y2}/MPPx_{y1}$$
$$= -p_1/p_2 \qquad (16.8)$$

Both the $RPTy_1y_2$ and the isorevenue line are negative, as indicated by the sign. By multiplying both by -1, the result is

$$RPTy_1y_2 = dy_2/dy_1 = p_1/p_2 \qquad (16.9)$$

An increase in the price of one of the outputs relative to the other will push the point of tangency toward the axis for the output that experienced the price increase. If the price of one output drops relative to the other, the production of the other output will be favored.

The path along which the farmer will expand his or her operation is a line that connects all points of tangency between the isorevenue lines and the corresponding product transformation curve. This line is called the output expansion path (Figure 16.2). To generate more revenue, the farmer must expand the resource base, or the availability of the input bundle x. As this happens, the farmer will move from one product transformation function to another along the output expansion path. If output prices are constant, most product transformation maps have underlying production functions that will result in an output expansion path with a constant slope.

Consider the data presented in Table 15.2 again, here presented in Table 16.2. Assume that soybeans sell for $9 per bushel and corn is $6 per bushel. The input combination where the rate of product transformation of corn for soybeans equals the price ratio is the combination between the combination 120 bushels of corn and 34 bushels of soybeans and the combination 111 bushels corn and 40 bushels soybeans. Total revenue for the first combination is $111 \cdot 6 + 40 \cdot 9 = \$1026$. Total revenue for the second combination is $120 \cdot 6 + 34 \cdot 9 = \$1026$.

Both combinations yield the same total revenue, but combinations on either side of these two combinations yield less total revenue. The exact point where revenue would be maximum lies between the two combinations yielding the same revenue. Tabular data can at best provide only an approximation of the true point where the rate of product transformation equals the inverse price ratio, as was the case here.

Not surprisingly, an increase in the price of one of the two outputs will tend to shift production toward the commodity that experienced the price

16.4 Constrained Revenue Maximization

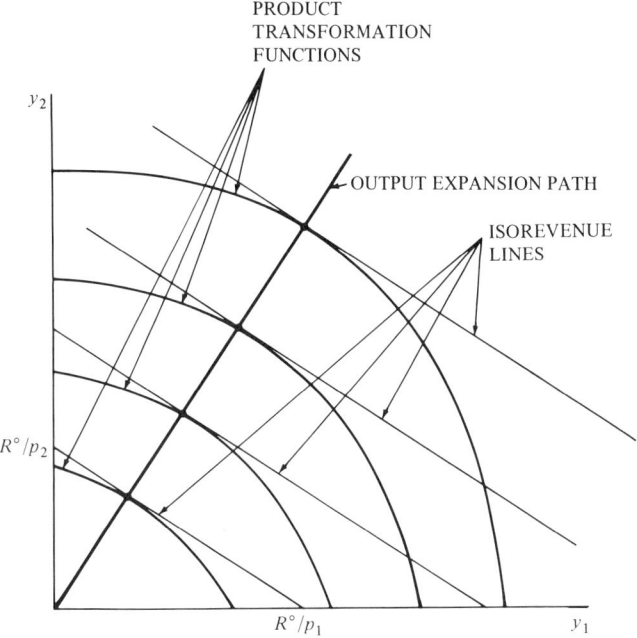

Figure 16.2 Product Transformation Functions, Isorevenue Lines, and the Output Expansion Path

increase and away from the other commodity. For example, if the price of corn remains unchanged, an increase in the price of soybeans will move the point of tangency between the product transformation function toward soybean production and away from corn production.

By observing what happens to the output of two products as the relative prices change, it is sometimes possible to discern the shape of the underlying product transformation function and the elasticity of product substitution. Suppose that the price of corn increased relative to soybeans. The expected result

Table 16.2 Rate of Product Transformation of Corn for Soybeans from a Variable Input Bundle x

Units of x Applied to Corn	Yield per Acre (bushels)	MPP of x in Corn Production	Units of x Applied to Soybeans	Yield per Acre (bushels)	MPP of x in Bean Production	RPT of Corn for Soybeans
0	0		10	55		
1	45	45	9	54	1	1/45 = 0.022
2	62	17	8	52	2	2/17 = 0.118
3	87	15	7	49	3	3/15 = 0.200
4	100	13	6	45	4	4/13 = 0.308
5	111	11	5	40	5	5/11 = 0.455
6	120	9	4	34	6	6/9 = 0.667
7	127	7	3	27	7	7/7 = 1.00
8	132	5	2	19	8	8/5 = 1.60
9	135	3	1	10	9	9/3 = 3.00
10	136	1	0	0	10	10/1 = 10.0

would be a significant but not total shift by farmers away from the production of soybeans and into the production of corn. The resources or inputs used in the production of soybeans can be used to produce corn, although inputs are not perfectly substitutable.

Now suppose that the two products are beef and hides. An increase in the price of hides would not cause the production of hides to increase relative to the production of beef at all. The technical relationship that requires each beef animal to have one and only one hide governs the shape of the product transformation function. No matter how high the price of hides, the farmer can still produce only one per animal. The elasticity of product substitution is as near zero as can be found in the real world anywhere.

Now assume that the two products are wool and lamb meat and that the price of wool relative to the price of lamb decreases. In a single production season, farmers with their existing flocks could increase lamb meat production relative to wool very little. They may be able to do so slightly by feeding out the lambs to larger weights. This suggests a single season elasticity of product substitution very near but not exactly zero.

However, if these price relationships persisted over time, farmers would sell the sheep capable of high wool production relative to lamb, and buy sheep capable of high lamb meat production relative to wool. The elasticity of product substitution is probably greater over several seasons than over a single production season.

Consider a situation where a farmer is producing two products y_1 and y_2. The $RPTy_1y_2$ is constant and the product transformation functions have a constant negative slope. Hence the elasticity of product substitution is infinite. If the absolute value of p_1/p_2 is greater than the absolute value of the $RPTy_1y_2$, the farmer will produce all y_1 and no y_2. If the absolute value of p_1/p_2 is less than the absolute value of $RPTy_1y_2$, the farmer will produce all y_2 and no y_1. If the absolute value of p_1/p_2 is the same as the absolute value of $RPTy_1y_2$, output of each product will be indeterminant. If the farmer is initially producing all y_2 and no y_1, an increase in the price of (p_1) relative to the price of y_2 (p_2) may not at first cause production to shift totally to y_1. As p_1 continues to increase, such that the price ratio p_1/p_2 exceeds the absolute value of $RPTy_1y_2$, production will suddenly shift entirely out of y_2 and into y_1.

16.5 Simple Mathematics of Constrained Revenue Maximization

The problem of maximizing revenue subject to a resource or input constraint illustrated in Figure 16.2 can be cast as a constrained revenue maximization problem and be solved mathematically via Lagrange's method.

The objective function is

$$\text{Maximize } p_1y_1 + p_2y_2 \qquad (16.10)$$

The constraint is the availability of the input bundle x, which is the equation for the product transformation function:

16.5 Simple Mathematics of Constrained Revenue Maximization

$$x^\circ = g(y_1, y_2) \qquad (16.11)$$

where x° is a fixed available amount of the input bundle x.

The Lagrangian is

$$L - p_1 y_1 + p_2 y_2 + \theta[x^\circ - g(y_1, y_2)] \qquad (16.12)$$

The corresponding first-order or necessary conditions are

$$\partial L/\partial y_1 = p_1 - \theta \partial g/\partial y_1 = 0 \qquad (16.13)$$

$$\partial L/\partial y_2 = p_2 - \theta \partial g/\partial y_2 = 0 \qquad (16.14)$$

$$\partial L/\partial \theta = x^\circ - g(y_1, y_2) = 0 \qquad (16.15)$$

By dividing equation (16.13) by equation (16.14), the result is

$$p_1/p_2 = (\partial g/\partial y_1)/(\partial g/\partial y_2) \qquad (16.16)$$

Since g is x,

$$p_1/p_2 = (1/MPPx_{y1})/(1/MPPx_{y2}) \qquad (16.17)$$

$$-MPPx_{y2}/MPPx_{y1} = -p_1/p_2 \qquad (16.18)$$

$$RPTy_1 y_2 = p_1/p_2 \qquad (16.19)$$

Equation (16.19) represents the same conclusion reached in Section 16.4. First-order conditions find the point where the slope of the isorevenue line is the same as the slope of the product transformation function. Both the isorevenue line and the product transformation function will be downward sloping.

Equations (16.13) and (16.14) may be rearranged in other ways. Some possibilities are

$$p_1/(\partial g/\partial y_1) = \theta \qquad (16.20)$$

$$p_2/(\partial g/\partial y_2) = \theta \qquad (16.21)$$

$$p_1/(\partial g/\partial y_1) = p_2/(\partial g/\partial y_2) = \theta \qquad (16.22)$$

$$p_1 MPPx_{y1} = p_2 MPPx_{y2} = \theta \qquad (16.23)$$

$$VMPx_{y1} = VMPx_{y2} = \theta \qquad (16.24)$$

Equation (16.24) represents the equimarginal return principle from the output side. The farmer should use the input bundle such that the last physical unit of the bundle returns the same *VMP* for both enterprises. The analysis assumes that the resource or input bundle is already owned by the farmer, and therefore the decision to produce will cost no more than the decision not to produce.

Maximization in a Two-Output Setting

The assumption that the input bundle is free or worth nothing if sold by the farmer seems unrealistic. More likely, the input bundle has a price. Assume that the price for a unit of the bundle is v. The constrained revenue-maximization problem then becomes one of maximizing revenue from the sale of the two products subject to the constraint imposed by the availability of dollars for the purchase of the input bundle.

The restriction in the availability of funds might be in the form of both owned dollars as well as the credit availability from the local bank, Production Credit Association, or other lending agency. Any interest charges for borrowed funds might be subtracted from C° before the problem is set up, so that C° represents funds actually available for the purchase of the physical input bundle. This cost constraint can be written as

$$C^\circ = vx \tag{16.25}$$

The Lagrangian is reformulated with the same objective function:

$$\text{maximize } p_1 y_1 + p_2 y_2 \tag{16.26}$$

The constraint is the availability dollars for the purchase of the input bundle x. Equation (16.27) is the product transformation function multiplied by the price of the input bundle v:

$$C^\circ = vx^\circ = vg(y_1, y_2) \tag{16.27}$$

The Lagrangian is

$$L - p_1 y_1 + p_2 y_2 + \phi[C^\circ - vg(y_1, y_2)] \tag{16.28}$$

The corresponding first-order (necessary) conditions are

$$\partial L/\partial y_1 = p_1 - \phi v \partial g/\partial y_1 = 0 \tag{16.29}$$

$$\partial L/\partial y_2 = p_2 - \phi v \partial g/\partial y_2 = 0 \tag{16.30}$$

$$\partial L/\partial \phi = C^\circ - vg(y_1, y_2) = 0 \tag{16.31}$$

By dividing equation (16.29) by equation (16.30), the result is

$$p_1/p_2 = (\partial g/\partial y_1)/(\partial g/\partial y_2) \tag{16.32}$$

$$RPT y_1 y_2 = p_1/p_2 \tag{16.33}$$

Equation (16.33) is the same conclusion reached in equation (16.19). First-order conditions find the point where the slope of the isorevenue line is the same as the slope of the product transformation function. The price of the input bundle does not affect the point of tangency between the product transformation function and the isorevenue line.

16.5 Simple Mathematics of Constrained Revenue Maximization

Equations (16.29) and (16.30) may also be rearranged in other ways. One possibility is

$$p_1/v(\partial g/\partial y_1) = \phi \qquad (16.34)$$

$$p_2/v(\partial g/\partial y_2) = \phi \qquad (16.35)$$

$$p_1/v(\partial g/\partial y_1) = p_2/v(\partial g/\partial y_2) = \phi \qquad (16.36)$$

$$VMPx_{y1}/v = VMPx_{y2}/v = \phi \qquad (16.37)$$

Equation (16.37) is the first order condition for revenue maximization subject to a cost constraint, assuming that the input bundle x has a price v. Equation (16.37) is the equimarginal return relationship that holds if the input bundle has a cost to the farmer. Equation (16.37) differs from equation (16.24) in that both sides of equation (16.37) has been divided by the price of the input bundle v.

Since the price of the input bundle is the same in the production of both outputs, these conditions suggest no change in the allocation of the input bundle between the production of y_1 and y_2 relative to the conclusions derived in the last example. Equation (16.37) states that the farmer should allocate the input bundle in such a way that the last dollar spent on the input bundle yields the same ratio of VMP to the cost of the bundle for both outputs.

This derivation does have an important advantage over the example in equation (16.24). The values for the Lagrangian multiplier (ϕ) that would result in maximum net revenue to the farmer now become apparent. The farmer would not spend an extra dollar on the input bundle x if it did not return the extra dollar. Profit maximization on the output side thus occurs when

$$VMPx_{y1}/v = VMPx_{y2}/v = 1 \qquad (16.38)$$

Equation (16.38) is the global point of profit maximization on the output side and can occur only when ϕ equals 1. A value for ϕ of greater than 1 suggests that the farmer has insufficient dollars for the purchase of enough x to globally maximize profits. Any point where the equality holds is a point on the output expansion path. The point of global profit maximization also lies on the output expansion path, and here the Lagrangian multiplier assumes a value of 1. Notice also that ϕ equals θ/v.

A pseudo scale line for each output can also be defined. An output pseudo scale line for y_1 would be a line on the map of product transformation curves connecting points where profits are maximum for y_1, but not necessarily for y_2. In other words, $VMPx_{y1}/v$ equals 1, but $VMPx_{y2}/v$ may not necessarily be 1.

Each pseudo scale line is derived from the profit-maximization point on a member of the family of the production functions transforming x into y_1, assuming that a portion of the input bundle x has been already allocated to the production of y_2. A similar derivation could be done to generate an output pseudo scale line for y_2. These output pseudo scale lines intersect at the global point of profit maximization, where

$$VMPx_{y1}/v_1 = VMPx_{y2}/v_2 = 1 \qquad (16.39)$$

16.6 Second-Order Conditions

In the product-product model, the point where the manager would prefer to be found is a point of tangency between the product transformation function and the isorevenue line. In factor-factor or input space, the point where the manager would prefer to be found is a point of tangency between the isocost line and the isoquant.

The point of tangency between the isorevenue line and the product transformation function does not look the same as the point of tangency between the isocost line and an isoquant. Isoquants are normally bowed inward or convex to the origin of the graph. Product transformation functions are normally bowed outward or concave to the origin of the graph.

The first-order conditions for revenue maximization subject to an input constraint are repeated here

$$L - p_1 y_1 + p_2 y_2 + \theta[x^\circ - g(y_1, y_2)] \tag{16.40}$$

$$\partial L/\partial y_1 = p_1 - \theta \partial g/\partial y_1 = 0 \tag{16.41}$$

$$\partial L/\partial y_2 = p_2 - \theta \partial g/\partial y_2 = 0 \tag{16.42}$$

$$\partial L/\partial \theta = x^\circ - g(y_1, y_2) = 0 \tag{16.43}$$

Equations (16.41), (16.42), and (16.43) are each differentiated with respect to y_1, y_2 and θ:

$$\partial(16.41)/\partial y_1 = -\theta \partial^2 g/\partial y_1^2 = -\theta g_{11}$$
$$\partial(16.41)/\partial y_2 = -\theta \partial^2 g/\partial y_1 \partial y_2 = -\theta g_{12}$$
$$\partial(16.41)/\partial \theta = -\partial g/\partial y_1 = -g_1$$

$$\partial(16.42)/\partial y_1 = -\theta \partial^2 g/\partial y_2 \partial y_1 = -\theta g_{21} = -\theta g_{12} \text{ (by Young's theorem)}$$
$$\partial(16.42)/\partial y_2 = -\theta \partial^2 g/\partial y_2^2 = -\theta g_{22}$$
$$\partial(16.42)/\partial \theta = -\partial g/\partial y_2 = -g_2$$

$$\partial(16.43)/\partial y_1 = -\partial g/\partial y_1 = -g_1$$
$$\partial(16.43)/\partial y_2 = -\partial g/\partial y_2 = -g_2$$
$$\partial(16.43)/\partial \theta = 0$$

The partial derivatives g_1 and g_2 are the marginal costs for the production of an additional unit of y_1 and y_2, respectively, expressed in physical rather than dollar terms. Had these second derivatives been found for the revenue-maximization problem constrained by dollars available for the purchase of x rather than physical units of x, then g_1 and g_2 would have been multiplied by the price of the input v. The term vg_1 is the marginal cost of an additional unit of y_1. The term vg_2 is the marginal cost of an additional unit of y_2.

Marginal cost is negative in stage III, since *MPP* is negative in stage III but is never negative in stages I and II. In stages I and II, an incremental unit of output can never be produced without any additional cost in terms of the input

16.6 Second-Order Conditions

bundle. Lagrange's method would not find a solution in stage III where the Lagrangian multiplier is negative.

The partial derivative g_{11} can be interpreted as the slope of the marginal cost function for y_1. The derivative g_{22} has the same interpretation for y_2. Marginal cost is again expressed in terms of physical input requirements rather than in dollar terms. The slope of marginal cost can be converted to dollars by multiplying by the input bundle price v, which would occur if the constraint were expressed in dollar and not in physical terms. Marginal cost is normally rising, except in stage III and perhaps in the early stages of stage I, for the input bundle x. This means that additional units of either y_1 or y_2 cannot be produced without incurring more and more additional cost or an increasing marginal cost. The cross partial derivatives ($g_{12} = g_{21}$) are needed to rule out production surfaces that appear as saddle points.

The Lagrangian multiplier θ is again interpreted as a shadow price, or imputed value of the input bundle x. The number θ is the increase in revenue associated with an additional unit of the input bundle. When MPP is positive (except for stage III for each input that is beyond the point of maximum output), the Lagrangian multiplier θ will also be positive.

Every component of the second-order conditions for constrained output and revenue maximization has an economic meaning. This economic meaning will lead to conclusions with regard to the probable sign on each component of the second order-conditions.

The second-order conditions for a constrained revenue maximization require that

$$\theta(g_1^2 g_{22} + g_2^2 g_{11} - 2g_{12}g_2 g_1) > 0 \tag{16.44}$$

Equation (16.44) is the determinant of the matrix:

$$\begin{matrix} -\theta g_{11} & -\theta g_{12} & -g_1 \\ -\theta g_{12} & -\theta g_{22} & -g_2 \\ -g_1 & -g_2 & 0 \end{matrix} \tag{16.45}$$

Since a negative value for θ would not be found in the solution, then

$$g_1^2 g_{22} + g_2^2 g_{11} - 2g_{12}g_2 g_1 > 0 \tag{16.46}$$

Equation (16.46) ensures that the product transformation functions are concave or bowed outward from the origin.

The first- and second-order conditions, taken together, are the necessary and sufficient conditions for the maximization of revenue subject to the constraint imposed by the availability of the input bundle x.

The price of the input bundle is positive. If the input prices are constant, the required sign on the second-order condition is not altered if the constraint is constructed based on the availability of funds for the purchase of x rather than the availability of x itself. The required second-order conditions would then be based on the determinant of the matrix

$$\begin{matrix} -\theta v g_{11} & -\theta v g_{12} & -v g_1 \\ -\theta v g_{12} & -\theta v g_{22} & -v g_2 \\ -v g_1 & -v g_2 & 0 \end{matrix} \qquad (16.47)$$

16.7 An Additional Example

Starting with production functions for y_1 and y_2, the product transformation function is constructed. The first-order conditions for revenue maximization subject to the constraint imposed by the availability of x are solved to determine the optimal amounts of y_1 and y_2 to be produced. The manager is then assumed to have the right amount of x needed to globally maximize profits in the production of both y_1 and y_2. The same level is needed irrespective of whether the problem is solved for the output or the input side.

The production functions for y_1 and y_2 are assumed to be

$$y_1 = x_{y1}^{0.33} \qquad (16.48)$$

$$y_2 = x_{y2}^{0.5} \qquad (16.49)$$

where x_{y1} and x_{y2} are assumed to be the quantities of x used in the production of y_1 and y_2, respectively.

The total availability of x is

$$x = x_{y1} + x_{y2} \qquad (16.50)$$

The inverse production functions are

$$x_{y1} = y_1^3 \qquad (16.51)$$

$$x_{y2} = y_2^2 \qquad (16.52)$$

Substituting equations (16.51) and (16.52) into equation (16.50), the equation for the product transformation function is

$$x = y_1^3 + y_2^2 \qquad (16.53)$$

The constraint imposed by the availability of funds for the purchase of x is

$$C^\circ = vx^\circ = v(y_1^3 + y_2^2) \qquad (16.54)$$

The Lagrangian that maximizes revenue subject to the constraint imposed by the availability of dollars for the purchase of x is

$$L = p_1 y_1 + p_2 y_2 + \theta[vx^\circ - v(y_1^3 + y_2^2)] \qquad (16.55)$$

The first-order conditions for the constrained maximization of equation (16.55) are

16.7 An Additional Example

$$p_1 - \theta 3 v y_1^2 = 0 \tag{16.56}$$

$$p_2 - \theta 2 v y_2 = 0 \tag{16.57}$$

$$vx - v(y_1^3 + y_2^2) = 0 \tag{16.58}$$

Now solve equations (16.56) and (16.57) of the first order conditions for y_1 and y_2, respectively:

$$p_1 = \theta 3 v y_1^2 \tag{16.59}$$

$$y_1 = (0.33)^{0.5}(\theta v)^{-0.5} p_1^{0.5} \tag{16.60}$$

$$p_2 = \theta 2 v y_2 \tag{16.61}$$

$$y_2 = (0.5)(\theta v)^{-1} p_2 \tag{16.62}$$

Production of y_1 and y_2 will decrease when the price of the input bundle v increases. Production of y_1 and y_2 will increase when the price of the output increases. The change in both cases will depend on the technical parameters of the underlying single input production functions. The farmer's elasticity of supply with respect to input prices for y_1 is -0.5, and for y_2 is -1. The farmer's elasticity of supply with respect to output prices for y_1 is 0.5, and for y_2 is 1.

Second-order conditions for constrained revenue maximization will be met if the underlying production functions for y_1 and y_2 are homogeneous of a degree less than 1.

Now substitute for y_1 and y_2 the corresponding values for x_{y1} and x_{y2}, and assume that the manager has enough x available so that profits with respect to the production of both y_1 and y_2 are maximum. This implies that the Lagrangian multiplier θ will be 1. Therefore,

$$y_1 = x_{y1}^{0.33} = (0.33)^{0.5} v^{-0.5} p_1^{0.5} \tag{16.63}$$

$$y_2 = x_{y2}^{0.5} = 0.5 v^{-1} p_2 \tag{16.64}$$

$$x_{y1} = 0.33^{1.5} v^{-1.5} p_1^{1.5} \tag{16.65}$$

$$x_{y2} = 0.5^2 v^{-2} p_2^2 \tag{16.66}$$

Insertion of prices for the input bundle v and the two output prices p_1 and p_2 into equations (16.65) and (16.66) yields the amount of x to be applied to y_1 and y_2 in order to globally maximize profits.

The own-price elasticity of demand by the farmer for the input bundle x in the production of y_1 is -1.5 and in the production of y_2 is -2. These are $1/(1 - e_p)$, where e_p is the production elasticity associated with the input bundle x in the production of each output.

The product-price elasticity of demand by the farmer for the input bundle x in the production of y_1 is 1.5 and in the production of y_2 is 2. These are obtained from the formula $-1/(1 - e_p)$. Each of these elasticities can be interpreted as the percentage increase in the demand for the input bundle x that accompanies a 1 percent increase in the output prices for y_1 or y_2. For both production functions, the input bundle own-price elasticity is the negative of the input bundle output-price elasticity.

The quantity of x to be used in the production of y_1 and y_2 could be obtained from a pair of input-side profit-maximization equations as well, and the same results with respect to how x should be allocated would be found.

Let

$$y_1 = x_{y1}^{0.33} \tag{16.67}$$

$$y_2 = x_{y2}^{0.5} \tag{16.68}$$

$$\Pi_{y1} = p_1 y_1 - v x_{y1} \tag{16.69}$$

$$\Pi_{y1} = p_1 x_{y1}^{0.33} - v x_{y1} \tag{16.70}$$

$$\Pi_{y2} = p_2 y_2 - v x_{y2} \tag{16.71}$$

$$\Pi_{y2} = p_2 x_{y2}^{0.5} - v x_{y2} \tag{16.72}$$

To find first-order conditions for maximum profits, set the first derivatives of both profit equations with respect to x_{y1} or x_{y2} equal to zero

$$\partial \Pi / \partial x_{y1} = 0.33 p_1 x_{y1}^{-0.67} - v = 0 \tag{16.73}$$

$$\partial \Pi / \partial x_{y2} = 0.5 p_2 x_{y2}^{-0.5} - v = 0 \tag{16.74}$$

Solving equations (16.73) and (16.74) for x_{y1} and x_{y2}, we obtain

$$x_{y1} = 0.33^{1.5} v^{-1.5} p_1^{1.5} \tag{16.75}$$

$$x_{y2} = 0.5^2 v^{-2} p_2^2 \tag{16.76}$$

which is the same result as obtained as from equations (16.65) and (16.66) for the derived demand elasticities with respect to input and product prices. The result again provides the quantity of x_1 and x_2 needed to maximize profits at the point where the Lagrangian multiplier equals 1.

16.8 Minimization of Input Use Subject to a Revenue Constraint

Any constrained maximization problem has a corresponding dual or constrained minimization problem. This dual problem can also be solved via Lagrange's method. The objective function in this case requires that input use be minimized for a specific amount of total revenue R

16.8 Minimization of Input Use Subject to a Revenue Constraint

$$\text{minimize } g(y_1, y_2) \text{ or } x \tag{16.77}$$

subject to the constraint that

$$R^\circ = p_1 y_1 + p_2 y_2 \tag{16.78}$$

The Lagrangian is

$$L = g(y_1, y_2) + \psi(R^\circ - p_1 y_1 - p_2 y_2) \tag{16.79}$$

The corresponding first-order conditions are

$$g_1 - \psi p_1 = 0 \tag{16.80}$$

$$g_2 - \psi p_2 = 0 \tag{16.81}$$

$$R^\circ - p_1 y_1 - p_2 y_2 = 0 \tag{16.82}$$

By rearranging and dividing equation (16.80) by equation (16.81), the familiar point of tangency is found where

$$RPTy_1 y_2 = dy_2/dy_1 = p_1/p_2 \tag{16.83}$$

Solving equations (16.80) and (16.81) from the first-order conditions for ψ yields

$$g_1/p_1 = \psi \tag{16.84}$$

$$g_2/p_2 = \psi \tag{16.85}$$

$$g_1/p_1 = g_2/p_2 = \psi \tag{16.86}$$

or

$$1/VMPx_{y1} = 1/VMPx_{y2} = \psi \tag{16.87}$$

Compared with the conclusions derived in equation (16.24), equation (16.87) appears upside down. In fact, the Lagrangian multiplier ψ is $1/\theta$ found in equation (16.24). If the problem is set up to maximize revenue subject to the availability of the input bundle x, the Lagrangian multiplier (θ) is interpreted as the increase in revenue associated with one additional unit of the input bundle. (Or the Lagrangian multiplier could be expressed as the decrease in revenue associated with a 1-unit decrease in the size of the input bundle.)

If the problem is set up to minimize input use subject to a revenue constraint, the Lagrangian multiplier ψ is the increase in input use needed to produce $1 of additional revenue. (Or the Lagrangian multiplier could also be expressed as the decrease in the use of the input bundle associated with $1 less revenue.)

Maximization in a Two-Output Setting

The second-order conditions for input bundle minimization subject to a revenue constraint require that

$$2p_1p_2g_{12} - g_{22}p_1^2 - g_{11}p_2^2 < 0 \tag{16.88}$$

Equation (16.88) is the determinant of the matrix formed by again differentiating each equation in the first-order conditions with respect to y_1, y_2 and the Lagrangian multiplier ψ

$$\begin{matrix} g_{11} & g_{12} & -p_1 \\ g_{21} & g_{22} & -p_2 \\ -p_1 & -p_2 & 0 \end{matrix} \tag{16.89}$$

Remembering Young's theorem, and multiplying both sides of the determinant by -1, we have

$$g_{22}p_1^2 + g_{11}p_2^2 - 2p_1p_2g_{12} > 0 \tag{16.90}$$

Now from the first-order conditions (16.80) and (16.81), substitute

$$p_1 = g_1/\psi \tag{16.91}$$

$$p_2 = g_2/\psi \tag{16.92}$$

$$(1/\psi^2)(g_1^2 g_{22} + g_2^2 g_{11} - 2g_1 g_2 g_{12}) > 0 \tag{16.93}$$

Since ψ is normally positive, these second-order conditions impose the same requirements on g_1, g_2, g_{12}, g_{22}, and g_{11} as before.

16.9 An Output Restriction Application

The example presented here illustrates the application of the product-product model to a problem in which the government restricts the quantity of a product that can be produced and marketed by the farmer. The federal government might attempt to establish a policy to support the price of certain crops by limiting the amount of output produced by the farmer. An output restriction is quite different from an acreage allotment. An acreage allotment restricts the amount of the input land to be used in the production of a commodity. An output restriction limits the quantity of the commodity that can be placed on the market.

The analysis presented here is an application similar to the acreage allotment application presented in Chapter 8. Output restrictions have been used less often than acreage restrictions by the government to control the production of commodities. The federal tobacco program provides a unique example. The government previously controlled the production of tobacco simply by limiting the acreage of tobacco that could be planted. Tobacco was treated by the government just like wheat. Farmers readily adapted to the acreage restriction as

16.9 An Output Restriction Application

the earlier model would predict. Only the very best land was used for tobacco production. Farmers made intensive use of chemical fertilizers and pesticides, and production per acre soared. However, the tobacco program was changed, and in recent years, farmers were allowed to only place a certain quantity of tobacco on the market. As of 1985, each farm now had a tobacco poundage rather than acreage allotment.

The impacts of a tobacco poundage allotment can be illustrated by using a model in product-product space. Let Y represent the commodity or commodities other than tobacco that a farmer might grow, and T represent tobacco. A series of product transformation curves between tobacco and other commodities are illustrated in Figure 16.3. In the absence of any restrictions on output of tobacco, the farmer is operating on the output expansion path where

$$VMP_{XT}/V_X = VMP_{XY}/V_X = \psi \qquad (16.94)$$

where VMP_{XT} and VMP_{XY} are the respective VMP's of the input bundle X in the production of tobacco and other commodities respectively. Let this point be represented by A in Figure 16.3.

Now suppose that the government imposes a poundage restriction. Let the poundage restriction be represented by the horizontal line labeled T^*. To comply with the restriction, the farmer must move back along the output expansion path to point B, which lies at the intersection of the output expansion path and the poundage constraint. Point B is represented by a point where

$$VMP_{XT}/V_X = VMP_{XY}/V_X = \eta \qquad (16.95)$$

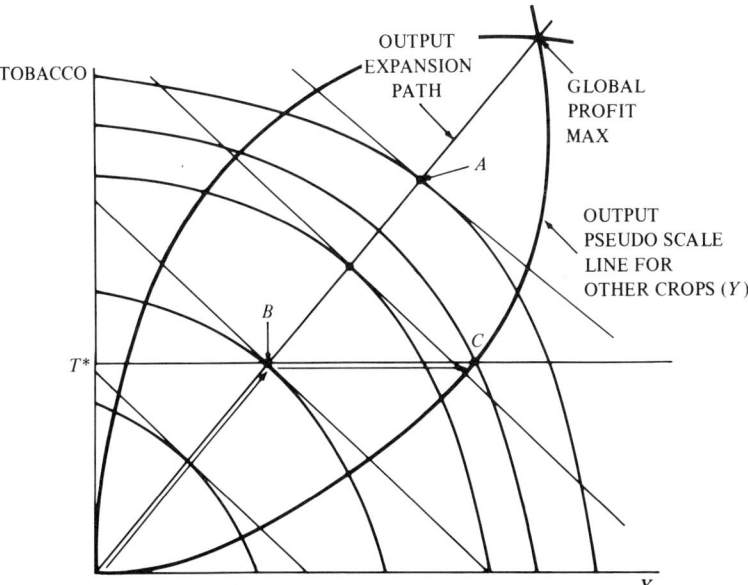

Figure 16.3 Output Quota

Both ψ and η are probably greater than 1, but η is larger than ψ. With the poundage restriction, the farmer has additional dollars available for the purchase of the input bundle X, but these dollars can only be used to produce commodities other than tobacco. The farmer will again move to the right along the constraint T^*. The farmer will probably not move to the point where the last product transformation function intersects the constraint T^*. If sufficient revenue for the purchase of the input bundle is available, the farmer will move to the product transformation function where

$$VMP_{XY}/V_X = 1 \qquad (16.96)$$

This point is not on the output expansion path, but is the point of global profit maximization for the input bundle X used in the production of other commodities Y. Tobacco production will remain constant at T^*. This point is C and represents a point on the output pseudo scale line for the production of the commodities represented by Y.

When the tobacco program was changed from an acreage allotment to a poundage allotment, tobacco production per acre declined, as would have been predicted by the earlier model. It is more difficult to determine if the production of other crops increased as a direct result of the tobacco poundage allotment, since tobacco has not in the recent past been grown in the absence of a government program.

The expected impact of the tobacco poundage program based on this model should be to increase the output of those crops requiring a similar bundle of inputs to tobacco but not affected by the quantity restrictions. The tobacco-producing areas of Kentucky have recently seen an increase in the production of labor intensive horticultural crops planted on small acreages in much the same manner as tobacco and requiring very similar inputs. This is the expected impact of an output restriction based on the product-product model.

Tobacco farmers have also used the tobacco poundage allotment system as a method of dealing with output uncertainty. Overproduction in good years can be stored and used to meet the output quota in years when nature is uncooperative and production is low.

16.10 Concluding Comments

Farmers respond to changes in relative prices for commodities by adjusting production levels toward the commodity that is experiencing the relative price increase and away from the commodity for which the price is decreasing in relative terms. If there is but a single input, or an input bundle already owned by the farmer, the optimal conditions for constrained revenue maximization require that the farmer equate the respective VMP's for each output.

The shape of the product transformation function determines the extent to which a farmer will adjust the output mix in the face of changing relative prices. If the elasticity of product substitution is near zero, the product transformation function is nearly a right angle, and the farmer will not adjust the mix of outputs in response to changing relative prices. However, to the extent that the elasticity of product substitution is positive, the farmer will respond to changing relative prices by adjusting the output mix.

The constrained maximization conditions on the product side look very similar to those on the input side. In both instances, the equimarginal return principle still applies. Farmers should allocate dollars in such a way that the last dollar used in the production of each product produces the same return. The product-product model can be applied to problems when the government implements policy to support prices by restricting the output of a particular commodity.

Problems and Exercises

1. Suppose that y_1 and y_2 sold for the same price. Using the data contained in Problem 1, Chapter 15, how much x would be applied to y_1 and y_2?

2. What would happen to your results in Problem 1 if y_1 were three times as expensive as y_2?

3. Show 10 possible combinations of output that could produce $1000 of revenue in y_1 sold for $5 and y_2 sold for $10. On the basis of these data alone, should the production of y_2 be favored over the production of y_1? Explain.

4. Suppose that the product transformation function is given by

$$x = 2y_1^2 + 3y_2^3$$

The price of y_1 is $5 and the price of y_2 is $4. Ten units of x are available. How much should be applied to y_1 and y_2?

5. Compare the interpretations of the Lagrangian multipliers for the following problems in a multiple-product setting.

   a. Output maximization subject to an input availability constraint.
   b. Revenue maximization subject to an input availability constraint.
   c. Global profit maximization on the output side in product space.
   d. Resource or input use minimization subject to a revenue constraint.

6. Suppose the government restricts the amount of a product that a farmer might sell. Will the farmer always continue to produce at a point where $RPTy_1y_2 = p_1/p_2$? Explain.

7. Will the output of other commodities always increase if the government restricts the amount of a particular commodity that might be sold by the farmer? Explain.

17
Two Outputs and Two Inputs

This chapter illustrates how the factor-factor model and the product-product model can be combined into a single model encompassing both the factor space and product space. First-order conditions for global profit maximization and for revenue maximization subject to the constraint imposed by the availability of dollars for the purchase of inputs are derived. An example of an intermediate product model is used to illustrate a possible application within agriculture.

Key Terms and Definitions:

Multiple-Input Multiple-Product Model
Equal Marginal Returns
Imputed Value
Intermediate Product Model
Quasi-general Equilibrium
Rate of Product Transformation Equals Marginal Rate of Substitution
Shutdown Condition

17.1 Introduction

Until now, production has been presented with models in which one or two inputs were used to produce a single output, or a single-input bundle was used to produce two outputs. These models could easily be illustrated using graphics, because no more than three axes were required (x_1, x_2 and y or y_1, y_2, and x), and the resultant graph contained no more than three dimensions. However, most farmers use many different inputs to produce many different outputs. Despite the fact that these models often cannot be illustrated using graphics, the same rules for maximization and minimization found to exist in factor-product, factor-factor, and product-product models still apply. It is now appro-

17.2 Two Inputs and Two Outputs: A Basic Presentation

Assume that the farmer uses two inputs, phosphate fertilizer (x_1) and potash fertilizer (x_2), in the production of two outputs, corn (y_1) and soybeans (y_2). Corn sells for $4.00 per bushel and soybeans sell for $8.00 per bushel. Units of phosphate fertilizer and potash fertilizer each cost $10.00. Data contained in Table 17.1 describe the yields and *VMP* values for each input in the production of each output.

The data presented in Table 17.1, although useful in illustrating the basic logic behind the equimarginal return principle, oversimplify the problem. The marginal product of each unit of 1 type of fertilizer is assumed to be independent of the availability of the other type of fertilizer. Thus the underlying production function for each output exhibits no interaction between the two inputs and therefore is additive rather than multiplicative.

Suppose that the farmer has available only $100, or enough to purchase a total of 10 units of fertilizer. Table 17.2 describes how each unit will be allocated. Units 1 and 2 produce the same *VMP* as do units 3, 4, and 5, and units 8, 9, and 10. So it does not matter which allocation is done first within these groups.

The general equimarginal return rule requires that

$$p_1 MPP x_1 y_1 / v_1 = p_2 MPP x_1 y_2 / v_1 = p_1 MPP x_2 y_1 / v_2$$
$$= p_2 MPP x_2 y_2 / v_2 = K \quad (17.1)$$

The *VMP* of each input in the production of each output will be the same and equal to some number K. The number K is actually a Lagrangian multiplier or an imputed value of an additional dollar available in the case for the purchase of fertilizer to be used in corn or soybean production.

Table 17.1 Two Inputs in the Production of Two Outputs[a]

Units of Fertilizer	Phosphate on Corn	$VMPx_1y_1$	Phosphate on Soybeans	$VMPx_1y_2$	Potash on Corn	$VMPx_2y_1$	Potash on Soybeans	$VMPx_2y_2$
0	70		30		80		20	
		80		40		60		80
1	90		35		95		30	
		60		40		60		64
2	105		40		110		38	
		40		24		40		48
3	115		43		120		44	
		20		16		20		24
4	120		45		125		47	
		8		16		12		8
5	122		47		128		48	
		0		16		8		0
6	122		49		130		48	
		−8		8		4		−8
7	120		50		131		47	
		−8		−8		0		−16
8	118		49		131		45	
		−16		−16		−4		−24
9	114		47		130		42	
		−20		−24		−8		−32
10	109		44		128		38	

[a] The price of corn is $4.00, the price of soybeans is $8.00. Units of either phosphate or potash cost $10.00.

Table 17.2 Allocation of Two Fertilizers to Two Crops

Unit	Fertilizer	Crop
1	Phosphate	Corn
2	Potash	Soybeans
3	Potash	Soybeans
4	Phosphate	Corn
5	Potash	Corn
6	Potash	Corn
7	Potash	Soybeans
8	Phosphate	Corn
9	Phosphate	Soybeans
10	Phosphate	Soybeans

In this example, the price of both inputs, v_1 and v_2, were the same at $10.00 per unit. The last unit of fertilizer applied in this example produced $40.00, except for the last unit of potash on soybeans, which produced $48.00. The correct allocation would have resulted in the same ratio of *VMP* to the price of the input in the production of each output. However, this is often not possible from a tabular data presentation. With this exception, K in our example was $4.00. The last dollar spent on each input gave back $4.00 in the production of each output.

The general profit-maximization relationship requires that

$$p_1 MPPx_1 y_1 / v_1 = p_2 MPPx_1 y_2 / v_1 = p_1 MPPx_2 y_1 / v_2$$
$$= p_2 MPPx_2 y_2 / v_2 = 1 \quad (17.2)$$

On the input side

$$MRSx_1 x_2 = v_1 / v_2 \quad (17.3)$$

in the production of each output. On the output side,

$$RPTy_1 / y_2 = p_1 / p_2 \quad (17.4)$$

for each input.

17.3 Some General Principles

Suppose that the production of two outputs is governed by two production functions, each with two inputs. Let the production functions for y_1 and y_2 be

$$y_1 = h(x_{11}, x_{21}) \quad (17.5)$$

$$y_2 = j(x_{12}, x_{22}) \quad (17.6)$$

where y_1 and y_2 denote outputs and h and j are production functions for y_1 and y_2, respectively. The first subscript on each x denotes the input, and the second

17.3 Some General Principles

subscript denotes the product to which it is applied. For example, x_{21} is input x_2 that is applied to y_1.

The total amount of x_1 and x_2 are used in the production of y_1 and y_2 are

$$x_1 = x_{11} + x_{12} \tag{17.7}$$

$$x_2 = x_{21} + x_{22} \tag{17.8}$$

Total revenue from the sale of y_1 and y_2 is

$$R = p_1 y_1 + p_2 y_2 \tag{17.9}$$

$$= p_1 h(x_{11}, x_{21}) + p_2 j(x_{12}, x_{22}) \tag{17.10}$$

where p_1 and p_2 are prices of y_1 and y_2, respectively. The total cost is the sum of the quantities of x_1 and x_2 multiplied by their respective prices

$$C = v_1 x_1 + v_2 x_2 \tag{17.11}$$

$$= v_1(x_{11} + x_{12}) + v_2(x_{21} + x_{22}) \tag{17.12}$$

Profit (Π) is revenue minus cost:

$$\begin{aligned} \Pi &= R - C \\ &= p_1 y_1 + p_2 y_2 - v_1 x_1 - v_2 x_2 \\ &= p_1 h(x_{11}, x_{21}) + p_2 j(x_{12}, x_{22}) - v_1(x_{11} + x_{12}) + v_2(x_{21} + x_{22}) \end{aligned} \tag{17.13}$$

Now let

$$h_1 = \partial h / \partial x_{11} \tag{17.14}$$

$$h_2 = \partial h / \partial x_{21} \tag{17.15}$$

$$j_1 = \partial j / \partial x_{12} \tag{17.16}$$

$$j_2 = \partial j / \partial x_{22} \tag{17.17}$$

The first-order conditions for maximum profit entail setting the first derivative of the profit function (17.13) equal to zero with respect to each input used in the production of each output:

$$\partial \Pi / \partial x_{11} = p_1 h_1 - v_1 = 0 \tag{17.18}$$

$$\partial \Pi / \partial x_{21} = p_1 h_2 - v_2 = 0 \tag{17.19}$$

$$\partial \Pi / \partial x_{12} = p_2 j_1 - v_1 = 0 \tag{17.20}$$

$$\partial \Pi / \partial x_{22} = p_2 j_2 - v_2 = 0 \tag{17.21}$$

Equations (17.18) to (17.21) can be rearranged in a number of ways. One way is

$$p_1 b_1/v_1 = p_2 j_1/v_1 = p_1 b_2/v_2 = p_2 j_2/v_2 = 1 \qquad (17.22)$$

The partial derivative b_1 is the marginal product of x_1 in the production of y_1 or $MPPx_1y_1$; j_1 is the marginal product of x_1 in the production of y_2 or $MPPx_1y_2$; b_2 is the marginal product of x_2 in the production of y_1 or $MPPx_2y_1$; j_2 is the marginal product of x_2 in the production of y_2 or $MPPx_2y_2$. So equation (17.22) can be rewritten as

$$p_1 MPPx_1y_1/v_1 = p_2 MPPx_1y_2/v_1 = p_1 MPPx_2y_1/v_2$$
$$= p_2 MPPx_2y_2/v_2 = 1 \qquad (17.23)$$

The farmer should allocate inputs between outputs in such a way that the last dollar invested in each input in the production of each output returns exactly a dollar. The Lagrangian multiplier in the profit maximization example is 1.

Another way of writing equations (17.18) to (17.21) is

$$-b_1/b_2 = dx_2/dx_1 = v_1/v_2 \quad \text{in the production of } y_1 \qquad (17.24)$$

$$-j_1/j_2 = dx_2/dx_1 = v_1/v_2 \quad \text{in the production of } y_2 \qquad (17.25)$$

The marginal rate of substitution of x_1 for x_2 must equal the inverse price ratio in the production of both outputs.

Yet another way of rearranging equations (17.18) to (17.21) is

$$(p_1 b_1/v_1)/(p_2 j_1/v_1) = 1 \qquad (17.26)$$

$$(b_1/j_1)(p_1/p_2) = 1 \qquad (17.27)$$

$$j_1/b_1 = p_1/p_2 \qquad (17.28)$$

$$dy_2/dy_1 = p_1/p_2 \quad \text{for input } x_1 \qquad (17.29)$$

$$RPTy_1y_2 = p_1/p_2 \quad \text{for input } x_1 \qquad (17.30)$$

Similarly,

$$j_2/b_2 = p_1/p_2 \qquad (17.31)$$

$$dy_2/dy_1 = p_1/p_2 \quad \text{for input } x_2 \qquad (17.32)$$

$$RPTy_1y_2 = p_1/p_2 \quad \text{for input } x_2 \qquad (17.33)$$

The rate of product transformation must be the same for both inputs in the production of the two outputs and equal the inverse product-price ratio.

17.4 The Constrained Maximization Problem

Of course,

$$h_1 = MPPx_1y_1 = v_1/p_1 \tag{17.34}$$

$$h_2 = MPPx_2y_1 = v_2/p_1 \tag{17.35}$$

$$j_1 = MPPx_1y_2 = v_1/p_2 \tag{17.36}$$

$$j_2 = MPPx_2y_2 = v_2/p_2 \tag{17.37}$$

In equations (17.34) to (17.37), the marginal product of each input in the production of each output must be equal to the corresponding factor/product-price ratio.

17.4 The Constrained Maximization Problem

The problem might also be set up in a constrained maximization framework. The objective function is the maximization of revenue subject to the constraint imposed by the availability of dollars for the purchase of x_1 and x_2.

Revenue is

$$R = p_1y_1 + p_2y_2 = p_1h(x_{11}, x_{21}) + p_2j(x_{12}, x_{22}) \tag{17.38}$$

Cost is

$$C^\circ = v_1x_{11} + v_1x_{12} + v_2x_{21} + v_2x_{22} \tag{17.39}$$

All notation is the same as in the example in Section 17.3. The Lagrangian is

$$L = p_1h(x_{11}, x_{21}) + p_2j(x_{12}, x_{22}) + \lambda(C^\circ \\ - v_1x_{11} - v_1x_{12} - v_2x_{21} - v_2x_{22}) \tag{17.40}$$

The corresponding first-order conditions for a constrained revenue maximization are

$$\partial L/\partial x_{11} = p_1h_1 - \lambda v_1 = 0 \tag{17.41}$$

$$\partial L/\partial x_{21} = p_1h_2 - \lambda v_2 = 0 \tag{17.42}$$

$$\partial L/\partial x_{12} = p_2j_1 - \lambda v_1 = 0 \tag{17.43}$$

$$\partial L/\partial x_{22} = p_2j_2 - \lambda v_2 = 0 \tag{17.44}$$

Equations (17.41) to (17.44) can also be rearranged in a number of ways. One way is

$$p_1h_1/v_1 = p_2j_1/v_1 = p_1h_2/v_2 = p_2j_2/v_2 = \lambda \tag{17.45}$$

Again, the partial derivative h_1 is the marginal product of x_1 in the production of y_1, or $MPPx_1y_1$; j_1 is the marginal product of x_1 in the production of y_2 or $MPPx_1y_2$; h_2 is the marginal product of x_2 in the production of y_1 or $MPPx_2y_1$; j_2 is the marginal product of x_2 in the production of y_2 or $MPPx_2y_2$. So equation (17.45) can be rewritten as

$$p_1 MPPx_1y_1/v_1 = p_2 MPPx_1y_2/v_1 = p_1 MPPx_2y_1/v_2$$
$$= p_2 MPPx_2y_2/v_2 = \lambda \quad (17.46)$$

The Lagrangian multiplier λ is the imputed value of an extra dollar available for inputs to be used in the production of y_1 and y_2 and allocated in the correct manner. These first-order conditions define a point on both the input and output expansion path.

17.5 An Intermediate Product Model

The intermediate product model is not quite a multiple-input multiple-product model, but it does have the key feature that factor and product space are brought together in a single model. Suppose that a farmer uses available inputs for the production of two products, grain or forage. The grain and the forage are in turn used in the production of beef. Grain and forage can be thought of as two outputs in product space but as two inputs in factor space. A product transformation function can be drawn that represents the farmer's possible combinations of grain and forage that can be produced from the set of inputs or resources available.

Superimposed on this product transformation function are a series of isoquants representing alternative levels of beef production, and each isoquant might represent a steer of a different weight (800, 900, 1000, 1100 pounds; and so on). The simple solution to the problem of maximizing beef production subject to the availability of inputs for the production of grain and forage is to find the point where the isoquant for beef production comes just tangent to the product transformation function. Here the output of beef is maximum, and the marginal rate of substitution of grain for forage in beef production equals the rate of product transformation of grain for forage production (Figure 17.1).

The solution illustrated in Figure 17.1 can be derived using Lagrange's method. Since grain and forage are inputs in one context but outputs in another context, call grain z_1 and forage z_2. The product transformation function for grain and forage is

$$x^° = g(z_1, z_2) \quad (17.47)$$

where $x^°$ is the bundle of inputs available for grain or forage production, g represents the product transformation function, z_1 is grain, and z_2 is forage.

The production function describing the transformation of grain and forage into beef is

$$b = f(z_1, z_2) \quad (17.48)$$

17.5 An Intermediate Product Model

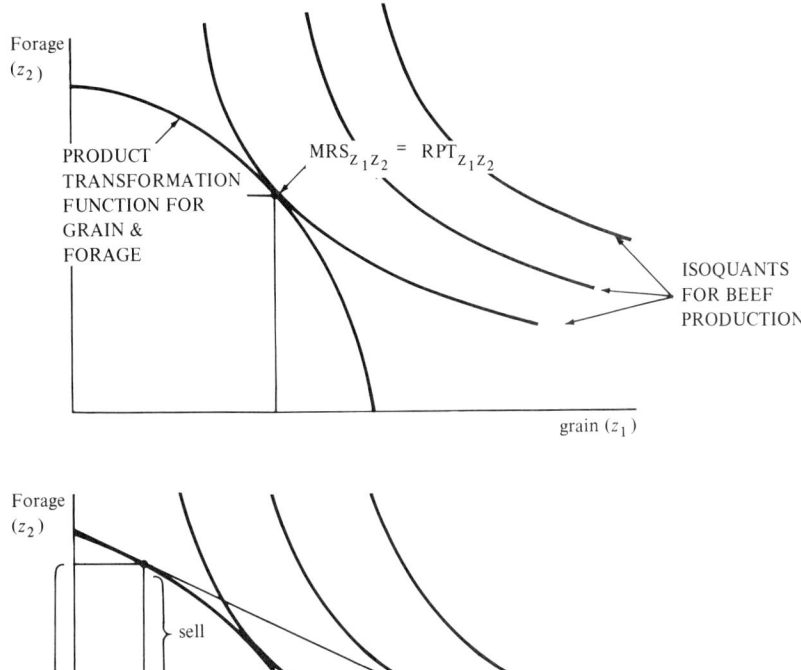

Figure 17.1 Intermediate Product Model

where b is the quantity of beef produced and f is the specific production function that describes the transformation of grain and forage into beef.

The Lagrangian can be set up as a constrained maximization problem. Beef production is maximized subject to the constraint imposed by the availability of the input bundle x used in the production of grain and forage. The Lagrangian is

$$L = f(z_1, z_2) + v[x^\circ - g(z_1, z_2)] \qquad (17.49)$$

Define

$$\begin{aligned} f_i &= \partial f/\partial z_i \\ g_i &= \partial f/\partial z_i \end{aligned} \quad \text{for } i = 1, 2$$

Two Outputs and Two Inputs

Then the corresponding first-order conditions for a maximum are

$$\partial L/\partial z_1 = f_1 - v g_1 = 0 \qquad (17.50)$$

$$\partial L/\partial z_2 = f_2 - v g_2 = 0 \qquad (17.51)$$

$$x - g(z_1, z_2) = 0 \qquad (17.52)$$

The first-order or necessary conditions for the maximization of beef production subject to the constraint imposed by the availability of the input bundle have economic interpretation.

For example, the Lagrangian multiplier (v) is the imputed value of an additional unit of the input bundle x in the production of beef b. The units on the Lagrangian multiplier are in pounds of beef resulting from the incremental or last unit of the input bundle used. The Lagrangian multiplier represents the shadow price or implicit worth of an additional unit of the input bundle x to be used in beef production. The Lagrangian multiplier tells how much additional beef would be produced from an additional unit of the input bundle x.

The partial derivatives f_1 and f_2 are the familiar marginal products of grain and forage to be used as inputs in the production of beef. The negative ratio of f_1/f_2 is also the familiar marginal rate of substitution of grain for forage (dz_2/dz_1).

The partial derivatives g_1 and g_2 are marginal factor costs of grain and forage expressed in terms of physical units of the input or resource bundle x used in their production. The negative ratio of g_1/g_2 is the familiar rate of product transformation of grain for forage (dz_2/dz_1).

The entire problem is solved relying only on physical or technical relationships governing the transformation of the input bundle into grain and forage and grain and forage into beef. Product and factor prices have not yet entered.

The first-order conditions can be rearranged. By dividing the equation (17.50) by equation (17.51), we have

$$-f_1/f_2 = dz_2/dz_1 = MRSz_1z_2 = -g_1/g_2 = dz_2/dz_1 = RPTz_1z_2 \qquad (17.53)$$

Equation (17.53) represents a point of tangency between the isoquant and the product transformation function, as illustrated in Figure 17.1. The marginal rate of substitution of grain for forage in beef production must equal the rate of product transformation of grain for forage.

Another possible statement of the first-order conditions is

$$f_1/g_1 = f_2/g_2 = v \qquad (17.54)$$

The marginal product of grain in the production of beef (f_1) divided by its marginal cost in terms of the input bundle x (g_1) must equal the marginal product of forage in the production of beef (f_2) divided by its marginal cost in terms of the input bundle x (g_2). These ratios should all be equal to the Lagrangian multiplier v.

17.5 An Intermediate Product Model

Suppose that all farmers faced the same product transformation function for grain and forage, the same isoquant map for beef production from grain and forage, and that grain and forage could only be used in the production of beef. Then the relative prices for grain that would prevail would be the prices defined by the ratio p_{z1}/p_{z2}, which would be equal to the marginal rate of substitution of grain for forage in factor space and the rate of product transformation of grain for forage in product space. If the technical parameters governing production by one farmer also apply to all farmers, the firm-level marginal conditions will lead to a market level determination of relative prices for each input or intermediate product.

In such a quasi-general equilibrium setting, all factor prices except one would be determined inside the model. The one price not so determined would become the price to which every other factor price would be compared. The relative prices of grain and forage could thus be determined internal to or endogenous to the model rather than as information coming from the marketplace determined outside the model.

The farmer has options not always recognized by the algebra of the marginal conditions. The market price for beef (p) will be determined not only by the technical parameters governing its production, but by other factors as well. Consumer utility functions for beef relative to other goods must enter. Eventually, consumer utility functions for beef will have an effect on prices in the marketplace, which, in turn, will affect the prices that farmers are able to pay for grain and forage in the production of beef. As a result, grain and forage prices will increase or decrease, since the demand for an input is a function of the product price.

However, in the short run, the price of beef may either exceed or be below its cost of production. Because all farmers may not have the same technical parameters governing grain, forage, and beef production, and because grain and forage can be put into uses other than beef production, there is no particular reason to believe that the market will at any particular point in time have found its long-run equilibrium as defined by the technical parameters governing the production of beef by each farmer, with input prices governed by the prices for beef in the marketplace.

One option the farmer has is to forget about beef production and sell the forage and grain. Total revenue from the sale of beef is

$$TR = pb \tag{17.55}$$

where p is the price of beef and b is the quantity produced. The input bundle required to produce beef (x_b) can be broken into several cost components:

$$TC = vx_b = p_{z1}z_1 + p_{z2}z_2 + \Sigma\, v_j x_j + \Sigma\, v_k x_k \tag{17.56}$$
$$\text{for all } j = 1, \ldots, m$$
$$k = m + 1, \ldots, n$$

where z_1 is grain and z_2 is forage. The subscript j represents each of m variable inputs used in the production of beef excluding the cost of the grain and forage, and k represents each of $n - m - 1$ fixed inputs used in beef production. The first set of inputs represents costs incurred only if beef is produced, while the second set of inputs represents those costs incurred regardless of whether or not beef is produced.

The farmer will produce grain and forage and use that to produce beef in the short run if

$$TR > p_{z1}z_1 + p_{z2}z_2 + \Sigma\, v_j x_j \tag{17.57}$$

where z_1 = grain
z_2 = forage
p_{z1} = price of grain
p_{z2} = price of forage
$\Sigma\, v_j x_j$ = all other variable costs except grain and forage

In other words, the farmer will produce beef in the short run only if variable costs are covered. In the long run, all costs are variable and therefore must be covered if production is to occur.

The farmer also faces a decision with respect to whether to produce grain and forage and sell them as commodities or to shut down entirely. For the farmer to shut down, the total revenue from the sale of beef must be less than the variable costs of production, including the market value of the grain and forage. Production of beef is then ruled out.

Costs incurred in the production of grain and forage can again be categorized as fixed or variable depending on whether each cost item would be incurred regardless of production. The farmer would shut down entirely if the total revenue from the sale of the grain and forage in the marketplace did not exceed the costs for variable inputs used in their production. In the long run, all costs are variable, and all must be covered for production to take place.

The farmer faces another option not recognized by the marginal conditions presented so far. Suppose that in the short run, the product transformation function for an individual farmer favors forage production relative to grain production. Market conditions also result in a higher relative price for forage than for grain. The farmer will be able to produce at the level indicated by the point of tangency between the product transformation function and the isorevenue line. The forage is sold on the market and the money is used to purchase grain.

The farmer can reach any point on the isorevenue line for grain and forage as long as the isorevenue comes tangent to a single point on the product transformation function. Any point can be reached by buying one of the products and selling the other, in this case, selling forage and buying grain. By definition, any point on an isorevenue line produces the same total revenue. By selling forage and buying grain, the farmer may be able to produce more beef than would have been the case if he or she had relied solely on the point of tangency between the product transformation function and the isoquant (Figure 17.1). The isorevenue line for grain and forage production is the isocost line for beef production.

17.6 Concluding Comments

This chapter has derived the necessary marginal conditions for global profit maximization and for constrained revenue maximization in a two-factor, two-product setting. The value of the marginal product of both inputs in the production of both outputs divided by the respective prices of each input must be the same for both inputs in the production of both outputs in the constrained maximization solution. In addition, global profit maximization (maximization of the difference between revenues and costs) requires that the equality be equal to 1.

The intermediate product model illustrates a situation in which prices for inputs and products might be determined by equating the rates of product substitution between products and the marginal rates of substitution between factors. Prices in such a model are determined within the model rather than taken as givens. If prices are assumed to be determined outside the model, a farmer may be able to take advantage of market conditions and produce a greater amount of output than would otherwise be the case.

Problems and Exercises

1. Assume that the following conditions exist. What should the farmer do in each instance?

Case	$VMPx_1y_1/v_1$	$VMPx_1y_2/v_1$	$VMPx_2y_1/v_2$	$VMPx_2y_2/v_2$
a	3	3	2	2
b	3	3	3	3
c	3	1	3	1
d	2	2	1	1
e	0	2	0	2
f	1	0	1	0
g	1	1	1	1
h	0	0	0	0
i	−1	0	−1	0
j	−1	−2	−2	−1

2. In a multiple-input, multiple-output setting, how does the solution differ if the farmer is interested in global profit maximization versus constrained revenue maximization? In Problem 1, which conditions represent points of global profit maximization? Which conditions represent solutions to the constrained revenue-maximization problem?

3. Explain what is meant by the term *intermediate product*.

4. In what instances might a farmer be able to produce a greater amount of beef than would be suggested by the amount of feed that the farmer could produce. If it is technically possible to produce beef from farm-grown feed, should a farmer always do so? Explain. What role does the distinction between fixed and variable costs play in determining whether or not a farmer should sell grain and forage in the market or produce beef?

18
General Multiple-Product and Multiple-Input Conditions

The necessary and sufficient conditions for maximization and minimization developed for the factor-factor model in Chapter 8 and for the product-product model in Chapter 16, can be extended to accommodate any number of inputs and outputs. This chapter illustrates three models. The first model extends the two-input factor-factor model to more than two inputs. The second model extends the two-output product-product model to more than two outputs. The third model combines the factor-factor and product-product models using many different inputs and outputs to derive a general set of conditions for constrained revenue maximization and global profit maximization.

Key Terms and Definitions:

Categorization of Inputs
First-Order Conditions
Second-Order Conditions
Necessary-Conditions
Sufficient-Conditions
Bordered Principal Minor
Resource Endowment
Input Requirements Function
Implicit Production Function
General Equimarginal Return
    Principle

18.1 Introduction

The models that have been developed can be extended to accommodate any number of inputs and outputs. Farmers usually operate in a situation where many inputs are used to produce many different outputs. A general set of rules for allocation of inputs and outputs is needed. In this chapter the factor-factor and product-product models are extended to accommodate more than two inputs and outputs. A general set of rules are developed that would apply in a multiple-product, multiple-input setting.

18.2 Many Inputs and a Single Output

Production economists frequently rely on models in which only two factors of production are used. However, there are few if any production processes within agriculture that use only two inputs. The inputs to a production process within agriculture are usually quite diverse.

For example, a production function for a particular crop might include inputs such as land, the farmer's labor, hired labor, fertilizer, seed, chemicals (insecticides and herbicides), tractors, other farm machinery, and irrigation water. A production function for a particular livestock enterprise might include as inputs such as land, the farmer's labor, hired labor, feeds such as grain and forage, buildings, veterinary services and supplies, and specialized machinery and equipment.

If the production economist were to rely on the two-input factor-factor model, the inputs used for the production of either crops or livestock would need to be combined into only two aggregate measures. Here problems arise, for the inputs listed above are very different from each other. A production function calls for inputs measured in physical terms. If such inputs as tractors and fertilizer are to be aggregated, they would have to be measured in dollar terms. Moreover, the tractor provides a stream of services over a number of years, while a high percentage of applied fertilizer is used up during the crop year and a question arises as to how the aggregation for the production function for a single cropping season should take place.

A better approach might be to categorize inputs as fixed or variable and then to extend the theory such that more than two variable inputs could be included in the production function. In such an approach, production and variable cost functions include only those inputs that the farmer would normally treat as variable within the production season. For crops, seed, fertilizer, part-time hired labor paid an hourly wage, herbicides, and insecticides would be included, but inputs such as tractors and machinery, full-time salaried labor, and land would be treated as fixed within the production function and would not be included in the production function and variable-cost equation.

The categorization of inputs as fixed or variable depends on the use which the farmer might make of the marginal conditions proposed by the theory. For example, if the farmer wishes to make use of the marginal conditions only to determine the proper quantity of fertilizer, pesticides, herbicides, and part-time hired labor to use in the production of a particular crop, the remaining inputs should be treated as fixed and not as part of the maximization process.

However, such a model would not provide the farmer with any information with respect to questions such as whether or not the renting of additional land would be profitable. If the farmer wanted the model to provide information with regard to the amount of land that could be rented at a profit, the acres of land could be treated as variable with a cash rent charge per acre as the price in the cost function.

Assume that a decision has been made with respect to which inputs are to be treated as variable such that the farmer can make an allocation decision, and the n different inputs in the production function represent only those categorized as variable. A production function using n different variable inputs can be written as

$$y = f(x_1, \ldots, x_n) \tag{18.1}$$

where n is the inputs to the production process to be treated as variable and under the control of the farmer. Each x represents one of the specific inputs used in the production process, whereas y may be the output from either a specific crop or livestock enterprise.

The cost equation for n inputs treated as variable by the farmer in a purely competitive environment is

$$C = v_1 x_1 + \cdots + v_n x_n = \Sigma x_i \quad \text{for } i = 1, \ldots, n \tag{18.2}$$

A general Lagrangian formulation for revenue maximization allowing for multiple inputs is

$$L = pf(x_1, \ldots, x_n) + \lambda(C^\circ - \Sigma x_i) \tag{18.3}$$

where p is the output price.

n different inputs can be varied, and the farmer can control the amount to be used of each. Let

f_1 denote the *MPP* of x_1 holding all other inputs constant
f_i denote the *MPP* of x_i holding all other inputs constant
f_n denote the *MPP* of x_n holding all other inputs constant

Then the first-order conditions for constrained revenue maximization in a many-input setting requires that

$$pf_1/v_1 = \cdots = pf_i/v_i = \cdots = pf_n/v_n = \lambda \tag{18.4}$$

$$pMPPx_1/v_1 = \cdots = pMPPx_i/v_i = \cdots = pMPPx_n/v_n = \lambda \tag{18.5}$$

$$VMPx_1/v_1 = \cdots = VMPx_i/v_i = \cdots = VMPx_n/v_n = \lambda \tag{18.6}$$

First-order conditions for constrained revenue maximization in a many-input setting require that all ratios of *VMP* for each variable input to the respective variable input price be equal and equal λ, the imputed value of an additional dollar available for the purchase of x. If the Lagrangian multiplier λ is 1, a point of global profit maximization on the input side has been achieved. Conditions presented in equations (18.4) to (18.6) represent the general equimarginal return principle in the n-factor case and are consistent with those developed in the two-factor case.

For every pair of inputs i and j,

$$dx_j/dx_i = v_i/v_j \tag{18.7}$$

18.2 Many Inputs and a Single Output

$$MRSx_ix_j = v_i/v_j \tag{18.8}$$

The slope of the isocost line must be equal to the slope of the isoquant for every pair of inputs. Equations (18.7) and (18.8) define a point of least-cost combination on the expansion path. These conditions are also consistent with those obtained in the two-factor setting.

The second-order conditions for a constrained maximization in the n-factor case differ somewhat from those derived in the two-factor setting. In the two-factor setting the determinant of the matrix of partial derivatives obtained by differentiating each of the first-order conditions with respect to x_1, x_2, and the Lagrangian multiplier was always positive. In the n-factor case, the second-order conditions require that determinant of the following matrix have the sign associated with $(-1)^n$, where n is the number of inputs:

$$\begin{vmatrix} f_{11} & \cdots & f_{1i} & \cdots & f_{1n} & -v_1 \\ \cdot & & \cdot & & \cdot & \cdot \\ \cdot & & \cdot & & \cdot & \cdot \\ \cdot & & \cdot & & \cdot & \cdot \\ f_{i1} & \cdots & f_{ii} & \cdots & f_{in} & -v_i \\ \cdot & & \cdot & & \cdot & \cdot \\ \cdot & & \cdot & & \cdot & \cdot \\ \cdot & & \cdot & & \cdot & \cdot \\ f_{n1} & \cdots & f_{n1} & \cdots & f_{nn} & -v_n \\ -v_1 & \cdots & -v_i & \cdots & -v_n & 0 \end{vmatrix} \tag{18.9}$$

In the two-input setting, the determinant of this matrix must be positive, but negative for three inputs, positive for four inputs, and so on. If the number of inputs is even, the determinant will be positive. If the number of inputs is odd, the determinant will be negative.[1] Moreover, the bordered principal minors in the n-input case alternate in sign. To illustrate, the bordered principal minors for the three-input case and the required signs for the determinants are

$$\begin{vmatrix} f_{11} & -v_1 \\ -v_1 & 0 \end{vmatrix} < 0 \quad \begin{vmatrix} f_{11} & f_{12} & -v_1 \\ f_{21} & f_{22} & -v_2 \\ -v_1 & -v_2 & 0 \end{vmatrix} > 0 \quad \begin{vmatrix} f_{11} & f_{12} & f_{13} & -v_1 \\ f_{21} & f_{22} & f_{23} & -v_2 \\ f_{31} & f_{32} & f_{33} & -v_3 \\ -v_1 & -v_2 & -v_3 & 0 \end{vmatrix} < 0 \tag{18.10}$$

The first-order conditions represent the necessary conditions for constrained revenue maximization in the many-input setting. If the first-order conditions hold, the second-order conditions as specified by the required signs on the determinants above are necessary and sufficient for constrained revenue maximization in a many-input setting. Second-order conditions rule out points of revenue minimization as well as saddle-point solutions. If the first- and second-order conditions hold and the Lagrangian multiplier is equal to 1, the global point of profit maximization on the input side has been found.

18.3 Many Outputs and a Single Input

Most farmers do not restrict production to a single output, but are involved in the production of several different outputs. The endowment of resources or inputs available to a farmer may differ markedly from one farm to another. Usually, it is not the physical quantities of inputs that are restricted, but rather the dollars available for the purchase of inputs contained within the bundle.

An input requirements function using a single-input bundle to produce many different outputs can be written as

$$x = g(y_1, \ldots, y_i, \ldots, y_m) \tag{18.11}$$

where m is the number of outputs of the the production process. Multiplying by the weighted price of the input bundle v yields

$$vx = vg(y_1, \ldots, y_i, \ldots, y_m) \tag{18.12}$$

where $vx = C°$, the total dollars available for the purchase of inputs used in the production of each output.

A general revenue equation for m different outputs produced in a purely competitive environment is

$$R = p_1 y_1 + \cdots + p_m y_m = \Sigma p_i y_i \quad \text{for } i = 1, \ldots, m \tag{18.13}$$

A general Lagrangian formulation for revenue maximization allowing for multiple outputs is

$$L = p_1 y_1 + \cdots + p_i y_i + \cdots + p_m y_m + \psi[vx° - vg(y_1, \ldots, y_i, \ldots, y_m)] \tag{18.14}$$

where $vx° = C°$, the money available for the purchase of the input bundle x.

Let g_i denote one over the *MPP* of x in the production of y_i holding all other outputs constant. Then the first-order conditions for constrained revenue maximization in a many-output setting require that

$$p_1/g_1 v = \cdots = p_i/g_i v = \cdots = p_m/g_m v = \psi \tag{18.15}$$

$$p_1 MPPxy_1/v = \cdots = p_i MPPxy_i/v = \cdots = p_m MPPxy_m/v = \psi \tag{18.16}$$

$$VMPxy_1/v = \cdots = VMPxy_i/v = \cdots = VMPxy_m/v = \psi \tag{18.17}$$

where v is the price of the input.

First-order conditions for constrained revenue maximization in a many-output setting require that all ratios of the *VMP* of x to the price of the input bundle (v) be equal, and equal ψ, the imputed value of an additional dollar available for the purchase of x. If the Lagrangian multiplier ψ is 1, a point of global profit maximization on the output side has been achieved.

Dollars available to the farmer and used for the purchase of the input bundle must be allocated in such a way that the last dollar spent in the production of each output returns the same amount for all the possible different outputs. In other words, if the farmer has found the optimal solution in the constrained case, the last dollar spent in the production of each output will generate the same return, whether the output is corn, beef, soybeans, wheat, or milk.

For every pair of outputs i and j,

$$dy_j/dy_i = p_i/p_j \tag{18.18}$$

$$RPTy_iy_j = p_i/p_j \tag{18.19}$$

The slope of the isorevenue line must be equal to the slope of the product transformation function for every pair of outputs. This equation defines a point on the output expansion path.

Second-order conditions require that determinant of the following matrix have the sign associated with $(-1)^m$, where m is the number of outputs:

$$\begin{vmatrix} -\psi v g_{11} & \cdots & -\psi v g_{1i} & \cdots & -\psi v g_{1m} & -v g_1 \\ \vdots & & \vdots & & \vdots & \vdots \\ -\psi v g_{i1} & \cdots & -\psi v g_{ii} & \cdots & -\psi v g_{im} & -v g_i \\ \vdots & & \vdots & & \vdots & \vdots \\ -\psi v g_{m1} & \cdots & -\psi v g_{m1} & \cdots & -\psi v g_{mm} & -v g_m \\ -v g_1 & \cdots & -v g_i & \cdots & -v g_m & 0 \end{vmatrix} \tag{18.20}$$

In the two-output setting, the determinant of this matrix must be positive, but negative for three outputs, positive for four outputs, and so on. This second-order condition rules out points of revenue minimization as well as saddle-point solutions. Again, the bordered principal minors must alternate in sign.

The first-order conditions comprise the necessary conditions for constrained revenue maximization in a many-input setting. If the required signs for the determinant of equation (18.20) and the bordered principal minors also hold, the conditions are sufficient. If the Lagrangian multiplier is equal to 1 and these sufficient conditions have been met, the global point of profit maximization on the input side has been found. The farmer is globally maximizing profits if the last dollar spent for the input bundle returns exactly a dollar in each farm enterprise.

18.4 Many Inputs and Many Outputs

The most realistic setting is one in which the farmer uses many different inputs to be treated as variable in the production of many different products. The farmer faces a series of decisions. Normally, he or she is constrained by limitations in the availability of dollars that can be used for the purchase of inputs, so the total dollars used for the purchase of inputs must not exceed some predetermined fixed level. The farmer must decide how the available dollars are to be used in the production of various commodities such as corn, soybeans, wheat, beef, or milk. The mix of commodities to be produced must be determined. The farmer must also decide the allocation of dollars with respect to the quantities of variable inputs to be used in each crop or livestock enterprise. Therefore, the mix of inputs to be used in the production of each of the many enterprises must be determined.

Marginal analysis employing Lagrange's method can be used to solve the problem under conditions in which many different factors or inputs to the production process are used in the production of many different commodities. The rules developed in the many-input, many-output case are the same as those derived in the two-factor, two-product case presented in Chapter 17. However, the mathematical presentation becomes somewhat more complicated.

In the problem with two inputs and two products, the equality that must hold contained four expressions, each representing a ratio of *VMP* for an input used in the production of a product relative to the price of an input. In a general setting allowing for many more inputs and outputs, there will be many more expressions in the equality. If there are m different outputs produced and every possible output uses some of each of the n different inputs, there will be n times m expressions in the equality representing the first-order conditions. For example, if a farmer uses six inputs in the production of four different outputs, the 24 ratios of *VMP*'s to input prices must be equated.

Suppose that the farmer uses n different inputs in the production of m different outputs. The farmer wishes to maximize revenue subject to the constraints imposed by the technical parameters of the production function, as well as the constraints imposed by the availability of dollars for the purchase of inputs. The revenue function is

$$R = p_1 y_1 + \cdots + p_m y_m \tag{18.21}$$

The production function linking inputs to outputs is written in its implicit form[2]

$$H(y_1, \ldots, y_m; x_1, \ldots, x_n) = 0 \tag{18.22}$$

In the implicit form, a function of both inputs and outputs (H) is set equal to zero. The inputs are treated as negative outputs, so each x has a negative sign associated with it.

The Lagrangian maximizes revenue subject to the constraint imposed by the technical parameters of the production function, and the availability of dollars for the purchase of inputs. The Lagrangian function is

$$L = p_1 y_1 + \cdots + p_m y_m + \psi[0 - H(y_1, \ldots, y_m; x_1, \ldots, x_n)] \\ + \lambda[C° + v_1 x_1 + \cdots + v_n x_n] \tag{18.23}$$

18.4 Many Inputs and Many Outputs

Since each input has a negative sign associated with it, it is appropriate that the second constraint be written as $C^\circ + \Sigma x_i$ rather than as $C^\circ - \Sigma x_i$.

Differentiating first with respect to outputs, the first-order or necessary conditions are

$$\partial L/\partial y_1 = p_1 - \psi \partial H/\partial y_1 = 0$$
$$\vdots$$
$$\partial L/\partial y_i = p_i - \psi \partial H/\partial y_i = 0$$
$$\vdots$$
$$\partial L/\partial y_m = p_m - \psi \partial H/\partial y_m = 0 \qquad (18.24)$$

For every pair of outputs, i not equal to j:

$$dy_j/dy_i = p_i/p_j \qquad (18.25)$$

The slope of the product transformation function or rate of product transformation must equal the slope of the isorevenue line or inverse output-price ratio. Moreover,

$$(\partial H/\partial y_1)/p_1 = \cdots = (\partial H/\partial y_i)/p_i = \cdots = (\partial H/\partial y_m)/p_m = 1/\psi \qquad (18.26)$$

Differentiating with respect to inputs, the first-order conditions are

$$\partial L/\partial x_1 = -\psi \partial H/\partial x_1 + \lambda v_1 = 0$$
$$\vdots$$
$$\partial L/\partial x_i = -\psi \partial H/\partial x_i + \lambda v_i \quad 0$$
$$\vdots$$
$$\partial L/\partial x_n = -\psi \partial H/\partial x_n + \lambda v_n \quad 0 \qquad (18.27)$$

For every pair of inputs, i not equal to j:

$$dx_j/dx_i = v_i/v_j \qquad (18.28)$$

The marginal rate of substitution must be equal to the corresponding inverse price ratio. Furthermore,

$$\psi(\partial H/\partial x_1)/v_1 = \cdots = \psi(\partial H/\partial x_i)/v_i = \cdots = \psi(\partial H/\partial x_n)/v_n = \lambda \qquad (18.29)$$

But

$$\psi = p_1/(\partial H/\partial y_1) = \cdots = p_i/(\partial H/\partial y_i) = \cdots = p_m/(\partial H/\partial y_m) \quad (18.30)$$

The m different expressions for ψ from equation (18.30) can be substituted each time ψ appears in equation (18.29). The multiplier ψ appears in equation (18.29) n different times, so the required m times n expressions are possible:

$$p_i(\partial H/\partial x_j)/(v_j\,\partial H/\partial y_i) = (p_i\,\partial y_i/\partial x_j)/v_j = p_i MPPx_j y_i/v_j \quad (18.31)$$

or

$$p_1 MPPx_1 y_1/v_1 = \cdots = p_i MPPx_1 y_i/v_1 = \cdots = p_m MPPx_1 y_m/v_1$$

$$\vdots \qquad \vdots \qquad \vdots$$

$$= p_1 MPPx_j y_1/v_j = \cdots = p_i MPPx_j y_i/v_j = \cdots = p_m MPPx_j y_m/v_j$$

$$\vdots \qquad \vdots \qquad \vdots$$

$$= p_1 MPPx_n y_1/v_n = \cdots = p_i MPPx_n y_i/v_n = \cdots = p_m MPPx_n y_m/v_n = \lambda \quad (18.32)$$

The ratios of the values of the marginal products to the respective input prices must be the same for each input in the production of each output and equal to the Lagrangian multiplier λ. The Lagrangian multiplier λ is the imputed value of an additional dollar available for the purchase of inputs, allocated according to these conditions. A value for the Lagrangian multiplier λ of 1 would imply global profit maximization in this setting.

Second-order conditions for the multiple-input, multiple-product case are not presented here, but would not be at variance with the second-order conditions presented earlier in the chapter. The final conclusion in the multiple-input, multiple-product setting is entirely consistent with each of the marginal conditions developed earlier in the text. The rules with respect to input allocation across various outputs can be looked upon as extensions to the simpler models rather than as something different.

18.5 Concluding Comments

This chapter has developed a general equimarginal return principle or rule that applies in a situation where a farmer uses many different inputs in the production of many different outputs. While the underlying conclusions in the case in which many factors are used to produce many different products do not differ from the conclusions reached in Chapter 17 for the two-input, two-output case, the derivation of these conclusions becomes somewhat more complicated. If n inputs are each used in the production of m different outputs, n times m different terms will appear in the equimarginal return equation.

18.5 Concluding Comments

Since farmers usually use several different inputs in the production of a number of different outputs, the equimarginal return expressions developed in this chapter perhaps come closest to applying to the actual situation under which most farmers operate. A farmer will have found a constrained maximization solution if the ratio of *VMP* to input price is the same for every input in the production of every output. Global profit maximization occurs when this ratio is 1 for all inputs and all outputs.

Notes

1. The slope of *MPP* or f_{11} is negative in stage II of the production function. If there are two inputs, f_{22} is also negative in stage II. If there are three inputs, f_{33} is also negative in stage II. Thus

$$f_{11} < 0$$
$$f_{11}f_{22} > 0$$
$$f_{11}f_{22}f_{33} < 0$$

   and so on. The fact that the required sign on the determinant changes as the number of inputs increases is a direct result of the fact that *MPP* is declining within stage II of the production function, where the optimal solutions would be found that meet both necessary and sufficient conditions for a maximum.

2. A function may be written in its implicit form. For example, the production function $y = f(x_1)$ can be written in its implicit form as $h(x_1, y) = 0$. However, if the implicit function $h(x_1, y) = 0$ is to be written as an explicit production function $y = f(x_1)$, or as the explicit cost function in physical terms $x_1 = f^{-1}(y)$, then the partial derivatives $\partial h/\partial x_1$ and $\partial h/\partial y$ must exist and be nonzero.

Problems and Exercises

1. Are the necessary and sufficient conditions for finding a point representing a solution to the constrained revenue maximization problem the same in an *n*-input, one-output setting, as in a two-input, one-output setting? Explain.
2. Are the necessary and sufficient conditions for finding a point representing a solution to the constrained revenue-maximization problem the same in a one-input, *n*-output setting as in a one-input, two-output setting? Explain.
3. What do the necessary conditions for constrained revenue maximization require in an *n*-output, *n*-input setting? What are the required sufficient conditions?
4. Suppose that in an *n*-input, *n*-output problem, the Lagrangian multiplier was found to be 3 for all inputs used in the production of all outputs. Interpret this Lagrangian multiplier. What if the Lagrangian multiplier were instead found to be 1? What would be the interpretation of a Lagrangian multiplier of zero. Could the Lagrangian multiplier be negative? Explain.

19
Enterprise Budgeting and Marginal Analysis

The development of budgets for individual crop and livestock enterprises may at first seem rather unrelated to the marginal principles developed in earlier chapters of this text, but these economic principles play an important role in determining how budgets for farm enterprises should be constructed. A number of questions arise. (1) What level of output should be chosen? (2) Upon what level of input use should the farm budget be based? (3) How should inputs that last for more than one season be handled? (4) What about potential economies and diseconomies of size for the enterprise? (5) what about uncertainty with respect to prices and output levels? Answers to these questions form the basis for this chapter.

Key Terms and Definitions:

Enterprise Budget
Decision Rule
Pecuniary Economies of Size
Nonpecuniary Economies of Size
Fixed-Input Allocation

19.1 The Development of an Enterprise Budget

Budgets for individual farm enterprises are widely used by farmers and others as planning devices for determining both what crops should be grown and livestock should be raised, and for determining how inputs should be allocated between enterprises. A farmer who does little other planning might devote considerable time to the development of individual enterprise budgets for each of the crop and livestock activities being considered.

Table 19.1 provides an example of a commonly used format for an enterprise budget. The example used here is corn. The enterprise budget is constructed on the basis of an acre. Output is listed first. A price for the output is

19.1 The Development of an Enterprise Budget

Table 19.1. Enterprise Budget for an Acre of Corn.

Gross returns			
Sale of grain	$ 3.00	× 110 bu	$330.00
Total returns			330.00
Variable costs of production			
Nitrogen	$ 0.25	× 125.00 lb	31.25
Phosphate	0.23	× 60.00 lb	13.80
Potash	0.13	× 60.00 lb	7.80
Lime	8.50	× 0.50 tons	4.25
Seed	1.00	× 16.00 lb	16.00
Chemicals	17.00	× 1.00 acres	17.00
Insurance	0.015	× 600.00 dollars	9.00
Repairs	0.015	× 600.00 dollars	9.00
Machinery operation	5.00	× 5.00 hr	25.00
Hauling	0.18	× 110.00 bu	19.80
Labor	3.50	× 5.00 hr	17.50
Total variable costs			170.40
Fixed costs of production			
Machinery depreciation	10.0%	× $ 300	30.00
Building depreciation	5.0%	× 300	15.00
Interest on machinery	8.0%	× 300	24.00
Interest on buildings	8.0%	× 300	24.00
Interest on land	8.0%	× 1500	120.00
Taxes	0.6%	× 1800	10.80
Total fixed costs			223.80
Total fixed and variable costs			394.20
Net returns over all costs			−64.20
(Return to management)			

assumed. The variable costs are listed. An assumption is made with regard to the amount to be used of each variable input. In the case of corn, the list includes inputs such as insecticides and herbicides, nitrogen, phosphate and potash fertilizer, and seed. Assumptions are made with regard to the price of each variable input item, and the corresponding cost of that item per acre is calculated. Labor to be used per acre is calculated, and a wage rate for that labor specified. Costs for fuel and repairs required to run the machinery needed to produce the crop are listed. Estimates of the amount of fuel to be used are made as well as its price per gallon.

Repair costs are frequently very difficult to estimate. It is difficult to know how much will need to be spent for the repair of a machine on a per acre basis before it is used, and implicit assumptions need to be made about the price of machinery repairs. These numbers are usually nothing more than guesses based on the farmer's past experiences with the machines used in conjunction with the enterprise. Engineering data may also be available for estimating repair costs.

The fixed costs are listed. A major fixed-cost item is the depreciation on the machinery, buildings, and equipment. Fixed costs should represent the costs associated with the wearing out of the inputs that are used in the enterprise for more than one season, but tax laws enter. Farmers are probably more aware of the concept of depreciation as defined by what is allowed as an expense under current federal tax law than they are of the true costs associated with the wearing out of the machine over a number of years of operation. Farmers are concerned with maximizing profit after taxes, so the number to be entered for depreciation becomes unclear. Taxes are also included here, and are usually relatively easy to determine on a per acre basis for the budget.

Another major fixed-cost item is the interest charge on borrowed money, or the opportunity cost of the farmer's own money invested in the farm. If the farmer uses entirely borrowed funds, the cost to be listed here is easy to determine, but if the farmer uses some of his or her own money, the money that is used should have an imputed value or shadow price attached to it based on the returns available in a risk-free alternative. For example, if the farmer could have earned 8 percent interest at the local bank, that represents a shadow price for the farmer's own money used in the corn enterprise. Another alternative for tenants is to show the cash, or cash equivalent rent.

Farmers usually respond by saying that their money invested in farmland, due to an appreciation in farmland values, in most years yields a return greater than what would have been received by putting the money in a bank account. This return would have occurred whether or not the farmer produced corn, but would not have occurred if the farmer had sold the farmland and exited from farming.

Fixed- and variable-cost items are summed and subtracted from gross returns obtained from the sale of the crop to determine profit on a per acre basis. Even here there are difficulties. Ideally, the profit should be representative of what is left over after every factor of production other than management has been paid, but problems occur. Farmers usually do not deduct an opportunity cost for their own money invested in the enterprise. Moreover, they usually do not charge on the budget for their own or family labor that is not a cash expense. The profit figure that often appears on an enterprise budget is actually a return to management and entrepreneurial skill as well as a return to the farmer's own money invested and to nonwage farm family labor.

The farm enterprise budget is a document based on a very comprehensive and complicated series of economic assumptions. The marginal principles outlined in earlier chapters can play a role in dealing with some of the issues associated with the development of a budget for a farm enterprise.

19.2 The Level of Output to Be Produced

One of the first questions a farmer must face is to determine the level of output to be produced and represented in the budget. The farm enterprise budget is usually developed on a per acre or per animal basis. However, a salient theme running through much of this text is that the cost per unit of output produced is not constant, but varies depending on the output level chosen. An enterprise budget, even if constructed on a per acre or per animal basis, must be based on a specific assumption with regard to the amount of the output that is to be produced. The basic problem here is that the level of output of a particular enterprise is one of the key pieces of information that the farmer desires as an outcome of the budgeting process. However, to develop the budget, the farmer must make an assumption about the level of output to be produced, particularly if fixed costs are to be determined on a per acre basis.

19.2 The Level of Output to Be Produced

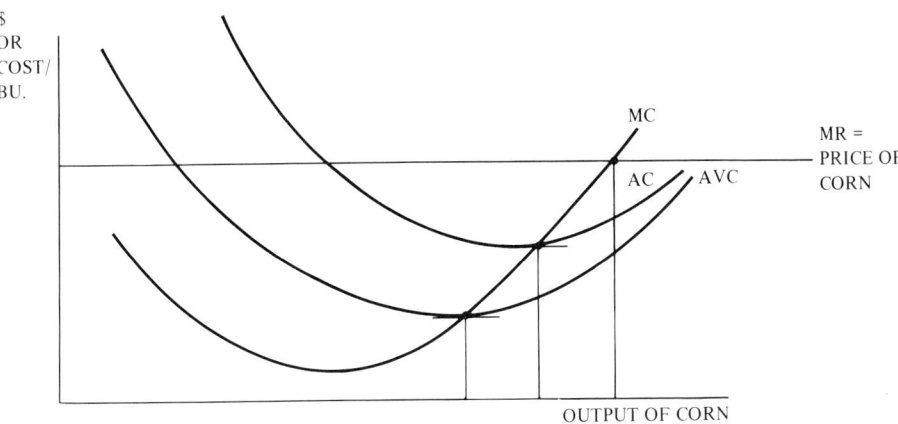

Figure 19.1 Output of Corn and the Per Bushel Cost of Production

A production economist would argue that if the entrepreneur is interested in maximizing profits, the level of output to be chosen is that output level where

$$\text{marginal cost} = \text{marginal revenue} = \text{product price}$$

Figure 19.1 illustrates a set of cost functions on the output side for corn production. The enterprise budget can at best represent only a single point in this series of cost functions. If the farmer produced but one commodity, the level of output for the enterprise budget should be equal to the profit-maximizing level where marginal cost and marginal revenue are the same.

However, farmers usually produce more than one product and have limitations on the availability of funds to purchase inputs for each enterprise. The equation marginal cost equals marginal revenue implies that no limitations exist in the availability of money needed to purchase inputs. Under this assumption, the farmer would produce at a level that maximizes profits in each enterprise. It is unlikely that a farmer would have all the money needed for the purchase of inputs, and will globally maximize profits.

The product-product model provides a better set of decision-making rules for determining the allocation of dollars for the purchase of inputs when the farmer produces many different outputs and faces constraints. The basic decision rule for the product-product model is

$$VMPxy_1/v = \cdots = VMPxy_i/v = \cdots = VMPxy_m/v = \psi \qquad (19.1)$$

where the notation is the same as defined in Chapter 16.

Equation (19.1) is the familiar equimarginal return principle on the output side. The rule implies that the farmer would attempt to make equal the ratio of returns to costs for all enterprises. Equation (19.1) also implies that the output level to appear on the farm budget for each enterprise would probably be less than that associated with the point where marginal revenue and marginal cost are the same.

19.3 The Variable-Input Levels

A second decision the farmer must make is to determine the level of the variable inputs to be used. The marginal cost equals marginal revenue rule generates an output level that maximizes profits. The output level that maximizes profits uses the amounts and combinations of inputs defined by the intersection of the pseudo scale lines.

The farmer interested in maximizing profits can either equate marginal cost to marginal revenue or can determine where the *VMP* for each input divided by its respective price equals 1. The first approach gives the solution in terms of output, while the second provides the solution in terms of the optimal quantities of each input to be used, but the two solutions are consistent. If each input is used at its profit-maximizing level by the (*VMP* = *MFC*) decision rule on the input side, the profit-maximizing level of output will be produced by the (*MR* = *MC*) decision rule on the output side.

If there are constraints or limitations in the availability of funds for the purchase of inputs, marginal analysis also provides a clear set of rules both with regard to how dollars should be allocated for the purchase of inputs as well as how the inputs should be allocated among enterprises:

$$p_1 MPP_1 y_1 / v_1 = \cdots = p_i MPPx_1 y_i / v_1 = \cdots = p_m MPPx_1 y_m / v_1$$

$$= p_i MPPx_j y_1 / v_j = \cdots = p_i MPPx_j y_i / v_j = \cdots = p_m MPPx_j y_m / v_j$$

$$= p_1 MPPx_n y_1 / v_n = \cdots = p_i MPPx_n y_i / v_n = \cdots = p_m MPPx_n y_m / v_n = \lambda \quad (19.2)$$

Constrained maximization indicates that inputs should be allocated to each output in such a way that the last dollar spent for each input returns the same amount for every farm enterprise. The input levels selected should be consistent both with this rule and with the output level specified for each enterprise budget.

However, farmers often have but partial knowledge of the *VMP*'s associated with each input to be used in the production of each output. Information is frequently obtained on a trial-and-error basis, which can be both expensive and time consuming for the farmer. There is little question as to the proper amount and allocation of each input, but the information needed to do this is often unavailable.

19.4 The Fixed-Input Allocation

A farm budget is frequently used as a planning device for the coming production season. Fixed inputs would thus include only those factors of production the farmer did not intend to change or control over the coming season. Conversely, variable inputs are factors of production which the farmer planned to control or alter during the upcoming season. Variable inputs are usually readily allocable to specific enterprises. In many instances, fixed inputs cannot readily be allocated to an enterprise.

Inputs not allocable to a specific enterprise have very little to do with marginal analysis. If fixed inputs cannot easily be allocated to a particular enterprise, they should not play a role in determining whether or not that enterprise should be pursued. If the ultimate goal of enterprise budgeting is to determine the output levels for each enterprise, perhaps those inputs that cannot easily be allocated to a particular enterprise should better be left out of the enterprise budget entirely.

The cost of fixed inputs does become important when the farmer determines the net farm income at the end of the growing season. In the long run, the farmer must cover all costs, fixed and variable, in order to survive, but in the long run, all costs are variable. The budget for an enterprise should not be looked upon as a document for determining the net farm income from that enterprise, but rather as a planning tool useful in managing the farm. Fixed inputs enter in only if the farmer is considering the purchase or the sale of the item at the time the enterprise budget is made, and then the input is more properly treated as a variable cost allocable to the enterprise.

For the purpose of enterprise budgeting, inputs allocable to the specific enterprise might better be categorized as durable or nondurable. Durable inputs are those that normally last more than one production season. Nondurable inputs are used up during the production season. The process of determining the cost per year of a specific durable input to appear in the enterprise budget is much easier once the farmer has determined that the durable input should be allocated to a specific enterprise.

19.5 The Economies of Size and Farm Budgets

As noted earlier, a farm budget assumes a specific level of output to be produced. However, costs per unit of output can vary substantially depending on the size of the operation. The assumed size of the operation can have a great deal to do with the specific numbers that appear in the budget.

As indicated in Chapter 9, economies of size usually arise from two sources. Pecuniary economies of size occur because the farm manager is able to purchase an input at a lower price per unit in large quantities than in small quantities.

Nonpecuniary economies of size occur because by expanding the level of output, the farmer can spread fixed costs and thus reduce average fixed costs per unit of output. But if fixed costs cannot be allocated to specific enterprises, the pecuniary economies of size issue is more properly dealt with as part of the total plan for the farm, outside the budget for a specific enterprise. Moreover, in the long run there are no fixed costs.

Nonpecuniary economies of size can also occur due to the possible specialization of inputs. As the size of the enterprise increases, the farmer can purchase input that are better suited to low-cost production.

Enterprise budgets can reflect pecuniary economies of size. Prices for variable inputs might be based on approximations of how much of each input will be purchased by the farm in total. In providing quantity discounts to the farmer, the fertilizer dealer does not care how much of the fertilizer is to be allocated specifically to the wheat, corn, and soybean enterprise.

19.6 Price and Output Uncertainty

To develop an enterprise budget, specific assumptions need to be made with respect to prices and outputs. If an enterprise budget is developed as a planning document, neither prices nor outputs will be known with certainty. If the farmer makes budgets at the start of the season, the farmer will be nearly certain of the prices for inputs needed and purchased at the start of the production season. For inputs purchased during the production season, there may be a degree of variability relative to budgeted amounts.

A decision must be made with regard to the price of the output or outputs produced by the enterprise. There will normally be a good deal of variability in output prices during the production season, but the farmer has tools available for dealing with this source of variability. For example, the futures market might be used to determine a specific price for the output at the end of the production season. If the output or commodity is affected by a government program, the price of the commodity may be supported at some specific level. Therefore, the problem of attaching a specific price to an output in an enterprise budget may not be as difficult as it initially seems.

Output uncertainty presents other problems. Despite a farmer's keen awareness of the *VMP*'s associated with each input in the production of each output in a normal production season, because of nature, the outcomes suggested by the enterprise budget may not become reality. Farmers usually make output predictions based on past experience with the enterprise in an average year, adjusted for any changes in the use of inputs as proposed in the budget. Ideally, this is the output level where marginal revenue and marginal cost are equal, or as an alternative, an output level such that the rates of product transformation for the output from each pair of enterprises equals the corresponding output price ratio.

19.7 Concluding Comments

Enterprise budgets are the planning tools perhaps most commonly used by farmers. Marginal analysis can provide a useful basis for the development of the appropriate numbers for an enterprise budget. Marginal analysis can be used to determine (1) the proper output level, (2) the amounts and combinations of inputs that will produce at greatest profit or least cost for a given output level, and (3) the proper size of the operation.

An enterprise budget is a planning document that specifies what might happen and also what almost surely will not always take place. It is not an accounting document designed to determine the overall profitability of the farm. The marginal rules developed in this text can play a key role in making the enterprise budget a more effective aid to farm planning.

Problems and Exercises

1. In an enterprise budget, how are variable costs distinguished from fixed costs?

2. Upon what basis might a farmer determine potential selling prices for the commodity or commodities produced by the enterprise?

3. In determining costs, what level of output should be chosen as the basis for making the enterprise budget?

4. Suppose that the farmer has available quantity discounts in the purchase of fertilizer and chemicals. How should such discounts be handled within the enterprise budget framework?

20 Decision Making in an Environment of Risk and Uncertainty

This chapter provides a very basic introduction to how risk and uncertainty can be incorporated into farm planning, with an emphasis on the marginal analysis developed in Chapters 2 to 18. Risk and uncertainty are defined. The role of farmer attitudes and objectives in determining particular strategies for dealing with risk and uncertainty is discussed. Expected prices and yields might be used to replace actual prices and yields in marginal analysis models. A simple marginal analysis model incorporating income variability is developed. Alternative strategies for dealing with risk and uncertainty at the farm level are compared.

Key Terms and Definitions:

Risk
Uncertainty
Risk–Uncertainty Continuum
Probability
Expected Income
States of Nature
Action
Consequences
Utility
Utility Function

Variance
Expected Price
Expected Yield
Income Variability
Insurance
Contract
Flexible Facilities and Equipment
Diversification
Government Program

20.1 Risk and Uncertainty Defined

Farmers face situations nearly every day in which the outcomes are uncertain. Nature has a significant impact on farming. For example, it may not rain or it may rain too much. Crops can get hailed out or insects and disease can destroy a crop. An apple or orange crop may get frost, and animals develop diseases and die. Thus farming is inherently linked to the path of nature.

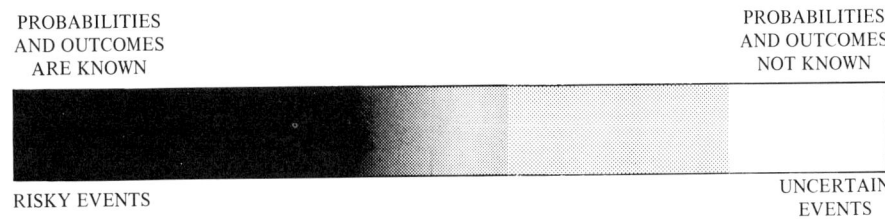

Figure 20.1 Risk–Uncertainty Continuum

The markets affect farmers to a great degree as well. Farmers complain that prices are high when they have nothing to sell and that prices are low when crop yields are high. Prices for agricultural commodities are largely determined by forces outside the control of the individual farmer. Farming takes place in an environment characterized by risk and uncertainty.

Frank Knight was the one initially responsible for making a distinction between the term *risk* and the term *uncertainty*. He argued that in an uncertain environment, possible outcomes and their respective probabilities of occurrence were not known. In a risky environment, both the outcomes and the probabilities of occurrence are known.

Some economists have suggested that to deal with risk, all that is needed is an insurance policy. The insurer can discover the outcomes and the probabilities of their occurrence and write a policy with a premium sufficient to cover the risk and net a profit to the insurer.

Uncertainty cannot be dealt with as easily. If the outcomes and the probabilities associated with each outcome are not known, the insurer would not be able to write a policy with a premium sufficient to cover the risk. Recently, some insurance companies have written policies designed to pay for losses resulting from the occurrence of very unusual events. It is difficult to believe that insurance companies have complete knowledge of the probabilities associated with these events, so distinguishing between risk and uncertainty on the basis of insurability is not the final answer.

Rather than to think of *risk* and *uncertainty* as dichotomous terms, it may be more appropriate to think of a risk–uncertainty continuum (Figure 20.1). At one end of the continuum lie risky events, in which the outcomes and the probabilities attached to each outcome are known. At the other end of the continuum lie uncertain events, in which neither outcomes nor probabilities of their occurrence are known. Many events taking place in farming lie between the polar extremes of risk and uncertainty. Usually, some but not all of the possible outcomes are known, and some but not all outcomes have probabilities attached to them. Much of farming lies midway on the risk–uncertainty continuum.

20.2 Farmer Attitudes Toward Risk and Uncertainty

One of the problems in dealing with risk and uncertainty is that individuals, including farmers, vary markedly in their willingness to take on, and preferences for, risk and uncertainty. No one would normally enter an environment char-

Table 20.1 Alternative Income Generating Strategies

Strategy	Income	Probability
A	$1,000,000	0.3
	−500,000	0.2
	0	0.5
B	100,000	0.3
	50,000	0.4
	0	0.2
	−20,000	0.1
C	50,000	0.7
	30,000	0.2
	0	0.1
D	30,000	0.4
	25,000	0.4
	15,000	0.2

acterized by risk and uncertainty without expectations of gains greater than would be the case in the absence of risk and uncertainty.

That individuals vary markedly in their willingness to take on risk and uncertainty can be illustrated with a simple class game. Suppose that a person is confronted with four different strategies. Each strategy will produce varying levels of income and have probabilities attached to each income level. The four strategies are outlined in Table 20.1. The outcomes and the probability of each outcome are known with certainty. The probability assigned to each strategy represents the expected proportion of times the specified income is expected to occur, relative to the total times the particular strategy (A, B, C, or D) is pursued. For each strategy, the probabilities sum to 1, indicating that for each strategy, only the three income levels are possible. Each member of the class might vote on the strategy that he or she would pursue.

One way to determine which strategy to pursue would be to calculate the expected income occurring as the result of each strategy. The expected income is the income resulting from the strategy weighted by its probability of occurrence. For strategy A, the expected income is $(0.3 \times 1,000,000) + (0.2 \times -500,000) + (0.5 \times 0) = \$200,000$. For strategy B, the expected income is $(0.3 \times 100,000) + (0.4 \times 50,000) + (0.2 \times 0) + (0.1 \times -20,000) = \$48,000$. For strategy C, the expected income is $(0.7 \times 50,000) + (0.2 \times 30,000) + (0.1 \times 0) = \$41,000$. For strategy D, the expected income is $(0.4 \times 30,000) + (0.4 \times 25,000) + (0.2 \times 15,000) = \$25,000$. So based on expected income, strategy A would always be pursued, despite the fact that strategy A also allows for the greatest potential losses.

The strategy that is pursued depends in part on the person's particular financial situation. Suppose that if a positive income was not achieved, the person would lack funds necessary to meet the basic needs of life, and would starve. Such a person would be reluctant to pursue any strategy other than D, but a person with $1 million already in the bank would probably choose strategy A. The worst that person could do is lose half of what he or she already had.

The strategy each person chooses is largely unrelated to intelligence or education. There is probably no relationship between the strategy that each person selects and his or her score on the last hour exam in agricultural production economics. College graduates would not necessarily tend to choose strategies different from high school graduates. All millionaires are not college graduates. Those in bankruptcy are not all high school dropouts.

Each person thus has a different preference for risk and uncertainty versus certainty that is very much intertwined with his or her own psychic makeup. So it is with farmers. Anyone can cite examples of farmers who pursued high-risk strategies that paid off. Examples of farmers who pursued high-risk strategies and went bankrupt are also commonplace, and there are numerous examples of farmers who pursued secure strategies, made a living at farming, but never became wealthy. Self-made millionaires vary widely in intelligence and education, but share a common characteristic in that they are willing to assume large amounts of risk with little, if any, fear if things should not go their way.

Professions vary in the amount of risk. The race car driver assumes enormous amounts of risk in the pursuit of a potentially high payoff. College professors and others in secure, stable occupations are frequently quite risk averse.

Farmers as a group probably prefer to take on more risk than college professors as a group. Nearly every extension agricultural economist has had the opportunity to work with farmers whose incomes exceed the income of the extension agricultural economist several times over. If farmers were not willing to assume some risk, they would have long ago chosen an occupation with a steady income with little variability from year to year. Rather, they let the whims of nature and the marketplace in large measure determine their annual incomes. Students from farm backgrounds sometimes attend an agricultural college in hopes of securing a job that has less income variability than was present on the farm back home.

20.3 Actions, States of Nature, Probabilities, and Consequences

A farmer must have alternatives open in order to make a decision. If two or more alternatives are not available, a decision cannot be made. The alternatives available to a farmer represent the *actions* or *strategies* open to the farmer. The set of actions should encompass the full range of alternatives open to the farmer. In the game in Section 20.2, the actions were represented by the alternative strategies. There are usually a finite number of actions or strategies open to the manager.

The *states of nature* represent the best guess by the decision maker with regard to the possible events that might occur. States of nature are assumed to be outside the control of the decision maker, and in combination with the decision maker's actions determine the outcomes for the decision maker.

Probabilities can be attached to each outcome. They represent the manager's guess as to the number of occurrences of a particular outcome relative to the total number of possible outcomes resulting from a particular strategy. For example, if a particular outcome is expected to occur 3 times out of 10, a probability of 0.3 will be assigned. If all outcomes for each strategy are delineated, the sum of the probabilities associated with each strategy will be 1. This was the case in the game in Section 20.2.

Consequences represent outcomes that are produced by the interaction of the manager's actions and the states of nature. Consequences represent what could happen to the manager. The various income levels represented the outcomes or consequences associated with each strategy in the game.

These terms can be further illustrated with another game. Suppose that the farmer is faced with two options, to grow wheat or soybeans. Assume that nature also has two states, one producing high yields and the other producing low yields. The income resulting from each combination of decision-maker strategies and states of nature, and the corresponding subjective probabilities attached to each state of nature. The resultant matrix is:

	State of Nature and Probabilities	
Action	High Yields: 0.6	Low Yields: 0.4
Grow Soybeans	$20,000	$ 3,000
Grow Wheat	$15,000	$10,000

The expected income if the farmer grows soybeans is

$$(0.6)(\$20,000) + (0.4)(\$3000) = \$13,200$$

The expected income if the farmer grows wheat is

$$(0.6)(\$15,000) + (0.4)(\$10,000) = \$13,000$$

If the farmer is interested in maximizing expected income, he or she would be better off to grow soybeans than wheat. However, the farmer might also be concerned with income variability.

20.4 Risk Preference and Utility

The farmer's willingness to take on risk is in large measure linked to his or her psychic makeup. The satisfaction or utility that a farmer receives from each outcome in large measure determines the strategy that he or she will pursue. The maximization of utility subject to constraints imposed by the availability of income is the ultimate goal of a farmer, or for that matter, anyone.

A utility function links utility or satisfaction to the amount of one or more goods that are available. Utility maximization becomes the criterion by which choices are made by the manager. A farmer's utility or satisfaction is not unrelated to his or her expected income, but it is not the same thing as his or her expected income either. If utility and expected income were the same thing, the farmer interested in utility maximization would always choose the strategy that yielded the highest expected income.

In the game outlined in Section 20.2, consider a possible strategy E that yielded $300,000 with a 0.5 probability, and $100,000 with a 0.5 probability. If expected income and utility were the same, everyone would be indifferent between this strategy and strategy A presented in Table 20.1. Most people prob-

20.4 Risk Preference and Utility

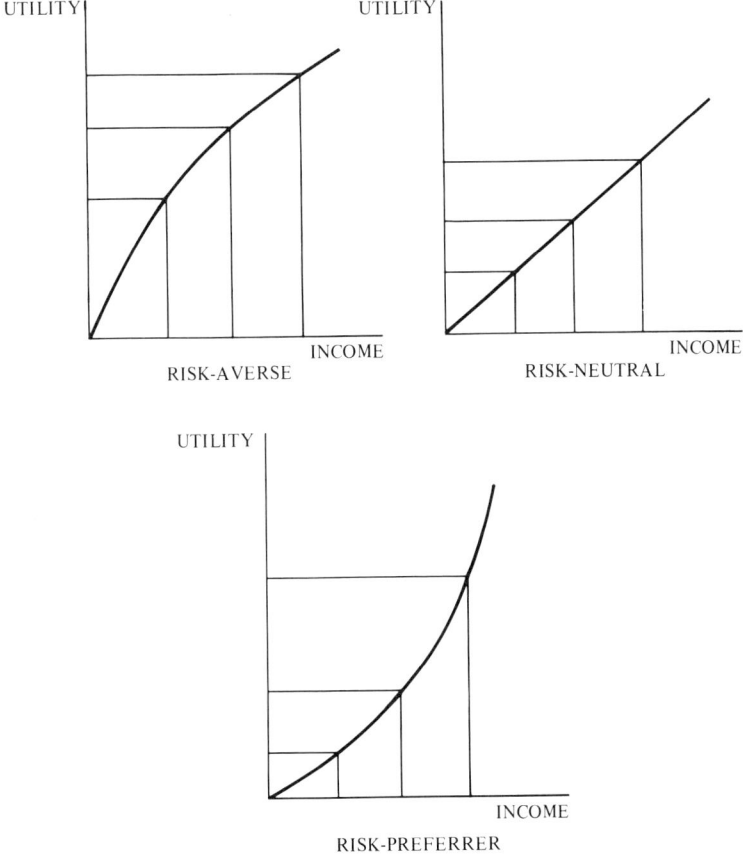

Figure 20.2 Three Possible Functions Linking Utility to Income

ably would strongly prefer strategy E to strategy A, despite the fact that both strategies yield the same expected income of $200,000. Clearly, there is more to maximizing utility than maximizing expected income.

A good deal of effort by economists has been devoted to proofs that utility functions for individuals and, in particular, for farm managers exist. Figure 20.2 illustrates three possibilities with respect to possible functions linking utility to income. Assuming that the farmer can achieve greater income only at the expense of taking on greater risk or uncertainty, the risk averter will have a utility function that increases at a decreasing rate as income rises. The utility function for the risk-neutral person will have a constant slope. The utility function for the risk preferrer will increase at an increasing rate.

One utility function that is sometimes assumed is the quadratic utility function

$$U = z + bz^2 \tag{20.1}$$

where z is some variable of concern that generates utility for the manager, such as income. Suppose that there exists uncertainty with regard to the income level, so that z is replaced by the an expected z or $E(z)$. Therefore, expected utility is

$$E(U) = E(z) + bE(z^2) \tag{20.2}$$

The expected value of a squared variable is equal to the variance of the variable plus the square of the expected value. Therefore,

$$E(z^2) = \sigma^2 + [E(x)]^2 \tag{20.3}$$

Hence

$$E(U) = E(x) + b[E(x)]^2 + b\sigma^2 \tag{20.4}$$

Thus utility is a function not only of expected income, but also its variance.

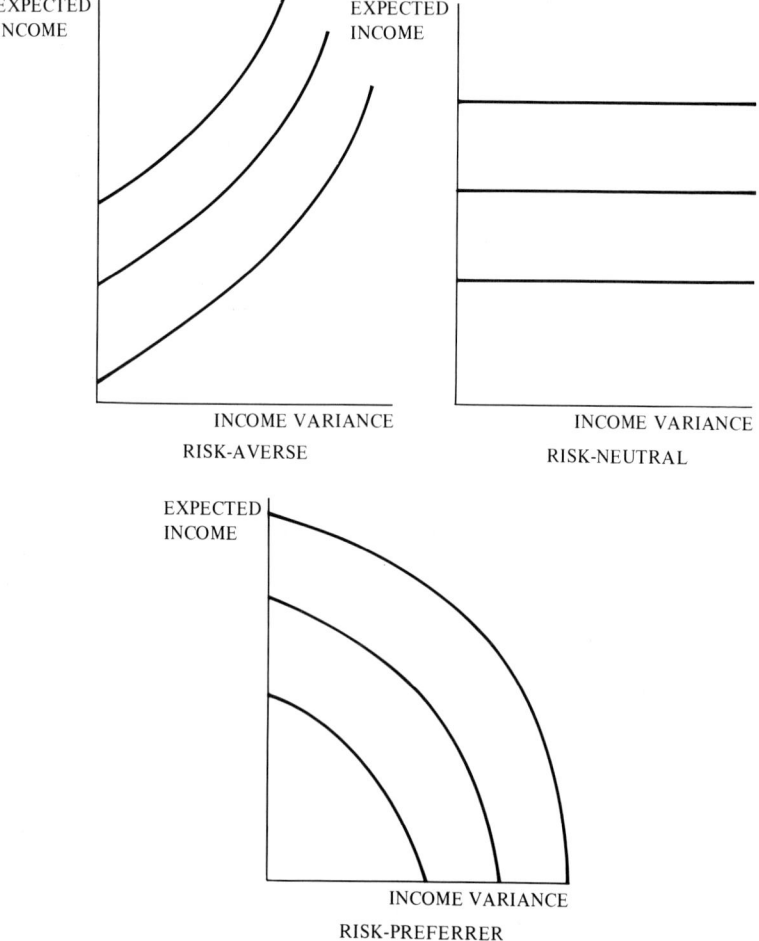

Figure 20.3 Indifference Curves Linking the Variance of Income with the Expected Income

Indifference curves that show possible combinations of income and its variance that yield the same amount of utility for the manager might be obtained by assuming that U equals $U°$ and taking the total differential of the utility function:

$$dU° = 0 = (1 + 2b)\, dE(x) + b\, d(\sigma^2) \qquad (20.5)$$

Therefore,

$$dE/d\sigma^2 = -b/[1 + 2bE(x)] \qquad (20.6)$$

The denominator $[1 + 2bE(x)]$ will always be positive. The shape of the indifference curves will depend on the value of b. If b is zero, the farmer neither desires nor dislikes risk. The farmer is risk neutral. If b is positive, the farmer loves risk, and indifference curves will have a negative slope. If b is negative, the farmer is risk averse and will have indifference curves sloping upward to the right. Figure 20.3 illustrates some possible relationships suggested by this utility function.

20.5 Risk, Uncertainty, and Marginal Analysis

The models in this text that used marginal analysis all assumed that input prices, output prices, and outputs were known with certainty. There exist several ways of incorporating risk and uncertainty into these models, while relying on marginal analysis as the basic tool for decision-making information.

One of the simplest ways of incorporating risk and uncertainty into a model might be to use expected prices or yields rather than actual prices or yields within the model. Just how yield and price expectations are formulated by farmers has been a topic of great concern to some agricultural economists.

An agricultural economist interested in the futures market might argue that one way a farmer formulates price expectations is by studying the prices on futures contracts for the month in which the crops or livestock are expected to be marketed. The futures market does not necessarily predict with a high degree of accuracy what the cash price will be some time in the future. However, the prices for futures contracts are an additional piece of information that the farmer might be able to use at least as a partial basis for developing expectations with regard to prices at marketing time. The farmer might also take advantage of the futures market to determine specific prices at the time of delivery, and these prices could be treated the same as a certain price within the model.

Farmers have many other sources of information with regard to expected prices. The news media, farm magazines, the agricultural extension service, the federal government, and private price forecasting agencies all devote considerable effort to providing price and general outlook information for farmers. One problem with this information is that the quality can vary widely. The farmer must not only study the forecasts obtained from each source, but also attach subjective probabilities with respect to its accuracy.

Farmers rely heavily on current and recent past prices as a means of formulating price expectations. If the cash price of corn at the start of the production season is high relative to soybeans, almost certainly there will be an increase in corn acreages irrespective of what prices are forecasted to prevail at the time the crop is marketed. Current and recent past cash prices may not accurately represent the prices that should be included in a profit-maximization model.

Yield or output expectations are usually largely based on past experience with the particular commodity. Suppose that a farmer experienced corn yields of 130 bushels per acre last year, 114 bushels per acre the year before, and 122 bushels per acre the year before that. A simple way of formulating a yield expectation might be to average the yield over the past three years. This would treat each of the past three years as equally important in the formulation of the yield expectation. In this example, the expected yield would be 122 bushels per acre.

Another way would be to weight more heavily data from the recent past relative to earlier data. Expected output becomes a distributed lag of past output levels. For example, a farmer might place a weight of 0.6 on last year's data, 0.3 on the year before, but 0.1 on the year previous to that. The weights representing the relative importance of each year's data are highly subjective but should sum to 1. The expected yield in this example is

$$y = 0.6(130) + 0.3(114) + 0.1(122) = 124.4 \text{ bushels per acre.} \quad (20.7)$$

Once price and output expectations have been formulated, they could be inserted directly into the model. The marginal conditions would then be interpreted based on expected rather than actual prices.

The major disadvantage of using expected price and output levels as the basis for formulating economic models is that the approach fails to recognize that price and output variability leads to income variability for the farmer. Only if the farmer is risk neutral is the expected profit maximum optimal for the farmer. Despite the fact that a model using expected prices and output levels leads to maximum profits when expected prices and outputs are realized, income variability when expected prices and yields are not realized may lead to severe financial problems for the farmer. Even if expected prices and outputs are accurate over a planning horizon of several years, the farmer must survive the short-run variability in order to make the long run relevant.

One way of incorporating such variability into a model would be to add additional constraints. Suppose that the farmer used an input bundle to produce two outputs, y_1 and y_2. Due to price and output instability, there is income variability associated with both y_1 and y_2. The income variability associated with y_1 is $y_1\sigma_1^2$, and the income variability associated with y_2 is $y_2\sigma_2^2$. The income variability associated with the first commodity may partially offset or add to the income variability from the second commodity. An interaction term or covariance term is needed. This term that adjusts for income variability interaction is $2y_1y_2\sigma_{12}$.

The total income variability (δ) is

$$\delta = y_1\sigma_1^2 + y_2\sigma_2^2 + 2y_1y_2\sigma_{12} \quad (20.8)$$

The farmer is interested in maximizing revenue subject to the constraint that income variability not exceed a specified level $\delta°$, and the constraint imposed by the availability of dollars for the purchase of the input bundle x. So the Lagrangian is

$$L = p_1 y_1 + p_2 y_2 + \psi(\delta^\circ - y_1 \sigma_1^2 - y_2 \sigma_2^2 - 2 y_1 y_2 \sigma_{12})$$
$$+ \eta[vx^\circ - vg(y_1, y_2)] \qquad (20.9)$$

The corresponding first-order conditions are

$$\partial L / \partial y_1 = p_1 - \psi(\sigma_1^2 + 2 y_2 \sigma_{12}) - \eta v g_1 = 0 \qquad (20.10)$$

$$\partial L / \partial y_2 = p_2 - \psi(\sigma_2^2 + 2 y_1 \sigma_{12}) - \eta v g_2 = 0 \qquad (20.11)$$

$$\partial L / \partial \psi = \delta^\circ - y_1 \sigma_1^2 - y_2 \sigma_2^2 - 2 y_1 y_2 \sigma_{12} = 0 \qquad (20.12)$$

$$\partial L / \partial \eta = vx^\circ - vg(y_1, y_2) = 0 \qquad (20.13)$$

If there were no income variability, the first-order conditions would be the same as the standard first-order conditions in the product-product model. Income variability could reduce or increase the output of y_1 relative to y_2. The signs on the income variance–covariance terms are indeterminate. Income variability can be incorporated into a standard model, but the key problem with this is that the farmer would need to be able to provide an indication of the variances and covariances associated with the incomes obtained from the commodities being produced.

20.6 Strategies for Dealing with Risk and Uncertainty

A farmer has a number of strategies available for ameliorating the impacts of risk and uncertainty. Each of these strategies reduces losses when nature is unfavorable or the markets turn against the farmer, but also reduce potential profits when nature and the markets are favorable.

20.6.1 Insure against risk

If an insurance policy is available, income variability due to that source of risk can be reduced by purchasing the policy. People purchase fire insurance not because they expect their house to burn down, but because the cost of the insurance is low relative to the potential loss that could occur should the house burn. Insurance policies work best when the probability attached to the occurrence of the event is low, but if the event occurs, the result would be catastrophic. In other words, insurance should be used in situations where there is a low probability of a large loss.

Crop insurance plans have the effect of making the farmer's income from one year to the next more even, despite the fact that the farmer may pay in the form of premiums somewhat more than is returned in the form of claims over a 10-year period. The premium cost reduces potential profits in years without a crop loss. Only if the risk of crop failure on a particular farm substantially exceeds the risks on which the premiums were based will returns from the insurance policy more than offset premium costs.

20.6.2 Contracts

The futures market can be thought of as a device which allows farmers to contract for the sale of a specified commodity at a specified price for delivery at some future point in time. Thus the futures market is a mechanism to reduce or eliminate price uncertainty by determining prices to be paid after harvest, or at the point when the commodity is ready for market. Although price and income variability will be reduced, in a rising market, the farmer will limit potential gains if prices are determined at the start of the production season.

The futures market is but one contractual arrangement for eliminating price uncertainty. Any contractual arrangement that at the start of the production season specifies a price to be received at the end of the production season will eliminate price uncertainty. Contractual arrangements are commonly used for commodities such as broilers, horticultural crops, and sunflowers. Any contractual price would work well in a marginal analysis model, since it represents price certainty.

20.6.3 Flexible facilities and equipment

If a farmer is to adjust to changing relative product and input prices, it must be possible to adapt buildings and equipment lasting more than one production season to alternative uses as input and output price ratios change. Figure 20.4 illustrates some possibilities. The long-run product transformation function represents the possibilities open to the farmer before buildings are built and equipment is purchased (curve A). Once the durable items have been built and capital committed, two possibilities exist.

Specialized facilities will allow production to take place on the long-run planning curve if relative price ratios turn out to be as expected over the long

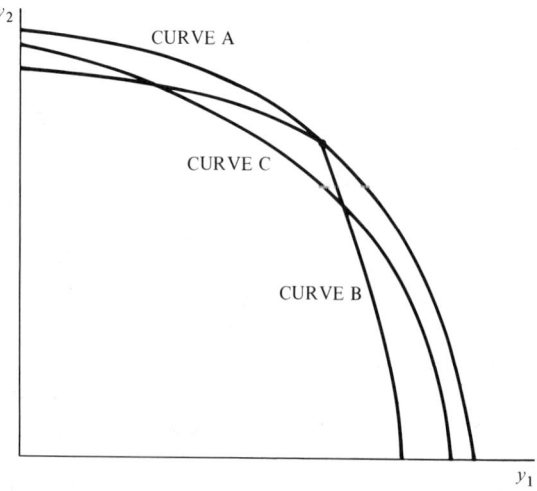

Figure 20.4 Long-Run Planning: Specialized and Nonspecialized Facilities

term. But production drops off dramatically if the use of the buildings and equipment is changed to produce another mix of outputs in response to changing relative prices (curve B). A milking parlor is an example of a livestock facility ill adapted to other uses. Specialized harvesting equipment for a new crop not previously grown by the farmer (such as sunflowers in a farming area devoted to wheat and other small grains) is another example.

If a good deal of price variability is expected, a better strategy might be to construct buildings and to purchase machinery and equipment adapted to a wide variety of uses with little additional cost (curve C). A point on the long-run planning curve is never achieved under any conceivable output price ratio. A barn suited for the production of many different classes of livestock is an example of a flexible facility. In grain production, planting tillage and harvest equipment adapted to an array of different crops represents flexible equipment. The farmer is better off under extreme price variability with flexible facilities and equipment. The farmer is better off with the specialized facilities if price variability is not extreme.

A farmer who attempts to deal with price uncertainty by choosing to build or purchase machinery and facilities adaptable to a diverse array of uses is, in effect, choosing facilities allowing for a greater elasticity of substitution on the product side. A facility suitable only for the production of one commodity, or two commodities in an exact fixed proportion to each other, would lead to a zero elasticity of substitution on the product side.

20.6.4 Diversification

Diversification is a strategy long used by farmers for dealing with both price and output uncertainty. The idea behind a diversification strategy is to let profits from one type of livestock or crop enterprise more than offset losses in another enterprise. Diversification may also make more effective use of labor and other inputs throughout the year, thus increasing income in both good years and bad. To deal most effectively with price and income variability, the enterprises on the diversified farm must have prices and outputs that move opposite to each other.

It does little good to attempt to reduce output variability by both growing wheat and raising beef cattle, if wheat yields are low when rainfall is inadequate, and at the same time, beef cattle cannot be adequately fed on pastures with inadequate rainfall. To guard against uncertainty associated with drought, the farmer would need to find an enterprise in which the output is not as rainfall dependent, and this may be difficult.

The strategy may be more effective for dealing with price uncertainty. Beef and grain prices sometimes move together, but not always, nor do beef and pork prices always move in tandem. The ideal strategy would involve locating commodities whose prices always move in opposite directions. While a farmer who diversifies may substantially reduce income variability and make more effective use of certain inputs, income could also be reduced relative to what would have occurred had production of only the high-priced commodity taken place. The diversified farmer also bears a cost in not as effectively being able to take advantage of pecuniary and other internal economies open to the specialized counterpart.

20.6.5 Government programs

The federal government long has been heavily involved in programs that provide price and income support for farmers. Agricultural policy during the 1970s moved away from mandatory programs and toward programs that allow the farmer to decide for himself or herself whether or not to participate. Most government programs have been directed toward the reduction of price, rather than output uncertainty, but the wheat and feed grain disaster programs of the 1970s are examples of programs designed to support farm incomes when output levels are low.

Net farm income for the United States is rather unrelated to output in a particular year. The 1983 drought throughout much of the midwestern grain-producing areas dramatically reduced output of key crops such as corn, although net farm income was higher in 1983 than in 1982, when drought was not widespread but prices were lower. A farmer's income increases when success is achieved at growing a crop in which other farmers had widespread failures.

Government price support programs that place floors under which commodity prices are supported are usually thinly disguised mechanisms for supporting farm incomes. Such programs increase incomes and support the welfare of every farmer who participates, large and small. Participation in a program will normally reduce income variability, and to the extent that tax revenues for supporting prices come from nonfarm consumers, long-term income may also be larger than would have been the case if the program had not been in place.

When given a choice, occasionally farmers will find it to their advantage not to participate in a government program. The decision can be made by first calculating net revenue when the farmer participates. This usually means a restricted output (y) at a high price. Net revenue based on nonparticipation is then calculated assuming more output but a lower price. However, the decision by the farmer to participate or not participate will be based both on the extent to which participation in the program will reduce income variability as well as increase net income.

Recently, the federal government has been making attempts to move away from federal price support programs. For programs that remain, increasingly farmers are being asked to pay for the full cost of government price support programs, including the cost of storage of commodities in excess supply. The recent move toward a no net cost tobacco program could be an indication of potential programs for other commodities.

When government support prices exceed levels at which supply and demand are in equilibrium, surpluses of the price-supported commodities occur. Most commodities cannot be stored indefinitely, and storage costs can quickly become rather high. In the past, the government has used the school lunch program to dispose of surplus, government-owned commodities. Recently the government has distributed surplus dairy products occurring as a result of the price support program to low income and elderly residents. Unfortunately, the federal government does not have the option of giving away cigarettes to low-income or elderly people, or making chewing tobacco an approved vegetable on the school lunch menu.

In the past, government programs have both reduced income variability and raised net farm incomes. Utility is increased because incomes rise and variability in incomes is reduced. A no-net-cost program would only reduce income variability. Therefore, a no-net-cost government program could increase utility if farmers were not risk neutral. However, incomes to farmers (and utility) over the long term would be reduced because of the cost to farmers of operating the government program.

20.7 Concluding Comments

This chapter has provided a very basic introduction to the problem of taking into account risk and uncertainty in economic analysis. Specific models incorporating risk and uncertainty could easily fill an entire textbook. The simplest approaches for including risk and uncertainty involve replacing actual prices and yields with the respective expected values. However, price and income variability leads to income variability, which in turn, affects the farmer's utility or satisfaction.

While marginal analysis can form the basis for some models that include risk and uncertainty, other models are based on approaches that do not require the traditional framework. Included in the latter category are approaches involving games such as those outlined in Section 20.3. The reading list at the end of this text includes a number of articles dealing with risk and uncertainty using a variety of modeling approaches.

Problems and Exercises

1. Calculate the expected income on the basis of the following data:

Income	Probability
$100,000	0.2
20,000	0.5
−50,000	0.3

2. Why are expected income and utility not the same thing?
3. Why do farmers not always choose to pursue the strategy with the greatest expected income?
4. Discuss possible states that nature might assume in farming, and possible actions a farmer might take in dealing with these states of nature.
5. Suppose that an enterprise with a greater expected income also resulted in a greater input variability than that for another enterprise. How could this situation be considered within a marginal analysis framework?
6. Suggest strategies that a farmer might use to deal with risk and uncertainty.

Reference

Knight, Frank H. *Risk, Uncertainty and Profit.* Boston: Houghton Mifflin, 1921.

21 Time and Agricultural Production Processes

Chapters 2 to 18 treated production processes in a comparative statics framework, and the time element was largely ignored. This chapter introduces time as an explicit component of marginal analysis. Goals for farmers other than profit maximization over a single production period are introduced. Time is introduced as an explicit variable within a single period planning model. Basic procedures for discounting or compounding revenues and costs over several production periods are outlined, and a profit maximization model in which revenues and costs occur over several production seasons is presented.

Key Terms and Definitions:

Alternative Goals
Long-Run Profit Maximization
Accumulation of Wealth
Time as an Input
Macroeconomic Policy
Inflation
Real Interest Rate
Net Worth
Discounting
Compounding
Present Value
Multiple-Period Production

21.1 Introduction

Throughout much of this text, the implicit assumption has been that farmers during a single production season are interested in maximizing profits or in maximizing revenue subject to constraints. Although these may be valid goals for a farmer within a single production season, farmers do not normally enter farming, produce for one season, and then exit. Farmers look at the occupation over a time period of 20 years or more. They normally do not expect to exit from farming within a short period. As a result, most farmers have goals and objectives that go beyond single season profit or constrained revenue maximization. These goals and objectives may not be totally inconsistent with short-run profit or constrained revenue maximization, but they may not be entirely consistent either.

In addition to having an impact on the goals of the decision maker, time influences agricultural production in other ways. Time can be thought of as a scarce resource or input that must be allocated in a manner consistent with the goals of the farm manager. A dollar earned some time into the future cannot be treated the same way as a dollar earned today. Revenues and costs must be discounted or compounded. Time is an inherent part of virtually all agricultural finance issues. Marginal analysis can be used as a basis for making decisions within a time frame encompassing several production periods.

21.2 Alternative Goals of a Farm Manager over Many Seasons

21.2.1 Long-run profit maximization

Just as a farmer is interested in maximizing profits in a single production season, a farmer might also be interested in maximizing expected long-run profit. The maximization of profit over a 20-year period may not entail making the same set of choices that would be made if the farmer were interested in maximizing profit in each of 20 successive single-season production periods.

Long-run profit maximization may require making larger expenditures on durable inputs such as land and machinery, for example, early within the 20-year period. A farmer interested in long-run profit maximization over a number of years has a long-run planning horizon and will make investment decisions with expected payoffs some years away consistent with the long-run goal. The decisions made by farmers are not unrelated to the length of the planning horizon.

There are many examples of farm enterprises that must inherently involve a planning horizon of more than one year. The farmer who starts a pick-your-own strawberry enterprise is a year and a half or more away from revenue from the sale of the strawberries. A person planning to grow apples or Christmas trees on land not previously used for that purpose must be interested in long-run rather than short-run profit maximization. If all farmers were interested only in single-season profit or constrained revenue maximization, they would never go into such enterprises.

A goal of long-run profit maximization will frequently require short-run profit and income sacrifices during the early years of the planning horizon, with the hope or expectation of making greater profits during the latter years. However, a dollar today is worth more than a dollar obtained a year or more from now. A dollar today could earn interest in a bank. This is forgone income until the dollar is earned. Inflation makes a dollar earned today more valuable than the same dollar earned a year from now. These elements must enter if a farmer is interested in finding a decision path that maximizes profits over a long term planning horizon.

Moreover, season-to-season variability in profits or farm income is often greater if long-run rather than short-run profit maximization is the goal. The variability is of importance to the extent that it influences the survival of the farm firm at some point during the planning horizon. Short-run survival is essential to long-run profitability, and hence long-run profits are subject to the constraint that the firm survive in the short run.

21.2.2 Accumulation of wealth

Farmers sometimes seem less interested in their own incomes than in ensuring that their children inherit a lot of farmland. Some might argue that the accumulation of wealth or net worth, usually in the form of farmland, is more important to most farmers than the goal of maximizing long-run profits. The maximization of long run profits and the accumulation of wealth in the form of farmland are not entirely inconsistent goals, but neither are the two goals entirely consistent.

Some nonfarm businesses pride themselves in paying consistent annual dividends to their stockholders. However, aggressive companies are more likely to reinvest such profits in the firm. If these reinvestments are successful, the price of the stock in the company will increase. Farmers make similar choices. A farmer might spend profits from last season's crop on family living expenses. A farmer interested in maximizing single-season profits might use part of last year's profits to purchase inputs such as fertilizer for this year's crop, with the hope of increased profits for the coming year. A farmer interested in the accumulation of wealth might more likely use part of last year's profits as a down payment on additional land, and the profitability of the crop for the coming season may be reduced to a degree. The balance between these three uses provides important clues with respect to the underlying goals of the farm manager.

21.2.3 Other goals

Farmers, much like consumers, are subject to peer pressure. Nearly every farmer wants to be recognized by his or her neighbors as a good farmer. This peer pressure manifests itself in curious ways. Some farmers enter contests designed to see who can produce the greatest yields for a given crop. Yield maximization is almost always inconsistent with profit maximization. Livestock shows may be enjoyable for farmers. Often there is no clear link between the characteristics of livestock deemed important in the show ring and profit maximization. However, large profits may be made if there are others who believe that such characteristics are desirable. Money can be made if a buyer desiring the particular traits can be found.

Farm machinery provides another example. Examples of farmers who appear to have as their primary goal the accumulation of the best set of farm machinery can easily be found. A self-respecting farmer would not want to be placed in a situation whereby his or her tractor was considered by the neighbors to be somehow inadequate, even though it may provide excellent service at low cost. Such peer pressure even extends to the color or brand of farm machinery, with certain brands being favored in certain areas.

The quality of life has a great deal to do with specific decisions made by the farmer. Some farmers produce cattle not to make a profit but rather to enjoy the associated life-style (to the consternation of ranchers who are at-

21.3 Time as an Input to the Production Process

tempting to produce cattle for a profit). A home on 10 acres represents a desirable hobby farm for some workers in urban areas.

Farmers normally do not think of time as an input to the production process, but time can be thought of as an input. Labor is an input only to the extent that it provides a stream of services over time that presumably increase the profitability of the firm. Farm machinery is not an input in the sense that fertilizer and seed are inputs to the production process. Rather, the farm machinery also provides a stream of services over time. It is the stream of services, not the machinery itself, that contributes to the profitability of the firm. Time suitable for performing planting, tillage, and harvest activities is limited by weather conditions, and field time used to perform one operation cannot be reused to perform another field operation.

Much of farm management involves the allocation of the scarce resource time in such a way that profits to the farm are maximized. Consider a farmer who has available during a single production season a limited number of hours $(T°)$ suitable for the performance of planting (T_p), tillage (T_t), and harvest (T_h) activities. Assume that the farmer produces two crops, corn and soybeans. The farmer has already determined the acreage of y_1 and y_2 to be grown and is interested in allocating available time to each crop. Revenue is sum of the output of the two crops multiplied by their respective prices $(R = p_1 y_1 + p_2 y_2)$. The output of each crop is a function of the time available in planting, tillage, and harvest operations for that crop. That is $y_1 = y_1(t_{p1}, t_{t1}, t_{h1}); y_2 = y_2(t_{p2}, t_{t2}, t_{h2})$.

Form the Lagrangian,

$$L = p_1 y_1(t_{p1}, t_{t1}, t_{h1}) + p_2 y_2(t_{p2}, t_{t2}, t_{h2})] \\ + \rho(T_p - t_{p1} - t_{p2}) + \gamma(T_t - t_{t1} - t_{t2}) + \psi(T_h - t_{h1} - t_{h2}) \quad (21.1)$$

where y_1 is corn, y_2 is soybeans, t_{p1} is the time used in the planting operation per unit of output y_1, and t_{p2} is the time used in the planting operation per unit of output y_2; t_{t1} is the time used for tillage operations per unit of output y_1, t_{t2} is time used for tillage operations per unit of output per unit of output y_2; and t_{h1} is the time used for harvest operations per unit of y_1.

Then the first-order conditions for single-season maximization of revenue subject to the constraint imposed by the the time available for planting, tillage and harvest operations are

$$p_1 \partial y_1 / \partial t_{p1} = \rho \quad (21.2)$$

$$p_2 \partial y_2 / \partial t_{p2} = \rho \quad (21.3)$$

$$p_1 \partial y_1 / \partial t_{t1} = \gamma \quad (21.4)$$

$$p_2 \partial y_2 / \partial t_{t2} = \gamma \quad (21.5)$$

$$p_1 \partial y_1 / \partial t_{h1} = \psi \quad (21.6)$$

$$p_2 \partial y_2 / \partial t_{b2} = \psi \tag{21.7}$$

$$T_p - t_{p1} - t_{p2} = 0 \tag{21.8}$$

$$T_t - t_{t1} - t_{t2} = 0 \tag{21.9}$$

$$T_t - t_{b1} - t_{b2} = 0 \tag{21.10}$$

By rearranging equations (21.2) to (21.7) we have

$$p_1(\partial y_1 / \partial t_{p1}) = p_2(\partial y_2 / \partial t_{p2}) = \rho \tag{21.11}$$

$$p_1(\partial y_1 / \partial t_{t1}) = p_2(\partial y_2 / \partial t_{t2}) = \gamma \tag{21.12}$$

$$p_1(\partial y_1 / \partial t_{b1}) = p_2(\partial y_2 / \partial t_{b2}) = \psi \tag{21.13}$$

The Lagrangian multipliers in this problem can readily be interpreted as the imputed values for an additional unit of available time in the planting, tillage, or harvest seasons for each crop, in terms of revenue to the farm. For each operation, the farmer should allocate time in such a way that the last unit of time results in the same marginal increase in revenue for both outputs y_1 and y_2. In general, the Lagrangian multipliers ρ, γ, and ψ will not necessarily be the same value but will depend both on how much time is required for the operation per unit of output and how much time is available.

The Lagrangian multipliers indicate the imputed value of time in each period in the production of various commodities. If the magnitudes of the shadow prices or Lagrangian multipliers are large for a particular period, the available time is posing a severe restriction on production of the various products. A Lagrangian multiplier near zero for a particular period suggests that although time in that particular period is of some positive value in the production process, it does not pose a severe restriction.

The example presented here is only illustrative. The farmer will probably break time down into weekly or perhaps even daily increments. In a daily model, each day would have its own Lagrangian multiplier but the same marginal rules for allocating time between enterprises would apply. These rules suggest that the farmer should do first the operation that contributes the most to the revenue for the entire farm.

A similar approach could be used determining the sequencing of events for allocating farm machinery use, as well as determining the sequencing of chores to be done in allocating hired labor each day between enterprises. Mathematical programming models have been used in Kentucky, Indiana, and in other states in extension work with farmers. A primary objective of these models is to determine how available field time, labor and machinery should be allocated between corn and soybean production. The sequence of events taking place during the production season is divided into a calendar of weekly events. Farmers specify the available field time, labor, and machinery during each week of the production season, and the model allocates each time-related input according to the rules suggested here. Thus results provide an indication of how time related inputs should be allocated during each week of the growing season.

21.4 Time, Inflation, Interest Rates, and Net Worth

A dollar earned a year from now is not the same thing as a dollar earned today. A dollar spent today is not the same thing as a dollar spent a year from now. There are two reasons for this. First, a dollar earned today could have been placed in the bank and interest would have accrued. That interest is forgone if the dollar is earned a year from now. Moreover, the opportunity cost of a dollar spent today is the interest that could have been earned if the dollar had not been spent today. Current government policy at the federal level over time plays a significant role in determining the profitability of agriculture over time.

For example, the rate of inflation affects agriculture over time. Because of inflation, a dollar earned a year from now is less valuable than a dollar earned today. A dollar borrowed today can be paid back with cheaper dollars earned a year from now. Interest rates paid by banks on savings and charged by banks on loans should reflect these intertemporal differences in the value of a dollar. The interest rate charged or paid by banks less the inflation rate is sometimes called the *real interest rate*. Thus the interest rates charged or paid by banks reflect not only the real interest rate, but also the general rate of inflation in the economy.

Interest rates on low-risk investments, such as savings accounts insured by the federal government, are also of concern. The imputed value of dollars not invested in the farm can be represented by the return in a risk free investment. During the 1970s, inflation was often greater than 10 percent, but banks were allowed to pay only $5\frac{1}{4}$ percent on many savings accounts. The result was a negative real interest rate (the interest rate less inflation) on savings.

Banks made loans to farmers and others at interest rates below the general rate of inflation. They could do this because rates were broadly based on the interest rates they were paying savers. Farms were purchased at low interest rates, and because of inflation, loans were paid back with ever cheaper dollars. The policies were good for farmers and others who purchased land with borrowed dollars, and as a result, farmers wishing to take advantage rapidly bid up farmland prices and increased their net worth. The result was a massive transfer of net worth from savers to farmers who purchased land with borrowed money and from savers to other debtors, particularly debtors who put borrowed money into real estate. Not surprisingly, savers took their money out of banks and put it into land, houses, and other real estate.

Starting in the mid-1970s, the government began to deregulate interest rates paid to savers. By 1986, banks were free to determine for themselves the interest rates to be paid on any savings account. Interest rates were no longer cheap relative to the rate of inflation. The result was a transfer of net worth away from debtors and toward savers. It no longer made as much sense for farmers to borrow money for the purchase of farmland, for farmers would be usually now paying interest rates above, not below, the general rate of inflation. One impact on farmers of bank deregulation has been to make the implicit worth (imputed value, shadow price, or Lagrangian multiplier) of their own funds invested in a low-risk alternative such as an insured savings account greater than was true when interest rates on savings accounts were regulated. As a result, saving accounts now appear relatively more attractive than investment in the farm business. In addition, the cost of borrowing funds increased, meaning that farmers would invest borrowed funds in the farm business only if there was a potential for a high potential return on the investment.

By the mid-1980s, the farm export market had become weak in part because of high interest rates and a desire on the part of foreign countries to hold dollars. Because of the strong dollar, U.S agricultural commodities were expensive to foreign countries, and the general price level for agricultural commodities in export was weak. Farmers no longer bid up the price of farmland, and land values in many instances declined.

Macroeconomic policies pursued over time by the federal government can and do have a significant impact on decisions made by farmers. Time affects the opportunity cost or imputed value for dollars that could be invested in farming or as an alternative, in a low-risk savings account. Moreover, over time, inflation and deflation can increase or decrease the value of a farmer's real estate holdings and other assets, thus affecting net worth. The profitability of agriculture in a particular year is closely linked to the export market, which, in turn, is tied to exchange rates for foreign currency, interest, and inflation rates in the United States. Agriculture does not operate in a static, timeless environment at the macroeconomic level.

21.5 Discounting Revenues and Costs

Discounting is used to determine what a specific amount of revenue obtained at some future point in time would be worth today or to determine the current amount of a cost incurred at some future point in time. The examples presented here illustrate how to calculate discounted present values for a stream of revenues that occur over a period of several years, but the same approach could be applied to costs that do not all occur at the start of the production period.

21.5.1 The present value of a dollar

The present value of a dollar earned one period from now can be determined by dividing the dollar by 1 plus the market rate of interest. If the interest rate is 8 percent and the period of time is one year, the present value of a dollar is $1/1.08 = \$0.926$. Suppose that the dollar is instead earned five years from now. The present value of that dollar is $1/(1.08)^5 = \$0.681$. Suppose that an enterprise generates a dollar in revenue at the end of each of five years. The present value of the $5 thus generated is

$$1/(1.08) + 1/(1.08)^2 + 1/(1.08)^3 + 1/(1.08)^4 + 1/(1.08)^5 = \$3.99$$

(21.14)

21.5 Discounting Revenues and Cost

A general rule for determining the present value (PV) of a dollar earned at the end of each of n years is

$$PV = \Sigma \, 1/(1 + i)^n \qquad (21.15)$$

where $n = 1, N$
N = number of years
i = market interest rate.

21.5.2 Discounting revenues with the present value formula

The amount of money returned at the end of the year will probably vary from year to year. For example, if at the end of year 1, 40 dollars is returned; year 2, 50 dollars; year 3, 20 dollars; year 4, 10 dollars; and year 5, 100 dollars, the present value formula provides the value of the revenues at the start of year 1

$$PV = 40/(1 + i) + 50/(1 + i)^2 + 20/(1 + i)^3 \\ + 10/(1 + i)^4 + 100/(1 + i)^5 \qquad (21.16)$$

A general present value formula is

$$PV = \Sigma(R_j/(1 + i)^j) \quad \text{for all } j = 1, \ldots, n \text{ where } n \text{ is the number of years.}$$

R_j is the revenue from the jth year.

A farmer may consider the purchase of a machine that will return 100 dollars per year in increased revenue above any variable costs to run the machine and keep it in repair. At the end of five years, the machine is worn out but has a salvage value of $150. The present value formula can be used to determine what the farmer could afford to pay for the machine for an interest rate of 8 percent

$$PV = 100/(1.08) + 100/(1.08)^2 + 100/(1.08)^3 + 100/(1.08)^4 \\ + 100/(1.08)^5 + 150/(1.08)^5 = \$501.36 \qquad (21.17)$$

The discounted revenue from the machine is $501.36. The farmer can afford to pay up to $501.36. The current price of the machine could be subtracted from its present value (PV) to obtain the discounted net present value (NPV). If the NPV is positive and the assumptions are correct, the farmer will make money on the investment.

Such an approach could easily be applied to a large durable goods investment such as a farm tractor. The major problem is in obtaining the needed revenue data for the machine. Ideally, returns should represent the marginal revenue attributed to the machine with costs other than the purchase price of the machine subtracted. It is sometimes difficult to determine the revenues that should properly occur as a result of owning the new machine. For example, a larger tractor may result in increased revenues because of improved timing of planting, tillage, and harvest operations, but these revenues are sometimes difficult to measure.

Another issue involves the determination of the expected life of the tractor and its salvage value at the end of the expected life. The true expected life is normally very different from the assumed life that is allowed for federal tax purposes. The proper interest rate to be used is another problem. For example, the interest rate could be one of the interest rates charged by the local bank on borrowed funds, or it could be one of the rates paid on a savings account.

The present value formula has been modified to determine the present value of an asset with an infinite life span, such as a piece of land. The present value formula for an asset with an infinite life span is

$$PV = R/i \qquad (21.18)$$

where R is the annual return attributable to the asset over all costs other than the asset itself, and i is the assumed interest rate. For example, cornland with a return of $300 per acre over all costs other than the cost of the land, is worth $300/i$ dollars per acre. If the interest rate is 10 percent, the land is worth $3000 per acre. If the land is selling for $2500 dollars per acre, its net present value is 3000 − 2500 or 500 dollars per acre.

21.5.3 Compounding revenues and costs

The discounting process presented in Section 21.5.2 makes it possible to determine what revenues and costs occurring over a period of years would be if all were measured at the start of the production period. Compounding is the process used to determine revenues and costs at the end, not the beginning of the planning horizon. The examples used here apply to costs, but the same approach could be used to determine revenues at the end of the planning horizon.

The process of discounting revenues and costs may be an unfamiliar one, but the process of compounding revenues and costs should be familiar to anyone who has purchased an item with borrowed money. The process of compounding costs involves nothing more than the accumulation of the loan amount (or principal) and interest charges over the time span that the item is owned.

Suppose that a farmer purchases a truck for $10,000. The farmer intends to sell the truck at the end of three years for $6000. The farmer could have instead used the money to buy a certificate of deposit to mature in three years with a 10 percent interest rate compounded annually. At the end of the first year the truck cost the farmer $10,000(1.10) = \$11,000$. At the end of the second year, the truck cost $11,000 (1.10) = 10,000(1.10)^2 = \$12,100$. At the end of the third year, the truck cost $12,100(1.10) = 10,000 (1.10)^3 = \$13,310$. If, at the end of the third year, the farmer sells the truck for $6000, the cost of the truck was 13,310 − 6000 = $7310 over the assumed three years of ownership.

If the farmer borrows the money for the purchase of the truck from the bank, the interest charge on the loan could be used. However, the example becomes more complicated in that the farmer will likely pay back the loan in monthly or annual installments. This means that over the three years, the farmer will have, on the average, owed the bank far less than the full $10,000, and the interest payments would be based on what was actually owed. However, if the truck had not been purchased, the payments the farmer would have made to the bank on the loan over the three years would have instead been put in a savings account which would have earned interest. The interest on the savings account represents an opportunity cost that should also be charged to the truck.

A general formula for compounding costs is

$$C = C_{n-1}(1 + i) + C_{n-2}(1 + i)^2 + \cdots + C_0(1 + i)^n \qquad (21.19)$$

where C is the total costs incurred to the end of the nth year, C_0 is the cost at the start of the first year, C_{n-1} is the cost incurred at the start of the nth year, C_{n-2} is the cost incurred at the start of the $(n - 1)$th year, n is the number of years, and i is the assumed interest rate.

A similar formula could be used to discount revenues, except that revenues usually occur at the end rather than the start of the year.

21.6 Polyperiod Production and Marginal Analysis

Marginal analysis can be applied to problems in which there is time between the occurrence of costs and the return of revenue from the sale of the product. To do this, compounding or discounting is used to compare revenues obtained at the end of a year with costs occurring at the start of the year. The approach can then be expanded to take into consideration production decisions involving enterprises where both costs and returns occur over a period of several years.

Suppose that a farmer incurs production costs for output y_1 at the start of the year, but revenues do not result until the end of the year. The total revenue is

$$TR = p_1 y_1 \qquad (21.20)$$

where y_1 is output and p_1 is the price of the output.

The total cost (TC) is a function of output:

$$TC = c(y_1) \qquad (21.21)$$

Revenues occur at the end of the year, so they are discounted to the start of the year:

$$PV = TR/(1 + i) = p_1 y_1/(1 + i) \qquad (21.22)$$

Costs occur at the start of the year and need not be discounted.
The profit equation discounted to the start of the year is

$$\Pi = TR/(1 + i) - TC \qquad (21.23)$$

First-order conditions require that the slope of the production function be equal to zero:

$$d\Pi/dy_1 = (dTR/dy_1)[1/(1 + i)] - dTC/dy_1 = 0 \quad (21.24)$$
$$= p_1/(1 + i) = c'(y_1)$$

In a purely competitive model, marginal revenue and price are the same thing. The discounted marginal revenue or price ($p_1/(1 + i)$) must equal the marginal cost [$c'(y_1)$].

The problem could also be solved for first-order conditions at the end of the production season. Costs would be compounded, but revenues occurring at the end of the production season would not be compounded. The total compounded cost would be

$$TC(1 + i) = c(y_1)(1 + i) \quad (21.25)$$

Profit is

$$\Pi = TR - TC(1 + i) \quad (21.26)$$
$$= p_1 y_1 - c(y_1)(1 + i)$$

The first-order conditions again require the slope of the profit function to be zero:

$$d\Pi/dy_1 = p_1 - c'(y_1)(1 + i) = 0 \quad (21.27)$$

$$p_1 = c'(y_1)(1 + i) \quad (21.28)$$

$$p_1/(1 + i) = c'(y_1) \quad (21.29)$$

In general, the marginal conditions remain the same regardless of whether the problem is solved at the start or the end of the year.

Now suppose that a farmer produces two commodities in which revenues occur at the end of the year but costs occur at the start of the year. The farmer has the choice of producing commodity y_1, which returns revenues in each of the years in a three-year planning horizon; or producing commodity y_2, which does not bring any returns in years 1 and 2, but does bring a large return at the end of year 3. Both commodities incur costs for each year that are assumed to be paid at the start of each year. The market rate of interest is i, and the farmer wishes to choose the combination of y_1 and y_2 that will result in maximum discounted profits over the three-year period.

The discounted revenue from the sale of y_1 at the end of year 1 is

$$R_{11} = p_{11} y_1/(1 + i) \quad (21.30)$$

where R_{11} is the revenue obtained from y_1 at the end of year 1 discounted to the start of year 1, and p_{11} is the price of y_1 at the end of year 1.

21.6 Polyperiod Production and Marginal Analysis

The revenue from the sale of y_1 produced during year 2, discounted to the start of year 1, is

$$R_{12} = p_{12} y_1 / (1 + i)^2 \qquad (21.31)$$

where R_{12} is the revenue obtained from y_1 at the end of year 2 discounted to the start of year 1, and p_{12} is the price of y_1 at the end of year 2.

The revenue from the sale of y_1 produced during year 3, discounted to the start of year 1, is

$$R_{13} = p_{13} y_1 / (1 + i)^3 \qquad (21.32)$$

where R_{13} is the revenue obtained from y_1 at the end of year 3 discounted to the start of year 1, and p_{13} is the price of y_1 at the end of year 3.

Since y_2 does not generate any revenues at the end of years 1 and 2, the revenue from y_2 can be calculated from the formula

$$R_{23} = p_{23} y_2 / (1 + i)^3 \qquad (21.33)$$

where R_{23} is the revenue obtained from y_2 at the end of year 3 discounted to the start of year 1, and p_{23} is the price of y_2 at the end of year 3.

The present value of all revenues in all periods from the sale of y_1 is

$$R_1 = R_{11} + R_{12} + R_{13} \qquad (21.34)$$

The present value of all revenues in all periods from the sale of y_2 is

$$R_2 = 0 + 0 + R_{23} \qquad (21.35)$$

since revenues from y_2 occur only at the end of period 3.

Costs for the production of y_1 and y_2 accrue in each year, despite the fact that y_2 only produces returns in year 3. Costs in each year are assumed to be a function of the output level. Since the costs for year 1 occur at the start of year 1, they need not be discounted. Costs occurring at the start of year 2 are discounted by the factor $1 + i$, and costs occurring at the start of year 3 are discounted by the factor $(1 + i)^2$.

Total discounted costs for the production of y_1 are

$$C_1 = C_{11} + C_{12} + C_{13} \qquad (21.36)$$

where C_1 is total costs over the three-year period;
C_{11} is $c(y_{11})$ or the costs of producing y_1 in year 1 paid at the start of year 1
C_{12} is $c(y_{12})/(1 + i)$, or the costs of producing y_1 in year 2 paid at the start of year 2
and C_{13} is $c(y_{13})/(1 + i)^2$, or the costs of producing y_1 in year 3 paid at the start of year 3

Total discounted costs for the production of y_2 are

$$C_2 = C_{21} + C_{22} + C_{23} \qquad (21.37)$$

where C_2 = total costs over the three year period
$2C_{21} = c(y_{21})$ or the costs of producing y_2 in year 1 paid at the start of year 1;
$C_{22} = c(y_{22})/(1 + i)$, or the costs of producing y_2 in year 2 paid at the start of year 2
$C_{23} = c(y_{23})/(1 + i)^2$, or the costs of producing y_2 in year 3 paid at the start of year 3

Profit is discounted revenue less discounted costs for both products

$$\Pi = R_1 + R_2 - C_1 - C_2 \qquad (21.38)$$

The necessary conditions for profit maximization require that the slope of the profit function be equal to zero with respect to both outputs

$$\partial \Pi / \partial y_1 = \partial R_1 / \partial y_1 - \partial C_1 / \partial y_1 = 0 \qquad (21.39)$$

$$\partial \Pi / \partial y_2 = \partial R_2 / \partial y_2 - \partial C_2 / \partial y_2 = 0 \qquad (21.40)$$

$$\partial R_1 / \partial y_1 = \partial C_1 / \partial y_1 \qquad (21.41)$$

$$\partial R_2 / \partial y_2 = \partial C_2 / \partial y_2 \qquad (21.42)$$

Discounted marginal revenue must equal discounted marginal cost for both outputs. For outputs y_1 and y_2,

$$\partial R_1 / \partial y_1 = p_{11}/(1 + i) + p_{12}/(1 + i)^2 + p_{13}/(1 + i)^3 \qquad (21.43)$$

$$\partial R_2 / \partial y_2 = p_{23}/(1 + i)^3 \qquad (21.44)$$

$$\partial C_1 / \partial y_1 = c'(y_{11}) + c'(y_{12})/(1 + i) + c'(y_{13})/(1 + i)^2 \qquad (21.45)$$

$$\partial C_2 / \partial y_2 = c'(y_{21}) + c'(y_{22})/(1 + i) + c'(y_{23})/(1 + i)^2 \qquad (21.46)$$

If second-order conditions are met, these conditions would determine the allocation between the production of y_1 and y_2 that would globally maximize discounted profits under the assumed interest rate. These relationships can be rearranged to show that the ratio of discounted marginal revenues to discounted marginal costs should be equal to 1 in the production of both outputs.

If the farmer were constrained by the availability of inputs required to produce y_1 and y_2, the ratio of discounted marginal revenues to discounted marginal costs should be the same for the production of both outputs. However, in this case, the ratio would be equal to a number greater than 1.

21.7 Concluding Comments

This chapter has illustrated a number of ways in which time can be incorporated into economic analysis. The labor, machinery, and field time available to a farmer during each period within the calendar of events occurring for a production season are limited, and available time within each period must be allocated consistent with the equimarginal return rule. Time is of even greater concern within a multiperiod production framework. Goals and objective of farmers may change as the length of the planning horizon is altered. Application of the equimarginal return rules within a planning horizon encompassing many production periods involves either the compounding or discounting of revenues and costs. However, even within a multiple-period framework, the equimarginal return rules still apply.

Problems and Exercises

1. Outline alternative goals a farmer might pursue other than short-run profit maximization. Are there possible goals in addition to those listed in this book?

2. Why does compounding and discounting become an inherent part of marginal analysis in a multiperiod framework?

3. Suppose that an enterprise generates $1000 in revenue in each of five years. The interest rate is 9 percent. What is the present value of the stream of revenue generated over the five-year period?

4. Assuming an interest rate of 10 percent, how much is an acre of land worth that generates $200 in returns over costs (other than interest and principal payments on the land)? Why are farmers frequently willing to pay more than this value for an acre of land?

5. Suppose the following schedule of revenues and costs:

Year	Revenue at End of Year	Costs at Start of Year
1	$2000	$1000
2	3000	2000
3	2000	4000
4	5000	1000
5	2000	1000

a. Calculate the present value of revenues over costs at the start of year 1.
b. Calculate the future value of revenue over costs at the end of year 5.

22. Linear Programming and Marginal Analysis

This chapter provides a basic overview of linear programming, and discusses its relationship to the maximization and minimization techniques used for the factor-factor and product-product models. The assumptions of linear programming are given. The fixed-proportion production function, which forms the basis for linear programming, is compared with the linear production function. A simple linear programming problem is illustrated using graphics, and solved numerically using the simplex solution algorithm. An application of linear programming to a small farm resource allocation problem is presented.

Key Terms and Definitions:

Classical Optimization Methods
Operations Research
Linear Programming
Mathematical Programming
Computer Programming
Algorithm
Nonlinearities
Linearity
Additivity
Divisibility
Nonnegativity
Single-Valued Expectations

Fixed-Proportion Production Function
Linear Production Function
Activities
Resource Constraints
Inequality Constraint
Feasible Solution Area
Simplex Algorithm
Slack Variables
Duality
Personal Microcomputer

22.1 Introduction

This book has made extensive use of what is sometimes referred to as classical optimization methods. Classical optimization methods involve the maximization or minimization of a function subject to one or more constraints. To do this, a new variable called a Lagrangian multiplier is added for each constraint, and the maximization or minimization entails setting the partial derivatives of the Lagrangian function with respect to each variable, including the Lagrangian multipliers, equal to zero. The Lagrangian multipliers can be interpreted as the increase (or decrease) in the function to be maximized (or minimized) associated with a relaxation of the constraint by 1 unit. Lagrangian multipliers have substantive economic interpretation for a diverse array of problems.

Classical optimization methods are but one method for maximizing or minimizing a function subject to one or more constraints. The field of operations research is broadly concerned with problems of constrained maximization or minimization. Operations research has applications in economics and agricultural economics, as well as in many other areas in which problems are found that involve finding the optimal value of a function subject to one or more constraints.

Mathematical programming is another general term commonly used to describe problems that involve constrained maximization or minimization. The term *algorithm* as in mathematical programming algorithm is used to refer to a method or procedure for solving a mathematical programming problem.

Students sometimes confuse mathematical programming with computer programming. The two terms are entirely different. *Computer programming* refers to the process of providing a computer with a set of instructions to tell it what calculations to perform. Mathematical programming algorithms usually require many calculations, and therefore can quickly become complicated. A computer is usually used to perform the large number of complicated calculations, so computer programming is often needed to solve mathematical programming problems. However, small mathematical programming problems can be solved without the aid of a computer. Moreover, computer programs can be written that have nothing to do with maximizing or minimizing a function subject to constraints.

The problems in this text that involved maximizing or minimizing a function subject to a constraint are actually mathematical programming problems. The procedure that involved setting the partial derivatives of the Lagrangian function equal to zero could be thought of as the algorithm for solving the problems. The graphic representation could be thought of as the graphical solution to a specific mathematical programming problem. No computer was needed to find a solution.

22.2 Classical Optimization and Linear Programming

Mathematical programming can be divided into two major subcategories, nonlinear programming and linear programming. The problems that involved constrained maximization using the Lagrangian function are examples of nonlinear programming problems. In every case, either the objective function was nonlinear, or the constraint was nonlinear, or both. The production function $y = f(x_1, x_2)$ can be either a linear or a nonlinear function. The production function $y = A x_1^a x_2^b$ is clearly nonlinear. The constraint $C = v_1 x_1 + v_2 x_2$ is clearly linear. Becoming familiar with classical optimization methods makes one familiar with a specific procedure or algorithm for solving certain nonlinear programming problems.

Linear programming involves the maximization or minimization of a linear function subject to linear constraints. Unlike classical optimization problems, in which at least one of the functions was nonlinear, with linear programming, every function is linear.

It may come as a surprise that linear programming has broad application to agricultural economics. Most of marginal analysis is dependent on relationships that involve nonlinearities. The most basic example is the law of diminishing returns. Cost and production functions are seldom linear. Isoquants and product transformation functions are usually curved, meaning that there is no limit to the number of possible solutions (combinations of inputs or outputs) as relative prices on inputs and outputs change.

The assumptions underlying linear programming in some ways are more restrictive and in other ways are less restrictive than the assumptions inherent in classical optimization techniques. Classical optimization required at least one of the functions to be nonlinear. If isoquants or product transformation functions did not have continuously turning tangents, a single unique solution to the constrained maximization problem would not exist. Isoquants and product transformation functions represented in linear programming models never have continuously turning tangents. Nonlinear functions are approximated with short or piecewise linear segments. If an isoquant or product transformation function is nonlinear, any change in the relative prices will result in a change in the quantities of the inputs used or the products produced. With certain linear programming problems, even large changes in relative prices will not lead to a change in the relative quantities of inputs used or products produced.

With classical optimization methods, corner solutions that involved the use of none of certain of the inputs, or production of none of certain of the outputs were not allowed. All constraints must hold in strict equality. This is because derivatives are defined only on open sets. Corner solutions are commonplace with linear programming. Inputs are not often fully utilized and therefore constraints need not hold in strict equality. Possible outputs are not necessarily always produced. Classical optimization methods are therefore more flexible in that all functions do not have to be linear, but less flexible in not allowing for corner solutions.

22.3 Assumptions of Linear Programming

Five basic assumptions underlie any linear programming model. These assumptions are (1) linearity, (2) additivity, (3) divisibility, (4) nonnegativity, and (5) single-valued expectations. Mathematical programming techniques other than linear programming can sometimes be used for problems in which one or more of the assumptions of linear programming have been violated.

Linearity. The objective function and the constraints in a linear programming problem are linear. If the linearity assumption does not hold, one of the nonlinear programming techniques is required. Classical optimization methods are well known, but many other advanced techniques are available for solving optimization problems involving one or more nonlinear functions. A technique called *quadratic programming,* for example, can be used when the objective function is quadratic in form.

Additivity. Suppose that in order to produce a unit of y_1, 2 units of x_1, and 3 units of x_2 are required. Two units of output will require 4 units of x_1 and 6 units of x_2. Five hundred units of y_1 will require 1000 units of x_1 and 1500 units of x_2. Hence constant returns to scale exist. The additivity assumption is fundamental to the use of linear programming in production economics.

Divisibility. If 1 unit of y_1 can be produced using 1 unit of x_1 and 1 unit of x_2, then $\frac{1}{2}$ unit of y_1 can be produced with $\frac{1}{2}$ input of x_1 and $\frac{1}{2}$ unit of x_2. One-tenth of a unit of y_1 can be produced by using one-tenth of a unit of x_1 and one-tenth of a unit of x_2. The divisibility assumption becomes silly for certain categories of agricultural inputs. A linear programming problem might call for a solution that requires 1.457 bulls and 3.567 tractors. A technique called *integer programming* will force the solution to contain only integer values for inputs that cannot be divided, such as a tractor or a bull.

Nonnegativity. The solution should not require that negative quantities of an input or resource be used. The usual solution algorithms for linear programming models do not allow for negative quantities of inputs to be used nor negative outputs to be produced. Zero quantities for both outputs and inputs are allowed.

Single-Valued Expectations. Linear programming models assume that coefficients such as input requirements and prices are known a priori with certainty. For example, if wheat, corn, and soybeans are to be included as possible enterprises within a linear programming model, the prices for which these commodities sell must be known in order to construct the model. If certain coefficients are not known with certainty, one of the stochastic programming techniques might be used.

22.4 Technical Requirements and Fixed-Proportion Production Functions

The production function underlying a linear programming model is sometime called a *fixed-proportion production function*. The fixed-proportion function is sometimes written as

$$y_1 = \min(a_1 x_1, a_2 x_2) \tag{22.1}$$

Production is determined by the most limiting input. Suppose that $a_1 = 4$ and $a_2 = 6$; and that 10 units of x_1 is available and 15 units of x_2 is available. The output of y_1 is determined by the smaller of $4 \times 10 = 40$ or $6 \times 15 = 90$. In this example, y_1 would be 40.

The fixed-proportion production function is very different from the linear production function:

$$y_1 = a_1 x_1 + a_2 x_2 \tag{22.2}$$

The linear production function assumes that inputs x_1 and x_2 can substitute for each other. The marginal product of x_1 is a_1 and the marginal product of x_2 is a_2. The $MRSx_1x_2$ is $-a_1/a_2$.

With the fixed-proportion production function, one input does not substitute for the other, but rather, inputs must be used in fixed proportions with each other. The isoquant map for a fixed proportion production function is a series of right angles with a production surface similar to that illustrated in case 1 of Figure 12.2. The isoquant map for the linear production function consists of isoquants with a constant slope of $-a_1/a_2$. The surface is as illustrated in case 5 of Figure 12.2.

22.5 A Simple Constrained Maximization Problem

Suppose that the following objective function is to be maximized subject to constraints:

$$\text{Maximize } 4y_1 + 5y_2 \tag{22.3}$$

where y_1 and y_2 are two commodities. The 4 and 5 represent the price per unit of y_1 and y_2, respectively. The constraints are:

$$\text{Resource or input } x_1: \quad 2y_1 + 1y_2 \leq 12 \tag{22.4}$$

$$\text{Resource or input } x_2: \quad 1y_1 + 2y_2 \leq 16 \tag{22.5}$$

There are 12 units of resource or input x_1 available, and 16 units of resource or input x_2 available. Units of commodity y_1 each require 2 units of x_1 and 1 unit of x_2. Units of commodity x_2 each require 1 unit of x_1 and 2 units of x_2.

All the available x_1 and x_2 need not be used, as indicated by the inequality signs. The matrix

$$\begin{array}{ccc} y_1 & y_2 & \\ 2 & 1 & x_1 \\ 1 & 2 & x_2 \end{array} \tag{22.6}$$

represents the technical input requirements for x_1 and x_2 needed to produce 1 unit of y_1 and y_2. In this example both x_1 and x_2 are needed in order to produce either y_1 or y_2, but this need not always be the case, and some of the input requirements could be zero. The columns of matrix (22.6) are sometimes referred to as the *activities*, while the rows are referred to as *resource constraints*.

This linear programming problem and its solution can be illustrated using a graph with y_1 on the horizontal axis and y_2 on the vertical axis (Figure 22.1). Suppose that only y_1 were produced. According to the first constraint, 12/2 or 6 units could be produced. Therefore, the first constraint intersects the y_1 axis

22.5 A Simple Constrained Maximization Problem

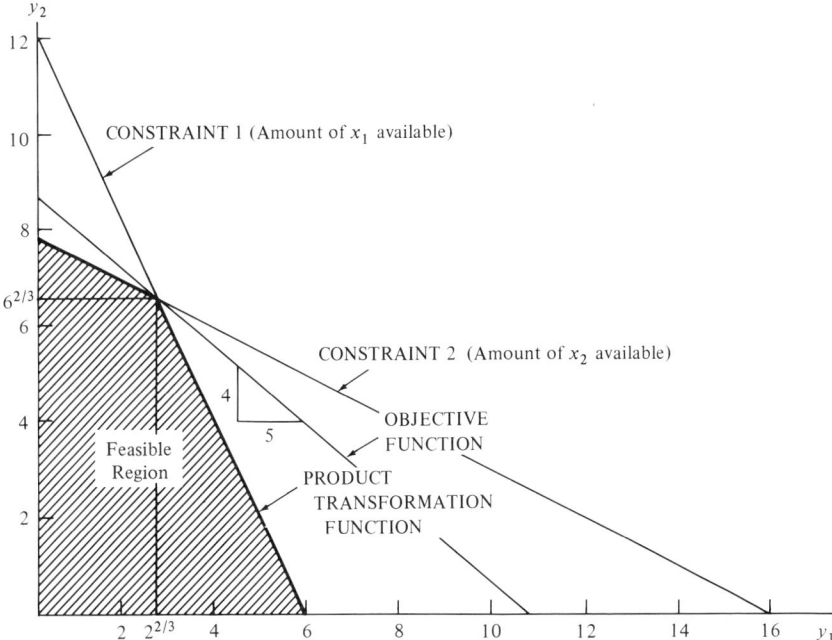

Figure 22.1 Linear Programming Solution in Product Space

at 6 units. Now suppose that only y_2 were produced. According to the first constraint, 12/1 units or 12 units could be produced. The first constraint intersects the vertical axis at 12 units. The slope of the first constraint would be 12/6 or 2:1.

If only y_1 were produced, the second constraint would intersect the y_1 axis at 16/1 or 16. If only y_2 were produced, the second constraint would intersect the y_2 axis at 16/2 or 8. The slope of the second constraint would be 8/16 or 1:2. If y_1 appears on the horizontal axis, and y_2 appears on the vertical axis, the slope of each constraint is equal to the coefficient on y_1 divided by the coefficient on y_2.

The area inside both constraints represents the feasible solution area. The feasible solution area looks like a diagram representing a product transformation curve. The product transformation curve is made up of portions of each constraint that lie inside the other constraint. Instead of being a smooth, continuously turning curve, this product transformation curve is approximated with two linear segments, each with a different but constant downward slope. The constraints intersect at the point where the slope of the linear segments of the product transformation function change.

If less than $2\frac{2}{3}$ units of y_1 is produced, the slope of the product transformation function is the same as the slope of the second constraint. If more than $2\frac{2}{3}$ units of y_1 is produced, the slope of the product transformation function is the same as the slope of constraint 1. The slope of the product transformation function where the two constraints intersect and the output of y_1 is exactly $2\frac{2}{3}$ units is undefined.

The objective function is identical to the revenue function in the product-

product model. The slope of the objective function will also be equal to the coefficient on y_1 divided by the coefficient on y_2 or 4:5 in this example.

A small linear programming problem can be solved with only some carefully drawn graphics. The solution represents the largest possible revenue consistent with the specified constraints. This means that the revenue function must be pushed as far as possible from the origin of the graph, but still touching the feasible solution area represented by the area inside both constraints.

For this problem, there are but three possible solutions, not counting $0y_1$, $0y_2$. However, if the objective function has exactly the same slope as one of the constraints, all y_1 can be produced, all y_2 can be produced, or the combination of y_1 and y_2 that occurs at the point where the two constraints intersect can be produced. If the objective function has the same slope as one of the constraints, an infinite number of combinations of y_1 and y_2 can be found that maximize the objective function.

The first solution would to be to produce all y_2 and no y_1. Constraint number 2 (the availability of x_2) would limit the production of y_2 to only 8 units, despite the fact that there is enough x_1 to produce 12 units. The remainder of x_1 would be unused, or in disposal. For this corner solution to occur, the relative price ratio of y_1 and y_2 (p_1/p_2) would have to exceed the slope of the second constraint, which in this problem is 1:2. This would imply that the price of y_2 would need to be more than twice the price of y_1. If all y_1 were produced, revenue for this problem would be 5 × 8 or $40.

The second solution would be to produce all y_1 and no y_2. In this case, constraint 1 (the availability of x_1) would limit production of y_1 to only 6 units, and x_2 would be in disposal. For this solution to occur, the relative price ratio of y_1 and y_2 (p_1/p_2) would have to be less than the slope of the second constraint, which in this problem is 2:1. This would imply that the price of y_2 would have to be less than half the price of y_1, or that y_1 is more than twice the price of y_2. If all y_1 were produced, revenue for this problem would be 4 × 6 or $24.

The third solution would be to produce the mix represented by the intersection of the two constraints. A carefully drawn graph will reveal that this mix is $2\frac{2}{3}$ units of y_1 and $6\frac{2}{3}$ units of y_2. For this solution to occur, the price of y_2 would need to be less than twice the price of y_1, but greater than one half the price of y_1. This implies a price ratio of

$$1/2 < p_1/p_2 < 2/1$$

The price ratio for this problem of 4/5 falls within this range. If this combination were produced, revenue would be $4 \times 2\frac{2}{3} + 5 \times 6\frac{2}{3} = \$44$. The $44 represents the maximum revenue possible given the price ratios and the two constraints. Both of the other possible solutions yield less revenue.

One final possibility exists. Suppose that the slope of the objective function were exactly the same as the slope of one of the two constraints. If the slope of the objective function were exactly $\frac{1}{2}$, as would be the case if the relative prices were $\frac{4}{8}$, then the solution that produced all y_2 would result in the exact same revenue as the solution that produced a combination ($8 \times 8 = 8 \times 6\frac{2}{3}$

+ 4 × $2\frac{2}{3}$ = 64). In that case, the linear programming problem would maximize the function either if all y_2 or the combination of y_1 and y_2 were produced. Any combination consistent with the constraints that called for the production of more than $6\frac{2}{3}$ units of y_2 would also result in the same revenue. In this case there is not a single solution to the linear programming problem.

If the relative prices were in the ratio 2/1, such as 8/4, the solution that produced all y_1 would result in the same revenue as that obtained from the combination (8 × 6 = 8 × $2\frac{2}{3}$ + 4 × $6\frac{2}{3}$ = 48). The same problem would result. If this were to occur, computer routines designed to solve linear programming problems usually warn the user that the solution is not unique.

22.6 Other Approaches for Solving Linear Programming Models

The graphical presentation of a linear programming problem is useful in establishing the linkages between linear programming and the product-product model. However, the diagrammatic approach cannot be used for problems that involve the production of more than two outputs. Diagrams become messy for problems involving a large number of constraints. Numerous algorithms are available for solving linear programming problems. The simplex algorithm is widely known. For small problems, the simplex algorithm is simple enough that the needed calculations can be performed by hand.

Computer programs based on the simplex algorithm for solving linear programming problems are available. However, most computerized algorithms used in agricultural economics make use of algorithms for solving linear programming problems that are more complicated to understand than the simplex algorithm but require fewer calculations by the computer. The problem of developing algorithms that solve various mathematical programming problems while minimizing the required computer time is a major research effort at some universities.

Algorithms for solving linear programming problems on a small, personal microcomputer are available. The size of the problem in terms of the number of columns (or activities) and the number of rows (or constraints) place limits on the size of the problem that can readily be solved on a small computer within a short period.

Currently available from several vendors are algorithms that will solve linear programming problems up to 100 × 200 in matrix size, and within a few minutes on a personal computer at least 256K in size. Large university computers are able to solve very large linear programming problems within minutes or even seconds of computer time.

The solve time for a linear programming problem seems to increase exponentially, rather than linearly, with the addition of rows and columns. A problem with 100 rows and 100 columns would probably take substantially more than twice as much time to solve as one with a 50 × 50 matrix. Large and complex mathematical programming problems still require large and fast computers for quick solutions.

22.7 The Simplex Method

The problem presented graphically in Section 22.4 will be solved using hand calculations with the aid of the simplex method. The problem was

$$4y_1 + 5y_2 \tag{22.7}$$

where y_1 and y_2 are two commodities. The 4 and 5 represent the price per unit of y_1 and y_2, respectively.

The constraints are

$$2y_1 + 1y_2 \leq 12$$

$$1y_1 + 2y_2 \leq 16 \tag{22.8}$$

$$y_1, y_2 \geq 0 \tag{22.9}$$

where the coefficients on y_1 and y_2 represent the technical requirements for x_1 and x_2 per unit of output. Input x_1 has 12 units available and x_2 has 16 units available.

The first step is to introduce two new variables, called *slack variables* (s_1 and s_2). Slack variables are used to convert the inequalities into equalities. One is required for each inequality constraint. The slack variables can each be thought of as a garbage dump for holding units of input x_1 or x_2 not being used in the solution. The coefficients on slack variables are initially zeros in the objective function. The coefficient on a slack variable that appears in an equation is 1, and the coefficient on the slack variables not appearing in an equation is zero. At the start, no y_1 or y_2 is produced, and therefore the value of the objective function is zero. The problem is then rewritten as

$$2y_1 + 1y_2 + 1s_1 + 0s_2 = 12 \tag{22.10}$$

$$1y_1 + 2y_2 + 0s_1 + 1s_2 = 16 \tag{22.11}$$

$$4y_1 + 5y_2 + 0s_1 + 0s_2 = 0 \tag{22.12}$$

The 12 and 16 in equations (22.10) and (22.11) are sometimes referred to as the right-hand side (RHS), since they appear on the right-hand side. The right-hand side represents the availability of inputs or resources x_1 and x_2. The problem can be rewritten as follows:

Row \ Column	y_1	y_2	s_1	s_2	RHS
x_1	2	1	1	0	12
x_2	1	2	0	1	16
Objective	4	5	0	0	0

(22.13)

22.7 The Simplex Method

The usual place to start is to bring in units of the output or activity with the largest price or coefficient in the objective function. This would be y_2. However, it really makes no difference, and y_1 could be chosen. In this example, the conventional rule is followed and y_2 is chosen. Thus y_2 becomes what is called the *pivotal column*.

Since the objective function is to be maximized, the most limiting input must be determined. Each unit of y_2 requires 2 units of x_2 and 16 units of x_2 are available. Each unit of y_2 requires 1 unit of x_1 and 12 units of x_1 are available. Thus x_2 is most limiting ($16/2 = 8 < 12/1 = 12$). The row labeled x_2 becomes what is called the *pivotal row*.

Every element in the x_2 row is divided by the coefficient that appears at the intersection of the pivotal row and the pivotal column, 2 in this case. This results in a table with a new row x_2 labeled nx_2

Row \ Column	y_1	y_2	s_1	s_2	RHS
x_1	2	1	1	0	12
nx_2	$1/2 = 0.5$	$2/2 = 1$	$0/2 = 0$	$1/2 = 0.5$	$16/2 = 8$
Objective	4	5	0	0	0

(22.14)

The new x_1 row (nx_1) is found by subtracting from the old x_1 row the product of the element in the nx_2 row and the column under consideration times the element at the intersection of entering column y_2 and the x_1 row. Suppose that the element to appear in column y_1 of row x_1 is to be found. That number will be $2 - 0.5 \times 1$. The number 2 appears in the old x_1 row for column y_1, a 0.5 appears in row nx_2 for column y_1, and 1 appears at the intersection of the entering y_2 column and the x_1 row. Following the same rule, the corresponding new element at row x_1 and column y_2 is $1 - 1 \times 1 = 0$. Similarly, the new element at row x_1 and column s_1 is $1 - 0 \times 1 = 1$, and so on. This results in the new matrix

Row \ Column	y_1	y_2	s_1	s_2	RHS
nx_1	1.5	0	1	-0.5	4
nx_2	0.5	1	0	0.5	8
Objective	4	5	0	0	0

(22.15)

A similar approach is used on the objective function row. The new element for the intersection of the objective row and column y_1 is $4 - 0.5 \times 5 = 1.5$. The new element for the intersection of the objective row and the right-hand side is $0 - 8 \times 5 = -40$. This number is the negative of the current objective function value. Notice also that 40 was the profit in the graphical solution when only y_2 entered. The completed matrix is

Row \ Column	y_1	y_2	s_1	s_2	RHS	
nx_1	1.5	0	1	−0.5	4	
nx_2	0.5	1	0	0.5	8	
nObjective	1.5	0	0	−2.50	−40	(22.16)

If all numbers appearing in the columns representing outputs are 0 or negative, the optimal solution has been found. In this example, the value at the intersection of the y_1 column and the new objective row is positive, indicating that production of y_1 will further increase profits. Following the same procedure, a new table is constructed. However, this time the entering row is y_1. The resultant new table is

Row \ Column	y_1	y_2	s_1	s_2	RHS	
nnx_1	1	0	0.67	−0.33	2.67	
nnx_2	0	1	−0.33	0.67	6.67	
nnObjective	0	0	−1.00	−2.00	−44.00	(22.17)

The optimal solution has been found that maximizes revenue from the sale of y_1 and y_2 subject to the two constraints. The 2.67 and 6.67 represent the output of y_1 and y_2, respectively. The −44.00 is the negative of the objective function value. The solution produces $44 of revenue. All this information was available from the graphical solution.

However, a new piece of information is also available. The numbers appearing in the objective function row and the slack columns labeled s_1 and s_2 are the negatives of the imputed values of an additional unit of x_1 and x_2, respectively. If one additional unit of x_1 were available, it would, if allocated properly, contribute 1 additional dollar to revenue. An additional unit of x_2 would contribute 2 dollars to revenue. These are the shadow prices for x_1 and x_2. These shadow prices indicate the maximum amount that the manager would be willing to pay for the next unit of x_1 and x_2.

The shadow prices obtained from a linear programming model can be interpreted in exactly the same manner as the Lagrangian multipliers obtained using classical optimization methods. In both cases they represent the change in the objective function associated with a relaxation of the corresponding constraint by 1 unit.

If the shadow price for an additional unit of an input is $2.00, 1000 additional units of the input are not necessarily worth $2000 to the farmer. The shadow prices really apply only to the next unit of the input. Shadow prices usually decline in discrete steps as the availability of the input is increased. To be perfectly accurate, the incremental unit of the input should be infinitely small, or Δx should be dx. The same interpretation problem occurs with Lagrangian multipliers in a classical optimization model.

If the linear programming solution does not use all available units of an input, its shadow price, or implicit worth will be zero. Additional units of an input already in excess have an imputed value of zero and are worth nothing to the farmer.

22.8 Duality

In earlier chapters it was shown that any constrained maximization problem can be converted into a corresponding constrained minimization problem, and that any constrained minimization problem can be converted into a corresponding constrained maximization problem. The use of the inputs becomes the function to be minimized, the revenue function becomes the constraint.

Any linear programming problem can be converted to its corresponding dual. The primal problem might involve either the maximization or minimization of an objective function subject to constraints. If the primal is a constrained maximization problem, the dual will be a constrained minimization problem. If the primal is a constrained minimization problem, the dual will be a constrained maximization problem.

The constrained revenue maximization problem found the combination of outputs y_1 and y_2 that maximized revenue subject to the constraints and was similar to a constrained revenue maximization problem in product-product space. The corresponding dual is a constrained minimization problem. The use of inputs x_1 and x_2 is minimized subject to a revenue constraint. The problem is similar to that of finding the least cost combination of inputs in factor-factor space.

The dual of the maximization problem is

$$\text{minimize } 12x_1 + 16x_2 \tag{22.18}$$

where x_1 and x_2 are imputed costs of inputs or resources. The constraints are

$$2x_1 + 1x_2 \geq 4$$

$$1x_1 + 2x_2 \geq 5 \tag{22.19}$$

$$x_1, x_2 \geq 0 \tag{22.20}$$

Notice that the rows of the primal are the columns of the dual. The columns of the primal are the rows of the dual. The right-hand side is made up of coefficients that formerly were prices of outputs. The objective function to be minimized has coefficients that formerly were values for input availability on the right-hand side. Less than or equal to constraints now are greater than or equal to constraints.

The dual can also be solved graphically, but the axes are now inputs x_1 and x_2 rather than outputs y_1 and y_2. The first constraint will intersect the x_1 axis at 2, and the x_2 axis at 4. The second constraint will intersect the x_1 axis at 5 and the x_2 axis at 2.5 (Figure 22.2).

This time the feasible solution area lies outside of both constraints. The feasible solution area is again bounded by the two constraints. The line follow-

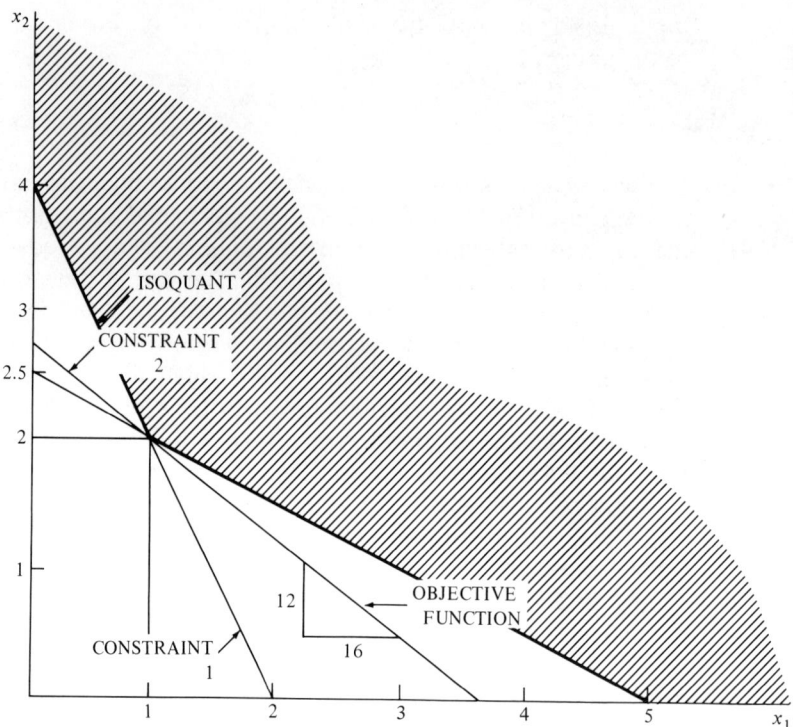

Figure 22.2 Linear Programming Solution in Factor Space

ing the portion of each constraint outside the other constraint represents an isoquant constructed of two linear segments rather than a product transformation function.

The objective function is similar to an isocost line in factor-factor space. The slope of the objective function is $-v_1/v_2$, where $v_1 = 12$ and $v_2 = 16$. Again, three solutions are possible. All x_1 can be used, all x_2 can be used, or a combination of x_1 and x_2 can be used. A carefully drawn diagram indicates that the combination would be 1 unit of x_1 and 2 units of x_2. These numbers look familiar.

The minimization problem can be solved via the simplex method. The procedure is the same as for the maximization problem with two exceptions. Since the constraints are greater than or equal, the slack variables must have negative rather than positive signs when they appear. In the maximization problem, the entering row was selected on the basis of the input that was most limiting or the smallest ratio of the right-hand-side value to the corresponding coefficient for the row in the column selected for entry. In the minimization problem, the row would be selected on the basis of the largest ratio of the right-hand-side value to the corresponding coefficient in the row for the column considered for entry.

However, it is not necessary to solve the dual if the primal has already been solved. The value for the objective function will be the same for both problems. The optimal levels of y_1 and y_2 in the primal are the shadow prices

Table 22.1 Enterprises and Net Revenues over Variable Costs

Enterprise	Units	Revenues over Variable Costs
Corn	Acres	$45 per acre
Wheat	Acres	$32 per acre
Oats	Acres	$20 per acre
Sows	10 sows	$2400 per 10 sows
Steers	10 steers	$1400 per 10 steers
Layers	10,000 layers	$5400 per 10,000 layers

for x_1 and x_2 in the dual. The optimal values for x_1 and x_2 (the 1 and 2) in the dual are the shadow prices for the primal problem. The same solution will result regardless of whether the primal or dual is solved.

22.9 An Application

The use of linear programming in agricultural economics is illustrated with a simple problem. The problem is purposely kept small in order to shorten the explanation. The problem illustrates how linear programming might be used as the basis for developing a much larger farm planning model. The farmer has the choice of the enterprises listed in Table 22.1. Net revenues per unit of each enterprise over variable costs are listed.

The farmer has 100 acres of land. Steers, sows, and layers are kept in confinement, so incremental units will not require any more land. The farm has a wheat allotment limiting wheat acreage to no more than 12 acres. Only 50 of the 100 available acres are suitable for the production of row crops. The production of grain crops will require access to no additional capital, but the production of hogs, steers, and layers will require capital for the purchase of needed animals and feed. Labor is broken into three periods, January to April, May to August, and September to December. Table 22.2 lists the resource or input availability that will comprise the right hand side. Table 22.3 provides the resource or input requirements for each enterprise.

The linear programming model was solved with a standard computer algorithm for linear programming problems. Table 22.4 provides the levels for

Table 22.2 Inputs or Resources on the Farm

Input	Amount
Total land	100 acres
Row crop land	50 acres
Wheat allotment	12 acres
January–April labor	1600 hours
May–August labor	2000 hours
September–December labor	1600 hours
Capital	$20,000

Table 22.3 Input Requirements by Enterprise.

Enterprise	Input Requirement per Enterprise Unit
Corn	
Total land	1 acre
Row crop land	1 acre
Wheat allotment	None
January–April labor	5 hours
May–August labor	1 hour
September–December labor	3 hours
Additional capital	None
Wheat	
Total land	1 acre
Row crop land	None
Wheat allotment	1 acre
January–April labor	1 hour
May–August labor	2 hours
September–December labor	3 hours
Additional capital	None
Oats	
Total land	1 acre
Row crop land	None
Wheat allotment	None
January–April labor	1 hour
May–August labor	2 hours
September–December labor	3 hours
Additional capital	None
Sows	
Total land	None
Row crop land	None
Wheat allotment	None
January–April labor	300 hours
May–August labor	300 hours
September–December labor	300 hours
Additional capital	$8000
Steers	
Total land	None
Row crop land	None
Wheat allotment	None
January–April labor	200 hours
May–August labor	20 hours
September–December labor	100 hours
Additional capital	$6000
Layers	
Total land	None
Row crop land	None
Wheat allotment	None
January–April labor	900 hours
May–August labor	900 hours
September–December labor	850 hours
Additional capital	$17,000

Table 22.4 Linear Programming Enterprise Solution

Corn	50 acres
Wheat	12 acres
Oats	38 acres
Sows	None
Steers	None
Layers	1.17647 units or 11,764.7 layers
Net returns over variable costs	$9746.94

each enterprise as determined by the model and the value of the objective function when the solution was found. Shadow prices or imputed values for an additional unit of each input are found in Table 22.5.

The shadow prices in Table 22.5 indicate what the farmer could afford to pay for an additional unit of an input. These shadow prices are the same as Lagrangian multipliers in that they give the increase in the objective function (in this case, returns over variable costs) of an additional unit of the input. This farmer could afford to pay up to $20 to rent an additional acre of land. If the land were suitable for row crops, it would be worth $25. If additional wheat allotment could be secured, up to $12 could be paid for an additional acre. Excess labor is present in all periods, so an additional unit is worth nothing. The shadow price on additional capital represents the maximum interest rate the farmer could afford to pay for the next unit of capital, in this case more than 31 percent.

22.10 Concluding Comments

This chapter has illustrated some of the linkages between linear programming and the marginal analysis models developed earlier in the text, and provided an illustration of a practical resource allocation problem that can be modeled with linear programming. A comprehensive linear programming model designed for farm planning would include far more detail, breaking down items such as labor into weekly or even daily periods, and including far more possible enterprises or activities.

Table 22.5 Imputed Values or Shadow Prices for Inputs

Total land	$25
Row crop land	$20
Wheat allotment	$12
January–April labor	0 (241.18 hours not used)
May–August labor	0 (791.18 hours not used)
September–December labor	0 (300.00 hours not used)
Additional capital	0.31765

Linear programming models that do a comprehensive and detailed job of allocating inputs among enterprises have a tendency to quickly become very large and can require a large computer to solve and/or a substantial amount of computer time. The model presented here is cheap to solve, costing only 16 cents using the MPS solver on the University of Kentucky IBM 3083 computer, so it lends itself to experimentation. The model provides an indication of the types of problems a larger and more detailed model would be able to solve.

Problems and Exercises

1. Does linear programming tighten or weaken the assumptions underlying classical optimization methods? Explain.

2. Solve the following linear programming problem by hand, using the simplex method outlined in the text.

$$\text{maximize } 2y_1 + 3y_2$$

subject to

$$3y_1 + 4y_2 \leq 20$$
$$1y_1 + 6y_2 \leq 24$$

Now find a computer program for solving the problem, and solve the problem on the computer. Compare the results with your hand solution. Now solve the dual with the same computer program, and compare the results.

3. What happens to the solution if the price of y_1 increases to $10? Does the second resource become more valuable as measured by its shadow price?

4. Are a Lagrangian multiplier obtained from a classical optimization problem and a shadow price obtained from a linear programming problem the same thing? Explain.

5. Explain why the maximum number of possible solutions to a linear programming problem can be no greater than one more than the number of constraints.

6. Set up on the computer the farm planning problem contained in this chapter, and solve. Compare the results with those obtained in the text. Are the results presented in the text accurate? Now change the prices on one of the outputs and observe what happens to the optimal solution and the shadow prices on each input or resource.

23
Frontiers in Agricultural Production Economics Research

This chapter provides an introduction to topics of current interest to agricultural economists conducting research on problems of importance in agricultural production economics. The chapter is organized around three major topic areas: (1) the treatment of management in a production function, (2) technological change and its link to a production function, and (3) unresolved conceptual issues relating to the estimation of production functions from actual data.

Key Terms and Definitions:

Management Functions
Risk Bearing
Entrepreneurship
Technological Change
Estimation of Production Functions
Correlation

23.1 Management and Agricultural Production Functions

The manager of a farm performs three functions; the manager (1) selects the amount of each output and mix of outputs to be produced in the production process, (2) determines the proper quantity of each input to be used and allocates inputs among the various outputs, and (3) bears the risk associated with the production and marketing of the products. Some agricultural economists use the term *entrepreneurship* to describe the manager's risk-bearing function. The marginal conditions outlined in this book play a key role in determining how a farm manager might best perform functions (1) and (2). As indicated in Chapter 20, the manager's willingness and ability to bear risk depends in large measure on his or her psychic makeup.

23.1.1 Alternative approaches to management

Some agricultural economists have attempted to treat management just as any another input to the production function, to be measured and treated in much the same way as inputs such as seed and fertilizer. Such an approach might yield a production function such as

$$y = A x_1^a x_2^b M^c \qquad (23.1)$$

where y is an output, x_1 and x_2 are two variable inputs, and M is management with an elasticity of production of c. With a specification such as equation (23.1), management enters the production function in a multiplicative fashion, and the marginal products of all the other inputs contain management in them.

An attempt is then made to locate or develop some measure of the skill of the manager. A sometimes used measure is the years of education of the farm manager. Analyses based on this idea have rarely, if ever, yielded anything. Usually, the researcher finds that the measure of management was unrelated to output, and the faulty measurement of the management skill is blamed for the bad results.

Agricultural economists who attempt to deal with the concept of management using an approach such as this might better find fault with the conceptual logic. Management is not an input as such. Rather the skill of the manager largely determines the amount of the other inputs to be used in the production process, as well as how these inputs are to be allocated in the production process. Good managers are those who know and can make use of the marginal principles and are willing to assume the requisite amounts of risk.

Moreover, although marginal principles can be learned in a class in production economics, farm managers without the benefit of a college course have often become aware of and make use of these principles, even though they may not be aware of the formal logic. A good deal of marginal analysis is nothing but a formal presentation of common sense; and many people have common sense with regard to decisions with respect to how much input should be used, even though they lack the formal training in agricultural economics.

Formal education may do little to change the manager's psychic makeup. The well-educated manager would not necessarily be willing to assume greater amounts of risk than the manager who lacked an extensive formal education. It is not surprising that education is not necessarily a good measure of a manager's skills.

Another approach is to assume that management is not a separate variable but rather, influences the production elasticities on the remaining variables of the model. Such logic would lead to a production function with variable elasticities of production

$$y = A x_1^{a(M)} x_2^{b(M)} \qquad (23.2)$$

where a and b are individual production elasticities which are each a function of the "level" of management M.

This model suggests that a given quantity of fertilizer will somehow produce greater output on the farm of a skilled manager than on the farm of a

23.1 Management and Agricultural Production Functions

manager who lacks skill. Just what the skills are that make a difference is not clear. Good managers have no magical skills that make it possible for them to get around the technical relationships that govern and limit the amount of output that can be produced from a given amount of input, but they are keenly aware of the amount and allocation of inputs needed to produce the greatest net revenue within the constraints imposed on the farm.

A final possibility is that the manager's skills are embodied in the coefficient or parameter A. This example is similar to the first example except that management is not treated as a separate variable. The parameter A in a Cobb–Douglas type of production function is a sort of garbage dump, embodying the collective influences of everything that the researcher did not wish to treat as an explicit input in the production function. One possible equation for A is

$$A = M^c \theta \tag{23.3}$$

where θ is the parameter with the management variable excluded.

This approach leads back to the same equation as that listed in the first approach, but possibly avoids the problem of having to find a separate measure of management. The alternative of not measuring management as a separate variable assumes by default that the manager's skills do not vary across farms, which may be equally incorrect.

23.1.2 Management and profit maximization

Some economists have traditionally aggregated inputs into four categories: land, labor, capital, and management. In fact, the treatment of management in an agricultural production function as a separate variable probably had its roots in this input categorization. Each input category receives a payment. Land receives rent, labor receives wages, capital receives interest, and management receives profit. Profit is what is left over after all other inputs or factors of production have received their payments.

The model of pure competition in long-run equilibrium yields zero profit. It is not entirely clear whether this means that the manager's skills go unrewarded. If the manager's skills were unrewarded, the manager of a firm operating in a purely competitive long-run equilibrium is indifferent to producing or shutting down. But if the manager were getting no return for his or her skills, he or she would be better off shutting down the operation, rather than wasting time doing things that net no return. In short, it is not clear why any firm should want to produce in the long-run equilibrium of pure competition.

A critic might argue that in long-run competitive equilibrium, a manager's skills are no longer needed, and therefore it is not important that these skills go unrewarded. Moreover, long-run equilibrium is perhaps never achieved, and managers keep producing because of the potential short-run pure profits. This same critic might also say that it is foolish to think about such things because no industry operates in a purely competitive environment.

Even Euler's theorem is problematic. Should management be treated as one of the inputs to the production process to be paid its *VMP*? Or does management simply get what is left over after all other factors of production have received their respective *VMP*'s? If so, management gets a return only if the production function is homogeneous of a degree less than 1. But is it not proper for management to earn its *VMP* just like every other input? Maybe Euler's theorem applies only to the long-run competitive equilibrium, and a manager is not needed. Euler the mathematician derived an algebraic relationship and was rather unconcerned as to the competitive conditions under which economists might assume that the relationship held.

The treatment of management within a production function remains a serious and unresolved problem in agricultural production economics. Each approach for the treatment of management in the production function has logic behind it, but it is easy to find fault with each approach as well.

23.2 New Technology and the Agricultural Production Function

New technology usually comes in the form of an improvement in one or more of the inputs used in the production process. There are many possible impacts of new technology on agriculture.

An improvement in one of the inputs might raise its marginal product and increase the elasticity of production for that input, causing the slope of the new production function to be greater than the old production function at a given level of input use. An improvement in one of the inputs might cause the marginal product of one or more of the other inputs to the production process to increase. An increase in the slope of the production function will cause the *VMP* for all the affected inputs to rise, resulting in an increased profit-maximizing level of use for any input whose marginal product is affected by the technology. The development of hybrid seed corn not only raised the marginal product of seed, but undoubtedly also increased the marginal product of other inputs, such as nitrogen fertilizer.

A second and perhaps less likely possibility is that the new technology shifts the intercept but not the slope of the production function. Output with the new production function is increased relative to the old production function, but the marginal products of the inputs are unaffected. In this case, the profit-maximizing level of input use will not change, but the output will increase at the profit-maximizing level of input use.

A third possibility is that the new technology lowers the per unit cost of production. The new technology is adopted because with the new technology, one or more of the input prices are reduced. This amounts to a reduction in the price (v) of input x. As a result of the price reduction, the profit-maximizing level of input use will be increased. An example of a cost-reducing technology is the development of a new pesticide that is as effective as the old but at a lower per acre cost.

New technology will usually cause output to increase over time. Figure 23.1 illustrates some possible effects of new technology in a two-input setting. Diagram A illustrates a case in which the new technology makes input x_2 more productive relative to input x_1. Isoquants farther out are positioned closer and closer to the x_2 axis.

New technology could cause the per unit cost of the input to decrease, resulting in increased use of the input experiencing the price reduction for a

23.2 New Technology and the Agricultural Production Function

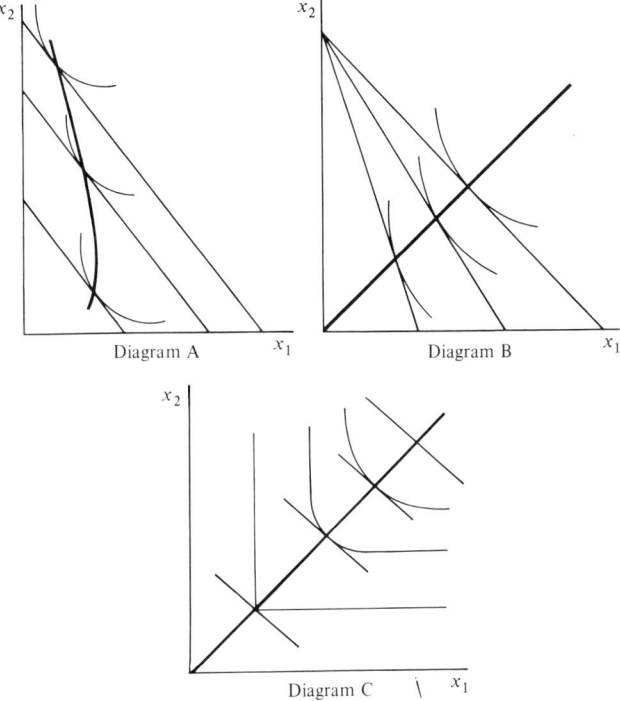

Figure 23.1 Some Possible Impacts of Technological Change

given budget outlay (diagram B). An example would be the development of a new herbicide that was as effective at controlling a particular weed but at a lower cost per acre than before. Such a new technology may or may not affect the use of the other inputs, depending on the shape of the isoquants.

New technology could also change the shape of the isoquants and therefore result in an increase in the elasticity of substitution (diagram C). A large elasticity of substitution is desirable in that it allows for significant changes in the mix of inputs that can be used to produce a commodity in the face of changes in relative input prices and technology that makes possible the substitution of cheap inputs for expensive inputs. Technology that allows a farmer to produce methane from farm manure is an example.

23.2.1 Some examples

Suppose that the production function is

$$y = a + bx + cx^2 \tag{23.4}$$

where $a, b > 0 \quad c < 0$

If the new technology shifts the entire production function without any change in the marginal product of x, the parameter a will have increased. It is unlikely that output would be produced in the absence of the input.

An increase in the marginal product of x could occur as a result of the parameter b becoming larger or as a result of the parameter c becoming less negative. This is the probable impact of much new technology.

Now consider the production function

$$y = a + bx_1 + cx_1^2 + dx_2 + ex_2^2 \tag{23.5}$$

where a, b, c, d, and e are parameters. New technology that affects x_1 will not change the marginal product of x_2.

Now suppose that the production function has an interaction term with a corresponding parameter f:

$$y = a + bx_1 + cx_1^2 + dx_2 + ex_2^2 + fx_1x_2 \tag{23.6}$$

New technology that affects input x_1 will probably change the parameters b, c, and f. Since the parameter f is part of the *MPP* for x_2 also, the new technology for x_1 will change the *MPP* of both x_1 and x_2. Normally, f would be expected to be positive, such that the new technology would increase the marginal product of x_2 as well. New technology might also increase the value of f, even if f were negative.

Suppose the Cobb–Douglas type of production function

$$y = Ax_1^a x_2^b \tag{23.7}$$

One explanation for parameter A of the Cobb–Douglas type of production function is that it represents the current state of the production technology at any point in time. A change in the parameter A will change the slope of the production function and the individual *MPP*'s for both inputs. The parameter A appears multiplicatively in each *MPP*. Moreover, changes in either a or b result in a change in the *MPP* for each input. Again a and b both appear in the *MPP*'s for x_1 and x_2.

If, as a result of the new technology, the price of one of the inputs declines, there will normally be an increase in the use of the input that experienced the price decrease. The use of the other inputs (that do not experience a price decrease) may increase, decrease, or stay the same, depending on whether the other inputs are technical complements, competitive, or independent.

23.2.2 Time and technology

For an agricultural economist dealing with a problem in a static, timeless environment, the impacts of new technology are of little concern. A production function estimated from single period cross-sectional data has as an underlying assumption the state of the technology that existed at the time for which the data are available.

However, if a production function is to be estimated from data over several production periods, technology does become of importance. Moreover, it is often difficult to find direct measures of the state of technology over time. Agricultural economists usually rely on some simple, if crude means such as the incorporation of a time variable into the production function. A simple time variable (for example, 1 for year 1, 2 for year 2, 3 for year 3, and so on) is a

23.2 New Technology and the Agricultural Production Function

very inaccurate measure of technology but may represent an improvement on a model that failed to recognize that technology changed at all.

Suppose that the production function was to be estimated as a Cobb–Douglas type of function

$$y = Ax_1^a x_2^b \tag{23.8}$$

The parameter A could be defined as

$$A = \alpha + \beta \tag{23.9}$$

where α is the parameter A with the impacts of technology (time) removed and β is the parameter associated with the change in technology. This approach would be most applicable in instances where there existed a gradual improvement in technology over a long period and it was difficult to determine which specific input categories are affected.

If the agricultural economist believes that the elasticities for only certain of the inputs are affected by the technology, the parameters for the affected inputs could be made a function of the measure of technology (in this case, time). For example, suppose that the new technology is thought to influence the elasticity of production for input x_1. The parameter a on x_1 could be defined as

$$a = \theta + \gamma T \tag{23.10}$$

where θ is the base production elasticity and γ is the change in the production elasticity with respect to a change in the technology per unit of time. More complicated functions could easily be developed that would allow for variable rates of change in the technology. The production function becomes a Cobb–Douglas type with variable production elasticities.

Another approach would be simply to estimate separate production functions for each year in the data series. This would amount to a series of still snapshots of the state of technology that existed for each period. An approach such as this can provide a good deal of information, since separate estimates of every parameter for every period are available, but a lack of the data needed for such a comprehensive approach may pose a problem.

Solow proposed a transcendental-like approach to the incorporation of technological change. Following his approach, a simple model would be

$$y = Ax_1^a x_2^b e^{rT} \tag{23.11}$$

where T is a measurement thought to represent technology, such as time, e is the base of the natural log, and r is the associated coefficient.

Such a model would allow for variable rates of change in marginal products as a result of the new technology. The function is readily transformed to its natural logarithms and estimated by ordinary least-squares regression. This approach is applicable in instances where it is not readily apparent which specific inputs are affected.

A similar approach would be to use the transcendental function

$$y = ax_1^{\alpha_1} x_2^{\alpha_2} e^{\gamma_1 T x_1 + \gamma_2 T x_2} \tag{23.12}$$

where T is the technology measure. The values for γ_1 and γ_2 would indicate the extent to which the new technology favors input x_1 or input x_2.

Approaches exist for dealing with technology in an agricultural production function. However, a major problem remains in that the variable technology is often difficult if not impossible to measure. Exceptions exist in instances where the specific technology is readily identifiable.

For example, successful studies have been conducted when the technology is similar to the development of hybrid corn, high-yielding rice varieties in international development, or a mechanized tomato harvester. The kind of technological change that usually takes place in agriculture is more gradual and less dramatic. Sometimes agricultural economists simply ignore gradual technological change and hope that the gradual changes associated with a general technological improvement do not significantly affect research results.

23.3 Conceptual Issues in Estimating Agricultural Production Functions

The estimation of agricultural production functions from survey data collected from farmers has been a very widespread activity by agricultural economists. A common approach might be to survey 100 farmers with regard to the quantities of seed, fertilizer, chemical, and other inputs used, and then attempt to estimate a single production function using the 100 farmers as individual observations in the data set. This research approach is becoming very popular in studies conducted in developing countries.

Major problems exist with this research approach. Some of the problems are readily apparent, while others are more subtle but of no less importance. One readily apparent problem stems from the lack of controlled experimental conditions. It may rain on one surveyed farmer but not on another. Soil conditions may vary from farm to farm, and managerial skills may differ from farm to farm. Yet a single production function will be estimated for all farms in the sample. Most researchers recognize that the lack of controlled experimental conditions represents a major problem with this approach to estimating agricultural production functions, and attempt to take steps to control for factors such as soil type and weather conditions.

Less well recognized but no less important are the problems associated with the behavioral objectives of the manager whose farm is part of the data set. Only one production function is to be estimated from the entire data set. Agricultural economists like to assume that farmers are profit maximizers or, as an alternative, seek to maximize revenue subject to a cost constraint. Prices for both inputs and outputs are largely given, and on a cross-sectional basis do not vary significantly from farm to farm.

If a single production function applies to all farms (an assumption basic to the estimation of the production function with farms as observations), information is complete, input and output prices are fixed and the same for all farms,

23.3 Conceptual Issues in Estimating Agricultural Production Functions

and farmers maximize profit, then all farmers should have found the point where *VMP* equals *MFC*. The data from which the production function is to be estimated do not consist of a series of points but rather, a single point. All farmers are using the same quantities of inputs and producing the same yields. To the extent that farmers are not all observed to be operating at the same point, one or more of the assumptions have broken down. Either the farmers do not know how to or cannot maximize profits, the same production function does not apply to all farmers, or input and output prices are not constant.

Suppose that farmers are not globally maximizing profits but rather, seek to maximize revenue subject to a cost constraint. In this case, all farmers would be operating on the same expansion path, but larger farmers would be operating closer to the point where profits are globally maximized, where λ equals 1. Again, the basic assumption of the analysis is that the same production function applies to all farmers in the data set. If the production function is homothetic, the expansion path is linear or has a constant slope, and input prices are constant. Each farmer's input bundle differs in size from the input bundle owned by the other farmers in the data set, but everyone's input bundle contains the same inputs in the same proportions.

If agricultural economists collect data from survey farms, farms with large outputs will use large amounts of fertilizer, chemicals, and other inputs. Smaller farms will use smaller amounts of fertilizer, chemicals, and other inputs. However, the proportions of each input in each bundle remain constant. When the statistical research is conducted, the agricultural economist discovers that the data series for the individual inputs are very highly correlated with each other. A large farmer using lots of fertilizer will also use lots of chemicals and other inputs; a small farmer uses small amounts of fertilizer, chemicals, and other inputs. This correlation leads to multicollinearity problems which, if severe enough, make it impossible to estimate the production elasticities for the individual inputs.

What is seldom recognized is that such problems should occur as a direct result of the assumption that farmers would like to be on the expansion path. To the extent that the individual input categories are not perfectly correlated with each other, either a single production function does not apply to all farmers, input prices vary from farm to farm, or farmers are not on the expansion path. The breakdown of any of these assumptions is not very comforting to those agricultural economists who understand marginal theory in a purely competitive environment.

Agricultural economists thus find themselves in a very difficult position. To the extent that the results of the analysis are stable enough to provide statistically significant estimates of individual production elasticities, one or more of the theoretical assumptions underlying the analysis has, to a degree, broken down. To the extent that individual production elasticities are unobtainable, the theoretical assumptions hold. However, this is of little consequence to agricultural economists in need of specific estimates of *MPP*'s and production elasticities. (See Doll for additional discussion of this problem.)

One approach to deal with this problem would be to abandon attempts to estimate agricultural production functions from nonexperimental farmer-generated cross-sectional data. Reliance might instead be placed solely on data obtained under controlled experimental conditions in agricultural experiment stations or other laboratory facilities. In the United States, such data do represent an important basis for the estimation of agricultural production functions. The problem here is that such data do not entirely reflect what is happening in an actual farm setting.

A gap exists between results obtained at an experiment station and on the farm. Experiment station yield trials may utilize a hand harvest not feasible or possible on large acreages on a farm. In the United States, as in most developed countries, the gap between experiment station and on-farm results is not that large, and perhaps adjustments could be made to take the gap into account. In developing countries the gap can be very large indeed, and agricultural economists working in these countries almost certainly need to know exactly what is happening on the farms themselves.

23.4 Concluding Comments

This chapter was called "Frontiers in Agricultural Production Economics Research" for a reason. The earlier chapters largely fit together as a neat package. Problems were proposed, models developed and analyzed, and solutions obtained. Unlike the earlier chapters, in this chapter problems are proposed and possible models presented, but no simple and neat solutions have been presented.

The issues presented in this chapter were chosen because they represent examples of highly significant and as yet unresolved problems confronting agricultural production economists. Much of agricultural economics research deals directly with problems such as these, and work on such problems is challenging. It is the author's hope that this book has stimulated both an interest in and an appreciation for the work of agricultural economists.

Problems and Exercises

1. What is management?
2. How might management be measured?
3. Outline alternative ways in which management might be incorporated into a production function. Explain the consequences of each approach.
4. What is new technology?
5. How might new technology be measured?
6. Is a time variable a proxy for new technology? Explain.
7. Outline alternative ways in which new technology might be incorporated into an agricultural production function. Explain the consequences of each approach.
8. Draw alternative isoquant maps representing the probable alternative consequences of new technology.

References

Doll, John P. "On Exact Multicollinearity and the Estimation of the Cobb–Douglas Production Function." *American Journal of Agricultural Economics* 56 (1974) pp. 556–563.

Solow, R. M. "Technological Change and the Aggregate Production Function." *Review of Economics and Statistics* 39 (1957) pp. 312–320.

Suggested Readings

1. General Economic Theory

Beattie, Bruce, and C. R. Taylor. *The Economics of Production.* New York: John Wiley, 1985.

Bilas, Richard A. *Microeconomic Theory,* 2nd ed. New York: McGraw-Hill, 1971.

Carlson, Sune. *A Study in the Pure Theory of Production.* New York: Kelley and Millman, 1965.

Cohen, K. J., and R. M. Cyert. *Theory of the Firm.* Englewood Cliffs, N.J.: Prentice-Hall 1965.

Ferguson, C. E. *The Neoclassical Theory of Production and Distribution.* Cambridge: Cambridge University Press, 1969.

Ferguson, C. E., and J. P. Gould. *Microeconomic Theory,* 4th ed. Homewood, Ill.: Richard D. Irwin, 1975.

Frisch, Ragnar. *Theory of Production.* Chicago: Rand McNally, 1965.

Hicks, J. R. *Value and Capital,* 2nd ed. Oxford: Oxford University Press, 1946.

Koopmans, Tjalling C. *Three Essays on the State of Economic Science.* New York: McGraw-Hill, 1957.

Leftwich, Richard H. *The Price System and Resource Allocation,* 3rd ed. New York: Holt, Rinehart and Winston, 1966.

Mansfield, E. *Microeconomics,* 3rd ed. New York: W. W. Norton, 1979.

Marshall, Alfred. *Principles of Economics,* 8th ed. New York: Macmillan, 1920.

2. General Agricultural Production Economics

Beattie, Bruce, and Wade L. Griffen. "Production Functions, Cost of Production and Associated Optimality Linkages: A Textbook Supplement." *Southern Journal of Agricultural Economics* 12:2 (1980) pp. 153–156.

Cramer, Gail L., and Clarence W. Jensen. *Agricultural Economics and Agribusiness,* 2nd ed. New York: John Wiley, 1982.

Doll, John P., and Frank Orazem, *Production Economics: Theory with Applications*, 2nd ed. New York: John Wiley, 1984.

Heady, Earl O. *Economics of Agricultural Production and Resource Use.* Englewood Cliffs, N.J.: Prentice-Hall, 1952.

Heady, Earl O. "Optimal Sizes of Farms Under Varying Tenure Forms Including Renting, Ownership, State and Collective Structures." *American Journal of Agricultural Economics* 53:1 (1971) pp. 17–25.

Johnson, Glenn L. "Agricultural Economics, Production Economics and the Field of Farm Management." *American Journal of Agricultural Economics* 39:2 (1957) pp. 441–450.

Lacewell, Ronald D., and Ron Knutson, "Research and Extension Issues in Production Economics." *Southern Journal of Agricultural Economics* 14:1 (1982) pp. 65–74.

Nelson, A. Gene, and Richard S. Johnston. "A Note on the Definition of the Economic Region of the Production Function." *American Journal of Agricultural Economics* 53:1 (1971) pp. 109–111.

Patrick, George. "Farmers' Goals: Uni or Multidimensional?" *American Journal of Agricultural Economics* 65:2 (1983) pp. 315–319.

Patrick, George, and Brian Blake. "Measurement and Modeling of Farmers' Goals: An Evaluation and Suggestions." *Southern Journal of Agricultural Economics* 12:1 (1980) pp. 199–204.

3. Mathematics as a Tool in Economics

Allen, R. G. D. *Mathematical Analysis for Economists*. New York: Macmillan, 1956.

Chaing, Alpha C. *Fundamental Methods of Mathematical Economics*. New York: McGraw-Hill, 1967.

Henderson, James M., and Richard E. Quandt. *Microeconomic Theory: A Mathematical Approach,* 3rd ed., New York: McGraw-Hill, (1980).

Samuelson, Paul A. *Foundations of Economic Analysis*. New York: Atheneum, 1970 (originally published in 1947).

Silberberg, Eugene. *The Structure of Economics (A Mathematical Analysis)*. New York: McGraw-Hill, 1978.

Varian, H. F. *Microeconomic Analysis*. New York: W. W. Norton, 1978.

4. Production Functions

Arrow, K., H. B. Chenery, B. Menhas, and R. M. Solow. "Capital Labor Substitution and Economic Efficiency." *Review of Economics and Statistics* 43:3 (1961) pp. 225–250.

Cobb, Charles W., and Paul H. Douglas. "A Theory of Production." *American Economic Review* 18:Suppl. (1928) pp. 139–156.

de Janvry, Alain. "The Class of Generalized Power Production Functions." *American Journal of Agricultural Economics* 54:2 (1972) pp. 234–237.

Debertin, David L. "Developing Realistic Agricultural Production Functions for Use in Undergraduate Classes." *Southern Journal of Agricultural Economics* 17:2 (1985).

Furtan, W. Hartley, and Richard S. Gray. "The Translog Production Function: Application to Saskatchewan Agriculture." *Canadian Journal of Agricultural Economics* 29:1 (1981) pp. 82–86.

Halter, A. N., H. O. Carter, and J. G. Hocking. "A Note on the Transcendental Production Function." *Journal of Farm Economics* 39:4 (1957) pp. 966–974.

Heady, Earl O., and John L. Dillon. *Agricultural Production Functions*. Ames, Iowa: Iowa State University Press, 1961.

Just, Richard E., David Zilberman and Eithan Hockman. "Estimation of Multicrop Production Functions." *American Journal of Agricultural Economics* 65:4 (1983) pp. 770–780.

Lau, L. J. "Profit Functions with Multiple Inputs and Outputs." *Review of Economics and Statistics* 54:3 (1972) pp. 281–289.

McFadden, D. "Further Results on CES Production Functions." *Review of Economic Studies* 30:1 (1963) pp. 73–83.

Mittlehammer, Ron C., Scott C. Matulich, and D. Bushaw. "An Implicit Form of Multiproduct–Multifactor Production Functions." *American Journal of Agricultural Economics* 63:1 (1981) pp. 164–168.

Mundlak, Yair. "A Note on the Symmetry of the Homogeneous Production Function and the Three Stages of Production." *Journal of Farm Economics* 40:3 (1958) pp. 756–761.

Mundlak, Yair. "Transcendental Multiproduct Production Functions." *Econometrica* 33:4 (1965) pp. 814–828.

Seagraves J. A., and Paseur, E. J. "On Defining Uneconomic Regions of the Production Function." *American Journal of Agricultural Economics* 51:1 (1969) pp. 195–202.

Spillman, W. J. "Application of the Law of Diminishing Returns to Some Fertilizer and Feed Data." *Journal of Farm Economics* 5:1 (1923) pp. 36–52.

Spillman, W. J. "Law of the Diminishing Increment in the Fattening of Steers and Hogs." *Journal of Farm Economics* 6:1 (1924) pp. 166–178.

Weaver, Robert D. "Multiple Input, Multiple Output Production Choices and Technology in the U.S. Wheat Region." *American Journal of Agricultural Economics* 65:1 (1983) pp. 45–56.

Zellner, A., J. Kmenta, and J. Dreze. "Specification and Estimation of Cobb–Douglas Production Function Models." *Econometrica* 34:4 (1966) pp. 784–95.

5. Production Processes over Time

Baker, Timothy G., and Bruce McCarl. "Representing Farm Resource Availability over Time in Linear Programs: A Case Study." *North Central Journal of Agricultural Economics* 4:1 (1982) pp. 59–68.

Bradford, Garnett, and Donald W. Reid. "On Optimal Replacement of Farm Tractors." *American Journal of Agricultural Economics* 65:2 (1983) pp. 326–331.

McConnell, Kenneth. "An Economic Model of Soil Conservation." *American Journal of Agricultural Economics* 65:1 (1983) pp. 83–97.

Shumway, C. Richard, Alberto Reyes, and Robert W. Blake. "Profitability and Risks in Dairy Feeding Programs: A Multiperiod Optimization." *Southern Journal of Agricultural Economics* 14:2 (1982) pp. 77–82.

Watts, Miles J. "Machinery Repair Functions and Depreciation." *North Central Journal of Agricultural Economics* 4:1 (1982) pp. 69–72.

6. Risk and Uncertainty

Anderson, J. R., J. R. Dillon, and J. B. Hardaker. *Agricultural Decision Analysis.* Ames, Iowa: Iowa State University Press, 1977.

Antle, John M. "Incorporating Risk in Production Analysis." *American Journal of Agricultural Economics* 65:5 (1983) pp. 1099–1106.

Brink, Lars, and Bruce McCarl. "The Tradeoff Between Expected Return and Risk Among Corn Belt Farmers." *American Journal of Agricultural Economics* 60:2 (1978) pp. 259–263.

Friedman, M., and L. J. Savage, "The Expected Utility Hypothesis and the Measurability of Utility." *Journal of Political Economy* 60:4 (1952) pp. 463–474.

Harris, Tiff, and Gene Nelson. "Dealing with Risk in Making Farm Decisions: An Introduction." Oregon State University Extension Service, 1978.

Jolly, Robert W. "Risk Management in Agricultural Production." *American Journal of Agricultural Economics* 65:5 (1983) pp. 1100–1113.

Just, Richard E. "An Investigation of the Importance of Risk in Farmers' Decisions." *American Journal of Agricultural Economics* 56:1 (1974) pp. 14–25.

Just, R. E. "Risk Aversion Under Profit Maximization." *American Journal of Agricultural Economics* 57:2 (1975) pp. 347–352.

Just, R. E., and R. D. Pope. "Production Function Estimation and Related Risk Concerns." *American Journal of Agricultural Economics* 61:2 (1979) pp. 277–284.

Scott, John R., and C. B. Baker. "A Practical Way to Select an Optimal Farm Plan Under Risk." *American Journal of Agricultural Economics* 54:4 (1972) pp. 657–660.

7. Marginal Analysis and the Farm Budget

Barnaby, G.A., Jr., and Larry Langemeyer. "A Procedure for Allocating Production Costs to Individual Enterprises in Farm Management Workshops." *North Central Journal of Agricultural Economics* 6:1 (1984) pp. 121–130.

Bradford, Garnett L., and David L. Debertin. "Establishing Linkages Between Economic Theory and Enterprise Budgeting for Teaching and Extension Programs." *Southern Journal of Agricultural Economics* 17:2 (1985).

Held, Larry, and Richard Zink. "Farm Enterprise Choice, Risk Return Tradeoffs in Cash Crop Versus Crop–Livestock Systems." *North Central Journal of Agricultural Economics* 4:2 (1982) pp. 11–20.

8. Mathematical Programming

Baumol, William J. *Economic Theory and Operations Analysis.* Englewood Cliffs, N.J.: Prentice-Hall, 1977, Chap. 12.

Boulding, Kenneth E., and W. Spivey, eds. *Linear Programming and the Theory of the Firm.* New York: McGraw-Hill, 1966.

Dorfman, Robert. *Application of Linear Programming to the Theory of the Firm.* Berkeley, Calif.: University of California Press, 1951, Chaps. 1 and 2.

Dorfman, Robert. "Mathematical or Linear Programming: A Nonmathematical Exposition." *American Economic Review* 43:5 (1953) pp. 797–829.

Dorfman, Robert, Paul A. Samuelson, and Robert Solow. *Linear Programming and Economic Analysis.* New York: McGraw-Hill, 1958.

Heady, Earl O., and Wilfred Candler. *Linear Programming Methods.* Ames, Iowa: Iowa State College Press, 1958.

Intriligator, Michael D. *Mathematical Optimization and Economic Theory.* Englewood Cliffs, N.J. Prentice-Hall, 1971.

Koopmans, Tjalling C., ed. *Activity Analysis of Production and Allocation.* New York: John Wiley, 1951.

Leftwich, Richard H. *The Price System and Resource Allocation.* New York: Holt, Rinehart and Winston, 1966, Chap. 18.

Naylor, Thomas H. "A Kuhn Tucker Model of a Multi-product Multi-factor Firm." *Southern Economics Journal* 31:4 (1965) pp. 324–330.

Naylor, Thomas H. "The Theory of the Firm: A Comparison of Marginal Analysis and Linear Programming." *Southern Economics Journal* 32:3 (1966) pp. 263–274.

Pfouts, Ralph W. "The Theory of Cost and Production in the Multi-product Firm." *Econometrica* 29:4 (1961) pp. 650–658.

9. Empirical Applications of Production Theory

Doll, John P. "A Comparison of Annual Versus Average Optima for Fertilizer Experiments." *American Journal of Agricultural Economics* 54:2 (1972) pp. 226–233.

Doll, John P. "On Exact Multicollinearity and the Estimation of the Cobb–Douglas Production Function." *American Journal of Agricultural Economics* 56:3 (1974) pp. 556–563.

Hall, Harry H. "Economic Evaluation of Crop Response to Lime." *American Journal of Agricultural Economics* 65:4 (1983) pp. 811–817.

Suggested Readings

Lee, Warren F., and Norman Rask. "Inflation and Crop Profitability: How Much Can Farmers Afford to Pay for Land?" *American Journal of Agricultural Economics* 58:5 (1976) pp. 984–990.

10. Costs, Size, and Scale

Gardner, Delworth, and Rulon Pope. "How Is Scale and Structure Determined in U.S. Agriculture?" *American Journal of Agricultural Economics* 60:2 (1978) pp. 295–302.

Pope, Rulon, and Richard Prescott. "Diversification in Relation to Farm Size and Other Socioeconomic Characteristics." *American Journal of Agricultural Economics* 62:3 (1980) pp. 554–559.

Schatzer, Raymond J., Roland K. Roberts, and Earl O. Heady. "A Simulation of Alternative Futures in U.S. Farm Size." *North Central Journal of Agricultural Economics* 5:1 (1983) pp. 1–8.

Stanton, B. F. "Perspective on Farm Size." *American Journal of Agricultural Economics* 60:5 (1978) pp. 727–737.

Tew, Bernard, Stan Spurlock, Wes Musser, and Bill R. Miller. "Some Evidence on Pecuniary Economies of Size for Farm Firms." *Southern Journal of Agricultural Economics* 12:1 (1980) pp. 151–154.

11. The Demand for Inputs to the Production Process

Debertin, David L., and Angelos Pagoulatos. "Energy Problems and Alternatives: Implications for the South." *Southern Journal of Agricultural Economics* 12:1 (1980) pp. 47–56.

Gunjal, Kisan R., Roland K. Roberts, and Earl O. Heady. "Fertilizer Demand Functions for Five Individual Crops in the United States." *Southern Journal of Agricultural Economics* 12:2 (1980) pp. 111–116.

Koizumi, Tetsunori. "A Further Note of the Definition of the Elasticity of Substitution in the Many Input Case." *Metroeconomica* 28 (1976) pp. 152–155.

Lau, L. J., and Pan Yotopoulos. "Profit, Supply and Factor Demand Functions." *American Journal of Agricultural Economics* 54:1 (1972) pp. 11–18.

Lianos, Theodore P. "The Relative Share of Labor in United States Agriculture, 1949–1968." *American Journal of Agricultural Economics* 53:3 (1971) pp. 411–422.

Pagoulatos, Angelos, David L. Debertin, and William L. Johnson. "An Econometric Analysis of Qualitative Choice Among Performance Characteristics of Agricultural Tractors." *Southern Journal of Agricultural Economics* 14:2 (1982) pp. 83–90.

12. Policy and Technological Change

Brandt, Jon A., and Ben C. French. "Mechanical Harvesting and the California Tomato Industry: A Simulation Analysis." *American Journal of Agricultural Economics* 65:2 (1983) pp. 265–272.

Ganguly, Pradeep. "Technological Change and the Relative Share of Labor: The Case of Tobacco Production in the U.S." *Southern Journal of Agricultural Economics* 12:2 (1980) pp. 105–110.

Reed, Michael. "An Analysis of Policy Alternatives for the U.S. Burley Tobacco Market." *Southern Journal of Agricultural Economics* 12:2 (1980) pp. 65–70.

Index

Acreage allotment, 145–148
Actions, 305
Activities, 334
Additional units, 20
Additivity, 333
Agricultural economics, 7
Agricultural production economics, 7
Agriculture and economics, 7
Algorithm, 331, 337
Allen, R. G. D., 200
Allocation of resources, 8
Aoun, Abdessalem, 209, 211
Approximate *MPP*, 27
Arrow, Kenneth, 203, 211
Assumptions
 of linear programming, 332–333
 of pure competition, 9–11
Asymptotic to the axes, 87–88
Attitudes of farmers, 303–305
Average cost, 65, 178
Average fixed cost, 65–69
Average physical product, 22
Average value of the product, 42
Average variable cost, 65–69

Berndt, E. R., 209, 211
Bordered principal minor, 287
Bowed inward, 86–87
Bowed outward, 241–242
Bradford, G. L., 191, 194
Brown, R. S., 209, 211
Budget, 295
Budget constraint, 115–118

Bundle of inputs, 122–123
Buyers, 9

Carter, H. O., 185, 193–194, 207
Cash rent, 142
CES production function, 202–206
Chenery, H. B., 203, 211
Choice of outputs, 8
Christensen, L. R., 207, 209, 211
Classical optimization, 132, 330–331
 and linear programming, 331–332
Cobb, Charles W., 182
Cobb–Douglas production function, 165–182
Cobb–Douglas type of function, 168
Cobb–Douglas with variable elasticities, 191
Comparative statics, 6
Competitive economic environment, 9
Competitive products, 244
Competitiveness, technical, 219
Complementary products, 245
Complements, technical, 218
Compounding, 324–325
Computer programming, 331
Consequences, 305–306
Constant elasticity of substitution, 202–206
Constant marginal rate of substitution, 88
Constant marginal returns, 21
Constant returns to scale, 156
Constrained cost minimization, 140–142
Constrained maximization, 334–337

Index

Constrained optimization, 132
Constrained output maximization, 138–140, 179–180, 223–224
Constrained revenue maximization, 132–138, 179–180, 255–262, 277–278
Constraint, 4, 115–118
Constraints, resource, 334
Consumer, 5
Consumption economics, 4–5
Continuous production function, 17
Contracts, 312
Convex to the origin, 86
Corner solution, 135–136
Correspondence, 16, 67
Correlation, 355
Cost minimization, 140–141
Cost of the input bundle, 158–161
Cost-share equation, 208–209
Critical values, 102, 108
Curvature
   production function, 21
   MPP, 31–33

de Janvry, Alain, 191, 193–194, 207
Demand, 6–7
Derivative, 25
Determinant of a matrix, 107
Diminishing marginal rate of substitution, 86–87
Discounting, 322–324
Discrete production function, 15–17
Diseconomies of scale, 151–153, 163–165
Diseconomies of size, 151–153, 163–165
Diversification, 313
Divisibility, 333
Doll, John P., 225, 355–356
Domain, 14–15
Douglas, Paul H., 182
Duality
   and the Cobb–Douglas, 176–179
   linear programming, 341–343
   of cost and production, 72–73, 158–161
Duncan, Marvin, 209, 211
Dynamic economics, 6
Dynamics, 6

Economic model, 3–4
Economic theory, 2–3
Economics
   defined, 1
   vs. agricultural economics, 7

Economies of scale, 153–155, 163–165
Economies of size, 151–153, 163–165, 299–300
Elasticity, 34, 215–218
Elasticity of demand, 215–216
Elasticity of input demand, 215–218
Elasticity of production
   and the Cobb–Douglas, 170
   defined, 34
   stages of production, 54–55
Elasticity of substitution, 195–211
   and the CES, 202–206
   and the Cobb–Douglas, 200–201
   and the translog, 206–209
   defined, 195–200
   empirical estimation, 209
   output side, 249–250
   policy applications, 201–202
Elements of a matrix, 107
Enterprise budgeting, 294–301
Entrepreneurship, 347
Envelope curve, 63–64
Equimarginal returns
   and pseudo scale lines, 126–127
   defined, 121
   general rules, 288–289, 291–292, 298
Euler, Leonhard, 162
Euler's theorem, 162–163, 349–350
Exact MPP, 27
Expansion path, 119–122
Exports, agricultural, 322

Factor-factor model, 11
Factor-product model, 11
Family
   of product transformation functions, 252–254
   of production functions, 89–91
Farm planning model, 343–345
Feasible region, 335
Feasible solution area, 335, 341–342
First derivative, 25, 31–32
First-order condition, 53, 101–109, 136–137, 286–292
Fixed cost, 63–65, 285–286
Fixed inputs, 18–20, 298–299
Fixed proportion of inputs, 84–85, 88
Fixed proportion production function, 333–334
Flexible facilities, 312–313
Foundations of Economic Analysis, 4
Free entry and exit, 10

Index

Function, 14–15
Function coefficient, 158
Function of a function, 231

Global maximum, 100, 108–109
Global profit maximization, 130–131
Goals, alternative, 317–319
Goals and objectives, 8
Government programs, 314–315
Graphics, 4

Halter, A. N., 185, 191, 193–194, 207
Heady, E. O., 142, 196–197
Henderson, James, 203–206, 211
Hocking, J. G., 185, 194, 207
Hockman, Eithan, 250–251
Homogeneous product, 10
Homogeneous production function, 155–157, 170
Homothetic production function, 120, 157

Implicit production function, 290, 293
Implicit worth, 59, 134
Imputed value, 58–60, 134, 345
Income variability, 306–311
Independence, technical, 218–219
Inflation, 321–322
Inflection point, 28, 43
Input bundle, 159–160
Input demand function, 212–225
　one-input setting, 213–215
　two-input setting, 219–223
　under constrained maximization, 223–224
Input price variation, 233–234
Input requirements function, 288
Insurance, 311–312
Integer programming, 333
Interest rate, 321–322
Intermediate product, 278–282
Intermediate run, 19–20
Inverse production function, 73–76
Inverse price ratio, 116, 255
Irrational stage of production, 53
Isocline, 119
Isocost line, 116–117
Iso-outlay line, 116–118
Isoquant
　and ridge lines, 89–91
　and the Cobb–Douglas, 171–172

　and total derivatives, 95
　defined, 85, 99–100
　shape, 196
Isoquant map, 117
Isorevenue line, 254–255

Joint products, 246
Jorgenson, D. W., 207, 211
Just, Richard E., 250–251

Klein, L. R., 200, 211
Knight, Frank, 303, 315
Koizumi, T., 200, 211

Lagrange, Joseph-Louis, 132
Lagrange's function, 132
Lagrange's multiplier, 132–141, 331
Lagrangian function, 132, 139–140, 224
Lau, L. J., 207, 211
Law of diminishing returns, 20, 184
Law of diminishing marginal returns, 20, 240
Law of the minimum, 83
Lease design, 142–145
Least cost combination of inputs, 119, 138, 140
Length of run, 18–20
Linear programming, 12, 330–346
　applications, 343–345
Linear in the coefficients, 168
Linear in the parameters, 168
Linearity, 332–333
Local maximum, 100, 108–109
Long run, 19–20
Long-run average cost, 63–64, 152
Long-run marginal cost, 64

Macroeconomics, 5–6, 322
Management
　and production functions, 347–349
　and profit maximization, 349–350
　approaches to, 348–349
　functions of, 8, 347
Many inputs, 285–287
Many outputs, 288–289
Many outputs and many inputs, 289–293
Marginal analysis, 12, 309–311, 325–328
Marginal conditions, 127–128
Marginal cost, 65–73, 76–79, 178–179

Index

Marginal factor cost, 44
Marginal physical product, 22, 93
Marginal product function, 24
Marginal rate of substitution
  and marginal product, 91–93
  defined, 86
Marginal rate of technical substitution, 86
Marginal revenue, 69–72, 228–230
Marginal value of the product, 232–233
Market price, 9
Mathematical programming, 331
Mathematics, 4, 11
Matrix, 107
Matrix algebra, 107–108
Maximization defined, 99–102
Maximum APP, 29
Maximum MPP, 29
Maximum profit, 70–71
Maximum TPP, 29
McFadden, Daniel, 200, 211
Menhas, B., 203, 211
Microcomputer, 337
Microeconomics, 5–6
Minimization defined, 100–101
Minimum profit, 70–71
Mobility of resources, 10
Monopoly, 11
Multicollinearity, 355

Necessary conditions, 52–53, 102–109, 136–137, 321–322
Neoclassical production function, 28–29
Net worth, 321–322
Nonlinear programming, 331–332
Nonnegativity, 333
Nonpecuniary economies, 299

Oligopoly, 11
Orazem, Frank, 225
Output maximization, 111–112, 253–254
Output level, 296–298
Output price variation
  input side, 230–233
  output side, 227–230
Output restriction, 268–270
Output uncertainty, 300

Partial derivatives, 93–96
Pecuniary economies, 152, 299
Perfect competition, 10

Personal microcomputer, 337
Pivotal column, 339
Pivotal row, 339
Polynomial production function, 192–193, 351–352
Polyperiod production, 325–328
Present value, 322–323
Price flexibility, 228–229
Price uncertainty, 300
Primal, 341
Principal minor, 107
Probability, 305
Producer, 5
Product-product model, 12, 337
Product transformation curve, 240, 246–249
Product transformation function, 252–253
  CES type, 250
  Cobb–Douglas type, 250
Production economics, 4–5
Production elasticity
  neoclassical function, 36–37
  one-input case, 34–36
  vs. MPP and APP, 37–38
Production function
  conceptual issues, 354–356
  defined, 14–18
  fixed-proportion, 333–334
  for the bundle, 122–123
  links to cost function, 76–77
Production possibilities
  for a farm, 240–242
  for a society, 238–240
Production surface
  CES, 203–206
  Cobb–Douglas, 173–175
  polynomial, 192–193
  Spillman, 184–186
  transcendental, 190–191
Profit, 5, 43
Profit function, 109–111
Profit maximization, 41, 45
  and the Cobb–Douglas, 175–176
  general conditions, 234–236
  long run, 51–52, 317–318
Pseudo scale line, 124–127, 134
Pure competition, 10, 226–227
Purely competitive model, 11

Quadratic programming, 333
Quandt, Richard, 203–206
Quasi-general equilibrium, 281

Range, 15
Rate of product transformation, 243–244
Rate of technical substitution, 86
Real interest rate, 321
Resource constraints, 334
Resources, 1
Returns-to-scale parameter, 157
Ridge lines, 89–93, 189
Right-hand side, 338
Risk, 8, 302–315, 347
Risk preference, 306–309
Risk–uncertainty continuum, 303

Saddle point, 105–108
Scale, 153–155
Samuelson, Paul, 4, 13
Second derivative, 32–34
Second-order condition, 53, 101–109, 136–137, 262–264, 287, 289, 292
Sellers, 9
Shadow price, 60, 134, 340, 345
Shared rent, 142
Shephard's lemma, 208–209
Short run, 19–20
Short-run average cost, 63–64
Short-run marginal cost, 63–64
Sign, 31–34
Simplex method, 338–341
Single-valued expectations, 333
Size, 151–153, 299–300
Slack variables, 338
Slope, 31–34
Smith, Adam, 4, 13
Solow, R. M., 203, 211, 353, 356
Solutions, possible, 336
Solve time, 337
Stage I, 54
Stage II, 54
Stage III, 54
States of nature, 305
Static economics, 6
Statics, 6
Strategies, 305
Sufficient conditions, 52–53, 102–109, 136–137
Sunk costs, 20, 63
Supplementary products, 244–245
Supply, 6–7
Supply function, 77–79

Survey data, 354–356
Synergistic effect, 83, 86

Taylor's series expansion, 210
Technical competitiveness, 218–219
Technical complements, 218
Technical independence, 218–219
Technology
  and agricultural production functions, 350–352
  and time, 352–354
Theory, 2
Third derivative, 32–33
Three stages of production, 53–57
Time, 316–329
Total cost, 65, 69–70
Total derivative, 93–96
Total factor cost, 41
Total physical product, 16–17, 40–41
Total resource cost, 41
Total revenue, 69
Total value of the product, 40–41
Transcendental-like function, 353
Transcendental production function, 185–187, 354
Translog function, 206–210
True Cobb–Douglas, 169
Two-input transcendental, 185, 187–191
Two outputs and two inputs, 272–278

Uncertainty, 8, 300, 302–315
Unitary elasticity, 229
Utility, 5, 149, 306–309

Value of the marginal product, 42
Variable cost, 62–69, 285–286
Variable input, 18–20
Variable input prices, 233–234
Very short run, 19–20
Viner, Jacob, 64
Von Leibig, J., 83

Wants, 1
Wealth accumulation, 318
Wealth of nations, 4
Webb, Kerry, 209, 211

HD
1433
.D43
1986

11.00

HD
1433
.D43

1986